DIGITAL YOUTH

Emerging Literacies
on the World Wide Web

NEW DIMENSIONS IN COMPUTERS AND COMPOSITION

Gail E. Hawisher and Cynthia L. Selfe, editors

Digital Youth: Emerging Literacies on the World Wide Web
Jonathan Alexander

Role Play: Distance Learning and the Teaching of Writing
Jonathan Alexander and Marcia Dickson (eds.)

Datacloud: Toward a New Theory of Online Work
Johndan Johnson-Eilola

At Play in the Fields of Writing: A Serio-Ludic Rhetoric
Albert Rouzie

Sustainable Computer Environments: Cultures of Support in English
Studies and Language Arts
Richard Selfe

Doing Literacy Online: Teaching, Learning, and Playing
in an Electronic World
Ilana Snyder and Catherine Beavis (eds.)

forthcoming

Webbing Cyberfeminine Practice: Communities, Pedagogy
and Social Action
Kristine Blair, Radhika Gajjala, and *Christine Tully* (eds.)

Lingua Franca: Towards a Rhetoric of New Media
Colin Brooke

Aging Literacies: Training and Development Challenges for Faculty
Angela Crow

Labor, Writing Technologies and the Shaping of Composition
in the Academy
Pamela Takayoshi and Patricia Sullivan (eds.)

Integrating Hypertextual Subjects: Computers, Composition, Critical
Literacy and Academic Labor
Robert Samuels

DIGITAL YOUTH

Emerging Literacies on the World Wide Web

Jonathan Alexander
University of Cincinnati

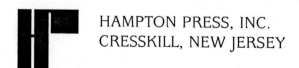

HAMPTON PRESS, INC.
CRESSKILL, NEW JERSEY

Printed in the United States of America

Library of Congress Cataloging-in-Publication Data

Alexander, Jonathan.
  Digital youth : emerging literacies on the World Wide Web /
  Jonathan Alexander
      p. cm. -- (New dimensions in computers and composition)
  Includes bibliographic references and indexes.
  ISBN 1-57273-650-X -- ISBN 1-57273-651-8
    1. Computers and literacy. 2. World Wide Web. 3. Composition
  (Language arts). 4. Youth--Effect of technological innovations on.
  I. Title. II. Series

LC149.5.A43 2005
302.2'244'0285--dc22

                                                       2005052512

Hampton Press, Inc.
23 Broadway
Cresskill, NJ 07626

CONTENTS

ACKNOWLEDGMENTS

A book only comes together through the efforts of many people, even if only one name appears as author on the title page. Without a doubt, this book would certainly *not* have been possible without all of the students who have inspired me to consider their writing more carefully—and respectfully. Their work, their ideas, and their insights are present throughout this book. Colleagues also played their part, and I want to thank Gail Hawisher, Cindy Selfe, Marcia Dickson, Jackie Rhodes, Will Hochman, and Margaret Barber for their continued guidance and mentoring; they are among the best friends a working scholar could have. I also thank the anonymous reviewers of my original manuscript; their insights helped give the book shape and a finer focus.

As I have been working in the field of computers and writing studies for the last decade, I have had the opportunity to work with editors who have published my work in various journals, both print and online. I thank those editors (and their reviewers) for their assistance in prodding me to refine—and extend—my thinking. The book borrows in part from that earlier work. Excerpts or short passages, radically revised, have been drawn from the following original publications: "The 'YOUth & AIDS Web Project': Web Publishing as Service Learning in First-Year Writing Courses," published in *Dialogue: A Journal for Writing Specialists*, 8(2), Spring 2004; "Digital Spins: The Pedagogy and Politics of Student-Centered E-Zines," published in *Computers & Composition*, 19(4), December 2002; "Ravers on the Web: Resistance, Multidimensionality, and Writing (about) Youth Cultures," published in *Kairos*, 7(3), Fall 2002 (http://english.ttu.edu/kairos/7.3/binder2.html?coverweb.html#de); "Introduction to the Special Issue: Queer Webs: Representations of LGBT People and Communities on the World Wide Web," written as guest editor for a special edition of *The International Journal of Sexuality and Gender Studies*, entitled "Queer Webs: Representations of LGBT People and Communities on the World Wide Web," 7(2 & 3), April/May 2002; "Homo-pages and Queer Sites: Studying the Construction and Representation of Queer Identities on the World Wide Web," published in the same issue of *The International Journal of Sexuality and Gender Studies*; a review of Steven Johnson's *Interface Culture*, written for the *Resource Center for Cyberculture Studies* (http://www.com.washington.edu/rccs/books/johnson.html); a review of Robert Yagelski's *Literacies and Technologies: A Reader for the Contemporary Writer*, published in *academic.writing* (http://aw.colostate.edu/reviews/yagelski_literacies_2001.htm); "Literacy/Motion," a review of *The Emerging Cyberculture: Literacy, Paradigm, and Paradox* (edited by Stephanie B. Gibson and Ollie O. Oviedo), published in *Kairos*, 6(1) (http://english.ttu.edu/kairos/6.1/reviews/alexander/); "Composing the Social: Bruce McComiskey's *Teaching Composition as Social Process*," published in *academic.writing* (http://aw.colostate.edu/contents/contents_ns4.htm).

At times, direct financial assistance came in very gratifying and useful forms. The collection and analysis of material in Chapter 5 was assisted by a research grant from the Gay and Lesbian Alliance Against Defamation (GLAAD), which published some of the findings in that chapter under a separate cover; some of this material was also used in the introduction to a special issue of *Computers & Composition*, entitled, "Sexuality, Technology, and the Teaching of Writing," which I guest edited with Will Banks, another good friend and super smart colleague (*21*(3), September 2004).

Finally, I dedicate this book to Mack McCoy, without whose interest in and knowledge of computers and the Internet—and without whose unflagging support—this book would not have been possible.

"HIDDEN LITERACIES"

AN INTRODUCTION

Literacy is changing.

Or, more specifically, what it means to be "literate" in our society is undergoing a transformation. Since the advent of the World Wide Web (WWW) in the mid-1990s, and the increasing use of Internet technologies throughout the West, digitally enabled mass communication has allowed millions to communicate with one another, have access to greater amounts of information, and share their own thoughts, desires, and dreams through web pages, e-mail, Instant Messaging, and other electronic venues. It is widely assumed by pundits, social critics, literacy specialists, educators, and many academics that computer-mediated communication impacts, alters, or at least shifts how we communicate, craft text, discover and disseminate information, and integrate visuals into our "textual" meaning-making.

In general, depending on which pundit or scholar one talks to, how we define what passes as "literate" in the Information Age is either shifting, for better or worse, or it is fundamentally changing in every conceivable way—for better or worse. But how so, specifically? What are some of the emerging, technologically enabled literacy practices, and how might they alter how we communicate, articulate our ideas and insights, and attempt to make and disseminate meaning? And what do these potential changes suggest about future literacies and literacy practices?

1

A humorous example of some potential shifts in literacy appeared in my e-mail inbox just this morning (September 16, 2003), sent to me by the director of the English Composition program at the University of Cincinnati. The following is an "Internet version" of *Romeo and Juliet*, pared down to the original story's bare essentials and peppered with e-mail "shorthand":

Romeo and Juliet—Internet Version

———————— Act 1 ————————
Login:
Romeo : R u awake? Want 2 chat?
Juliet: O Rom. Where4 art thou?
Romeo: Outside yr window.
Juliet: Stalker!
Romeo: Had 2 come. feeling jiggy.
Juliet: B careful. My family h8 u.
Romeo: Tell me about it. What about u?
Juliet: 'm up for marriage f u are. Is tht a bit fwd?
Romeo: No. Yes. No. Oh, dsnt mat-r, 2moro @ 9?
Juliet: Luv U xxxx
Romeo: CU then xxxx

———————— Act 2 ————————
Friar: Do u?
Juliet: I do
Romeo: I do

———————— Act 3 ————————
Juliet: Come bck 2 bed. It's the nightingale not the lark.
Romeo: OK
Juliet: !!! I ws wrong !!!. It's the lark. U gotta go. Or
die.
Romeo: Damn. I shouldn't hv wasted Tybalt & gt banished.
Juliet: When CU again?
Romeo: Soon. Promise. Dry sorrow drinks our blood. Adieu.
Juliet: Miss u big time.

———————— Act 4 ————————

Nurse: Yr mum says u have 2 marry Paris!!
Juliet: No way. Yuk yuk yuk. n-e-way, am mard 2 Rom.

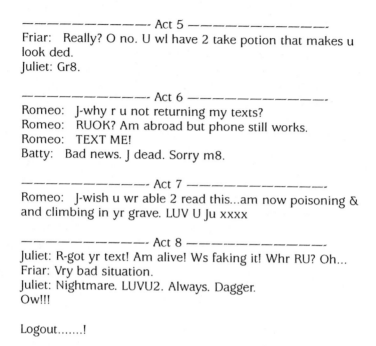

———————————— Act 5 ——————————.
Friar: Really? O no. U wl have 2 take potion that makes u
look ded.
Juliet: Gr8.

———————————— Act 6 ——————————.
Romeo: J-why r u not returning my texts?
Romeo: RUOK? Am abroad but phone still works.
Romeo: TEXT ME!
Batty: Bad news. J dead. Sorry m8.

———————————— Act 7 ——————————.
Romeo: J-wish u wr able 2 read this...am now poisoning &
and climbing in yr grave. LUV U Ju xxxx

———————————— Act 8 ——————————.
Juliet: R-got yr text! Am alive! Ws faking it! Whr RU? Oh...
Friar: Vry bad situation.
Juliet: Nightmare. LUVU2. Always. Dagger.
Ow!!!

Logout.......!

Although some might point to this as an example of how the Internet is
destroying our language, how it takes the beauty, artistry, and craft of a
powerfully written play and reduces it to a series of cheap visual and textual puns, others might argue that a multifaceted literacy is at work here.
After all, *Romeo and Juliet*, through repeated performance over 400 years,
has become something of a cultural cliché, and the language of its lovers is
frequently held up in many venues (television, radio, casual conversation)
for a bit of good-humored mockery—as is perhaps appropriate because the
play is, at least in part, about the overblown, overly dramatic emotions of
teenage love. But more than this, this "Internet version" points to continued delight in textual manipulation and word play. Moreover, it introduces
the element of *visual* play, in which numbers and other graphics (such as
the ampersand) are used to make meaning and assist in creating the parody. Certainly, the "reduction" mimics the speediness of Internet communications, the efficiency with which one can send a message and disseminate
information. And we should worry over such speediness and the value we
place over it, asking ourselves what is lost in the rush to type and click
"send." At the same time, though, I can't help but think that some effort,
and more than a little creativity, went into the composition of this "e-ver-

sion" of *Romeo and Juliet*. And that compositional effort, as well as the willingness to play with literacy and its many possible practices, has begun intriguing a number of scholars in a number of different disciplines.

Personally, as a computer user, writer, and scholar, I can certainly relate to the added dimensions of such playfulness enabled by the new communications technologies. In his autobiographical work, *Extra Life: Coming of Age in Cyberspace,* David S. Bennahum has done an admirable job of chronicling and examining the experiences of growing up at a time when computers were just becoming widespread, nearly household appliances. His title refers to the possibility of gaining an "extra life" while playing a video game if one performs particularly well. The question implicit in the title, however, asks us to query what kind of "extra life," if any, our increasingly intimate relationship with technology affords us. Or, to put the question in terms that N. Katherine Hayles has given: How have our increased interactions with computer technologies contributed to making us "posthuman"? For Bennahum (and for Hayles as well), that extra life has been mostly positive, embracing a rebellious ethos, and perhaps ethic, of experimentation:

> As computers entered our homes we were defining a new culture through gleeful experimentation, one that with the Internet in the 1990s would become dominant, capturing as much attention as did rebellion in the 1960s or jazz in the 1920s. (qtd. in Yagelski, 188)

Indeed, for some youth of my generation (I'm 36 as of this writing), and for many more in younger generations, the computer figures as an "accomplice" in adolescent rebellion, in an attempt to define one generation over and against previous generations. It is more than just a communications tool. It is an *identity* and *world-making* tool. In fact, the increasing use by American youth of computer technologies has prompted *Wired* magazine to call the latest generation of youth "born digital" and *Net Family News* identifies them as "digital kids," because there were "approximately 26.9 million 2- to 18-year-olds online in North America alone by the end of [the year 2000]" ("Born Digital"; "Our 'Digital Kids'").

Many scholars in a variety of fields, from communication and English studies to sociology and the graphic arts, have begun studying the impact of the Internet on how we communicate and make meaning, on how we are literate in the so-called Information Age. But, despite the growing scholarly interest in technologically enabled literacies, we have much to learn, particularly given the degree to which literacy practices and forms of communication seem to proliferate as new communications platforms are invented and used. Dennis Baron, writing in 1999, could still say in the conclusion to his essay "From Pencils to Pixels: The Stages of Literacy Technologies," that, "After more than a decade of study, we still know relatively little about how people are using computers to read and write" (83). Even more recently, Kathleen Blake Yancey, in her keynote address for the 2004 Conference on College Composition and Communication, offered the following observation, reflecting on more than a decade of both scholarly observation and day-to-day use and development of a variety of technological literacy practices:

> James Gee documented new genres of literacy that children acquire through playing video games. In *Smart Mobs*, Howard Rheingold chronicled the use of multiple, interacting telecommunication devices by people around the world who want to gather immediately, who seek new kinds of social and political interaction, and for whom multitasking seems completely normalized. Roz Helderman in *The Washington Post* identified instant messaging as the teenager's preferred communicative mode. Readers note their book preferences on Amazon.com's Listmania and then provide commentary on blogs and wiki's. Inside school, students in first-year composition create in digital portfolios new multimedia representations documenting, connecting, and synthesizing their learning across and beyond campus. Collectively, these formal accounts paint a portrait of digital writing as an underground economy of composition and communication, one functioning largely outside of school, and one whose success is measured by the social goals people meet day in, day out. (http://www.ncte.org/profdev/conv/cccc04/featured/114905.htm)

Yancey suggests, correctly I believe, that such "digital writing" comprises an "underground economy of composition and communication"—one that embraces and envisions possibilities of literacy that stretch beyond the classroom, beyond our purview (and even knowledge) as "authorities" on literacy, writing, and communication.

Granted, as Baron points out, the population "online," when compared to the rest of the population, in the country and the world, is relatively small, which makes the "underground economy" a fraction of the population in general and the literate population in particular. But, purely anecdotally, as I have taught writing in computerized classrooms over the last decade, I have noticed that more and more of my young adult students come to class not only with knowledge of computer and Internet technologies, but with an expectation that we will use them, and perhaps even compose for dissemination via the Web. Even the number of such students with their own Web sites seems to have risen dramatically.

Moreover, my experience as an educator and as a literacy advocate has convinced me that these particular youth, some of the primary users of these new technologies, are showing us some of the ways in which literacy is being redefined, recast, and reshaped as more and more communication occurs via networked platforms. Surely, this is a relatively small percentage of both "students" in higher education and "youth" with access to technology, but it is my contention that we can see, experience, and analyze some of the changing dimensions of literacy and literate practices in the ways in which such "digital youth" are using the new communications technologies, particularly the WWW. Put another way, these digitally savvy students, I believe, are among those at the forefront of rethinking and re-imagining the possibilities of electronically enabled literacy.

A WHOLE LOT OF WRITING GOING ON, 1.0: YOUTH WRITING

Just recently, I was reminded of the importance of writing, particularly writing on the Web, to a variety of youth with Internet access. I received the following e-mail during the summer of 2003, and I was excited by what I read:

> The Cowgirl Superstars and Vivid, a Northern Kentucky Zine Machine, present:
>
> The CINCINNATI ROCK + READ FEST 2
> Saturday, August 9, 2003
> 7:30 p.m., $5, all ages
>
> In celebration of an often overlooked sector of Cincinnati's thriving underground art scene, The Cincinnati Rock and Read Fest brings together some of the tri-state's hottest literary minds for a one-night marathon convention and concert.
>
> Zinesters, self-published authors, literacy advocates and literary avant-gardists from every walk of life will convene to share their words and works, to offer a sampling of local literary arts to concert-goers and to enjoy hot, new, home-grown rock and roll.

A true adventure in literary and musical experimentation, the R&R will be held in the recently opened third floor gallery of S.S. Nova. Independent publishers from the tri-state and beyond will showcase their wares, offering a rare networking opportunity for a community that is often completely underground or visible only online. Attendees include local favorites XRay Magazine and Theory of Everything, politically oriented Friction Magazine from Akron and Dayton's punk rock Pool Party Magazine. Literacy in Northern Kentucky (LINK), an adult literacy advocacy group, will join the festivities by providing statistics, reading material and information for those interested in volunteering.

Writers can't solely depend on each other for inspiration, and so the R&R pays homage to a source of continual divine inspiration for many contemporary artists: rock and roll. Bands include locals The Woos (eclectic pop-core), Humans Bow Down (astro-punk fusion), Film Caught Fire (uber-indie rock) and Dayton's Murder Your Darlings (calculated chaos rock).

The Cincinnati Rock and Read Fest 2 is not to be missed.

Vivid invites all independent publications to join them at the show to trade, distribute and network. Table space will be provided for anyone interested in distributing.

As a literacy advocate, I was thrilled that such an event was occurring in the city in which I live. It's inspiring to me when young people put on display and show off their own writing, their own work, to expand what passes for literacy and literate practice. These are youth who believe in the power of the word, in the possibilities of changing their worlds through writing. I wanted to take every one of them to class with me, to model for all of my students the continued importance and value of writing in the contemporary world.

As I browsed through the booths at the Fest, talking and mingling with the authors, editors, and illustrators, I was also surprised by how many zinesters had developed companion Web sites for their writing projects. Both *XRay* and *Friction Magazine* have extensive Web sites, with much content on them that doesn't make its way into print. Their work was intricate and complex, frequently mixing genres of prose and poetry, and combining visuals, images, and text. My mind turned to the many students I have taught over the past few years who have proudly shown me their own Web sites, who have often wanted to submit their composition assignments, their rhetorical analyses, or their text-based arguments, as Web sites or in a Web portfolio. Their work was comparably complex, involving inventive uses of FLASH and Java scripts, as well as creative uses of visual puns and parodies. I didn't have to go to The Cincinnati Rock + Read Fest 2 to be inspired by how some youth are using technology to write their own lives; it had been happening right under my own nose, in my own classrooms.

Others, too, have noted how many nonprofessional writers, especially younger writers, are experimenting with a wide variety of writing forms, particularly forms that are technologically enabled, and such work has prompted scholars in a variety of disciplines to explore this writing more fully. In general, the study of "nonacademic" and "nonprofessional" literacies, of ways people communicate beyond the world of school and work, is gaining interest. A recent scholarly collection, *Popular Literacy: Studies in Cultural Practice and Poetics*, focuses attention on such literacies, and editor John Trimbur, a noted English studies scholar, explains the attraction of them:

> I became increasingly interested in how people use reading and writing for their own ends—the hidden and unofficial literacies they use to negotiate their way in the world. . . . What's involved when people divert the means of communication from official purposes to serve their own ends—whether in small quotidian ways or linked to popular movements for social change? (ix)

Increasingly, much of that "diverted" communication is mediated through computer technologies and the Internet. In the concluding chapter of *Popular Literacy*, "Understanding Popular Digital Literacies," Lester Faigley notes how such "popular literacies" are experienced, experimented with, and explored through technology, particularly the Internet:

> In 1981 Thomas Miller and I conducted a survey of 200 college-educated people writing on the job, stratified according to type of employer and type of occupation. We found that everyone in an occupation that requires a college education wrote on the job and wrote frequently. Nearly three-fourths of the people sampled claimed to devote 10 percent or more of their work time to writing, but few reported to write much while off the job. For many people who have access to the Internet, that situation has changed. They may be using work time for personal writing, but they are nonetheless writing for purposes other than work. (257)

Given all of this work, this writing, an obvious question arises: What are all of these people writing about?

Sometimes, it is easier to answer such a question when we look at specific groups. For instance, Randal Woodland, writing in "'I plan to be a 10': Online Literacy and Lesbian, Gay, Bisexual, and Transgender Students," reflects on how "younger gay men carried on a full online life that was for many entirely separate from the other parts of their lives," and, in the process, he "recalled some hints I'd gotten of the hidden literacies of students, capacities for writing and self-expression that go on outside our classes and that we may never see" (77). Others have noted similar activity among youth writers in general. Writing in "Using Digital Tools to Foster Critical Inquiry," Richard Beach and Bertram C. Bruce suggest the following:

> While adolescents may continue to use media to construct themselves according to the values of a consumerist, narcissistic world, we would argue that their emerging participation in digital technologies portends the possibilities of alternative ways of constructing identities. Many adolescents are turning away from the represented worlds of much of broadcast media . . . to participate in shared communal experiences mediated by digital tools. (149)

Based on my own experiences, and inspired by the scholarship I was beginning to see, I too began exploring the number of ways in which my students, generally young, college-aged youths, were using Internet technologies to communicate. I had been inspired by their efforts, by their intimate engagement with writing and with diverse literacy practices, and, with their permission, I wanted to explore some of their "hidden literacies," to find out what they were writing about, what inspired them, and how they were using the new communications technologies as literacy tools. I also wanted to address a gap in scholarship about their use of technology, a gap often glossed over, even by the most intelligent authors and critics. For instance, in *Literacy in the New Media Age*, Gunther Kress acknowledges an obvious impact of technology on writing—the increase of authorial output:

> And yes, there is more writing than ever before. Let me make two points. The first is, who is writing more? Who is filling the pages of websites with writing? Is it the young? Or is it those who grew up in the era when writing was clearly the dominant mode? The second point goes to the question of the future of writing. Image has coexisted with writing, as of course has speech. In the era of the dominance of writing, when the logic of writing organized the page, image appeared on the page subject to the logic of writing. . . . In the era of the dominance

of the screen, writing appears on the screen subject to the logic of the image. Writing fits in how, where and when the logic of the image-space suggests. The effects on writing . . . will be inescapable. (7–8)

Kress raises the right kinds of questions, I think, but he skips over the question that might itself lead to some of the most interesting answers to his questions: "Is it the young?"

I believe it may be. And although some may think the Internet passé, I contend that some of the most exciting work in writing, in authorship, in literacy development, is still occurring on the Internet in general and on the Web in particular. In an interview for a collection appropriately titled *Digital Delirium*, Hakim Bey said the following about "Logging On" to the Internet:

Disinformation—the internet as psychic swamp—disembodied egos—information vampires. "We have a Web [SIC] page."
What to do with all these badly-designed gadgets? If I put the PC [personal computer] into an olde oaken cupboard, like rich people used to do with their TVs, I'd feel like an idiot—but if I leave it in plain sight it offends me at every moment with its smug space-age yuppie shape and designer beige plastic intrusiveness. I admit, these feelings scarcely amount to the *high moral ground*.
But please: let's have no more posturing about "the next stage of evolution" either.
Let's talk about something else. (154)

Okay, yes—the hoopla is over, but many youth with Internet access and Web-authoring skills are still writing the Web. And they are writing it in ways that are creative, dynamic, and boundary-pushing. The question is, are we paying attention? And what can we learn from the literacies with which such digital youth are playing on the Web?

That is the primary purpose of this book: First, to draw our attention to a critical examination of the emerging literacy practices of American youth, generally college-aged, who are composing for the Web, and, second, to excavate and examine some of the "underground economy" of communication that some of these e-savvy youth are creating and engaging.

Before we launch into this analysis, it is worth considering, if only briefly, the importance of studying such writing, as well as setting some useful parameters and establishing some workable definitions for this domain of inquiry. In the remainder of this introduction, then, I'll consider important questions of methodology, such as how we can study "digital youth" writing intelligently and productively and what we hope to learn as educators and scholars of literacy from such an analysis.

METHODOLOGICAL CONSIDERATIONS: CONDUCTING INTERNET RESEARCH

The "digital youth writing" examined here comes from a variety of sources. However, considering the large number of communications platforms that youth with e-access and skills use—ranging from chatrooms and e-mail to cell phones and text messaging—it is not possible to address adequately the entire spectrum of how youth with Internet access use communications technologies to write their lives and represent themselves. Therefore, the scope of this book is largely limited to the Web, which has become one of the most widely used forums through which digital youth communicate, express notions of identity and community, and build a sociopolitical sense of self through "writing." As Lisa Nakamura writes, "The web is the most popular incarnation of the Internet, and at the time of this writing [2002] comes the closest . . . to constituting a 'public sphere,' a virtual agora where users can meet and exchange the kind of discourse that builds community" (109).

Even the Web itself, however, is a dauntingly large domain of study, and I have thus consulted and worked closely with some key evolving methodologies for studying content on the Internet in general and the Web in particular. Indeed, in *Doing Internet Research: Critical Issues and Methods for Examining the Net*, Steve Jones writes that "Internet research . . . must avoid being prescriptive. But it is extremely difficult for it even to be descriptive, given the ever-changing networks involved, the mutating software and hardware, and the elastic definitions" (xiii). This is particularly true of the WWW, whose pages and sites are variously updated daily, appear and disappear overnight, or are left abandoned due to lack of interest or resources necessary to maintain them. Given this, scholars and researchers have been developing a few principles of Internet and Web research to guide our work in understanding and analyzing the Web. Let me flesh out a few such principles here to explain how I have undertaken my analysis.

In their seminal article, "Analyzing the Web: Directions and Challenges," Ananda Mitra and Elisia Cohen borrow from literary criticism and discourse analysis to propose a "critical text work" for examining and interpreting "texts" on the Web. In general, the two authors maintain that a text on the Web "has a set of specific characteristics predicated by its hypertextuality. These characteristics include the nonlinear nature of the text, its global reach, and its use of the multiple images borrowing from different media" (192). The hypertextual nature of the Web, which has garnered commentary and critique since its inception, is the primary dynamic around which most any aspect of "writing," "authoring," or "composing" on the Web must be analyzed. Summarizing Mitra and Cohen's work in his book, *An Introduction to Cybercultures*, David Bell identifies six key features of Web texts that Mitra and Cohen highlight in their analysis: "intertextuality, nonlinearity, a blurring of the reader/writer distinction, 'multimedianess,' 'globalness,' and ephemerality" (193). Each of these, arising out of the use of hypertext as a dominant mode of constructing sites, deserves comment, and, in all of my analyses, I have attempted to point out how the writers whose work I examine experiment in particular with intertextuality, nonlinearity, and a "blurring of the reader/writer" distinction. Additionally, the increasing use of multimedia, especially visuals and videos, deserves particular comment and analysis. In general, these four dimensions of Web texts are at the core of my discussions of how some youth are using the Web, but, as is seen here, we also have occasion to discuss both the "globalness" (or lack thereof) of the Web and the "ephemerality" of Web compositions.

These last two deserve special consideration before proceeding.

Certainly, important work is being done in studying the interconnectedness of and interrelationship between the Internet and various moves toward globalization. In *Global Literacies and the World Wide Web*, editors Gail E. Hawisher and Cynthia L. Selfe argue broadly that the "Web [is] an environment for global literacy practices" (1), and theirs is among the first collections that

> begins the examination of such culturally specific literacy practices—authoring, designing, reading, analyzing, interpreting—on the Web. . . . The overarching goal of the volume is to test the commonly accepted premise that the Web provides individuals around the globe with a common and neutral literacy environment within which international communications are authored, read, and exchanged. (3)

Contributors to Hawisher's and Selfe's collection examine a range of sites and literacy practices from several different nations and cultural groups. Ultimately, the editors see in the play of identities depicted by the Web the development of new literacies of self. In their "Conclusion: Inventing

Postmodern Identities: Hybrid and Transgressive Literacy Practices on the Web," the editors discuss the impact of globalization on the Web, commenting on how such globalization offers shifting sources of identity construction, resulting in changing identities and changing literacies to describe and represent those identities. They maintain that "individuals who use the Web are multiply defined" (287), and that we can view the Web as a site of changing understandings of both literacy and identity—with both personal *and* political ramifications:

> In this electronic environment of rapid and disturbing social change where conventional social formations and institutions are being deconstructed, personal and group identity—as expressed through language and literacy practices—is, in [Manual] Castells' words, "fast becoming the main, and sometimes the only source of meaning. . . . People increasingly organize their meaning not around what they do but on the basis of who they are, or believe they are" (Castells, 1996, p. 3), and they define their primary identities in their everyday literate practices within the networked society. (279)

The deconstruction of "conventional social formation and institutions" and the emphasis on "personal and group identity" brings with it new possibilities for political coalition. Summarizing the work of Donna Haraway, Hawisher and Selfe suggest that "geopolitical identities no longer satisfy in a world where we must act not out of 'natural identification'. . . but only out 'of conscious coalition, of affinity, of political kinship'" (280). Such analyses lead Hawisher and Selfe to argue that the Web "provides a site for transgressive literacy practices that express and value difference; that cling to historical, cultural, and racial diversity; and that help groups and individuals constitute their own multiple identities through language" (15). More broadly, the beauty of *Global Literacies and the World Wide Web* is its wonderful panorama of literacy practices to be found across the Web, and consequently across the globe, and the editors' and contributors' focus on "culturally specific literacy practices—authoring, designing, reading, analyzing, interpreting—on the Web"—serves as a good model for the kind of work I have attempted in these pages, a close reading and textual analysis.

I must admit, however, that my analyses have been much more narrowly focused than those offered by Hawisher and Selfe, and, consequently, the commentary in this book does not forward "global" claims about how people use the Web—quite the contrary. Rather, I have focused (a) on a particular set of representations on the Web, that of "youth," and (b) on a set of literacy practices arising out of a particular group's attempt to represent itself, its ideas, and its concerns. Because the majority of digital youth who actively use the Web live in the highly industrialized West, the sites I analyze and discuss are inevitably those of youth from largely first-world nations. They are also, consequently, frequently composed by white youth. This should not be surprising. In *Cybertypes: Race, Ethnicity, and Identity on the Internet*, Lisa Nakamura notes that "Web demographics are always in flux. It has been known for some time, however, that racial minorities use the web less than do whites" (108). Still, I have attempted to incorporate issues of race and ethnicity, and I am pleased with the diversity of sites I have collected for analysis and commentary. And although I offer a much narrower focus, perhaps sacrificing a global view of the Web, I think such an approach potentially provides us a more in-depth analysis of specific Web practices, particularly among a prominent group of Web users. More provocatively, we might see how these Web composers figure—or refuse to figure—their use of the Web in terms of "globalness."

A narrowed focus is troubled, however, by questions of ephemerality. In particular, given the ever-changing—and huge—nature of the WWW, how can I tell that my analyses are sufficiently representative of what such digital youth are doing on and with the Web? This is not an insignificant question for Web studies in general. David Bell's *An Introduction to Cybercultures* offers a useful chapter on "Researching Cybercultures" in which he outlines some of the challenges—and possibilities—of conducting research into cybercultures. In the course of his discussion, Bell succinctly highlights the "question of verifiability" as one that haunts studies of cybercultures or any Internet-based study (195). To wit, how can I know that what I am pointing out can be "verified" by others? For Bell, such a question arises out of the sheer volume of Web sites available for analysis: "How many links do we need to follow in order to get a sense of an 'area' of the web? If we look at ten sites on a topic, does it matter that there might be a hundred more we haven't seen?" (194). I don't know that I have a good answer for this question. The Web is so extensive that I could not, even if I tried, visit and study every page relevant to my inquiry.

Given such limitations, some scholars of the Internet have proposed what we might call a "provisional ethnography" as the best method for researching Web texts. For instance, Christine Hine, in *Virtual Ethnography*, maintains that when approaching a study of online communication, an ethnographic approach might work well:

> An ethnography of the Internet can look in detail at the ways in which the technology is experienced in use. In its basic form ethnography consists of a researcher spending an extended period of time

immersed in a field setting, taking account of the relationships, activities and understandings of those in the setting and participating in those processes. The aim is to make explicit the taken-for-granted and often tacit ways in which people make sense of their lives. The ethnographer inhabits a kind of in-between world, simultaneously native and stranger. They must become close enough to the culture being studied to understand how it works, and yet be able to detach from it sufficiently to be able to report on it. (4–5)

At the same time, Hine correctly notes that a "holistic understanding of the Internet seems a futile undertaking. . . . However hard the ethnographer works, she or he will only ever partially experience the Internet" (63). As such, it is best to acknowledge—up front—the provisional nature of this work. Bell summarizes well some of Hine's principles for conducting and reporting on Internet-based research, and a few points are worth emphasizing:

- Virtual ethnography is "interstitial" temporally—it is not inhabited 24 hours a day, so immersion can only be intermittent.
- Virtual ethnography can only ever be partial, and can never reflect the totality of the Internet.
- The ethnographer is also a participant using the media of cyberspace, and so reflexivity about online experiences should be foregrounded. (200)

I have taken these principles to heart, and I note throughout that the ideas forwarded, much like the sites examined, must necessarily be provisional in nature and should not be construed as representative of how *all* (or even a clear-cut majority of) digital youth use the Web or wish to be represented via the Web. Indeed, I don't think such a totality exists; the diversity of users and their interests are simply too great.

As such, I have eschewed examining a breadth of sites so that I could delve deeply into a *sampling* of sites, building case studies of them and incorporating comments from interviews with their authors into my analysis. In each chapter, I highlight the work of a former student (all under 30 years of age at the time of this writing), who shared with me his or her "hidden literacies" and Web-authoring experiments. After being inspired by the work I saw, I asked the students to provide additional sites for me to examine, perhaps sites that had inspired *them*. I also conducted my own Web searches for yet more sites by digital youth who were, in their own ways, pushing the boundaries of Web expression and literacy practice.

Each chapter is composed of analyses of a mixture of such sites. David Bell notes that some cyber-oriented ethnographers are recommending "multi-sited ethnography," combining both "online and off-line elements" (197), and I have actively pursued this line of analysis. Each chapter surveys a few sites that seem representative of the rhetorical issues or Web genres at which I am looking, and I provide an in-depth case study of a couple of sites whose authors I have interviewed at length. Complete interviews are included at the end of most chapters.

I would be remiss if I did not acknowledge how the use of youth as a conceptual category is problematical in several ways unless it is carefully qualified and delimited. So let me be clear, even if I risk being repetitive: I do not mean the term youth to be totalizing in any way. After all, youth *cannot* encompass all of the varieties of subcultural affiliations and identities perhaps implied by the term, and the possibilities for examining the way youth use technology to communicate, represent themselves and their concerns, and construct strategic literacies are, if not limitless, still multiple and complex, and they are further inflected by a number of social, cultural, and political forces that cannot be fully interrogated in one book. As such, I want to make it clear from the outset that I am focusing in this book on a particular subset of all the people who could legitimately be classified as "youth." Specifically, I want to draw critical attention to the kinds of Web-authoring and digital literacy practices of the kinds of students who frequently appear in first-year composition courses in colleges and universities. Even more specifically, the group I am interested in is comprised of these college youth who bring with them, often into the classroom, interest in, knowledge of, and frequently great facility with composing in Web-based venues and for Web publication. This is, admittedly, a particularly small group of students, but I believe these "e(lectronic)-savvy youth" or digital youth (as I refer to them throughout this volume) are showing us significant ways in which they engage—and expand—notions of electronically enabled or enhanced literacies. Given such a delimitation, my analyses can hardly be exhaustive, but I *do* believe they can productively speculative. Furthermore, youth itself will become a term that the writers we examine—both critics and youth themselves—interrogate as an ideological figure, a constructed category that variously has its own political uses and limitations and that often serves a repository for fantasies about the future of technology, literacy, and writing.

And finally, because the potential inquiry into this subject could be mind-bogglingly huge with respect to the sheer number of communications platforms available and the variety of ways a multitude of digital youth utilize these platforms, I have limited the scope of my study in one other way. Specifically, I have chosen not to examine fan cultures on the Web, which have been attracting much scholarly attention on their own, with many articles, books, and even conferences devoted to the study of how fans, typically young people, use the Web to write of their appreciation for popular culture. In particular, "fan fiction" and "slash" have gained much attention and have been inspired, for instance, by the work of Henry Jenkins and his book, *Textual Poachers: Television Fans and Participatory Culture*. Given the increasing prominence of this work, I want to turn our attention to other Web genres, such as youth's use of personal homepages, informational sites, e-zines (electronic magazines), and activist sites.

IDEOLOGICAL CONSIDERATIONS: YOUTH USING THE WEB

Beyond sampling and discussing via such case studies the diversity of emerging writing and literacy practices that some digital youth are experimenting with on the Web, I have also attempted to place these practices in larger contexts of how such youth view themselves in various cultural and sociopolitical matrices. In "The New Literacy Studies," Brian Street makes the following argument:

> Research into "vernacular" literacies within modern urban settings has begun to show the richness and diversity of literacy practices and meanings despite the pressures for uniformity exerted by the nation-state and modern education systems. . . . An understanding of literacy requires detailed, in-depth accounts of actual practice in different cultural settings. It is not sufficient, however, to extol simply the richness and variety of literacy practices made accessible through such ethnographic detail: we also need bold theoretical models that recognize the central role of power relations in literacy practices. (430)

Inspired by Street's call to recognize and analyze the "power relations" embedded in all "literacy practices," I use the following chapters not only to "extol . . . the richness and variety of literacy practices" that digital youth are deploying via the Web, but to trace some of the ways in which they are using these practices to forward particular social, cultural, and political ends—often in sharp contradistinction to the assumptions many make about digital youth and their political investments (or lack thereof).

Specifically, I take a few of the more prominent "mythologies" and popular beliefs about youths' use of technology and examine them against some
relevant actual practices. In many ways, examining debates about digital
youth and technology is interesting by itself in terms of unearthing and
understanding the ideologies at play in such debates. But the way that digital youth actually *use* the new communications technologies tells an even
more intriguing story about changes in literacy practices and the use of
technology to make sense of the world and intervene in its construction
and interpretation.

    Given this, the discussion here frequently proceeds as a series of "con-
frontations"—between e-savvy and digital youth and their representation,
particularly with regard to how they are figured in relationship to and use
technology. I analyze the various dominant ways in which scholars, critics,
and pundits view youth and technology, and then discuss some digital
youth's responses to them by examining how such youth use technology to
refigure themselves—often in contradistinction to their "mythological" representations by others, such as critics, pundits, academics, and other ideologues. In the process, we see how use by many youths of the new communications technologies has resulted in the development of several
emerging literacy practices—practices that might help define the future of
writing, as potentially fostered by electronic media such as the Web.
Specific questions driving this inquiry include the following: How are digital youth and their relationship to technology represented, and what do
such representations tell us about both youth and technology—as categories and ideological figures? How do digital youth variously represent
themselves with the new communications technologies? What can these
representations tell us about such youth's relationship to technology? How
might digital youth's use of technology prompt experimentation with new
literacies and literacy practices, and how does the development, proliferation, and consumption of representations of youth via technology reflect
those literacies and practices? Finally, what are the pedagogical implications of the ways such digital youth use and represent themselves with
technology on our understanding of literacy?

    To answer such questions, I draw, throughout this book, on the work of
three fields of critical inquiry—cultural studies, subcultural studies, and the
emerging field of cyberculture studies.

    In terms of examining representations, mythological and otherwise,
cultural studies theorists maintain that representations are inevitably, if
complexly, related to ideologies, and in general, I agree with Diana George
and Diane Shoos that "Representation is never innocent. It has real effects
and repercussions" (125). As such, cultural studies' attention to the inter-

section between language/representation and ideology/politics is a powerful methodological tool for understanding representations of youth and technology. How might such an analysis proceed? Speaking specifically about media representations, Carla Freccero offers several questions that can frame our discussion of the representation of youth and technology. In particular, she asks the following:

> What work are they [the media] doing? What motivates the representation? What does the representation say about the representers and the imagined viewers of such representation? What elements are combined in a cultural representation? What contradictions get highlighted? (15)

Moreover, for cultural studies theorists, texts are never simply static representations of ideologies or beliefs. For James Berlin and others influenced by cultural studies, texts *engage* ideology—ways of knowing the world, ways of being in the world, ways of being shaped by and shaping the world—by "reproducing" or "resisting" it. As Berlin puts it in "Composition and Cultural Studies," "texts are imbricated in economic, social, and political arrangements—[and] are indeed ideological . . . texts are products of culture and . . . reproduce or resist culture in related ways" (49). This study of how youth and technology are co-represented attempts to examine some of these connections between representation and ideological systems, as well as how some digital youth sometimes attempt to intervene in those representations, resisting them to create their own texts and images forwarding their own ideological investments.

Indeed, because this work also examines the way identities, cultures, politics, and representations are acts of *resistance,* I have found it useful to consider the work of writing studies specialists who theorize the ways in which writing can be used to intervene critically and productively in resisting predetermined and limiting notions of self and agency. In this regard, the work of bell hooks is especially significant. In *Outlaw Culture: Resisting Representations,* hooks argues for turning our attention—as scholars and pedagogues—to an interdisciplinary cultural studies that offers us "practical engagement with cultural practices and cultural icons who are defined as on the edge, as pushing the limits, disturbing the conventional, acceptable politics of representation" (4–5). For example, hooks offers astute readings of how hip-hop music and culture talk to us about race relations in America and how pop singer and sex icon Madonna offers us opportunity to reflect on shifting gender and sexual roles. In many ways, examining the way some digital youth use technology gives us just such "practical engagement" with "pushing the limits" of self and community expression, of meaning-making with digital communication platforms, and of the uses and potential abuses of electronic literacy.

The "boundary-crossing" that hooks proposes is hardly just an academic exercise in interdisciplinarity. Rather, according to hooks, we must fight "cultural fascism"—the "open demand for separatist politics, embracing notions of inclusion and exclusion, whether based on shared gender, race, or nationality." For hooks, such cultural fascism "seriously impedes all progressive effort to create a culture where border crossing enables both the sharing of resources and the production of a culture of communalism and mutuality." Moreover, such "fascism" slows the "exchange of knowledge, or the formation of new epistemologies" (6). With this in mind, the ultimate goal of the critical engagement hooks proposes is to "decolonize minds and imaginations," and hooks maintains that "cultural studies' focus on popular culture can be and is a powerful site for intervention, challenge, and change" (4). In terms of studying the representation of youth and technology, hooks' formulation asks us to be sensitive to how some youth use the new communications technologies in the "exchange of knowledge" and perhaps even in the "formation of new epistemologies." Digital youth do both—in inventive and startling ways. Indeed, citing Gary Clarke, cultural theorist John Storey says that "cultural studies should focus on 'the activities of all youths to locate continuities and discontinuities in culture and social relations and to discover the meaning these activities have for the youths themselves'" (219). And, as is seen here, youth deploy a number of "continuities and discontinuities" to disrupt their representation of themselves and their relationship to technology and to refigure it—and themselves—with their own literacies.

However, although I may begin with the work of hooks and Berlin for theoretical inspiration, I note how their formulations sometimes fall short of explaining the dynamics we are seeing—particularly with regard to the use of technology as a tool for resistance. For instance, hooks suggests that "a culture of communalism and mutuality" is the shared goal of cultural "outlaws." However, many of the digital youth writing practices I examine may seem to partake of an "outlaw" spirit, but their goals are hardly communal mutuality. As such, I draw on the work of *subcultural* theorists to explain some of the more complex dynamics of how some youth, in various subcultural formations, shape their own self-representation. In her general introduction to *The Subcultures Reader*, Sarah Thornton suggests that "studies of subcultures are attempts to map the social world and, as such, they are exercises in representation" (Gelder 1). And those representations, as we shall see, are often remarkably complex. In "Posing...Threats,

Striking...Poses: Youth, Surveillance, and Display," Dick Hebdige argues that "the politics of youth culture is a politics of gesture, symbol, and metaphor, that it deals in the currency of signs and that the subcultural response is, thus, always essentially ambiguous" (403). More specifically, Hebdige suggests the following:

> Subculture is, then, neither simply an affirmation or a refusal, neither simply resistance against symbolic order nor straightforward conformity with the parent culture. It is both a declaration of independence, of Otherness, of alien intent, a refusal of anonymity, of subordinate status. It is an *insubordination*. And at the same time, it is also a confirmation of the fact of powerlessness, a celebration of impotence. Subcultures are both a play for attention and a refusal, once attention has been granted, to be read according to the Book. (404).

In many ways, Hebdige's conceptualization will apply to some of the discussions here concerning how some digital youth use technology to represent themselves, their concerns, and their interests in technology—as simultaneously an act of resistance to the "parent culture" and also, frequently, as a "celebration of impotence," often articulated through nostalgia, irony, or fantasy. Such fantasy, however, is not without an *edge*, suggesting the development of *critical* literacies in response to how youth and technology are represented.

Indeed, if subcultural expressions are a "play for attention and a refusal . . . to be read according to the Book," then they are also *literacy* practices—albeit ones that may or may not be recognized by the "dominant" or "majority" culture. Several cyberculture studies specialists have devoted much time and energy to exploring the emerging literacy practices found in interactive, online forums. The questions they pose and the theories they proffer can assist us in understanding digital youth writing practices—and help us analyze how such youth use technology to communicate their views and to construct their worlds. In this regard, I am particularly thinking of the work of Sherry Turkle, Donna Haraway, as well as "cyber-writing" specialists Jay David Bolter, whose appreciation of the "writing" possibilities afforded by the new communications technologies is tempered by a critical sense of how literacy might change in unexpected—and perhaps even undesirable—ways.

The insights of these and other scholar-critics are sprinkled throughout this book, but I have perhaps been most inspired *methodologically* by the work that Gail Hawisher and Patricia Sullivan do in their article, "Fleeting Images: Women Visually Writing the Web"—a model piece of scholarship that combines and uses much of the critical work just described here. In this essay, Hawisher and Sullivan analyze both how women are represented and represent themselves on the Web, with a particular focus on visual imagery. They summarize their work as follows:

> With these images, then, we begin to see how some women (both in and out of the field of writing) visually represent themselves on the Web and how they themselves get represented. When others control the Web images, we see women represented commercially in ways that seem familiar to us—as objects to be ogled, objects to stimulate, commodities to be bought and sold. . . . But there are also examples of women writing their own visual representations in cyborg territory. These women begin to forge new social arrangements by creating a visual discourse that startles and disturbs. (287)

I appreciate Hawisher and Sullivan's attention to both the ways some "digital" women are represented and how they chose to represent themselves, to acts of cultural cooptation and sociopolitical resistance. My intention in this book has been to apply a similar approach to the study of how some digital youth are represented and represent themselves. I believe that understanding both in relation to one another offers us insight into how some youth use representations already in existence to craft their own, often through creative acts of resistance and re-appropriation. I offer one substantive caveat and qualification, worth bearing in mind: Just as Hawisher and Sullivan cannot speak for all women writing the Web, so too can I not speak for all digital youth writing the Web.

I actually experimented in some earlier work with an approach similar to Hawisher and Sullivan's; in that work, I analyzed how young gays and lesbians with Internet access use the Web and other online forums to create and critique a sense of self, identity, and community. In the process, I discovered a number of surprises, particularly the growing sense among some *queer* digital youth that the diversity of images of "gay" identity and community—on the Web, for instance—challenges perceived senses of *stable*, even monolithic gay identity, culture, and community. For such youth, finding a rich and varied online queer community is often both a "relief" *and* a site of "cognitive dissonance," in that many competing notions of what it means to be gay—with consequent implications for gay culture and politics—proliferate throughout the Web. On further reflection, I surmised that this might also be true of representations of youth in general, which circulate dizzyingly through magazines, the Web, radio ads, print ads, novels, television; so *many* representations are just begging to be "read," and they can be used both to undertake a *critical* understanding of representation *and* to explore a sense of the *multidimensionality* of representation in a "digital age." And, like gay youth trying to negotiate a number of possible identities and communities online, any number of youth encountering their representation both with and via technology have the opportunity to explore and negotiate such representations through an increasing number of interactive online forums, several on the Web alone. Moreover, they have the chance to create new *possibilities* of representation.

A WHOLE LOT OF WRITING GOING ON, 2.0: CHAPTER SUMMARIES

It should be obvious by now that a critical examination of digital youths' use of technology to represent their lives and their concerns may tell us much about our culture's developing relationship with the new communications technologies. Moreover, analyzing how some digital youth themselves process, understand, and interact with such technologies may also give us insight into how to negotiate our own relationships with both youth and technology. And, perhaps most importantly, I believe that undertaking such a study can show us the kinds of emerging literacy and authorial practices that some digital youth are drawn to, that they cultivate, and that they help develop as they represent *their* worlds to us. With that said, I examine in the following chapters both the debates surrounding digital youths' use of technology and a variety of possible emerging compositional and literacy practices in the Web texts that some youth are creating.

To explore this nexus of ideas and texts, I have divided the book into three sections, "Literacy Possibilities—and Problems," "Literacy Practices," and "Activist Literacies." Let me explain each, and their accompanying chapters, in a bit more detail.

The two chapters of the first section, "Literacy Possibilities—and Problems," analyze more thoroughly the debates surrounding digital youths' use of technology and the potential impact of such technologies on literacy, writing, and such youths' articulation and representation of their own concerns and issues. Chapter 1, "Technology, Literacy, and Digital Youth," traces such debates from the 1990s to the present, and I pay particular attention to how "youth" is figured as an ideological element—in both utopian and dystopian visions of the impact of technology on literacy. I begin with this debate in an attempt to situate my project within the context of ongoing discussions and concerns about technology and literacy, and, in the process, I note the need to take a bit more seriously both the actual literacy practices of some digital youth, and the kinds of emerging literacy practices that such youths' use of technology might herald. In Chapter 2, "Uses and Abuses of Hyperbole, or, the Case of Douglas Rushkoff's Digital Kids," I introduce how some youth themselves have entered into this debate, with provocative Web texts that situate such youths' own concerns about literacy and technology within the utopian/dystopian debate. I begin the chapter with an analysis of one of the major enthusiasts about the potentially utopian ways in which e-savvy youth use technology, Douglas Rushkoff, whose controversial book, *Playing the Future*, figures such youth as "digital kids" leading us into a future of electronically enabled "cooperation and community." After detailing some of Rushkoff's ideas, I examine raver culture, one of the youth subcultures, that Rushkoff lauds, and I test his enthusiasms against some of the ways that raver youth actually use communications technology, such as the Web. The hyperbolic enthusiasm that Rushkoff promulgates isn't shared by all digital youth, many of whom use hyperbole itself to interrogate and critique glib formulations of technology in general and the Web in particular as necessarily enabling greater cooperation and community building. Rather, some of these youth develop and deploy challenging Web literacies to explore their evolving and complex understanding of how technologies such as the Web can—and can not—be used to communicate, build community, and create alternatives spaces for exploring identity.

The three chapters in the Part II, "Literacy Practices," turn our attention directly to a variety of Web-based literacy practices by focusing attention on how many digital youth use Web technologies and technologically enabled literacies in different Web genres, such as the personal homepage, the e-zine, and the activist site. Throughout, attention is focused on what kinds of compositional practices characterize digital youth writing on these pages, as well as what those compositional practices reveal about how such youth use the Web to construct and complicate notions of identity, community, and politics. For instance, Chapter 3, "Ironies of Self: Rewriting the Personal Homepage," examines a popular mode or genre of Web writing, the personal homepage. The chapter explores how some youth use this standard genre to make some surprisingly complex—and political—statements about issues of identity and representation. In particular, the work I examine deploys tropes of irony and self-irony to complicate what it means to have a "marketable identity" on the Web. Chapter 4, "The Personal and the Political: E-Zines, Community, and the Politics of Publication," extends this discussion to another popular Web genre, the e-zine, which many digital youth are using to forward their own sociopolitical vision of the world. Using the Web's interactive features, some youth problematize our notions of "readers" and "writers" in the cause of advancing a more egalitarian, participatory sense of social and political interaction *through writing*. The chapter concludes with a case study of *X-Ray*, a Cincinnati-based dual desktop and Web-publishing venture, that highlights some inventive ways in which some digital youth use the Web to address complex political issues and build a community of writers. In Chapter 5, "Writing Queer Digital Youth: A Case of Identity and Community on the Web," I discuss a specific group or subset of youth who are using the Web to explore notions of identity, community, and politics. It has been argued for years that the WWW has been a significant source of information for queer youth with Internet access, particularly those in rural areas who do not have access to urban gay culture. As such, the Web's ability to disseminate information is often lauded as powerful, far-reaching, and potentially life-saving. But queer digital youth are putting the Web to use in other ways, and for other ends, as well. In this chapter, I detail how some lesbian, gay, bisexual, and transgender youth are using Web literacies in ways that gesture toward a political vision and narration of the queer self that might differ from older notions of gayness and queer politics. As such, this chapter extends the work in the preceding two chapters by looking at how a particular group— queer digital youth—write their lives on the Web.

The preceding three chapters, on personal homepages, e-zines, and queer youth sites, show some youth actively using a variety of Web genres and literacies to explore, experiment with, and expand notions of identity and community. The chapters in the remaining section of this book, "Activist Literacies," take up the question of how some digital youth use the Web as a tool for activist work, or as a tool for intervening directly in sociopolitical debates. The work that such youth do along these lines both challenges and critiques hopes for the political possibilities of the Web and offers us a glimpse of the kinds of literacy and Web practices that some digital youth think *are* useful when engaging in a political intervention. For instance, Chapter 6, "Digital Youth Activism: Rethinking the Web as a Tool for Social Change," offers a case study of how some youth are reconfiguring their use of the Web to forward their political and activist agendas. In this particular case, an analysis of the youth-run International Middle East Media Center, we see some youth taking a very tempered, practical, and pragmatic approach to the Web, which they see not as a utopian medium for the dissemination of information and community-building, but as a support for other media in the construction and diversification of information. Such a realignment speaks to a heightened awareness of the potential—and limitations—of the Web as a literacy and authoring tool. In contrast, Chapter 7, "Literacies in Action: The YOUth and AIDS Web Project," details and explores some of the ways that my students and I have attempted to use what we've learned about digital youth and youth writing on the Web to create an informational *and activist* site for college-aged youth about HIV and AIDS. What is startling and engaging about this project is how the young people with whom I have worked wanted to take responsibility for their own representation in terms of their sexuality and sexual practices, particularly at a time when the cultural and political climate seems to want to squelch open discussion of sexuality among young people. In response, students negotiated the creation of an online forum to disseminate *their* understanding of the significance of safer sex education—primarily through the use of visual rhetoric, narratives, and text-based arguments about the need to pay attention to the reality of sexually transmitted infections. Furthermore, they experimented with information dissemination itself as a critical tool of resistant intervention. A critical assessment of this project complements our sense of the possibilities of paying attention to what digital youth are doing with writing on the Web.

In general, some of the writing strategies and literacy practices discussed in these chapters and interviews will seem familiar, in a postmodern sort of way. For instance, we find that the youth composers under consideration here seem interested in tropes of manipulation and play—manipulating media images, texts, and even whole genres through hyperbole, irony, and parody. Such play is not unlike that seen above, in the "e-version" of *Romeo and Juliet*. In fact, we may not be seeing the emergence of radically *different* literacies—but perhaps different literacy *emphases*. For instance, hyperbole, hardly a new literacy practice, seems to enjoy much greater *critical* play among digital youth writing on the Web than do other forms of critique more common in print. The question explored here, then, is *why* are these emphases utilized via the Web and other digital communications media? What is "youths'" attraction to them? Part of the answer to this will lie in an examination of the greater flexibility afforded by the Web, for instance, in creating complex forms of communication; in particular, the digital ease of "cutting and pasting," manipulating images, reproducing text, and adding sound (and video) files seems to invite parody, pastiche, and hyperbolic distortion.

At the same time, and perhaps despite the postmodern penchant for word and image play, I also note a fairly pervasive emphasis on deploying these literacy practices in the service of a variety of activist projects and sociopolitical goals. This may be these youths' most significant contribution to writing and literacy: *a reassessment of how compositional play can be political work*. In some ways, this should not be surprising; in a media-saturated society, the creative use of media for both self-expression and world (re)making seems an obvious way to attempt to enter into important conversations about identity, community, and politics. The creativity and inventiveness with which some digital youth enter these conversations via the Web is the subject of this book.

And, ultimately, I argue that digital youths' emerging literacy practices on the Web reveal a much more complex and nuanced view of technology than the utopian/dystopian debates suggest. Specifically, many such youth seem actively engaged in exploring how the Web can represent their ideas, their interests, and even their political investments, but they are also simultaneously aware of the limitations of such representation in effecting substantive political change. Nonetheless, they experiment widely with a variety of older and emerging Web literacies, figuring their work, not as revolutionary (or apocalyptic), but as intervening in localized disputes over meaning and representation. Granted, I can only claim in these pages to note a few trends, but I think they are significant trends that deserve further attention and scholarship. My choices for discussion will, of necessity, seem idiosyncratic. And they are, because they represent both a combination of my interests and what is available for me to study. At the same time, I argue that my choices, idiosyncrasies aside, represent an intriguing spectrum of youth engagement with new communications technologies—and they are, at least, suggestive of some of the possibilities for the future of literacy and the future of writing.

A PEDAGOGICAL POSTSCRIPT
TO THIS INTRODUCTION

Recently, a colleague, another writing instructor and professor of English, forwarded me a link to a FLASH site (http://www.homestarrunner.com/sbemail64.html), and she suggested that I would appreciate its humor. In this site, which plays like a little comedy routine, two students are chatting electronically, and one, Kyle Smith, asks the other, "Strong Bad," to write his English paper for him. Kyle *could* write it, but he just doesn't want to. Strong Bad agrees, and, as the FLASH site plays, we see Strong Bad compose a truly horrible three-paragraph "essay" on the "hustle and bustle" of contemporary life. Strong Bad chats away to a friend while writing the paper, which he spices up by giving Kyle a "cool" nickname: "The Yellow

Dart." After adjusting the single-spacing to triple-spacing, Strong Bad is done, ready for several hours of video-game playing. This little Web-based joke pokes fun simultaneously at the lack of interest many students have in writing *and* instructional fears about how computer technologies enable students to "skirt" writing skills development: They can request, perhaps even "borrow" text easily from a variety of electronic "sources," and they can manipulate visual dimensions of their writing to make it seem more substantial than it actually is. These are not inauthentic fears: Some students *do* plagiarize from Web and Internet sources; others use every word-processing trick they have to "expand" their writing; yet others don't even take advantage of the most basic kinds of computer technologies to help them compose their papers, such as spell-checking.

Fortunately, the joke, like all jokes, rests on a bit of truth exaggerated to make a point. And, although the point is a salient and significant one, it is only one among many truths about how such digital youth use technology to write.

Indeed, this book arises out of my work as a writing specialist and a teacher of writing, and my conviction that many digital youth use communications technologies in ways that are startling and unexpected, in ways that query our sense of the possibilities of those technologies, and in ways that presage future implications for writing and literacy. As such, my work joins and, hopefully, extends that of others in the field of English studies, as well as other students and scholars of writing and literacy. For instance, two literacy educators and scholars, Richard J. Selfe and Cynthia L. Selfe, ask a pivotal question about technology and literacy in their essay, "Critical Technological Literacy and English Studies: Teaching, Learning, and Action": "What are our roles for teaching students how to think about and respond to technology as it continues to shape our lives and as we continue to affect its design and use in society?" (348). For all of those concerned with the impact of the new communications technologies on literacy, on how we read and write, this is an excellent, even pressing question.

Yes, what *are* our roles? As we attempt to answer such a question, I propose another one: What do our students have to teach *us*? Beyond teaching students and youth how to consume the new media, we need to be sensitive to how many youth are already *using* new media themselves. Nancy Kaplan notes the following in "Knowing Practice: A More Complex View of New Media Literacy":

> If our definition of literacy in this post-print era fails to include construction (configuration) we will have a cognitively impoverished user, one who cannot transfer working knowledge from one technological

environment to another. Serious education for the 21st century needs
to operate out of a new model of literacy, one that allows the space of
literacy to sustain both interpretation and configuration. (http://iat.
ubalt.edu/kaplan/ssgrr01.pdf)

Kaplan is concerned with making sure that students are given every opportunity to experience, explore, and experiment with new media, to experience it as both interpreter *and* participant. I contend that many youth
already are active participants—on their own terms, in their own spaces,
and in their own ways. It is with an eye toward appreciating, analyzing, and
understanding those terms, spaces, and ways that I invite readers to consider my comments, analyses, and thoughts in the remainder of this book.

PART I

LITERACY POSSIBILITIES— AND PROBLEMS

1

TECHNOLOGY, LITERACY, AND DIGITAL YOUTH

The increased use in the United States of computer technologies and the Internet during the 1990s prompted Lucy Rollin, in her reference guide *Twentieth-Century Teen Culture by the Decades*, to note what has since become a truism: "Nothing has changed teen life—indeed all life in the Nineties—as much as the Internet. This link-up of millions of computers . . . opened the world to teens in unprecedented ways, and they have been instrumental in creating that new world through their ability to manipulate the technology" (323). E-mail, chat, online gaming, personal Web pages with guestbooks and message boards, and a host of other interactive media— these allow not just for the exchange of information but the potential development of alternative communities and worldviews.

With the increased use of computer technologies has come a corresponding flurry of criticism—both pro and con—about the influence of such technologies on a wide variety of youth who are exposed to and use them. In particular, debates about the impact of such technologies on *literacy* and *literacy practices* frequented the pages of national newspapers, magazines, and journals, and in many ways these debates continue to rage. Periodic newspaper articles, for instance, report on English teachers either complaining about how Instant Messaging seems to be corroding their students' ability to spell (e.g., "Yo, can u plz help me write English?" in *USA*

Today, March 31, 2003[1]) or how Web-based classroom systems such as Blackboard or Web CT allow students to share papers easily and profit from peer review of their work in dynamic and innovative ways. For instance, in "A Young Writers' Round Table, via the Web" (August 14, 2003), Lisa Guernsey acknowledges both the fears and the hopes surrounding young people's use of computer technologies to aid and develop their writing and literacy skills:

> Parents worry that children are cutting and pasting paragraphs from Web sites rather than writing their own. Adults wonder if instant messaging, with its compressed spelling and syntax, might be stunting writing development.
>
> But in patches around the country, teachers say that online technology is now becoming a powerful tool for improving, rather than undermining, students' writing skills. E-mail exchanges and public Web pages give students audiences for their work. Online bulletin boards allow students to post drafts to be read by their peers. Sites like www.scholastic.com and teenwriting.about.com collect and publish writing so students can see what others in their age group are capable of. Specialized software enables teachers to distribute student drafts anonymously without spending hours at a copying machine.
>
> For many students, this means that their words are being read seriously by their peers for the first time. Instead of turning in a paper that seems to end up in a black hole, only to resurface a few weeks later with a few comments from a teacher, pupils get rapid feedback from other students in their class or elsewhere. (http://www.nytimes.com/2003/08/14/technology/circuits/14peer.html ?ex=1061950041&ei=1&en=0384f06529293737)

Such hopes, however, are hardly new. In 1994, even before the advent of the World Wide Web (WWW), literacy and writing studies scholars such as Lester Faigley were hailing the use of computer technology to teach writing and literacy skills. In *Fragments of Rationality: Postmodernity and the Subject of Composition*, Faigley asserted that networked computer technologies offer students the opportunity "of exploring how identity is multiply constructed and how agency resides in the power of connecting with others and building alliances" (199). Since then, academic conferences, special

---

[1] See http://www.usatoday.com/life/2003-03-31-chat_x.htm for the complete story.

issues of scholarly journals, and entire journals themselves, such as the online journal *Kairos* (http://english.ttu.edu/kairos/), focus on teaching writing and literacy skills with the Web and the Internet. More and more books are published focusing on explaining, exploring, and promoting the "new media," such as Lev Manovich's *The Language of New Media* (2001), and a new genre of writing textbooks, which I examine later in this chapter, focuses on the pedagogical usefulness of such media and the literacies they are enabling—literacy practices which Gregory Ulmer refers to as "electracy" in *Internet Invention: From Literacy to Electracy*, the title of his tech-savvy composition textbook.

At the very least, as Dennis Baron characterizes the situation in "From Pencils to Pixels: The Stages of Literacy Technologies," "The computer, the latest development in writing technology, promises, or threatens, to change literacy practices for better or worse, depending on your point of view" (70). There are many contentious views debating what that "change [in] literacy practices" will be, and they generally all suggest that the stakes of such change are potentially high. After all, if Walter Ong is correct in his assertion that "writing is a technology that restructures thought" (19), then the technologies used in crafting that writing might very well shape, if not restructure, how we think. Or, as Baron argues, the computer is just one item in a "series of communication technologies," and studying such technologies is essential because "different technologies interact with literacy in often unexpected ways" (vi).

Frequently, the figure of "youth" has been used in these arguments to represent a number of divergent and competing views about the usefulness and desirability (or not) of the new technologies. These views have ranged from dreams of utopian democracies enabled technologically through direct online participation and discussion to a belief that the "free-wheeling" and seemingly chaotic nature of Internet communications will ultimately undermine our ability to make collective sense of the world and lead to a consequent deterioration of shared values and views. Given these extremes, "youth" are portrayed either as leaders in embracing democracy-enhancing technologies or as victims of chaotic platforms that erode our ability to communicate effectively and coherently.

Henry A. Giroux, borrowing from the work of sociologist and cultural critic Dick Hebdige, suggests that whenever the figure of "youth" is raised in public debate as a category of concern, ideological issues are not far behind:

> In our society, youth is present only when its presence is a problem, or
> is regarded as a problem. More precisely, the category "youth" gets

mobilized in official documentary discourse, in concerned or outraged editorials and features or in the supposedly disinterested tracts emanating from the social sciences at those times when young people make their presence felt by going "out of bounds," by resisting through rituals, dressing strangely, striking bizarre attitudes, breaking rules, breaking bottles, windows, heads, issuing rhetorical challenges to the law. ("Doing Cultural Studies" 229)

Two points are salient here. First, the figure of "youth" is mobilized to attract attention to the debate, to stir interest, and perhaps even to claim a high moral ground in forwarding a disinterested position: After all, participants in the debate are arguing about our *children's* future, not out of our own sense of potential losses and gains (or so they say). Second, as Giroux suggests, some youth themselves are, at times, the direct cause for "outraged editorials and features," for heated debate; that is, some youth's involvement in boundary-pushing "rituals" or subcultural practices often provokes concern about their values, motives, and intentions.

In the case of the impact of technology on *literacy*, I think that much of the debate's heat comes from both quarters. On one hand, ideologues, pundits, and scholars have vested interests, as is seen shortly, in forwarding particular claims about the current state of literacy; in an increasingly multicultural world, and in one in which more and more people from divergent backgrounds are communicating online, there is a perceived increase in pressure to make sure we understand one another, to make sure we're "all on the same page," digitally or otherwise. On the other hand, some youth with Internet access and Web-authoring skills have themselves laid down a "rhetorical challenge" through their widespread use of the Internet and the Web, among other technological communications marvels, in often innovative, provocative, and even unsettling and disturbing ways; increasing use among American e-connected youth of e-mail, the Web, chatrooms, and Instant Messaging signals a range of communication that many adults can't always control—and that they might consequently find threatening.

I do not want to rehearse in their entirety these fairly well-known debates from the 1990s—and the flurry of consternation, dread, and glee that the increasing use of the new communications technologies has often provoked. Indeed, a comprehensive reckoning might not be possible, as the debate has produced a voluminous amount of scholarship and writing. Many people, from many different fields, are thinking about the impact of computer technologies on literacy, not to mention their impact on youth with access in particular. "Digital Literacy and Rhetoric: A Selected

Bibliography" by Carolyn Handa, published in 2001 in the scholarly journal *Computers and Composition*, lists more than seven pages of bibliographic entries. Handa cautions against thinking of the list as complete or exhaustive, even though she compiled her list from disparate fields, including visual literacy and rhetoric, technical communication, rhetorical theory, art, hypertext theory, sociology, semiotics, and even architecture. The diversity of disciplinary interest in the issue is itself an indication of the perceived far-reaching consequences of increased technological literacy and mediation of communication through computer networks.

Still, given the variety of questions (and concerns) raised as part of this debate, and given the central role that the figure of "youth" has played in it, any discussion of "youth and technology" must take into consideration these pedagogical and sociopolitical discussions about the impact of computer technology on literacy in general and the literacy education of youth in our country in particular. Moreover, it is useful to note how the figure of "youth" has circulated in and among such discussions as an ideological element. Through an examination of this debate, we see how *literacy*—and technology's potential impact on it, both pro or con—is a central concern of how youth with Internet access use technology. We also discover that what's missing in this debate is a real understanding or analysis of what digital youth (as I referred to them in the introduction) are *actually doing* with the new communications technologies, such as the Web. Analyzing this debate, then, should set the stage for a closer analysis in the following chapters of how digital youth use network technologies in general and the Web in particular as literacy tools and compose their lives, interests, and investments through them.

In general, we can understand the debate about youth, literacy, and technology as focusing on the following questions, which set up an intriguing binary opposition: Will computer technologies foster both greater access to and understanding of information, and will they assist in helping students learn to communicate effectively in a complex world? Or will their ease of use prompt uncritical dissemination and promulgation of useless "information," contributing to the growing glut of info-trash surrounding us? Of particular concern is the perceived move from traditional *print* literacies to *electronic* literacies—from the relative stability of the "text," the printed word, to the seeming ephemerality of digital communication, such as that on the ever-changing Web. Certainly, the pro/con nature of the debate itself suggests a limiting or even reductive understanding of the implications for increased use of technology in communication and meaning-making. Examining both "sides," however, will give us a sense of where the binary falls short, and will open up for us some other possibilities of thinking about the complex interrelationship between technology and literacy.

LITERACY LOST

Henry Giroux, a prominent educator and scholar, was among the first to note and to draw other scholars' and educators' attention to the fact that many youths' literacies are shaped not in the classroom, but in the mass media:

> Teens and other youth learn how to define themselves outside of the traditional sites of instruction, such as the home and the school. . . . [L]earning in the post-modern age is located elsewhere—in popular spheres that shape their identities, through forms of knowledge and desire that appear absent from what is taught in schools. The literacies of the post-modern age are electronic, aural, and image based. (http://www.gseis.ucla.edu/courses/ed253a/Giroux/Giroux3.html)

Giroux is well aware that the "literacies of the post-modern age," those most attractive to many youth, are indeed increasingly "electronic, aural, and image based." Not everyone, however, greets this news appreciatively. For instance, in "Uses and Gratifications of the Web among Students," Samuel Ebersole studied how a group of American public school students used the Web, and he concluded, perhaps a bit woefully, that

> Students were found to be visiting commercial sites at a much higher proportion than those in other domains. Also, the commercial sites received the lowest rating for "suitability for academic research" of all the domain names. And while students reported their purpose for using the WWW as "research and learning" fifty-two percent of the time, the coders found only twenty-seven percent of the sampled sites to be "suitable" for that purpose. (http://www.ascusc.org/jcmc/vol6 /issue1/ebersole.html)

Given such findings, one has to wonder, just what *are* young people with Internet access looking at?

Neil Postman has been among the most vocal critics of contemporary Western society's seeming glamorization of technology, and he has been particularly harsh in his assessment of the potential influence of technology on the realm of education. His comments are most pointed when it comes to issues of literacy. In *Technopoly*, he argued that the "world of the printed word" is characterized by "logic, sequence, history, exposition, objectivity, detachment, and discipline," whereas the "world of television," a metynomic stand-in for technology as a whole, emphasizes "imagery, narrative, presentness, simultaneity, intimacy, immediate gratification, and quick emotional response" (16). The differences between the two worlds has crucial consequences for children's literacy and education:

> Children come to school having been deeply conditioned by the biases of television. There, they encounter the world of the printed word. A sort of psychic battle takes place, and there are many casualties—children who can't learn to read or won't, children who cannot organize their thought into logical structure even in a simple paragraph, children who cannot attend to lectures or oral explanations for more than a few minutes at a time. (16–17)

More than a few assumptions are at work in such a passage, including the relatively unexamined causal relationship between immersion in television and poor success in school. Arguing broadly, Postman maintains that children "deeply conditioned by the biases of television" are essential illiterate, and because they "cannot organize their thought into logical structure," they seem incapable of critical thinking, at least as we've known it. Interestingly, however, Postman seems open to the possibility—or inevitability—of change. The characteristics of the "world of television" could come to dominate definitions of not just "success" but of literacy itself:

> [Children] are failures, but not because they are stupid. They are failures because there is a media war going on, and they are on the wrong side—at least for the moment. Who knows what schools will be like twenty-five years from now? Or fifty? In time, the type of student who is currently a failure may be considered a success. The type who is now successful may be regarded as a handicapped learner—slow to respond, far too detached, lacking in emotion, inadequate in creating mental pictures of reality. (17)

Despite the seeming "openness" to change, I can't help but detect a sense of loss in such a passage, a sense that something important is passing in changing conceptions of literacy and sociocultural fluency.

In many ways, Sven Birkerts, like Postman, is concerned with the future impact of technology on literacy, and his concern often manifests itself as a focus on *youth* and their literacy practices. In "Into the Electronic Millennium," Birkerts maintains that we are in a liminal time, with our practices of communication and meaning making moving from traditional print literacies to electronic media. For Birkerts, such a shift is not without substantial consequences: "Transitions like the one from print to electronic media do not take place without rippling or, more likely, *reweaving* the entire social and cultural web" (123). Like Postman, Birkerts raises the spectre of the effect of "electronic media" on children. Citing a number of sources, he suggests that "our educational systems are in decline"; more specifically, "our students are less and less able to read and comprehend their required texts, and . . . their aptitude scores have leveled off well below those of previous generations" (123). Again, as in Postman, the logic seems faulty, glossing over stark and unsupported claims and resting on unexamined contexts for such a decline in aptitude scores.

But Birkerts is not without some philosophical sophistication, and he links the rise of "electronic media" to the prevailing postmodern condition:

> The postmodern artifact manipulates its stylistic signatures like Lego blocks and makes free with combinations from the formerly sequestered spheres of high and popular art. Its combinatory momentum and relentless referencing of the surrounding culture mirror perfectly the associative dynamics of electronic media. (123)

Curiously, Birkerts and Postman identify a similar trend: the move from formerly *discreet* categories or entities comprising literacy—the ability to rationally categorize and understand discreet differences, for instance—to what Birkerts calls "associative dynamics" or to what Postman alludes to as "simultaneity." The assumption or implication propounded here, I believe, is that such "associative dynamics" are purely "free form" and thus without meaning; in other words, in embracing the freeplay of meanings, we lose our ability to *discriminate*, and thus to make critical judgments.

Others have raised similar concerns, particularly about the effect of hypertext, or the linking of multiple documents (as on the Web), on reading and comprehension. For instance, in the aptly titled essay, "The Effect of Hypertext on Processes of Reading," Davida Charney maintains that "the freedom that hypertext allows readers also makes it more difficult for them to make sense of texts, to extract information from them, and to register that information in long-term memory" (vi, *Literacy: A Critical*

Sourcebook). You'll note the progression: First, readers supposedly will have difficulty making sense of and retrieving information from texts; then, their memories themselves are affected by the shifts in reading. More broadly, some have argued that the ease of information retrieval enabled by the hypertextual nature of the WWW is itself potentially an impediment to the development of critical thinking skills. Even some of those who have embraced technological innovation, such as Bruce Sterling, a noted science-fiction author and futurist, and author of *Tomorrow Now: Envisioning the Next Fifty Years*, have speculated skeptically on the future of literacy as it may be shaped by e-savvy digital youth. In an interview touching on young people's use of the Web, Sterling offers cautionary comments, particularly about the Web and search engines:

> There is a Google blindness. It's a kind of common wisdom generator, but it's not necessarily going to get you to the real story of what's actually going on. . . .
>
> It is a form of literacy that's really peculiar. Socrates used to talk about this: "The problem with writing is that no one memorizes the Iliad any more. You've got to just know all of it. And how can you call yourself an educated man if you cannot recite Book Three, not missing a single epithet?" He's got a point there.
>
> It has a profound effect on literary composition. I've got Google up all the time. It gives you this veneer of command of the facts which you do not, in point of fact, have. It's extremely useful for novelists but somewhat dangerous if you're pretending to be a brain surgeon. (Godwin: http://www.reason.com/0401/fe.mg.cybergreen.shtml)

Access to information, of course, does not automatically lead to a critical ability to understand, analyze, use, and question that information—a fact potentially lost in the ease and speed with which information can be downloaded. Such points are well taken and worth the attention of those invested in the future of literacy practices.

At the same time, as Birkerts puts it, changes in literacy practices are inevitable, and they are driven by different technologies used to mediate text and communication:

> The context cannot but condition the process. Screen and book may exhibit the same string of words, but the assumptions that underlie their significance are entirely different depending on whether we are staring at a book or a circuit-generated text. As a nature of looking—at the natural world, at paintings—changed with the arrival of photogra-

phy and mechanical reproduction, so will the collective relation to language alter as new modes of dissemination prevail. (128)

I cannot disagree. But for Birkerts, the change is threatening. He argues later in his essay that we are seeing a consequent loss of history, or a "flattening of historical perspectives," largely to blame on a postmodern condition exacerbated by the increasingly widespread use of technology, which also leads to "language erosion" and a "waning of the private self" (129-130). Postman would probably agree, having characterized the "world of television" with such loaded words as "presentness," "simultaneity," "immediate gratification," and "quick emotional response." Such characteristics do not seem as intelligent or thoughtful as those seemingly enabled by more traditional literacy and critical thinking practices, such as categorization, comparison, contrast, and judgment. Instead, these new characteristics cater to the world of the senses and pleasure; instead of the "private self" contemplating rationally, we have pleasure-seeking youth insisting on "immediate gratification."

Even those who muster a bit more hopefulness about this "shift" figure it in terms with a strong undertow of loss. For instance, the following passage from Julian Dibbell's "The Writer a la Modem, Or, The Death of the Author on the Installment Plan" is worth examining in full; for, like the title of the essay, the excerpt betrays a sense of slow but impending loss:

> What will change just as inevitably, however, is the network of social relations that writing both defines and is defined by, and my own encounter with the online economy of textual production tells me this change will be as sweeping as what followed in the way of Gutenberg's invention. I have seen the writing on the bulletin board, and it promises an irreversible diffusion of authorship throughout the social body, a blurring past all recognition of the line between reader and writer. The structure of written word grows more diffuse as well—the intense coherence of heroic individual efforts gives way to the drifting dialogue of message bases and the trippy collaborative fictions of MUDs. And good luck trying to cull any regulating canon from this woozy corpus. You'll find no center in the haze of ephemerae: even if you do, it will not hold. (qdt. in Yagelski, 116)

Dibbell wants to be hopeful, but his apocalyptic allusions—the handwriting on the wall from the book of Daniel, the echo of a line from Yeats' "Second Coming"—reveal hesitancy at best, dread at worst. Moreover, much like Birkerts' claim that the proliferation of electronic media will lead to the "waning of the private self," Dibbell bemoans the loss of the "intense coherence of heroic individual efforts." In contrast, collaboration and dialogue are characterized as "drifting" and "tripp . . . fictions," reminiscent of the dreaded, meaning-reducing (or meaning-emptying) "associative dynamics." Reading through such passages, I wonder if we are seeing here nostalgia for one type of humanism—that of the heroic individual, a modernist construct who may or may not ever have existed.

LITERACY REGAINED

Many other writers and critics have been far more optimistic (or at least generously neutral) in their assessment of the impact of "electronic media" on both e-savvy youth and their notions of literacy.

Granted, some are a bit *over* optimistic. In *Interface Culture: How New Technology Transforms the Way We Create and Communicate*, Steven Johnson argues enthusiastically that the emergence of computer technology and interface design, the "bridge" between computers and their users, such as the metaphor of the "desktop" on many users' operating systems, constitutes a fundamental "paradigm shift" in our culture's information processing that is comparable to former paradigm shifts in communication—such as those represented by Charles Dickens' innovations in the novel and fictional narrative. For instance, Johnson argues at one point, "Where Dickens's narrative links [in his novels] stitched together the torn fabric of industrial society, today's hypertext links attempt the same with information" (116). When not casting such backward glances, Johnson speaks exuberantly of sweeping changes in prose often full of the language of "revolution" and techno-hype:

> The digital revolution will surely transform stock markets and library research and credit profiles, as the pundits on the business pages have been predicting for years. But it also promises to transform our experience of the world, just as the Industrial Revolution transformed the experiences of nineteenth-century Westerners. This book is in part an attempt to imagine the nature of this new experience, to sketch out its properties in advance. (40)

As attractive as such thinking can be, I am generally leery of these kinds of grand statements, if only because history has its own hindsight—a vision to which we are not yet privy. More to the point, Johnson never really makes good on demonstrating that computers, their interfaces, and the digital revolution in general have been as transformative as the Industrial Revolution. In general, the problem with arguing through analogies, however, is that similarities don't reproduce the context in which an innovation actually becomes an innovation, something truly transformative.

In fact, one could argue that another of Johnson's theses—that we cannot even imagine the uses to which technology will be put—undermines the entire project of suggesting that our current technologies are transformative; for, by Johnson's own logic, we cannot envision how our current technology will be used, or if it will be used, in the transformative ways he suggests. Indeed, in reading the conclusion to *Interface Culture*, one senses that Johnson knows that his book has ultimately made more claims than it can deliver, and he offers a more qualified thesis: "We will come to think of interface design as a kind of art form—perhaps the art form of the next century" (213).

Backing away from such grand assertions, other writers have focused on more specific ways in which the new communications technologies are shaping literacy in general and written communication in particular. For instance, Constance Hale and Jessie Scanlon's writing handbook and style guide, *Wired Style: Principles of English Usage in the Digital Age*, is an attempt to distill for prose stylists some of the perceived changes wrought on our use of the language by the increasing use of computer technologies, such as word processing, e-mail, and the Web. In summary, they offer "10 Principles for Writing Well in the Digital Age":

1. [Recognize that] The Medium Matters
2. Play with Voice
3. Flaunt Your Subcultural Literacy
4. Transcend the Technical
5. Capture the Colloquial
6. Anticipate the Future
7. Be Irreverent
8. Brave the New World of New Media
9. Go Global
10. Play with Dots and Dashes and Slashes (2–24)

Looking over this list, I can't help but think that critics of technology, such as Birkerts and Postman, might have a point. This list doesn't seem to promote the serious critical inquiry and sustained attention that technology's detractors believe are necessary for reading and critical thinking. Instead of encouraging a critical engagement with texts and with writing, this list seems to privilege playful individualism, or what Hale and Scanlon refer to as the "voice of the quirky, individualist writer" (7). To be fair, Hale and Scanlon are quite serious about the play they propose. For instance, they suggest that "Writing with power and clarity about technology requires more than just spelling out acronyms, more than regurgitating PR [public relations] talk. Grasp the technologies, then describe them with vivid language and clear metaphors" (11). Playfulness does not mean sacrificing clarity of expression—a cardinal goal throughout Hale and Scanlon's guide. Furthermore, their advice about being "irreverent" opens up possibilities for critique: "When we say 'Be irreverent,' we encourage you to do the following: Welcome inconsistency, especially in the interest of voice and cadence. Treat the institutions and players in your world with a dose of irreverence. Play with grammar and syntax. Appreciate unruliness" (15). Embedded in this appreciation for "unruliness" is a willingness to *critically* engage the world around us, to ask questions of it, to refuse to treat it and its assumptions as foregone conclusions. As such, sustained thinking is perhaps not so far from this technological playfulness as it might at first appear.

Both Johnson and Hale and Scanlon offer some general thoughts, even some youthful thinking, about some potentially positive impacts of the new communications technologies on how we communicate and on how we define literacy. Their enthusiasm is infectious, if at times under-developed. In contrast, other writers have addressed the concerns of technological nay-sayers a bit more directly, entering the debate with vigor and insight. Jay David Bolter, probably thinking of Postman and Birkerts, announced in *Writing Space: The Computer, Hypertext, and the History of Writing*, that the "shift from print to the computer does not mean the end of literacy" (2). In particular, Bolter questions the notion that electronic literacy necessarily translates into "woozy" diffusion:

> An electronic book is a fragmentary and potential text, a series of self-contained units rather than an organic, developing whole. But fragmentation does not imply mere disintegration. Elements in the electronic writing space are not simply chaotic; they are instead in a perpetual state of reorganization. They form patterns, constellations, which are in constant danger of breaking down and combining into new patterns. This tension leads to a new definition of unity in writing, one that may replace or supplement our traditional notions of the unity of voice and of analytic argument. The unity or coherence of an electronic text derives from the perpetually shifting relationship among all its verbal elements. (9)

In many ways, Bolter takes us to the point where Birkerts stops thinking about the *potential* of electronic media and texts—and then pushes us a little bit further to see not the end of literacy but a *refiguring* of literacy.

George P. Landow traces some of that refiguring in his influential text, *Hypertext 2.0: The Convergence of Contemporary Critical Theory and Technology*. For Landow, networked communication in general and hypertext in particular do not spell the end of literacy but a realignment of what kinds of discourse practices are privileged as literate. For instance, Landow noticed, when working with his students on constructing hypertextually enhanced documents, that "all hypertext webs, no matter how simple, how limited, inevitably take the form of textual collage, for they inevitably work by juxtaposing different texts, often appropriating them as well" (171). Landow reads such as appropriation as an affirmation of certain high-level literacy practices. Even when he's qualified in tone, his appreciation for what hypertext offers literacy is easily detectable:

> I am not much concerned to allay potential fears of this new form of writing by deriving it from earlier avant-garde work . . . here I am more interested in helping us understand this new kind of hypertext writing as a mode that both emphasizes and bridges gaps and that thereby inevitably becomes an art of assemblage in which appropriation and catachresis rule. This is a new writing that brings with it implications for our conceptions of text as well as of reader and author. It is a text in which new kinds of connections have become possible. (176–7)

Certainly, as Landow points out, hypertext brings with it potential "implications" for literacy, for our "conceptions of text as well as of reader and author." But it also helps writers deploy documented literacy practices, such as juxtaposition and catachresis—skills that have been examined since the beginning of the study of rhetoric. Granted, the ancients may have thought of catachresis as a rhetorical "vice" because it signaled the "use of a word in a context that differs from its proper application" (http://humanities.byu.edu/rhetoric/Figures/C/catachresis.htm). But its similarity to tropes such as metaphor nonetheless suggests its potential rhetorical usefulness.

Moreover, and speaking in terms of "new kinds of connections," the potential for interactivity, for both sharing and co-creating electronic texts, offers new possibilities for communication and meaning making, as Bolter argues: "The conceptual space of electronic writing . . . is characterized by fluidity and an interactive relationship between writer and reader. These different conceptual spaces foster different styles and genres of writing and different theories of literature" (11). Indeed, the *interactivity* afforded by the new communications technologies is among the most frequently cited *benefits* of electronic media in creating texts and communicating. For instance, using Walter Ong's notion of "secondary orality," "language that is a blend of written and spoken communication," Laura J. Gurak argues that "cyberliteracy" is "not purely a print literacy, nor is it purely an oral literacy. It is an electronic literacy—newly emerging in a new medium—that combines features of both print and the spoken word, and it does so in ways that change how we read, speak, think, and interact with others" (14). More importantly, however, for Gurak, "cyberliteracy is not simply a matter of learning how to keep up with the technology or how to do a Web search. . . . Cyberliteracy means voicing an opinion about what these technologies should become and being an active, not a passive, participant" (27).

Along such lines, Sherry Turkle notes, in "Seeing Through Computers: Education in a Culture of Simulation," three characteristics or "lessons of computing" that youth (roughly defined as those under age 30 with Internet access) experience in their encounter with technology: "simulation, navigation, and interaction"—with interaction garnering particular comment and praise (qtd. in Yagelski, 330). To wit, Turkle describes how such youth frequently use the possibilities of simulation *and* interaction afforded by technologies to critically intervene in the world around them. For instance, she cites the use of computer simulations, such as *SimCity* or *SimHealth*, in contemporary educational contexts, in which students have the opportunity to collectively—if virtually—build social institutions, learn from the mistakes of the past, and experiment with radical (and radically new) social structures. Extrapolating from such experiences, Turkle suggests that the increasing "cultural pervasiveness of simulation" could be taken as a "challenge to develop a new social criticism. This new criticism would discriminate among simulations. It would take as its goal the development of simulations that help their users understand and challenge their model's built-in assumptions" (qtd. in Yagelski, 336). Turkle's comments are, as usual, highly suggestive, and it's worth noting—as I attempt to do later in this book—how many youth intimately engaged with computer technology are trying to develop that "new social criticism," a criticism that challenges older views of the world and older models of meaning making. Indeed, others have noted similar possibilities. As recently as 1998, Don Tapscott, in *Growing Up Digital: The Rise of the Net Generation*, argued that some e-connected youth are "breaking free from the one-way, centralized media of the past and are beginning to shape their own destiny. And evidence is mounting that the world will be a better place as a result" (33).

Tapscott's enthusiasm aside (I return to him in Chapter 4), Nancy Kaplan's essay, "Literacy Beyond Books: Reading When All the World's a Web," offers perhaps the most lucid and compelling critique of those who have nay-sayed technology, particularly the Web's effect on literacy and various practices of reading and writing. As can be expected, many of the concerns that Kaplan addresses focus on hypertext, and she is attuned to the way that digital youth figure in this heated debate: "According to many professors of literature, the field claiming ownership of advanced literacy, hypertext—especially in the ubiquitous form of the World Wide Web—threatens to erode the ability of young adults to read with acumen and insights" (208). In general, the issue is one of reading: "the most serious and heated conversations about literacy in what Bolter has termed 'the late age of print' seem to have arisen in disputes about what hypertexts in general and the Web in particular do to reading practices" (210). A main concern seems to be, according to Kaplan's summary of Myron Tuman's work in *Word Perfect* (1992), that "hypertexts discourage deep reading and encourage reading surfaces, skimming, and frenetic motion" (213). In the process, "critical reading," or sustained and engaged examination of ideas via a text, is lessened, if not lost altogether. Such a view directly contradicts the best hopes of writers such as Turkle or Tapscott.

To address this critique, Kaplan offers a slight shift in emphasis. She suggests that, "Unlike writing activities, reading episodes leave no visible traces behind them" (215). So, perhaps, a study of how hypertexts are put together and composed might reveal the intellectual and critical work at play in them. Kaplan then offers us the following definition of literacy through which we can debate the value of hypertext and its impact of literacy: "the most important or highest form of literacy manifests itself as a sustained, critical engagement with ideas expressed verbally and presented in visible language." Using such a definition should help us "to determine whether print per se creates the necessary conditions and hypertexts per se do not" (220). For much of the remainder of her essay, Kaplan convincingly demonstrates that "the hypertext author's decision about the scope of a node [a page with links] constitutes an occasion for invention, a decision driven by aesthetic or rhetorical considerations" (221). As such, the process of linking, or creating links in hypertext, is itself a fundamentally critical engagement with the texts that a hypertext author is using, constructing, and reconstructing through his or her linkages. Moreover, as Kaplan argues, "Craft and artistry emerge in the design of [hypertextual] space, sculpted from the decisions writers make about the boundaries of nodes, the suggestiveness of link cues, and the patterns of links" (229–230). In building such a case for the critical components of *authoring* in hypertext, Kaplan hopes to demonstrate that comparable critical faculties are needed, and developed, in *reading* hypertext. She hints, for instance, that the "doubleness" of links—in other words, "the links taken and those passed by"—might usher into being a "particular reading" strategy that rests on attention to detail and critical thinking (227).

Kaplan builds a strong, generally convincing case in her essay. But even she must admit, in her conclusion, that "We are not clairvoyant, and probably cannot adequately imagine the sorts of reading and writing practices people who do not grow up in a print culture may yet develop" (232). As such, she returns us to the beginning of her essay and her earlier evocation of the figure of youth, of generations to come who may be immersed in the Web and other networked communication technologies. What will *their* "reading and writing practices" be?

TECHNOLOGY AND LITERACY: QUESTIONS OF PEDAGOGY

Such a question, and the debate to which it alludes, is not without its pedagogical implications as well, for writing instructors, literacy specialists, social scientists, and cultural studies scholars. Indeed, many educators and pedagogues have become intensely concerned with both the impact of communications technologies on literacy practices and meaning making in general and how best to instruct students in using these emerging technologies. At the very least, teaching students—or at least alerting them—to ways in which they can navigate the onrushing flood of information enabled by computer, particularly Internet and Web technologies, is becoming a crucial task. But more than this, many pedagogues and scholars of teaching are suggesting that we take stock of the changes in communication and literacy taking place around us. Or, to borrow Cynthia Selfe's title from her book, *Technology and Literacy in the Twenty-First Century: The Importance of Paying Attention*, we need to be "paying attention" to what technology and its intertwining with literacy have to tell us. Others agree. In their introduction to *Literacy Theory in the Age of the Internet*, Todd Taylor and Irene Ward argue the following: "Instead of being frustrated by the disorientation brought on by [technological] changes, we suggest that teachers and researchers embrace the current uncertainty and theoretical disarray as the most reasonable way to negotiate new notions of literacy as they appear on the horizon" (xvi).

Such "paying attention," even embracing "the current uncertainty and theoretical disarray," can take several guises. Richard Selfe and Cynthia Selfe, in "Critical Technological Literacy and English Studies: Teaching, Learning, and Action," argue for investigating, understanding, and utilizing in our literacy pedagogies the concept of "critical technological literacy," which "recognizes the complex links that now exist between literacy and technology at the beginning of the twenty-first century" (345). Interestingly enough, the Selfes' article appears in Robert Yagelski's collection *The Relevance of English: Teaching that Matters in Students' Lives* (2002), a book whose title alone signals some professional soul-searching in the broader field of English studies, on the part of those most concerned with issues of literacy and how to instruct youth in becoming literate citizens. To help us understand how technology is increasingly interpolated in this endeavor, the Selfes pose two interrelated questions:

> What are our responsibilities for educating students about technology, especially as these issues relate to the practice of literacy in this country and in other places around the world? In what specific sites can this education best take place? . . .

> What are our roles for teaching students how to think about and respond to technology as it continues to shape our lives and as we continue to affect its design and use it in society? (376–7)

The questions ask us not only to consider what technologies are increasingly important in literate communication, but also what kind of *relationship* we have with those technologies.

Many have attempted to address the first question: "What are our responsibilities for educating students about technology?" For instance, early in the debate on technology, education, and literacy, Esther Dyson promoted the educational benefits of the Internet and the Web. In *Release 2.0: A Design for Living in the Digital Age*, Dyson wrote the following:

> Optimists are excited about the possibilities of the Web and its multimedia content for education, for information, for building a worldwide infrastructure of understanding. They marvel at how easy it is to find information. They also trust that children can learn by themselves, exploring the geography of Africa one day and the wonders of bio-

> chemistry the next. They can watch a video of Charles de Gaulle giving his victory speech, and then link to a page of historical context, an English translation, or a map of Europe in 1945. (91)

The Internet, for Dyson, connects kids to schools, resources, their parents, and one another in potentially pedagogically effective ways. To explain her position, Dyson uses an example in which students (always having fun) post up Web sites to describe and advertise their various interests, connect with students at other schools with similar interests, and expand their understanding of the world by coming into contact with a host of others via the Internet: "Pretty soon, kids who hadn't taken much interest in school started staying late to work on their pages. . . . The amazing thing is, you've worked harder in school than you ever did before, and you thought you were just having fun. (Don't tell anyone!)" (83).

Of course, Dyson is aware of some potential drawbacks: Although the Internet "encourages participation," it also might put you in touch with people who are not interested in your well being. As such, "there still needs to be someone to guide you. . . . The good news is that the Net *does* allow you to experiment more safely than you could in 'real life'" (95, 96). Given such benefits and relative safety, Dyson's optimism leads her to encourage us not simply to "consume" the Internet, but to be a "producer" as well, putting up web pages and starting online communities (284–5). As such, Dyson sees educational uses of network technologies, most notably the Web, as directly tied to developing literacy skills.

Recent research seems to support Dyson's views regarding the potential benefits of promoting the use of computer technologies in educational settings. In an article in the *Journal of Technology, Learning, and Assessment*, Amie Goldberg, Michael Russell, and Abigail Cook analyzed 35 articles studying the use of computers to teach writing. The article, entitled "The Effect of Computers on Student Writing: A Meta-Analysis of Studies from 1992 to 2002," offered the following conclusion:

> These articles . . . indicate that the writing process is more collaborative, iterative, and social in computer classrooms as compared with paper-and-pencil environments. For educational leaders questioning whether computers should be used to help students develop writing skills, the results of the meta-analyses suggest that on average students who use computers when learning to write are not only more engaged and motivated in their writing, but they produce written work that is of greater length and higher quality. (http://www.bc.edu/research/intasc/jtla/journal/v2n1.shtml)

Granted, this is a study primarily focused on the use of word processing technologies, but I have noted similar gains in college-level writing courses in which students not only write with word processors but also work toward publishing their writing on the Web, for instance, via e-zines and other Web-based forums. Web publication in particular, with an instructor's guidance of course, seems to promote a fair amount of meta-cognition about one's writing, as well as increased care and concern for how students represent themselves and their ideas to a reading and Web-browsing public (See Alexander, "Digital Spins").

The potential benefits of using technology to teach writing and literacy skills have not been lost on textbook publishers, and numerous recent textbooks offer testimony to the increased importance of considering technology in general and networked computing in particular in literacy training and skills development. If I limit myself to my field, English Studies, and if I even limit myself further to listing the books *sent to me* by publishers, I still see an impressive number of handsome texts.

Some are basic guides for students, helping them navigate various Internet venues and platforms, particularly with an eye toward conducting research. These include books and guides such as Carol Lea Clark's *A Student's Guide to the Internet* (1996), Eric Crump and Nick Carbone's *English Online: A Student's Guide to the Internet and then World Wide Web* (1997), Jeanette A. Woodward's *Writing Research Papers: Investigating Resources in Cyberspace* (1997), and H. Eric Branscomb's *Casting Your Net: A Student's Guide to Research on the Internet* (1998). Others have focused primarily on teaching students techniques for composing with hypertext and authoring web pages, such as William Condon and Wayne Butler's *Writing the Information Superhighway* (1997), Victor J. Vitanza's *Writing for the World Wide Web* (1998), and Margaret W. Batschelet's *Web Writing/Web Designing* (2001). Inevitably, some are directed at instructors in an attempt to get them "up to speed," with some of the most notable being Daniel Anderson, Bret Benjamin, Christopher Busiel, and Bill Paredes-Holt's *Teaching Online: Internet Research, Conversation and Composition* (1998) and Sibylle Gruber's *Weaving a Virtual Web: Practical Approaches to New Information Technologies* (2000).

Besides instructing readers about technologically and network-enhanced writing processes and modes, a neat group of texts offers readings on the *culture* of the Internet, attempting to educate students about cyberculture and the changing ways in which people interact socially (and even politically) via the Internet. Books in this category include Hawisher and Selfe's *Literacy, Technology and Society: Confronting the Issues* (1996), Vitanza's *CyberReader* (1996, 1999), Richard Holeton's *Composing*

Cyberspace: Identity, Community, and Knowledge in the Electronic Age (1998), and Yagelski's *Literacies and Technologies: A Reader for Contemporary Writers* (2001). Yagelski's is not only the most recent, but perhaps the most notable in its fleshing out for students the nature, sides, and ramifications of the debate about the impact of technology on literacy. Indeed, one of the most attractive features of *Literacies and Technologies* is that Yagelski pulls no intellectual punches; the selections frequently offer substantial portions of works by some of the leaders in the growing field of literacy and technology studies, including Neil Postman, Jay David Bolter, Umberto Eco, Sherry Turkle, and Richard Ohmann. At the same time, it is refreshing to see more general and even classic pieces on literacy by authors as varied as Henry David Thoreau, Malcolm X, E. D. Hirsch, Paulo Freire, Jimmy Santiago Baca, and June Jordan. Including such pieces allows Yagelski to contextualize and historicize the debates about technology and literacy. And although it would be very easy to "stack the deck" with essays that mostly laud the ways in which technology facilitates writing and the exchange of ideas, Yagelski readily concedes that not everyone is pleased with the way computers are shaping the way writers and readers think, and he includes pieces by Wendell Berry ("Why I Am Not Going to Buy a Computer") and Sven Birkerts.

But although many instructors, scholars, and critics understand that technology impacts how we write (and read), not everyone agrees that the new technologies will necessarily foster new literacies, and thus they question the value of thinking pedagogically along the lines of Bolter's and Landow's insinuation that a new writing, perhaps a new form of literacy, is emerging. In 2002, in fact, in an issue of *Kairos*, an "online journal exploring the intersections of rhetoric, technology, and pedagogy," you could read wildly divergent opinions about the "new-media" and its promotion (or not) of new literacies. For instance, in "New Media and the Slow Death of the Written Word," Mark Zeltner points out that some writing theory specialists, such as Gregory Ulmer, have "envisioned a new form of literacy called 'electracy' being created by our use of electronic forms of communication like e-mail, multi-user domains and the web." In the face of such "electracy," though, Zeltner does not believe that the "new-media" will "create a new kind of literacy or destroy old concepts of literacy" (http://english.ttu.edu/kairos/7.2/binder.html?sectionone/zeltner/NM).

Many others, however, see very real effects on literacy instruction and pedagogy stemming from engagement with electronic communication platforms, and their pedagogies and textbooks reflect such perceived effects. Alice L. Trupe argues in "Academic Literacy in a Wired World:

Redefining Genres for College Writing Courses" that we need to reexamine the teaching of the "academic essay" and the literacy skills it implies so that we can make room for a more pressing question: "How should an undergraduate writer demonstrate *academic* literacy in a wired world?" (italics added; http://english.ttu.edu/kairos/7.2/binder.html?sectionone /trupe/WiredWorld.htm). The implication here is that the teaching of "traditional" literacy practices may not be sufficient for understanding and participating in the kinds of writing that students will encounter—and produce—in an increasingly "wired" world.

Some textbook authors have begun to address this issue, such as Libby Allison and Kristine L. Blair, authors of *Cultural Attractions/Cultural Distractions: Critical Literacy in Contemporary Contexts*, a textbook that presents a series of readings about "reading and writing the texts of the information age" (3). The authors' goal is not just to present a set of readings about changes in literacy practices in the "Information Age," but also to invite students to participate in those changes: "many activities and projects suggest that you try new formats in addition to the tried-and-true printed essay. These formats, such as Web pages, posters, videos, advertisements, brochures, letters, e-mail, and newsgroup posts, can be created and distributed through the very kinds of media and technology you will be studying" (3–4). Other textbooks do similar work, such as Daniel Anderson, Bret Benjamin, and Bill Paredes-Holt's *Connections: A Guide to On-Line Writing*, which "represents something of a bridge between traditional print-based writing and these newer forms of electronic composition" (5). And many of the exercises and writing prompts in Beth E. Kolko, Alison E. Regan, and Susan Romano's *Writing in an Electronic World* assume electronic formats and audiences, with corresponding discussions of how technology impacts our literacy practices.

Attempting to examine electronically enabled literacies from a sociocultural perspective, Jeff Rice's recently released textbook, *Writing About Cool: Hypertext and Cultural Studies in the Computer Classroom*, is designed to help students interrogate the relationships among writing, technology, and a sense of "coolness," broadly defined as a marker of the desirable. More broadly, Rich is attempting to show students the connection between technological and literacy practices and how culture is produced, disseminated, consumed, and critiqued. Calling attention to how more people are steadily attributing "coolness" to interests and pursuits once thought of as "geeky," such as working with computers, Rice suggests that our relationship to technology and the literacy practices enabled by the new communications media are changing in ways that deserve our attention and interrogation (http://www.ablongman.com/ricecool1e/about.html).

Perhaps the most radical of the bunch, Gregory Ulmer's textbook, *Internet Invention: From Literacy to Electracy*, published in 2002, offers a complex, challenging, and compelling attempt to stretch our understanding of literacy into "electracy." Chidsey Dickson's review of this textbook in *Kairos* neatly summarizes Ulmer's goal: "Internet Invention asks us to consider how writing, particularly writing on the Web, serves as an alternative space for composing the 'self' in its various connections to the world" (http://english.ttu.edu/kairos/8.1/binder.html?reviews/dickson/index.html). For Ulmer, the "self" can be composed in the "alternative space" of the Web by encouraging students to explore, experiment with, and engage in "rhetorical and composition practices . . . [that] move [them] from consumers to producers of image discourse" (6). Ulmer's text pushes students from consumption into production by having them create a series of largely personal Web sites, comprising a "mystory," that uses images and text to interrogate the self's interconnectedness and interrelationships with the surrounding world. Through this process, the student/self should begin to see how that self is interpolated in, constructed by, and caught up in a dense social matrix of meaning making, mediated in large part by visuals delivered to us electronically. Or, in Dickson's words,

> The assemblages of pictorial and verbal imagery which flow from the [textbook's assignment] prompts into the genre of "mystory"[,] record or document . . . the arresting information, moments or figures from each of the major institutions or discourses "on the understanding that certain qualities of orientation towards problems and solutions persist across domains." This genre of Web writing or mystory captures/strikes into stability a first simulation of the "wide site": the intersection between "the anecdotes of one's life and the aphorisms of a particular discourse or institution."

This is complex stuff, particularly for students. But such a pedagogy is born out of the understanding that students need to understand—and interrogate—the "intersection" of one's own self narration (or identity?) with that constantly being told by the dominant, surrounding culture. And because much of that story is mediated by and imparted to us through images filtered through electronic media, engaging the visual only makes a certain amount of sense. Thus, literacy becomes electracy—with a powerful, social goal: the creation of sites into

> [a]n umbrella organization gathering through the power of digital linking all the enquiries of students around the world and forming them

into a "fifth estate," whose purpose is to witness and testify, to give voice to a part of the public left out of community decision making, especially from policy formation. (Ulmer, 1)

Such a goal seems visionary, even utopian, reflecting perhaps the hopes and dreams of cyber-enthusiasts, such as Turkle, Tapscott, and Johnson.

LITERACY AND TECHNOLOGY: QUESTIONS OF RELATIONSHIP

Others, however, have raised serious questions about our relationship to those technologies, how we interact with them and understand their presence in our lives—questions that lead us to the second question that Richard and Cynthia Selfe pose: "What are our roles for teaching students how to think about and respond to technology as it continues to shape our lives and as we continue to affect its design and use it in society?" I think the Selfes are primarily interested in a socio-critical approach to technology, one in which we take seriously issues of access to technology, and in which we do not take for granted or view as transparent either the effect of technology on our lives or our use of it in the shaping and reshaping of our words and our worlds. As such, their concern is a parallel to Heidegger's and the issues he raises in his famous tract, "The Question Concerning Technology," in which the philosopher asks us to consider carefully our relationship to technology and its potential for teaching us about Being. As the Selfes write, "According to Heidegger, it is the questioning relationship we establish in connection with technology, not the technology itself, that is so vitally important to our understanding of human beings and the human condition" (360).

Heidegger himself explains the significance of interrogating our relationship to technology this way:

The revealing that rules throughout modern technology has the character of a setting-upon, in the sense of a challenging-forth. That challenging happens in that the energy concealed in nature is unlocked, what is unlocked is transformed, what is transformed is stored up, what is stored up is, in turn, distributed, and what is distributed is switched about ever anew. Unlocking, transforming, storing, distributing, and switching about are ways of revealing. But the revealing never simply comes to an end. (297–8)

The language is arcane, even obtuse, but Heidegger suggests that technology will not reveal the nature of Being to us by being used to conquer and order the world; rather, as Nick Mansfield puts it in his summary of Heidegger's position, "Technology's ability to reveal the truth of the potential of the world is also the world's calling out to us, its challenging of us to recognize truth as our calling" (157). In this way, technology is, for Heidegger, "a mode of revealing" (295).

Given this concern with our relationship to technology, it is worth interrogating not just how we can teach students to use technology to enhance their literacy skills (or to maintain competence in an increasingly networked world), but the kinds of relationships digital youth are already forming with communications technology, over and beyond what pedagogues suggest is "class worthy." In other words, to borrow from Heidegger, we might begin asking such questions as, how might some youth already be using technology to help them "reveal the truth of the potential of [their] world"? Indeed, as the remainder of this book will make clear, I am beginning to suspect that some digital youth's and students' relationships with communications technologies might involve their own unique creation of literacy practices, of reading and writing modes and possibilities.

The subject of students' literacies, of their own engagement with texts over and beyond the literacies they learn in the classroom, has increasingly been the subject of discussion in English Studies circles. Indeed, some teachers and scholars of literacy have recently called on us to re-examine how we use—or fail to use and even acknowledge—students' own literacies in our classrooms. For instance, Christopher Schroeder, in *Reinventing the University: Literacies and Legitimacy in the Postmodern Academy*, advocates strongly for paying attention to students' literacies and for working with them in the classroom. He draws on an emerging tradition in writing studies instruction to support his assertion:

> Alternative literacies and discourses are surfacing in scholarship; they are also appearing in composition classrooms across the United States. [Patricia] Bizzell, in her article on hybrid discourses, argues that teachers of composition cannot ignore these alternative discourses if they are going to prepare students for success in other classrooms and other contexts, and in a related way, Peter Elbow, in "Inviting the Mother Tongue," advocates for the legitimacy of students' primary discourses

in classrooms conventionally dominated exclusively by academic literacies. Even before Bizzell and Elbow, however, others, such as Lillian Bridwell-Bowles, Xin Liu Gale, and Derek Owens, were calling for alternatives to conventional academic literacies as legitimate ways of learning and knowing in classrooms. (19)

To be clear, Schroeder is not interested in abandoning traditional literacies, but in taking students' literacies seriously, and in developing and fostering pedagogical spaces in which teachers can construct useful and meaningful literacies with students. He argues that,

If . . . the literacies of the classrooms that we construct have political and aesthetic values and enable students to construct their own, then we have fulfilled the promise of education. As such, constructed literacies offer teachers the materials through which and by which they can construct classrooms of hope or hopelessness, of potential or problems, even of intellectual life or death. (241)

Such work and goals are also reflected in the collection *Alt Dis: Alternative Discourses and the Academy*, edited by Schroeder, Helen Fox, and Patricia Bizzell.[2] The preface to this anthology, with contributions from some of the leaders in the field of writing studies, such as Peter Elbow, begins with a critique of how the 1974 Conference on College Composition and Communication resolution, "The Students' Right to Their Own Language," has largely been forgotten. This resolution advocated respect for students' native literacies, such as those stemming from racial, ethnic, or subcultural backgrounds and affiliations, and the editors contend that this resolution has not been followed or adopted by the profession at large:

. . . many academics, in writing programs and elsewhere, still require students to produce traditional academic discourse and penalize them if they do not. Many writing teachers still agonize over how, or whether, to equip their students to meet this requirement. But meanwhile, many academics and students have been developing new discourse forms that accomplish intellectual work while combining tradi-

---

[2]Playing with alternative discourses is not necessarily new to the field of English Studies in general or writing instruction in particular. For instance, take a look at *Blending Genre, Altering Style: Writing Multigenre Papers* by Tom Romano.

tional academic discourse traits with traits from other discourse communities. (viii)

Increasingly, I think, such "new discourse forms" include a variety of network-enabled texts, such as Web texts and other innovative electronic media. E-mail and Instant Messaging, not to mention the emerging use of "texting" via cell phones, have their own developing "traditions" of communication and literate practice—"traditions" that digital youth and e-savvy students are often at the forefront of constructing and disseminating.

Paralleling and even complicating this expanded understanding of literacy is a fundamental reconsideration by some scholars of the usefulness of thinking in terms of "literacy" at all, particularly the tradition of text-based engagement that the term literacy seems to imply. For instance, Christopher Schroeder's sentiments find an interesting extension in Anne Wysocki and Johndan Johnson-Eilola's innovative and increasingly influential essay, "Blinded by the Letter: Why Are We Using Literacy as a Metaphor for Everything Else?" In this ingenuously crafted article, which uses pictures and multiple fonts, the authors talk about revisioning our understanding of literacy, perhaps even abandoning the term altogether, especially when we attempt to describe the complex relationship and meaning-making practices that many are developing with various communications media. For Wysocki and Johnson-Eilola, "literacy" seems too "passive": "The connotations of literacy . . . suggest a process of mechanical and passive individual reception: the book gives us who we are, the book sets the limits for who we allows into the realms of privilege" (365). The new communications technologies, however, with their interactivity and multimedia formats, call for a different understanding of meaning making, communication:

> Here is the possibility of understanding our relation to our communication technologies as not being one through which we are passively, mechanically shaped. There is the possibility of seeing ourselves as not just moving through information, but of us moving through it and making and changing conscious constructions of it as we go. This is not about handing books to children or high-school dropouts or the underdeveloped, and hoping that they will pick up enough skills to be able to lose themselves in reading . . .; it is instead about how we all might understand ourselves as active participants in how information gets "rearranged, juggled, experimented with" to make the reality of different cultures. (366)

As such, Wysocki and Johnson-Eilola are committed to opening up a space for thinking about—maybe thinking beyond—literacy, reading, and writing, particularly as they are inflected by and mediated by networked technologies. Viewed another way, such scholars are speaking to us about fundamental changes in how we understand and articulate our relationship to technology and the meanings made and mediated by it.

A significant part of paying attention to changes in literacy, and to our changing relationship to the way meaning is made in the Information Age, involves being attuned to the ways in which visuals and visual rhetoric are significant components of communicating in electronic forums like the Web. Diana George, in "From Analysis to Design: Visual Communication in the Teaching of Writing," argues that,

> For students who have grown up in a technology-saturated and an image-rich culture, questions of communication and composition absolutely will include the visual, not as attendant to the verbal but as complex communication intricately related to the world around them. (32)

George is hardly alone, and many others have noted the increasing importance of "visual literacy" (a phrase to which Wysocki and Johnson-Eilola might object), and the need for pedagogues to pay attention to visuals in the teaching of communication, literacy, and writing skills. In "Visualizing English: Recognizing the Hybrid Literacy of Visual and Verbal Authorship on the Web," Craig Stroupe asks his colleagues in the field of writing and English Studies to consider the prominent role that visuals play on the Web, and to understand that "verbal literacy is not replaced or buried so much as layered *into* a more diverse amalgamation of literacies" (608). More specifically, he argues that, "As has long been the case in television production and print advertising, Web-based communication makes verbal expertise only one among many forms of literacy and professional/rhetorical authority, any one of which may provide the primary vision for the production as a whole" (608). Stroupe is concerned with English Studies' potential failure to recognize complex "literate" acts on Web sites, and he's well aware of what Richard A. Lanham noted as early as 1993 in *The Electronic Word: Democracy: Technology, and the Arts*: resistances to technology among many academics, particularly those who study writing, is strong:

> Apoplexy seems to come more naturally than apocalypse to literary scholars when we think about technology. Apoplectic rage and scorn has been the common response to commercial television; apocalyptic

soaring on the wings of new technology has been altogether less common. (25)

As such, Stroupe, among many others, is committed to helping his colleagues note, learn, explore, and appreciate the many "continuities between traditionally defined English studies and certain possibilities in the hybrid practices of popular and Web cultures" (629). And, hopefully, "By visualizing its mostly verbal practices, English Studies could . . . recognize its continuities with these extra-verbal cultures" (630). Again, writers such as Stroupe are raising questions of relationship, of how we interact with and make meaning with the new communications technologies, and they are concerned that we be attentive to how students, who, in George's words, "have grown up in a technology-saturated and an image-rich culture," may already have an altered relationship to literacy, reading, and authoring.

Schroeder, Johnson-Eilola, Wysocki, George, and Stroupe might suggest that those most intimately involved in teaching literacy should expand their sense of how meaning is made and communicated—particularly with reference to the many literacies, skills, and creative acts of meaning-making that some of our students bring with them into the classroom. At the same time, however, there are those who think that the current reconfiguring of what literacy means might lead us to into murky territory, muddying a term originally meant to make certain skill sets clear and opaque. In *Literacy in the New Media Age*, Gunther Kress suggests that we reserve the term literacy to refer to instances "when we make messages using letters as the means of recording that message" (23). More specifically, he argues that

> The new technologies of information and communication . . . bring together the resources for representation and their potential with the resources of production and the resources of dissemination. It is this conflation which has led to some of the too ready extension of the term "literacy": using the computer has aspects of all three. (23)

In many ways, he is right, and Wysocki and Johnson-Eilola might agree: We need a new term, or new set of terms, to refer to the complex dynamics of communicating via emerging electronic and networked technologies— terms that address the ways in which many people, particularly digital youth, are not just using writing, but also visuals, to simultaneously represent, produce, and disseminate their ideas, insights, views, and senses of self, community, and world.

LITERACY IN MOTION

Given Kress' challenge to think carefully about how easily and perhaps callously we deploy the term literacy, I conclude this chapter by taking a close look at a recent collection of essays that undertakes to examine the developing relationship between technology and literacy—and that, cumulatively, through its contributors' essays, suggests a new understanding of literacy. The collection, *The Emerging Cyberculture: Literacy, Paradigm, and Paradox*, is a book of many movements, which trace the ways in which new communications technologies are impacting current notions and conceputalizations of literacy. Indeed, the metaphor of movement runs tellingly throughout the collection of essays. In the introduction, the editors, Stephanie B. Gibson and Ollie O. Oviedo, point to the usefulness of this metaphor, suggesting that "Travel and navigation dominate the ways in which we talk about interacting in cyberspace" (15). We search, explore, find, seek, and get lost in the ins and outs, the ups and downs—in both the amount of information moving along fiber optic lines and cables, and in the number of communication platforms to choose from in representing our own individual and collective searches for meaning making. Curiously, this metaphor of movement appears in a number of different descriptions and studies of the Internet and the new communications technologies—so much so, that it has become a commonplace, a shorthand of expression: "Where do *you* want to go today?"

Images of the journey, the search, and navigation abound, as they must, for asking the scholarly question—"What do we make of all of this?"—begs the question of a journey and a move toward meaning. But what meanings are we moving toward? And how will the journey impact our meaning making? Moreover, what byways and alternate routes, what criss-crossing paths or new directions, might the metaphor of movement point to—or occlude?

To answer this question, I began to trace how this metaphor of movement is deployed in *The Emerging Cyberculture* in a number of discussions of the impact of technology on literacy. For instance, in the wide-ranging, theoretically inclined introduction, one encounters comments that beg the question of how else we could think of technology—and literacy—except in terms of movement and motion:

- "Now literacy, not yet recovered from the swapping in of the visual, is being pulled in yet another direction with the nonlin-

earity, nonsequentiality, and interactivity of several forms of
hypertext." (7)

- "For hypertext use, we need to understand, for instance, how to
navigate the 'space.'" (8)
- "The object of hypermedia seems, in fact, to be the creation of
work that has movement, change, and ultimately disappear-
ance as its integral qualities. The fixity of print, its motions of
closure, and its authority are summoned to account for themselves in the world of electronic literacy. What will be their legacy?" (11)

On one hand, these quotations speak to how the graphical interface of
many of the new communications technologies offer us a chance to move
through multiple texts, as well as between texts and images, with greater
ease and immediacy than ever before. And many of the contributor's figure this movement as progress, as potential, as possibility.

The journey toward/through meaning offered by the emerging cyberculture, then, is one between ever increasing bits of information, prompting perhaps new linkages, new ways of thinking about the information
moving around us.

But one also can't help but wonder what metaphorical baggage is
packed for this journey.

Indeed, the metaphor of movement carries with it assumptions about
the inevitability of progress that comes with technological innovation, as
well as the unexamined faith in technological movement ultimately leading to shifts in cultural thinking and meaning making. As the editors
assert:

- "Examination of other paradigm shifts shows that shifts in cultural belief systems expose to the light the endless paradoxes
and connections with which cultures live as a matter of course."
(16)
- "The new 'reality' of dimensions that we will eventually come
to understand about cyberspace demands new habits of
thought that will swiftly become commonplace." (18)
- "All new technology brings with it a moment's opportunity to
view the world as it shifts. The window opens for an instance,
the bright glare of myriad possibilities streams blindingly into
the room, and we are stunned." (19)

The image of the individual stunned belies the assumption here that new communication technologies are *moving* us into new habits of thought, new forms of literacy, and even new dimensions of consciousness. And, curiously, this becomes one of the central—if not always acknowledged—paradoxes of the collection. The sense one gets from a reading of *The Emerging Cyberculture* is one of paradox: We move to communicate, even as we are bound by the forms of communication surrounding us; but we also move the forms in new directions, only to be bound again by the necessity of communicating at all.

Ultimately, one reads this book, and perhaps experiences the entire debate itself, with a sense of literacy itself *as* motion, and we understand *The Emerging Cyberculture* as a book of many movements because literacy itself has always already been an entity of many movements, tempting us to trace it even as it changes in the tracing. And, as the editors tell us in their introduction—"in the virtual world all our expectations can be turned inside out" (14-15)—then so too can our expectations about literacy be turned—and moved—in different directions. For what is literacy but the motion that has always allowed us varied and multiple technologies to shape meaning—and the world? Keeping such a view in mind, tracing the new technologies' impact on literacy will ultimately tell us more about the function of literacy itself.

And that's part of the purpose of this book.

Although it may be "too early in the game" to determine which side is right—the dystopic nay-sayers critical of technology and its deleterious impact on literacy and culture, or the utopian visionaries who applaud emerging e-literacies with their interactivity and hypertextual complexities—it is clear that the new technologies *are* posing many challenges—and possibilities—for students and other young writers. And, as we've seen, a concern with "youth," often ideologically loaded, has been at the heart of debates about both the use of technology and its impact on our understanding of literacy. For instance, Postman's and Birkerts' use of the figure of youth, particularly *children*, in their arguments is intended to underscore the presence of a problem; they invoke a "save the children" strategy for both rhetorical and political ends. For Postman and Birkerts, the *stated* problem is technology, but perhaps it is also, if unconsciously, a problem of *youth*—of the youth who use, revel in, and promote the very technologies that Postman and Birkerts find so problematic. For example, Postman draws his distinctions between print and "televisual" literacies a bit too harshly, and I think that, if we pay attention to the literacy practices of youth who engage, play with, and manipulate various "electronic media," we'll actually see a wider and more creative deployment of both print and multimedia literacies that not only gives the lie to Postman's binary but interestingly deconstructs it. Furthermore, the "associative dynamics" that Birkerts fears as undermining rationality and leading to free form meaning un-making may constitute a *change* in literacy practices, but they are hardly the end of literacy; rather, I want to argue that the way digital youth, in particular, use them reveals a meaningful and critical use of media and technology that need not elide either an awareness of history or a sensitivity to historical perspectives. At the same time, my interest in examining the way such youth use communications technologies is hardly utopian. I *also* want to "test" Bolter's contention that "electronic writing," as a conceptual space, "fosters different styles and genres of writing." Certainly, much youth writing in virtual spaces—on the Web, for instance—*seems* different, but I want to interrogate what "different" means.

More pointedly, perhaps, I want to address what seems *missing* in all of the foregoing discussion—a "paying attention" to what digital youth and some our students are already doing with the new communications technologies, such as the Web. The flurry of concern and enthusiasm over changing literacies, from Postman and Birkerts to Bolter and Landow to slick new textbooks on cyberculture and electracies, doesn't often step back far enough, or long enough, to readily examine what some young people actually do with these technologies—how they write with them, how they experiment with them as literacy tools. There are some notable exceptions, such as Gregory Ulmer's *Internet Inventions*, but even this text is more directive in suggesting how students should write the Web, as opposed to honoring and examining the many ways in which some youth are already writing the Web. Put another way, what I think we should do is take Christopher Schroeder seriously when he suggests in *Reinventing the University* that *we* take seriously the literacies that some of our e-savvy students have been practicing on their own. What we need, perhaps, is to bring Schroeder's respect for such literacies to bear on an analysis of digital youths' engagement with the new and emerging communications technologies. Doing so might complicate, enliven, and invigorate our understanding of literacy—and of how literacy is always in motion, despite both the nay-sayers and the techno-hype.

Ultimately, my questions are simple, evoking and evoked by the likes of Schroeder or Wysocki and their reconsideration of literacy itself: How do *digital youth*, specifically the e-savvy youth coming into our college and university writing programs, use communications technologies, and what does their use say about the kinds of literacy practices fostered or enabled by technology? Where are *their* voices, and what do *their* literacy practices tell us about the new communications technologies and their possibilities for meaning making? Further, as Julian Sefton-Green suggests in *Digital Diversions: Youth Culture in the Age of Multimedia,* we need to "tease out the relationships between the traditional and new literacies" (10). What are those relationships, and how do they affect both "traditional" and "new literacies"? And what do digital youths' use of the multimedia technologies say about that relationship, if anything? In relation to such questions, I have also been thinking about my own position vis-à-vis the debate about the "shift" from print to electronic literacies. With so many competing representations, even "mythologies" about "youths'" relationship to and use of the new communications technologies, it is worth asking if *digital* youths' use of such technologies "lives up to" the hype—both positive and negative. Are the "myths" accurate? Whose interests do they serve? What notions of literacy—technological and otherwise—do they maintain and enable? What emerging notions of literacy might they elide?

Indeed, I am going to argue in these pages that many e-connected and e-savvy youth are deploying a number of interesting and surprising rhetorical strategies and compositional practices to resist the nearly mythological representations that others have created about them and their use of technology. These strategies also tell us much about *their* vision for the new communications technologies and the emerging literacy practices they are using to engage that technology. As such, the digital youth writing strategies and practices I describe and discuss in this book give the lie to fears of the "end of literacy" due to increased use of the Internet and the media; at the same time, these practices also foreshadow potential *changes* in rhetorical and literacy practices. Put simply, digital youth write their lives, interests, and ideas—and they are increasingly using the new communications technologies to do so. They represent themselves—many times in ways that critique our understanding of them and their personal and sociopolitical investments. And frequently, their writing critiques *our* investments in and ideologies about both youth *and* technology. Examining both—the politics and mythologies imbedded in the representations of digital youth and technology against actual digital youth practices of communication and meaning making—creates a complex but telling portrait of the (future?) use of the these technologies and the kinds of literacies that such youth are favoring and developing with communications technologies.

As such, I spend the remainder of this book examining the ways some digital youth understand their relationship to the new technologies and considering some of the ways *they* use communications technologies, particularly the Web, to create, disseminate, and interact with such representations, and the world around them. In the next chapter, I offer a critical reading of Douglas Rushkoff's exuberant and utopian appreciation of e-savvy youths' use of technology, particularly networked communications technologies, and I contrast some of his enthusiastic claims with some of the actual practices that some digital youth deploy, particularly in their Web writing. In the process, I hope to demonstrate that some youth are viewing their engagement with the Web and with emerging literacies in ways that belie the simplicity of the utopian/dystopian debate, and that point to fairly complex literacy practices and engagements. In the chapters that follow, I look a bit more closely at some of those specific practices as they are manifested in—and transforming—various Web genres, such as the personal homepage, the e-zine, and the activist site.

2

USES AND ABUSES OF HYPERBOLE, OR, THE CASE OF DOUGLAS RUSHKOFF'S "DIGITAL KIDS"

As discussed in the introduction and in Chapter 1, discussions of youth who use technology are often characterized by hyperbole—by exaggerations, for instance, of the dangers posed to naïve youth by technology, of the addictive features of computers and video games, and even of the utopian possibilities offered by some youths' use of technology. Of course, when hyperbole is present, contradiction isn't far behind, and it should not be surprising that debates about "youth and technology," when argued in such broad terms as "good" and "evil" and utopian and dystopian, will produce shallow and even naïve positions. At the same time, one of the most consistently used and critically powerful tools deployed by some writing-savvy youth in their self-representation is hyperbole, and some youth writers who use the new communications technologies do so to create sites of resistance (on the Web and otherwise) that use hyperbole to critique how they and their concerns, interests, and investments are represented.

In this chapter, I extend the discussion in Chapter 1 to explore in a bit more detail some of the hyperbolic arguments made about youth and technology, particularly those that promise either utopian or dystopian futures.

In particular, I look at the early work of Douglas Rushkoff, who was among the most vocal in lauding the potential social, nearly utopian benefits arising from some youth, particularly e-savvy youth with strong subcultural affiliations, and their use and embracing of technology. Although Rushkoff represents a fairly utopian view of digital youths' use of technology, some e-savvy youth themselves forward a much more critical understanding of technology, particularly media and networked communications technologies. As such, these youth too enter into the debate about the impact of communications technologies, such as the Web, on their own self-understanding and literacy practices. Such an analysis should set the stage for a more thorough exploration in the following chapters of other literacy practices used by digital youth to examine, explore, and understand their own use of the new communications technologies.

"DIGITAL KIDS" AND THE PROMISE OF THE FUTURE

Rushkoff, a media critic, author, and lecturer, has been particularly enthusiastic in his assessment of how some youth use the new communications technology, and he was among the first to suggest that such use held out the potential for personal, social, and political reform and transformation—on a global scale. Few are as prolific as Rushkoff and few are as hopeful—particularly about the power of e-savvy youth to change our world for the better. The author of several recent books, including the nonfictional *Cyberia, Media Virus, Coercion: Why We Listen to What "They" Say*, and the novels *Ecstasy Club* and *Exit Strategy*, Rushkoff also writes a monthly column, usually on technology and frequently about youth with interests in technology and strong subcultural affiliations, and he helped produce the *Frontline* documentary, *The Merchants of Cool*, which explores how companies create and market youth culture.

Much of Rushkoff's interest in technology dovetails with his advocacy for "media literacy." For Rushkoff, the careful examination of media is an important, even political act, one that is necessary if we are to become "literate" in a media-saturated society. According to his professional Web site, his work "analyzes the way people, cultures, and institutions create, share, and influence each other's values. He sees 'media' as the landscape where this interaction takes place, and 'literacy' as the ability to participate consciously in it" (http://www.rushkoff.com/bio.html). For Rushkoff, our "ability to participate" has been revolutionized through the introduction of interactive communications platforms, such as the Web. Although some bemoan the overwhelming number of technological innovations that threaten to distance us from each other or more "traditional" modes of literacy and knowing, Rushkoff sees the new communications technologies as offering possibilities for even *greater* interaction—and for creating new modes of knowledge. Far from being simply the "victims" of our technology, we are, in Rushkoff's view, responsible for becoming better acquainted with such technology in order to help (re)shape our world, embrace the future, and further our evolution as sentient beings.

Rushkoff is careful to place the emphasis *not* on the technology, but on its *use*. He is a staunch critic of unthinking and naïve appreciation of technology, and he holds philosophically to the tenets of "technorealism"—a stance purporting to lead us along the "middle way" between uncritical optimism and outright pessimism in our understanding and use of technology. Along with 11 other writers and critics of technology, Rushkoff is one of the founding members of Tehnorealism.org, whose manifesto can be found on the Web at http://www.technorealism.org. On their site, the authors argue that they "seek to expand the fertile middle ground between techno-utopianism and neo-Luddism," and they hold to such tenets as "Technologies are not neutral" and "The Internet is revolutionary, but not Utopian." Throughout, the site authors—and, in other works, Rushkoff—see our understanding and use of technology as a *literacy* issue, maintaining that "Information is not knowledge" and that "Understanding technology should be an essential component of global citizenship." More specifically, they argue that, "regardless of how advanced our computers become, we should never use them as a substitute for our own basic cognitive skills of awareness, perception, reasoning, and judgment." Of particular concern is the fear that *speed* of access and mass availability of information will overtake critical thinking about that information: "the proliferation of data is . . . a serious challenge, requiring new measures of human discipline and skepticism. We must not confuse the thrill of acquiring or distributing information quickly with the more daunting task of converting it into knowledge and wisdom."

Along these lines, training youth, particularly those who are increasingly immersed (in the West, at least) in technologically enhanced and network-saturated environments, to understand and use technology appropriately and with awareness is crucial, and the technorealists maintain that simply "Wiring the schools will not save them":

> The problems with America's public schools—disparate funding, social promotion, bloated class size, crumbling infrastructure, lack of stan-

dards—have almost nothing to do with technology. Consequently, no amount of technology will lead to the educational revolution prophesied by President Clinton and others. The art of teaching cannot be replicated by computers, the Net [SIC], or by "distance learning." These tools can, of course, augment an already high-quality educational experience. But to rely on them as any sort of panacea would be a costly mistake.

The technology figured here is technology as *tool*—and perhaps one that we have placed a bit *too* much faith in at times. Rushkoff and the other "technorealists" are, I think, justifiably skeptical of such faith, and their interest in promoting a "reasoned," even cautious approach to technology and its uses seems sensible. In particular, the emphasis on "awareness" and even "judgment" seems to promote critical thinking about technology—not a blind reliance on it. As such, the technorealists' approach concerns itself with technological *literacy* in the broadest sense, with becoming critically aware of both how we communicate and the role of our communications tools in shaping that communication.

What is interesting about Rushkoff, however, is that, although his enthusiasm for the technology itself is tempered with a healthy critical skepticism, his enthusiasm for the youth who *use* technology is hyperbolic—even fetchingly so at times. Rushkoff's thinking has roots in Gen-X attitudes and identity, having edited a now out-of-print anthology, *The Gen X Reader*. Willing to work with and through a stereotype, Rushkoff argues that Gen-Xers may have "dropped out of American culture (as it is traditionally defined), [but] they also stand as a testament to American ingenuity, optimism, instinct, and intelligence" (http://www.rushkoff.com/genxreader. html). For Rushkoff, such youthful optimism is *most* evident in Gen-Xers' and subsequent generations' use of technology. Specifically, Rushkoff believes that e-savvy youth and their seemingly inherent, nearly innate interest in technology will lead the way in changing our world—potentially for the better. Furthermore, as seen later in this chapter, he is an enthusiastic supporter of youth cultures, particularly those that utilize new technologies, and many of his books contain exuberant discussions of how e-savvy youth and their subcultural/countercultural use of technology can show us provocative and exciting new ways of being in the world and potentially usher us into the next stage of human evolution.

Rushkoff's most sustained examination of these convictions comes in *Playing the Future: What We Can Learn from Digital Kids*. Originally published in 1996, *Playing the Future* offers a provocative analysis of many American youth subcultures and interests, ranging from skaterpunks and ravers to anime fans and Saturday-morning cartoons. For Rushkoff, youth subcultures are, in general, more interesting, noteworthy, and even evolutionary because of their members' greater appreciation of and dependence on technology. As the author tells us in his introduction to the 1999 updated version of the book,

> many of the subcultures [I have] described . . . have grown in popularity . . . because they were so effective in appealing to a youth population intent on adapting to the coming cultural shift—a shift characterized by an increasing dependence on technology and media, as well as an awareness of the many challenges and opportunities that networking and its resulting interdependence will pose. Like our children, we will be required to step back from our seemingly disjointed and conflicting experiences, and to see them instead in the context of the new, chaotic landscape on which we will be conducting human affairs. (9)

Several points here are worth exploring in a bit more depth.

First, Rushkoff is convinced that we live in a *liminal* time, in which massive and substantial change is inevitable, resulting in a "cultural shift." In many ways, this "shift" is the advent of postmodernity itself and the seeming chaos of our multicultural, fragmented world. But this is not bad news. One of the main emphases throughout *Playing the Future* is on appreciating and embracing this *chaos*, particularly a chaos brought about by the various communications media and platforms that allow *numerous*, conflicting stories to be told—stories that "give the lie" to "linear thinking, duality, mechanism, hierarchy, metaphor, and God himself" (269). Indeed, for Rushkoff, the past is characterized, á la Lyotard, by grand, meaning-granting meta-narratives that organized human experience into an easy-to-follow, largely linear interpretive story that relied on demonizing dualities to create meaning. Rushkoff's argument proceeds by interrogating a series of these binaries: linear thinking/chaos, duality/holism; mechanism/animism; gravity/consensual hallucination; metaphor/recapitulation; god/nature. In each case, Rushkoff favors the latter term, believing that we are moving into a chaotic era in which we will do better to embrace the chaos and go with the flow as opposed to imposing a sense of hierarchy, no matter how comforting. In Rushkoff's view, the hierarchy will stifle innovation and creativity, leading to social decay and collapse.

Second, new communications technologies such as the Internet can play, have played, and will continue to play a huge role in problematizing older, more restrictive "stories" about meaning, in that the *interactivity* enabled by these technologies allows for more voices to participate in the

construction and representation of human "realities." Specifically, Rushkoff
argues that "Many media analysts, including myself, have outlined the way
our media evolved from a top-down, unidirectional forum into the interactive free-for-all it is today" (47). In this view, television is basically a "top-
down" medium, with content dictated by others and channeled into our
homes. In contrast, a chatroom provides—and prompts—more "give and
take," more discussion, more reality *building*, as opposed to reality *reception* from somewhere else. Rushkoff writes enthusiastically about such reality building:

> Through technology, they [e-savvy youth] gain the ability to create
> what William Gibson called, in his book *Neuromancer*, a "consensual
> hallucination"—a group exercise in world creation when reality is no
> longer ordained from above, but generated by its participants. Fully
> evolved video game play, then, is total immersion in a world from with-
> in a participant's point of view, where the world itself reflects the val-
> ues and actions of the player and his community members. Hierarchy
> is replaced with a weightless working out of largely unconscious preoc-
> cupations. (180–1)

Rushkoff is hardly alone in thinking enthusiastically about the ramifications
of increased interactivity on the representation and construction of reality
and meaning. Don Tapscott's *Growing Up Digital: The Rise of the Net
Generation* (1998) covers similar ground, arguing that today's e-savvy and
digital youth are "breaking free from the one-way, centralized media of the
past and are beginning to shape their own destiny. And evidence is mounting that the world will be a better place as a result" (33).

How are such digital youth to shape their, and our, destiny? Utilizing
the interactive features of, for instance, the Web, e-mail, chat, and other
communications platforms, youth with Internet access exchange ideas,
shape opinion, and create information more quickly and efficiently. In the
process, according to Tapscott, "These young people will bring and implement radical views regarding how business should be conducted and on
the process of democratic government" (304). And academics too have
waxed enthusiastically along similar lines. Writing at roughly the same
time in *Fragments of Rationality: Postmodernity and the Subject of
Composition*, Lester Faigley suggested that the mix of voices in online chats
and discussions might create polyvocal narratives, showing participants a
useful diversity of views and helping us acknowledge and appreciate our
differences: "[students] are forced to confront different ways of constitut-

ing meaning from experience and to negotiate those meanings with other students" (185). For Tapscott, Rushkoff, and Faigley, the future, at the end of the 1990s at least, looked bright—with e-savvy youth and their embracing of technology leading the way.

Finally, Rushkoff suggests that we are preparing, as a culture, as a species, to take the next step in our sociocultural and political evolution. Postmodern chaos and the new communications technologies are certainly daunting, but they present us with a challenge to rethink and reconceptualize our identities, our social structures, our politics, and our cultures. In fact, throughout *Playing the Future*, Rushkoff repeatedly deploys the terms evolution and evolutionary to describe the changes that our interactions with technology are bringing us. Of course, evolution, as a trope, usually implies progress, and Rushkoff is generally hopeful about the future—but only if we listen to our kids and what they're telling us about that future. Indeed, Rushkoff's youth, his "digital kids," are at the forefront of cultural change, sociopolitical evolution, and the embracing of technology. As Rushkoff puts it, "Our children . . . have already made their move. They are leading us in our evolution past linear thinking, duality, mechanism, hierarchy, metaphor, and God himself toward a dynamic, holistic, animistic, weightless, and recapitulated culture. Chaos is their natural environment" (269). Again, the narrative is pretty clear: Out with the modern, in with the postmodern; out with the linear, in with the . . . well, you get the picture. Granted, the going will be rough: Our new technologies have created great chaos, but working within and with that chaos will save us, leading to our progress as a race. Who are our guides? Digital youth. And how will they create positive change? With technology. Why? Only they truly realize, utilize, and appreciate its *interactive* possibilities: "The screenager sees how the entire mediaspace is a cooperative dream, made up of the combined projections of everyone who takes part" (181).

So, given Rushkoff's assessment, what lies ahead for us on our evolutionary path? Where are these digital youth taking us? And what values will surface through the "consensual hallucination," through the "cooperative dream"? Rushkoff's answers are almost always hopeful, positive, and even utopian: "In a chaotic cultural system, ideas generating tolerance, better survival, or higher levels of organization will continue to iterate" (266). Why? Because greater communication and interactivity will help us get to know one another better—and consequently appreciate our differences. And the ramifications of this are, according to Rushkoff, far-reaching, both socially and politically: "Our media promotes free communication, our economy promotes choice, and our religions are turning to participation over programming" (268).

The causal chain here is, at least, hopeful, but it rests on the assumptions that the majority of our citizenry uses technology and that that technology will necessarily increase our interactivity with one another. Moreover, it is not always quite clear in *Playing the Future* how greater interaction leads to more tolerance; this seems more of a hopeful outcome than a demonstrable sociological reality. Indeed, Rushkoff's use of Gibson's phrase "consensual hallucination" from the novel *Neuromancer* is telling, prompting us to reconsider his enthusiasm; after all, Gibson's visions of technology in *Neuromancer* and subsequent novels is often one of terror and control, in which individuals, through their interactions with technology, are at even *greater* risk for mind control and programming. Furthermore, the causal chain begs a whole other set of questions that are largely unanswered in *Playing the Future*. Specifically, Rushkoff suggests that, "Thanks to media and a willingness to use it, real people are going to gain the ability to influence the direction of our body politique. Our only choice is whether to arm them with the skills necessary to effect successful stewardship" (202). I think many literacy teachers would agree that we should "arm" our students with the skills to use technology, but what *are* those skills, and how will they be used? And in some ways, Rushkoff's visions seem more mystical than "techno-realistic." For instance, he tells us that "higher levels of dimensionality appear to be the goal of evolutionary development" (242) and that a "spirituality of self-modification and conscious evolution will move quite naturally to encompass technology as a force of positive change" (141). Such cryptic statements pepper Rushkoff's analysis, and their generality, though optimistic, isn't particularly revealing about *how*, specifically, e-savvy youth and technology will save us.

To be fair, Rushkoff offers a caution in *Playing the Future*: "the evolution of technology without an accompanying development in human interaction can only end in disaster" (94). In so many ways, this is ultimately what Rushkoff wants to tell us: We need to be worthy of the technological wonders we have created. How can we be worthy? By watching the kids and their unabashedly playful, nonhierarchial, nonlinear engagement with interactive technologies. This necessitates that we "grow up," and accept "the responsibility of self-determinism and the grace of nonlinear experience. Equally important, the screenager accepts the media and technology generating all this confusion as a partner in forward evolution" (105).

Rushkoff has faced vocal critics, notably Mark Dery and Richard Barbrook, who have attacked his breathless optimism, as well as perceived ideological contradictions between his embrace of sub- and countercultures in his writings and his work as a consultant for some multinational corporations (http://www.disinfo.com/pages/dossier/id176/pg1.html). But I think another set of questions—specific to youth and technology—begs to be asked. Is digital youth's engagement with technology playful, nonhierarchial, and nonlinear? Has Rushkoff accurately described the sense in which digital youth view—and use—technology? And, if so, what does this mean—in terms of their use of technology to represent their concerns and issues and to shape their worlds?

I've used *Playing the Future* and other of Rushkoff's works in a few undergraduate writing, literature, and technology literacy courses, and student responses are varied. Pedagogically, having students examine Rushkoff's representation of e-savvy youth is useful in a number of ways. First, students are introduced to the ways in which a cultural critic can construct and use a representation to further his or her particular social and political agenda. Second, because Rushkoff plays the future with such sweeping thrusts and parries, students have the opportunity to explore and critique his more audacious generalizations with the lived experience of their specific situations. But students' responses to the *content* of his work are even more interesting. On one hand, it is hard not to be flattered by his insistence that e-savvy youth and their openness to technology will save the world, despite the backwards glancing of adult Luddites. Indeed, students are often initially very sympathetic to *Playing the Future*, identifying with the role that Rushkoff lays out for them. On the other hand, though, a closer reading with students of Rushkoff's claims yields critique and growing skepticism.

For instance, students in a post-9/11 world have been quick to pinpoint and critique Rushkoff's seemingly naïve connections between youth who embrace technology and the inevitability of sociopolitical progress. Rushkoff holds to his conviction that clutching desperately to our old, modernist ways of thinking is bad and we should follow the children into the brave new world of technologically induced chaos. Future success is all but guaranteed in the larger evolutionary scheme of things. After all, "In a chaotic cultural system, ideas generating tolerance, better survival, or higher levels of organization will continue to iterate" (266). Such claims, and there are many such throughout *Playing the Future*, seem dubious in a world where many technologies, even the Web, have recently been used to visit terror and destruction on civilian populations.

Our discussions of Rushkoff's representation of digital youth and technology become all the more critical—and revealing—when we closely examine the examples from youth culture that Rushkoff uses to bolster his arguments. Specifically, we begin to question some of the assumptions about digital youth and technology—beginning with a critique of the mediascape as "cooperative dream."

RAVER RESISTANCE AND THE HYPERREAL

One of the specific youth subcultures that Rushkoff examines is raver culture. Raves are a contemporary countercultural phenomenon, emphasizing techno-music, dancing, drug experimentation, and community-building through the values of peace, love, unity, and respect (PLUR). Drawing on their interests in technology, many ravers have actively used Web space to promote their ideologies and agendas, and some easily found Web sites promote "rave culture" and the dissemination of PLUR and community specifically via the Internet. Indeed, rave culture in general and rave parties in particular often partake of the same energy and techno-savvy of other 1990s technologically "hip" countercultures, such as the cyberculture surrounding publications such as *Mondo 2000*. Most students with whom I work are at least somewhat familiar with rave culture, and a handful admits to having participated in raves. Others have seen either news reports about raves, and a few have cruised through raver oriented Web sites. Many characterize raves themselves as large "underground" parties, usually held in warehouses, with dancing, techno-music, and the ingestion of Ecstasy or other designer drugs.

For Rushkoff, however, the rave is much more than just a party. In his enthusiastic discussion of rave culture, Rushkoff maintains the following.

> The rave is self-consciously phase-locked, and self-consciously technological. Ravers use their computers and digital recorders to create their music and design their graphics. They embrace technology for its ability to sample and recombine sounds and images from throughout cultural history, and even more for technology's ability to forge a new global culture. Rave philosophy, as outlined on the back of a clothing label or "hang tag" (one of their main conduits for written communication) generally credits technology with promoting global community and cultural tolerance. (160)

This is a good example of how Rushkoff's mid-1990s utopian sensibility links technology to cultural change, inviting us to believe that computer networks, and the youth wired to and through them, can save us all from cultural stagnation and social desiccation. Indeed, for Rushkoff, the value of the rave lies not just in its function as a big "group hug," but in its inventive, even radical use of technology. For example, the rave "aesthetic involves cultural 'sampling'—the selection and recombination of sounds, images, and ideas from throughout history. This is a quite conscious effort to reach an eternal, timeless moment of bliss by recombining, overlapping, and juxtaposing imagery from multiple periods within a single beat of music or frame of film" (37).

Such bliss is also intimately *collective*, and Rushkoff waxes simultaneously mystical and political about ravers' use of technology:

> Rave parties, where thousands of kids dance to digital music, are planned as consciousness-altering events. The psychedelic drugs, music, and lights are designed to put everyone into a group trance. By the end of the evening (which means dawn) the kids hope to experience themselves and one another as parts of a single, metaorganism. It's both futuristic and intensely tribal, making use of technology to promote deeply spiritual agendas. (36)

What are those "spiritual agendas"? Rushkoff summarizes them as "unity, tolerance, individual expression, and global evolution" (36). Certainly, Rushkoff is borrowing from basic raver ideology and values, particularly as embodied in the acronym/slogan PLUR. Note, however, how the values Rushkoff identifies are in line with the values of tolerance and interactivity that he suggests characterize e-savvy youths' use of technology in general.

In forums besides *Playing the Future*, Rushkoff has praised the rave scene, even suggesting in a column entitled "Electronica: The True Cyberculture" that "rave culture embodies and defines the Digital Age." He argues the following:

> The first major impact of computers and the Internet on our culture has been in the music and club communities of young people. Cheap micro-processing technology put high-quality sound synthesizers and mixing studios in the hands of musicians who never had access to professional recording equipment before. These young musicians, generally members of the countercultural communities who had already embraced computer technology, were profoundly changed by their ability to manifest in sound almost anything they could imagine.

Oddly, the sentiment here is both nostalgic and utopian. On one hand, Rushkoff sees ravers as embodying a "countercultural" sensibility with roots in the youth cultures of the 1960s; these are revolutionaries whose only difference from their hippie forefathers and mothers is their use of technology to further their ends. On the other hand, and perhaps *because* Rushkoff wants to keep the countercultural dream alive, his vision of raves is utopian, even ecstatically and hyperbolically so:

> Electronic music embodies and amplifies the core values of the origi-
> nal Internet community: there is no boss, anyone can participate, and
> the more contributions from around the world, the better. The object
> of a rave dance is to join a large group together, at least temporarily,
> into a single, joyful, coordinated being. How much closer to the utopi-
> an dreams of the Internet can a cultural movement get?
> (http://www.rushkoff.com/ecstasyclub.html)

It is hard not to see such thinking as hyperbolic, specifically when articulating the kinds of utopian promises that Internet technologies seemed to
carry with them: an interactive and united world. Moreover, the tone is
reminiscent—in spirit, if not in theoretical sophistication—of Donna
Haraway and her "Cyborg Manifesto." These "countercultural communities" seem intent on creating, in Haraway's words, an "oppositional consciousness" that is not, as Nick Mansfield puts it, "hung up on its own
essence and truth, but every forging new coalitions and interconnections"
(Haraway, *Simians*, 156; Mansfield, 160).

Rushkoff's enthusiasm seems, at time, gushing, and it is worth asking
if the reality of raves lives up to his representation. Student reactions are
telling in this regard. Most are often intrigued but also a little skeptical of
Rushkoff's enthusiasm. In particular, those who have actually attended
raves question the seeming "inevitability" of "global community and cultural tolerance" arising out of the rave experience. Hierarchies in raves
seem inevitable, and certain seemingly arbitrary standards of dress and
even physical attractiveness belie ravers' insistence that they are wholly
invested in PLUR and tolerant community building. Moreover, raves seem
inevitably a part of *White* youth culture, with their frequent musical borrowings from hip-hop or other racial and ethnic subcultures elided or unacknowledged.

To further the discussion and put more representations into play, my
students and I have scoured the Web for available sources of information
about raves and raveculture, and we invariably find a hodge-podge of information, slowly and painstakingly building a picture of what raveculture
must be like. The majority of pages we find speak positively and enthusiastically about raveculture, such as any number of sites we found via
Google.com. Students frequently view the pages with a mixture of amusement and genuine interest, often commenting on the sophisticated graphics and the complex use of visual rhetoric on many of the sites. Some of
our most interesting discussions come, however, from pursuing Rushkoff's
suggested link about raveculture. When we attempted to access the site listed in the appendix to *Playing the Future*, http://hyperreal.com, we found

the site taken over by a commercial venture—not surprising for the Web in 2002. We *did* find Hyperreal.*org*, a site focusing on raver culture and "the spirit of raving," with numerous links, psuedo-philosophical and political discussions, and information about rave "etiquette." The site is, like many other raver sites, very enthusiastic about the rave experience, maintaining, for instance, that "The party becomes a spiritual ritual in which the music's machine-driven beats and transcendental sound timbres synchronize our bodies and souls to the rhythms of the universe" (http://hyperreal.org /raves/spirit/intro.html).

More specifically, through examining such sites, students steadily build a picture of raveculture as embracing, among other things, "techno-shamanism," which "explores the synergy between the mystical and the physical," using technology (such as music sampling and even artificially created drugs) to "sync" minds and bodies to one another and induce a sensation of unity (link no longer available). Such "synergy" should steadily produce greater tolerance for others as we link to them, enjoying states of technologically driven bliss. To promote this philosophy, Hyperreal provides a wealth of information to *inform* potential ravers, not just about rave philosophy and culture, but about drug safety and other practical aspects of the rave experience. In many ways, such sentiments seem in line with Rushkoff's appreciation of raves and their (and his) conflation of the spread of technology with greater social tolerance.

Screen shot of http://hyperreal.org/

Through such sites, students also see the creation of an online counterculture. Hyperreal is clearly a community effort, with numerous links leading
to contributors' postings detailing and debating the various uses of technology, music, drugs, and raves in furthering a sense of global unity and tolerance. In many ways, dissemination of such information is itself the primary
act of resistance, questioning the dominant culture's mistrust of drugs—
and technology, for that matter—and asserting the right to create its own
vision of the future. In terms of the dissemination of specific kinds of information, raver use of the Web is quite provocative; for instance, Hyperreal
offers *extensive* information about drug usage and links to yet other numerous sources for visitors to explore and learn. The authors of Hyperreal are
also quite candid and explicit about both the prevalence of drug usage at
raves and their connection to the rave experience of "synchroniz[ing] our
bodies and souls to the rhythms of the universe." And the use of the Web
as a *visual* tool is not ignored: Hyperreal's section on drugs is visually
sophisticated, presenting pictures of various forms of the many drugs discussed, drop down boxes providing cross references for information, and
additional color-coded links. In fact, Hyperreal's "Chemistry" section alone
could serve as a case study in the use of visual rhetoric on the Web.

As such, Hyperreal utilizes the Web's ability to link often compelling
visual rhetoric with information and writing contributed from a number of
sources to create a countercultural site. As stated, simply providing such
information serves as an act of resistance; providing it in such a sophisticated manner represents an understanding of the importance of considering the medium in crafting community-building communication forums.
Curiously, this links up with Rushkoff's understanding of how some youth
use technologies, such as the Web. For Rushkoff, "The screenage activist
assumes a certain level of intelligence on the part of the general population
and seeks to disseminate information, promote networking, and provoke
action in as natural a way as possible. It amounts to a restoration of arro-
gant, youthful optimism" (200).

What are the political implications of such a philosophy? I have to
admit that I am both intrigued and drawn to such optimism. In general,
there is a *lot* of attractive confidence and optimism here, particularly about
the potential for continued dissemination of information to affect our
social, cultural, and political institutions for the better. In fact, my use of
such materials and Web sites in class stems from my belief that Hyperreal
models a form of complex, participatory online writing that actively creates
and sustains a countercultural movement. And although I hardly support all
raver sentiments, such as illicit drug use, I think it is useful for students to
see how other youth create such sites of resistance via the new communi-

cations technologies. According to Carla Freccero, using such sites in class might take advantage of—and enhance—many students' emerging sense of technological literacy:

> What students have learned outside the classroom are the techniques of acquiring information from media, the technological processes that inform their production, and how to go about obtaining access to the technologies themselves—how to "consume" them. This is what advanced capitalist culture successfully teaches. What the cultural studies approach to popular culture in the classroom can provide, then, is an approach to technological cultures that seeks to understand the social meanings of the representations produced by those cultures: a way, in other words, to analyze these products. The result will be not only an "informed consumer" but someone who many be able to intervene to produce meanings in the language of the medium itself and intervene politically when those representations are used to support particular agendas. (4)

Rushkoff would agree too, I believe. And, in many ways, ravers use technology—from the Web to consciousness-altering drugs—to support their agenda, and even to intervene socially and politically to "support particular agendas."

At the same time, two issues concern me—and increasingly concerned my students. First, Freccero seems to assume that students come to us already knowing how to "consume" the information they are given, but I think it's worth questioning what "consumption" means. Is such consumption *critical*? Many of our college-aged students, for instance, certainly know how to *access* information, but *how* are they understanding it, and what are they doing with it? Rushkoff himself tells us that "information is not knowledge," but he seems willing to trust youth: "The screenage activist assumes a certain level of intelligence on the part of the general population and seeks to disseminate information, promote networking, and provoke action in as natural a way as possible" (200). However, based on my experience as an educator and writing instructor, I am skeptical that the dissemination of information, no matter how exuberant and participatory it is, actually leads to an understanding of how to "consume" it. Freccero herself may feel similarly, arguing as she does for utilizing a cultural studies approach in the classroom to help students interrogate and understand popular culture. Second, as *thorough* and *communal* as Hyperreal seems, we need to question what points of view might be elided in its construction, no matter how seemingly communal. In other words, we need to question Rushkoff's assertion that "The screenager sees how the entire mediaspace is a cooperative dream, made up of the combined projections of everyone who takes part" (181). My students weren't so sure, and their feeling was that, despite the participatory nature of the Web in general and Hyperreal in particular, some views, some images of raver youth and technology, would "win out" over others. This is the point where we began to think critically about what other representations of youth, particularly raver youth, might tell us about raver culture, the ideologies enabling it, and the information potentially elided by those ideologies.

For instance, considering the extensive and relatively unabashed commentary on drugs presented in a site such as Hyperreal, students questioned the information contained on the rave-positive Web sites with information they have gleaned from other sources, such as news broadcasts about the dangers of raves and their seeming promotion of the use of illicit substances. Some had seen prime-time television reports about raves and designer drugs such as Ecstasy, and they noted in particular that news features about raves on *Dateline* and *60 Minutes II* generated much commentary on discussion boards, in chat rooms, and on the Web—particularly at pro-rave sites such as Dancesafe.org (see http://www.dancesafe.org/ ubbthreads/ubbthreads.php). Many students easily see in such reports the "dominant culture" attempting to curtail and contain the counterhegemonic exuberance of raveculture, and they are—not unjustifiably, I think—suspicious of the mass news media's interpretation of rave culture.

However, they invariably return to raver-oriented Web sites with some critical questions. Let's take Hyperreal as an example. Most of my students know that many ravers experiment with various drugs, such as Ecstasy (or MDMA, 3-4 methylenedioxymeth-amphetamine), as part of their ritual. Indeed, of the four main links on the Hyperreal site, "Chemistry" is listed second, sandwiched between "music" and "raveculture." When students examined material on the site about Ecstasy, they discovered much medical and even legal information about the drug (http://www.erowid.org/ chemicals/mdma/mdma.shtml). Most startling are the narratives contained under a separate link, "Experiences," detailing the intense highs and "ecstatic" (pun intended) states of well-being and friendliness claimed as positive side effects of the drug. When first visiting the site, students were initially willing to take this information *at face value*—despite the fact that, for the most part, *no* documentation is given. On coming back to the site with other, more skeptical reports about Ecstasy, students took a closer look at what they saw. For instance, some students pointed out that concerns about potential damaging side effects of Ecstasy are largely relegated to the end of this page and at the end of another page specifically on

Ecstasy (http://www.erowid.org/chemicals/mdma/mdma_basics.shtml). The importance of the *placement* of information was not lost on these students—especially when they had reason to suspect that the information given may be biased. Similarly, for other safety and health issues, we had to look carefully to find "negative" or potentially anti-rave commentary. For instance, we searched diligently for information about "safe sex," which we finally found on a rather unattractive page (http://hyperreal.org/raves/spirit/caring/Safe_sex.html). Interestingly, this page is one of the *contributed* messages to the site, which speaks favorably of the possibility of community-based sites offering the opportunity for various members to contribute vital information. But we couldn't help but wonder how many people see this page or wade through the numerous postings searching for a *variety* of viewpoints or diverse information.

Our examination of this site in class reminds me of what Diana George and Diane Shoos argue about the "new" media, such as Web texts:

> Certain kinds of texts . . . can appear to be all-inclusive and interactive and yet lead to no action at all—they simply take on more voices, more length. Although the links we find in web pages are intriguing to follow, but they are often arbitrary links. They don't necessarily make an argument, present a position, or offer options, and (though this may be the information superhighway) they also will not lead us to all information available on a given subject. (125)

If we think about Hyperreal in terms of George and Shoos' conception of literacy, we see that the pages included in the site do take on more voices, more length, and the Web pages are often intriguing to follow. Moreover, I would contend that the pages *do* make an argument: They present a position, even a compelling one of countercultural resistance for students. But does the site offer options that "lead us to all information available on a given subject"? Of course not, and I am not asking that any one site provide us with or lead us to all relevant information; no one site can. But my students quickly pointed out how an ideology of participation—of the technologically fostered "cooperative dream"—glosses over information that might query it, even when that information might be vital or life-saving, such as information about drug usage. As such, it is worth being skeptical of the *hyper*bole of Hyperreal's techno-shamanistic claims of promoting "unity"—which, in this case, seems a rhetorically loaded claim that rests on the subtle suppression of information that might counter it. As such, our experience with Hyperreal taught us that the dissemination of information, as useful as it is, does not necessarily lead to an understanding of that information or the consideration of multiple viewpoints—viewpoints that might be helpful (even crucial) in allowing us to make informed choices about potentially participating in a rave experience. Indeed, if my students and I relied totally on Hyperreal for information about raveculture, I might agree with Rushkoff about the potential of raves and ravecultural to use technology to usher in a new area of globalization and tolerance—which is probably why Rushkoff recommends this site. However, using different media (such as television reports and other Web sites) to question this site helped us read the site more carefully, more critically, looking for the loose threads in the original site that could help us create a more complex, carefully considered picture of the rave experience.

HYPER-MOCKERY

Although Hyperreal seems to support many of Rushkoff's claims about digital youth's use of technology to transform the world, other sites about raves tell a very different story—one that not only critiques some of the more hyperbolic claims of sites like Hyperreal, but that show hyperbole itself being used as a techno-literacy practice to offer critique and alternative views on some techno-mythologies, such as raver transformation of the world through technology.

In particular, I am thinking of sites that are explicitly *anti*-rave in their sentiments, such as this aptly titled one: The OFFICIAL Anti-Rave Site! at http://www.i-mockery.com/antirave/. The site contains rants, a satirical series of frequently asked questions (FAQs) about raves and ravers, a link to anti-raver "products" (t-shirts and coffee mugs), and an interactive survey about the site, inviting one to bash raves as well. In general, the site is an exercise in hyperbolic parody, and it uses gross exaggerations and caricature to critique (and just plain make fun of) the rave scene. Cognizant of the multidimensional powers of the Web, the site's authors use multimedia in interesting, if at times annoying, ways. For instance, there is a Flash game, "Raver Meltdown," and an ongoing Web "soundtrack," both of which are designed to contribute to the site's anti-rave sentiments. The music in particular, according to the authors, is part of the rhetoric of the site:

> If you're wondering why you can't turn off the music with the on/off button, it is because I want you people to understand what I experienced at a rave. I had to listen to what seemed like the same annoying

song over and over again for over 8 hours. There was no way for me to turn it off. So yes, you all must suffer! That way you will really appreciate where we are coming from with this anti-rave site. (http://www.i-mockery.com/antirave/main.asp)

Other typical site texts and features include a series of articles, such as "Why Raves Must Be Destroyed" and "The Raver Holocaust," which contribute to the hyperbolic nature of the site.

Part of the hyperbole and even satire of this site is its similarity (whether conscious or not) to the Hyperreal site. For instance, the site mocks raver drug usage, and, in an interesting parallel to Hyperreal's "Chemistry" section, we find a section on "New Cocktails" (http://www.i-mockery.com/antirave/cocktails.asp), featuring a host of faux drug combinations, such as

Cocktail Name: "CRACK-0-MINTY POP ROX"

Ingredients: "Crack Cocaine" & "Coca Cola" & "Junior Mints"

How To Use: Put "Crack Cocaine" rocks into "Coca Cola" can and shake vigorously. Insert one "Junior Mint" into each nostril and inhale as much as possible so that the mints will be lodged well inside your nasal cavity. Now drink the shaken Crack/Cola mixture but DO NOT swallow. Hold your mouth closed tightly and hold your breath until you are just about ready to pass out. Just before you are about to pass out have a friend slap you on the back while you still keep your mouth closed tightly. The Crack/Cola mixture will be forced up into your nostrils and will shoot out the Junior Mints with amazing speed.

THE BUZZ: Everyone at the rave will see the two Crack/Coke/Snot-laced Junior Mints flying across the room and believe that they are being attacked by aliens. Everyone will fall to the ground and begin to cry and offer the aliens all of their drugs and neon accessories in exchange for the aliens sparing their lives. You can claim all of the drugs and accessories for yourself if you aren't unconscious or dead.

The humor of the site only increases if you've seen the original lists at Hyperreal that "The OFFICIAL Anti-Rave Site!" seems to be parodying.

Antipathy toward ravers seems to revolve around a set of interlocking concerns, particularly youth self-representation and style. The site author(s) argue that "Ravers are nothing more but a bunch of adolescents looking for an excuse to get fucked up on some drugs and get laid" (http://www.i-mockery.com/antirave/raver-holocaust.asp). As such, they are inappropriate representatives of youth cultures or concerns. To further the critique, the author(s) deploy *style* as a criterion: "I mean come on . . . you have to be pretty fucked up to enjoy that shitty music for eight hours straight" (http://www.i-mockery.com/antirave/raver-holocaust.asp). At best, ravers are derivative: "Ravers are no different than the new age 'Deadheads' (or pardon me, 'Phish-heads') that wander around America for the exact same thing . . . sex and drugs" (http://www.i-mockery.com/antirave/raver-holo-caust.asp). Ultimately the author of this piece returns to hyperbole and argues, rather heavy-handedly and in poor taste, for the "extermination" of raves and ravers—a "raver holocaust."

The use of style as a point of critique is noteworthy. Subculture studies theorist Dick Hebdige's work in *Subculture: The Meaning of Style* focused on British punks, but his insights are relevant to our discussion of the dissem-ination of rave culture online. For example, Hebdige points out that even a slippery concept such as style can be "pregnant with significance":

> Its transformations go against nature, interrupting the process of nor-malization. As such, they are gestures, movements toward a speech which offends the silent majority, which challenges the principle of unity and cohesion, which contradicts the myth of consensus. (18)

By focusing their critique on raver style, the authors of The OFFICIAL Anti-Rave Site! give the lie to any sort of "unity or cohesion" among youth about raves and raver ideology. Moreover, if unwittingly, they use a site graphical-ly similar to Hyperreal to problematize Rushkoff's contentions that raver use of technology promotes tolerance and mutual understanding across differences. Of course, any large movement is going to have its detractors, and it should be no surprise that many youth (like any diverse, artificially grouped set of people) are contentious in their cliques and ideologies. And, as Rushkoff himself would probably agree, the same technologies can be put to vastly different ends. There may be a "myth of consensus," but it is only a myth.

But the critique offered by the site stems not just from troubling a par-ticular view of youth, but from other concerns about the nature of commu-nication and representation in our digital age. We can uncover some of these concerns by examining the host site, I-Mockery, which supports a number of youth-oriented Web ventures and online rants. The site authors of the "I-Mockery" homepage claim that they are interested in offering their visitors amusement and entertainment, but they also claim to use that entertainment for particular ideological ends. Specifically, they argue the following:

I-Mockery is here to challenge people. Particularly people who take themselves or their beliefs/scenes/etc. far too seriously. We're big on finding humor in everything in life. In a world that constantly spoon-feeds us so much crap, we need to be able to laugh at ourselves a little. Comedy is essential. If you don't take yourself too seriously, you'll die laughing at the people who get enraged by the content of these pages. If you do take yourself too seriously . . . well, you're screwed. (http://www.i-mockery.com/about.asp)

The use of humor—particularly parody and hyperbole—is not just amusing but also a *critical* tool to probe and potentially deflate unexamined ideologies, beliefs, and positions. Such a critical use of hyperbole finds *many* expressions on the Web, with some of the most famous examples being that of *The Onion* online (at http://www.theonion.com) and Landover Baptist (at http://www.landoverbaptist.org/), which offer parodies, respectively, of news reporting and religious/fundamentalist political intervention. As in The OFFICIAL Anti-Rave Site!, such sites mimic the style, tone, diction, and even graphical designs and layout of other sites to prompt questioning—if not, to borrow from I-Mockery, to both engage and "enrage" us—about the views we are being asked to accept.

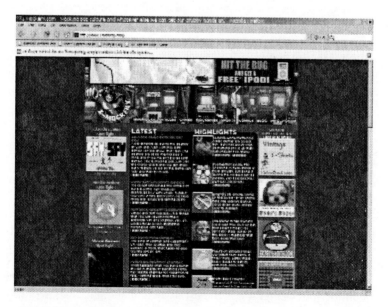

Screen shot of http://www.i-mockery.com/main.asp

In many ways, this is in line with Rushkoff's conception of literacy in the "digital age." According to his press page at Royce Carlton,

> [Rushkoff] challenges the popular opinion that government and business control our media and perceptions, and demonstrates how today's multi-channel world is far too chaotic to be controlled by any single force. In fact, he suggests that by learning to recognize and exploit the patterns in that chaos, we are more empowered than ever to challenge the status quo. (http://www.roycecarlton.com/speakers/rushkoff.html)

According to this view, literacy is an art of manipulation, encompassing both being able to recognize patterns of meaning in the onrush of information disseminated by multiple communications technologies and mix and to match them, or re-mix and match them—that is, in Rushkoff's terms, "exploit" them—in the creation of meanings that will "challenge the status quo." And in *Playing the Future*, Rushkoff suggests that one of the benefits of the new communications technologies is that they allow users to "splice" and "recapitulate" (his words) bits and pieces of various media in the creation of alternative meanings. Literacy then can be an act of resistance: Using the information bombarding us, much of it created by media conglomerates, in ways that query and question the beliefs we are invited to "buy into."

The reality of Web use, however, tells a more complex story that the one offered by Rushkoff. As Andrew Leonard points out in "Hits on Zits," a review of *Playing the Future*, much use of the Web by youth with access seems fairly mundane:

> After spending some time cruising teenager Web pages, I'm not rushing to kowtow to the new kiddie order. Screenager Web pages reveal concerns not so dissimilar from those of any pack of pre-Digital Revolution teenagers. Ninety percent of them are focused on bands, sports, movies, and zits. (http://hotwired.lycos.com/packet/packet/leonard/96/47/index3a.html)

Granted—to some extent. The limits of Leonard's own use of hyperbole—the prerogative of the reviewer—is revealed simply by examining the sites we've been discussing, such as Hyperreal and the I-Mockery sites, which use hyperbole to very different ends. Furthermore, the digital literacy that Rushkoff forwards—literacy as the art of technical manipulation of information—is just as likely to be turned to critique the community of cooperation as it is to advance it, as in I-Mockery contra Hyperreal. And it strikes me that *this* may be some digital youths' contribution to the Web and to technological literacy: not community and cooperation, but hyperbolic critique.

What's more fascinating from a *literacy* standpoint is that these "battles," as it were, are taking place in the textually and visually sophisticated—and often rhetorically loaded—spaces of the Web, with its ability to combine text, graphics, sound files, and interactive communications platforms. Using the work of Julia Kristeva in *La Revolution du Language Poetique*, Dick Hebdige argues for turning our attention to "the creation of subordinate groups through *positioning in language* . . . and the disruption of the process through which such positioning is habitually achieved" (*Subculture*, 140). I think that, given this formulation, we can read Hyperreal as positioning rave culture over and against the "dominant," mainstream culture, whereas The OFFICIAL Anti-Rave Site! simultaneously attempts to "disrupt" and problematize this positioning. Given this tug of war, this back and forth, what is ultimately revealing about some youths' use of technology is not so much the disagreements between the two groups, the ravers and the anti-ravers, but the *cultural territory* the two "factions" seem to be fighting over: namely, the claiming of the new communications technologies as a sphere within which to craft and disseminate alternative views and values. Raver sites advocate the nearly Rushkoffian sensibility of cooperative tolerance, whereas I-Mockery promotes critical hyperbole. As such, *consensus*, particularly the kind of tolerant, evolutionary "organicism" that Rushkoff promotes, does not seem to be the goal. If anything, the Web seems to allow for the relatively easy dissemination of more aggressively *opposing* views, and we may be seeing Webbed forms of what Umberto Eco calls "semiotic guerilla warfare" (150). Oddly, *both* positions are hyperbolic, eliding a negotiated middle ground between the two ends.

POSTMODERN NOSTALGIA, THE TRAP OF THE BINARY, AND THE ECSTASY CLUB

Is this community and interactivity then? Certainly, one could interpret Hyperreal and even I-Mockery as online "communities." Hyperreal almost seems bent on creating the kind of community of cooperation that Rushkoff envisions, which is probably why Rushkoff cites it in the bibliography to *Playing the Future*. And I-Mockery is a community of a different sort, albeit not the kind that Rushkoff and the collective authors of Hyperreal necessarily envision. It is, however, a critical engagement with information, even a *concern* with the relationship between information and knowledge (and *self*-knowledge) at a time when information seems so easily disseminated.

But I-Mockery's goal is not merely to get us to question the information we receive; it is also to make a comment about "quality control" and about the proliferation of information in the digital age:

> I-Mockery is here to help bring certain people and certain things into the public eye. Only in a horrible world like this does some teenage bimbo like Britney Spears become rich and famous while truly hardworking and genuine talents go on virtually unknown to the general public. Well never again, damnit. NEVER AGAIN! I-Mockery is here to help spread the word about many undiscovered/forgotten great things and great people! When it comes to the past, we're extremely sentimental bastards and we intend on keeping the greatest memories from our youth alive and well forever. So, if there's something great out there that you think needs better exposure, don't hesitate to write us about it! (http://www.i-mockery.com/about.asp)

As I've suggested, the emphasis on hyperbole as a mode of critique is a key feature among these youth-oriented Web sites. But the note of nostalgia, linking the satire to a strange conservatism, is noteworthy here as well. Although we are told that "comedy is essential," it is evident that the site favors unrecognized "talents." Is this a nod to the "authentic," in the midst of a highly mediated, digitized age? Indeed, I can't help but feel that the hyperbole lauded here barely masks a pining for the "authentic," and missing, values of a past popular culture, in which individual talent or genius was rewarded.

What might be some of those missing values, some of those concerns? Based on their comments, we can readily see a concern both with information overload and a seeming inauthenticity in the information given, as well as concerns about how the plethora of information made available via the Internet is being consumed or understood. After all, as we are told, "In a world that constantly spoon-feeds us so much crap, we need to be able to laugh at ourselves a little." Not surprisingly, I-Mockery is, as its name might suggest, not beyond a bit of self-reflexivity, but the authors take their ideological business seriously; even more so than Rushkoff, I think, there is a sense that a *critical* approach is needed in the overwhelming encounter with information. We need, as it were, standards to understand and differentiate the good from the bad. At the same time, the I-Mockery authors are nostalgic for the kind of pre-postmodern authenticity that Rushkoff bemoans as passé and anti-future.

John Fiske, writing in *Media Matters*, offers a possible explanation for the nostalgic sensibility we are seeing in the statements from the I-Mockery site authors. His comments suggest that the onrush of media images and venues, a characteristic of the postmodern world, can create a bit of dis-ease and discomfort:

> The postmodern promiscuity of images swamps any attempt to control them; it overwhelms any neat distinction between representation and reality, between fact and fiction. It refuses to allow "truth" a place in reality alone, for it cannot see that reality still has its own place for truth to make a home in. An image-saturated culture differs from a culture of controlled and organized representations not just in degree, but in kind. And this, postmodernism tells us, is what characterizes its world as generically different from the modern. (62)

Words such as "swamps" and "overwhelms" suggest that some might respond with resistance or nostalgia, itself a form of resistance to emerging trends and norms. At the same time that postmodernity is altering the "kind" of society in which we live, vestiges of the modern world linger:

> Although there is plenty of evidence of hyperreality around us, there is also evidence of modernism's dogged survival. The hyperreal may destroy the categories that once organized the differences between representation and reality or between different modes of representation, but our sense of those differences is not killed off as easily as postmodernism assumes. (62–3)

It is perhaps just this lingering modernity, its "dogged survival" into the realm of the postmodern hyperreal, that the I-Mockery composers are holding on to.

In many ways, however, I think there is also a nascent political sensibility here, one far more skeptical of techno-culture and information dissemination than that forwarded even by Rushkoff. Specifically, I-Mockery is responding to a capitalist co-optation that transforms subcultural and countercultural styles into marketable commodities. In "Posing . . . Threats, Striking . . . Poses: Youth, Surveillance, and Display," Dick Hebdige noted two "process[es] of recuperation" through which a subculture's resistant actions or style is "incorporated" into the "dominant mythology": one is the "conversion of subcultural signs (dress, music, etc.) into mass-produced objects (i.e., the commodity form)" and a second is the "'labeling' and re-definition of deviant behavior by dominant groups—the police, the media, the judiciary (i.e., the ideological form)" (131). Using examples from I-Mockery, we can see *both* of these processes occurring in a wide variety of media stars. For instance, Britney Spears, as a marketing construct, pack-ages "subcultural signs" such as youthful music and dress into a salable—and highly profitable—commodity. Furthermore, her sexualized antics, especially for one so young, are "re-defined" by a corporation (a "dominant group" in our culture): They are not "deviant" or "immoral," as they might have been labeled just a few decades ago, but empowered expressions of female sexuality. And they help sell stuff, too. From I-Mockery's perspec-tive, Spears may offer an example of how "authentic" artists, the real "tal-ents," have been eclipsed by the hyperreality of the rising media star, large-ly constructed and mediated through corporate use of technology. After all, Spears' music, videos, and performances make the most of recording industry technological know-how to create hyperreal spectacles, not other-wise possible without technological enhancement. Even the music itself is largely synthetically produced. At the very least, real talent, the lone romantic artistic youth, is often swamped by an ever-growing, smothering mound of technologically created "info."

In all fairness, I must point out that Rushkoff himself is not uncritical of his own enthusiasms—and not beyond a little nostalgia himself. His pri-mary self-critique comes in his first novel, *Ecstasy Club*. The novel, which is being made into a film by Screen Addiction films, explores raver sensi-bility and ideology, is an often ironic look at how the hyperbole of raver ide-ology—PLUR—is in need of critique, and avant-garde writers, ranging from Jeff Noon to Rudy Rucker to Julian Dibbell, have praised the novel for its insights and sophistication. William Gibson, who essentially invented the cyberpunk genre, called *Ecstasy Club* "A darkly comic contemporary fable: a brave, very funny, very knowing trip through the neo-psychedelic sub-strate of the wired world" (backcover blurb). The use of the word "fable" is telling: this is a story with a moral.

Rushkoff's Web site offers the following concise plot summary:

> When the young, hypertalented idealists who call themselves *Ecstasy Club* find an abandoned piano factory in Oakland, they make it the focus of a round-the-clock rave the likes of which the Bay Area has never seen before. They also make the factory a base camp in their search for a method of time travel that combines computer wizardry, esoteric spirituality and mind-altering substances. The club's mesmer-

ic leader, Duncan, and the story's resourceful narrator, Zach, actually manage to "break time" online, only to discover that an unsettling array of characters has beaten them to it. Government agents, corporate saboteurs, religious zealots and even the local cops are suddenly out to get the club. As they battle an ingeniously conceived conspiracy (think Thomas Pynchon meets *The X-Files*), Zach battles his own growing affection for Duncan's lover, Lauren, and begins to wonder whether enlightenment is all it's cracked up to be. (http://www.rushkoff.com/ecstasyclub.html)

The novel opens with a group of friends deciding to move into an abandoned piano factory, which will become not just their living quarters but the site of consciousness-expanding, mind-altering, and soul-developing raves; or, in the words of the narrator, Zach, "A conscious effort toward sustained bliss, enacted willfully. That was the whole point. Self-determination. Will over matter. Directed evolution. Renaissance . . . The second world creation, planned consciously by humans. . . . This is a revolution. A declaration of independence from status quo reality. We are attempting to intensify the overall level of novelty in the extant cultural organism, in order to change it. Mutate it" (2; 6; 18). Here are all the Rushkoffian tropes, catch-phrases, and slogans, encoded in a novel published 1 year after *Playing the Future*. Beginning with this basic scene, *Ecstasy Club* quickly becomes a novel of ideas in which Rushkoff rehearses—and perhaps even develops—some of his basic tenets and beliefs about media, e-savvy youth, and technology. But *Ecstasy Club* is hardly propaganda. The ideas are frequently given an ironic spin, not uncommon in the tradition of the novel, which often exists between the realm of the pure idea and the difficult or flawed enactment of the ideal in the realm of the all-too-human.

Indeed, the plot often exists to "test" as much as forward Rushkoff's ideas, with characters serving as failed spokespersons for various views or ideologies, from rave utopianism to cyberpunk paranoia. Zach, the narrator, tries to negotiate and navigate his way between the ideologies, all of which seem to compete for his attention and allegiance. His is perhaps the voice of reason, or the "normative" voice in the novel, but we have ample evidence to be skeptical of him too. Obviously intelligent and one of the more thoughtful founders of "The Ecstasy Club," Zach steadily questions his friends' goals and beliefs. Eventually, he hooks up with Lauren, and his interest in her stems not just from sexual and romantic attraction, but from the growing realization that she is "much more grounded. Practical. Real. Adult" (288). Or, as one student reviewer, Howard Ho, succinctly put it, "Only Zach is able to see through all this and find solace in conformity" (http://paradigm.asucla.ucla.edu/DB/issues/98/11.30/ae.ecstasy.html). Although Zach seems like a "sell-out," forsaking the cooperative ideals of the rave, Rushkoff maintains that the novel has a more pressing moral message:

> [*Ecstasy Club*] is cynical of alternative culture and of the people who would defend mainstream culture. The joke of this book is that the people who dedicate themselves so interminably to promoting evolution at all costs end up developing something that is much like fascism. And the people who are trying to prevent the development of human evolution at all costs end up fostering novelty. What I am trying to say is that any ideal carried out to an extreme that denies our natural human functioning is going to be detrimental, dangerous. (Eisenberg http://www.rewired.com/97/0630.html)

In the process of expounding on this moral, *Ecstasy Club* actually becomes a pretty strident critique of fanaticism, group-think, and the allure of cultish behavior—a moral perhaps most clearly seen in the novel's thinly veiled satiric representation of the Scientology organization.

In terms of the discussion explored in this chapter, *Ecstasy Club* ultimately shows us how difficult it is for the ravers in the group, despite impressive technological resources and phenomenal dedication, to *cohere* as a group, as an evolutionary, in-sync organism of cooperation and community. As Rushkoff puts it in an interview about the book,

> People have a hard time understanding how to come together as a group but also maintain their individuality. That's why I wanted to write a comedy—some people completely miss the satire. It's an allegory: going to a place to pursue religious freedom and ending up just as bad as the people you were running from. That's what the kids in the book experience—they want to come together as a group, but end up surrendering themselves to one specific individual. Duncan, the cult leader, sells out at the first possible opportunity. (Eisenberg http://www.omino.com/ ~ dom/clips/ecstasyclub.html)

Cooperation and community are the dream, but fanaticism is the unfortunate reality. Intriguingly, the novel, *Ecstasy Club*, serves as a foil to the more ecstatic views Rushkoff puts forward in *Playing the Future*, published just a year earlier.

But Rushkoff does not want to relinquish the dream, and he himself becomes somewhat nostalgic for the early, heady days when techno-utopia seemed just a mouse click away. In 2000, in *The Village Voice*, Rushkoff offered the following commentary as part of his contribution to a feature entitled "New Media Savants Check the Pulse of Silicon Alley":

> The best [sociological effect of the information technology revolution] has been the impact that the *idea* of interactive technology has had on humanity. We can now imagine what a complex, networked human society, functioning as a coordinated organism, might look and feel like. The worst effect, so far, has been computer-aided unconsciousness. We are using interactive technologies as marketing tools, applying our most powerful hypnosis and influence techniques to the World Wide Web. We are using the Internet to pace and lead ourselves into passive consumption. This is, most likely, because the only "value" we are programming into technology right now is monetary.
>
> For now, both the utopian and the nightmare scenarios we're all familiar with can serve us: Our communications technologies give us ways to envision a future where cooperation and community rule—and may motivate us to work towards that reality. Meanwhile, the fear of dehumanized, computer-driven consumer fascism might just give us enough pause to reconsider what it is we're building here. (http://www.villagevoice.com/issues/0003/griscom.php)

In some ways, I can't help but think that such nostalgia is generated by the *binary* thinking deployed, "the utopian and the nightmare scenarios"—a binary thinking that sees only one or the other possibility. Indeed, much of the philosophy that drives the plot of *Ecstasy Club*—and Rushkoff's own beliefs—is pretty dualistic: the battle between "the yin the yang, the right the left, the man the woman, Apollo and Dionysus" (306). Perhaps Rushkoff's blind spot in looking at the interactive communications technologies might lie in his insistence on imagining "networked human society" as a "coordinated organism." Such phrasing is more than a tad reminiscent of Rushkoff's praise in *Playing the Future* of "consensual hallucination," and the sense one gets is that this is an ideal, *the* ideal, eliding the possibility of any other significant use of the technology. We wouldn't want it any other way. Either "cooperation and community rule" or we are faced with "dehumanized, computer-driven consumer fascism."

But are these the only choices? Is there no negotiation between the two extremes? Are we caught between, on one hand, hyper-dreams of utopian tolerance and cooperation facilitated electronically, or, on the other hand, a constant need to deflate with hyperbole such dreams and their cooptation by "consumer fascism"? For even when we throw I-Mockery into the mix, we're confronted with some pretty stark binaries: You either laugh at yourself or you're "taken in" by the capitalist marketing machine. After all, when Zach himself cannot make the raver dream happen, he seemingly "retreats" to the "adult," "grounded" world—essentially, suburbia, the marketers' stronghold. Is Zach's retreat a move toward global cooperation and community? Or is it a nostalgia for a simpler time, a seemingly more authentic time, like that lauded by I-Mockery?

The limits of the binary—and the paucity of the options it offers—are even more sobering when we consider Jean Baudrillard's understanding of the hyperreal—a term the French critic has used to describe, not without a touch of his own nostalgia, "the generation by models of a real without origin or reality: a hyperreal" ("Simulacara," 166). In the vast technologically enabled play of information, we are creating—and entering—worlds of virtuality without referent, and thus with less discernible "meaning." Baudrillard describes the consequence for the meaningful exchange of information and our intervention into meaning-making in "Aesthetic Illusion and Virtual Reality": "Today . . . information is nothing more than the paradoxical confusion of the event and the medium, including all forms of intoxication and mystification connected to it" (200). This is Marshall McLuhan's mantra—"the medium is the message"—taken to an absurdist conclusion, a point that Hans Bertens underscores in *The Idea of the Postmodern*:

> Whereas for McLuhan the electronic revolution had definitely utopian aspects, for Baudrillard that revolution has effectively made us the helpless victims of a technological determinism that through its unassailable code serves the interests of a hyperreal, meaningless capitalist order. (156)

Read through this lens, Hyperreal—the Web site, the philosophy—seems like just a party. Synchronizing everyone to the same beat doesn't ever seem to escape the loop of information; in fact, we may be caught in a *feedback* loop—one that occupies youths' time without offering a substantive critique of the social order. Even more, Hyperreal's (and Rushkoff's, for that matter) sense of the rave as offering global "unity" seems an idea "without origin or reality"—a hyper-induced fantasy, or escapism at best. Conversely, I-Mockery uses hyperbole to critique a glib sense of technologically aided community, a free-form digital sensibility that blurs, if not erases, distinctions between self and other, even past, present, and future. I-Mockery worries that such blurring may result in our being "hoodwinked," in our inability to realize when we've been sold a bill of goods, in our being taken advantage of, in our being fed "crap"—in a loss of authentic self. But even this critique brings us back to another binary loop: postmodern freeplay versus postmodern nostalgia. We are either embracing the coming of the future or regretting the passing of the past.

As though cognizant of the strain of these binaries and their inability to offer us another space from which to think the impact of technology on literacy—and on conceptions of our selves and our potential for political agency—Rushkoff offers this curious re-interpretation of history towards the end of *the Ecstasy Club*:

> Then Duncan had a weird insight—I felt it, too. We saw that we could change history itself, and even the future, by seeing it differently. History itself is spin. Events are only real in the present tense—before they happen they're hype, and after they happen they're spin. The real substance of an event—if there even is any such thing—is inconsequential without pre-promotion and post-reportage. A rave is more about the flyers and the folklore than it is about the party; and the human condition is more about the future expectations and historical interpretation than anything else. Human evolution is just the give-and-take between hype and spin. Propaganda and consciousness are the same thing. (304–5)

Critics such as Sven Birkerts might see in this a conflation of history with hype, and a consequent erasure of historical perspective, eliding our chances of knowing who we are by comparison to what has come before. I think Rushkoff, however, sees this as a *reconceptualization* of history, perhaps as filtered through McLuhan—the medium, the "spin," *is* the message. Our hype is—or becomes—our history. In other words, if you can't escape the code, join it. I do not think this is meant as a crude reduction; rather, by hyperbolically conflating history and hype, Rushkoff hopes to open up spaces for resistant thinking and intervention. For instance, a careful and studied attention to the way we "hype," the way we "spin" ourselves—particularly in an increasingly digital age—might give us more insight into how we manipulate information for our own ends. In fact, this has been more and more one of Rushkoff's central preoccupations. In more recent books, such as *Media Virus: Hidden Agendas in Popular Culture* and *Coercion: Why We Listen to What "They" Say*, Rushkoff's tone is more paranoid, even more cynical, as he takes a turn toward conspiracy theories of how "they" control the media—and thus our minds. At the same time, he holds out the possibility of intervening in that control.

Questions, however, abound. Does remixing and matching *challenge* anything? Can technological collage be not just an aesthetic but a politic?

Is this a viable literacy practice, with discernible political ramifications for its deployment? Maybe. The hyperbole of I-Mockery's anti-rave site, relying as it does on remixing and matching bits and pieces of raver lore and philosophy, points out what's left un-thought in the rush to techno-global community. This is certainly a start. But we'll have to look for other literacy practices, other critical tools, perhaps even different ways of figuring technology, to see if we can move beyond this binary—and escape both the hyperbole of the technological utopia and the hyperbole of post-postmodern despair and nostalgia. The following chapters, I believe, show how some youth are working this binary over, how they are intervening in the production and dissemination of information (about themselves and other topics), and how they are exploring other literacy practices, those other critical tools, to express themselves and their emerging sense of identity and community.

PART II
LITERACY PRACTICES

3

IRONIES OF SELF

REWRITING THE PERSONAL HOMEPAGE

If the preceding chapters left us with a troubled binary—uncritical utopian views of subcultural youth and their potential use of technology versus overly critical assessments of postmodern hyperreality—then the following three chapters are probably situated in what I think is the fertile ground between those two extremes. Indeed, what I hope to show is that actual digital youth literacy practice on the Web, including such youths' understanding of the Web as a communications tool, is a bit more complicated, provocative, and suggestive than is figured by this binary. Put another way, what I want to do in this and the following chapters, then, is explore how some youth composers are writing the Web in ways that situate themselves, their ideas, and their meaning-making practices.

One prominent Web space in which we can see some digital youth composers deploying a variety of innovative literacy skills and practices is in the personal homepage. Gill Branston and Roy Stafford comment in *The Media Student's Handbook* that "The emphasis on publishing as an industrial activity has perhaps underplayed the pleasures of creativity that characterize many users' times spent on the Internet" (200). Certainly, one of the most prominent forms of creative, non-"industrial" writing found on the Internet is that of the personal homepage. Attempts to calculate the number of extant homepages yield varying results, but tallies are usually given in the millions. Charles Cheung, in "A Home on the Web: Presentations of Self on Personal Homepages," reports that "Tripod.com and Geocities.com claim over four million active homepage builders each . . . and Xoom.com claims a further two million (January 2000)" (43).

As a writing instructor, who has for the last 10 years taught primarily in networked environments, I can attest to the prominence of the home-page as a favored writing medium for many e-savvy youth, even if I haven't necessarily seen *millions* of student homepages. The attractiveness of the homepage as a writing space perhaps lies in its emphasis on the *personal*. In "Cyberspace of the People, by the People, and for the People: Predominant Use of the Web in the Public Sector," Debashis "Deb" Aikat writes, "The Web has empowered common people with the potential for disseminating information and ideas to the millions of people that com-prise the population of the Internet . . . personal Web pages have enriched the diversity of Internet content" (25). Such "enrichment" occurs as Web users become writers and composers themselves; as Cheung notes, "[the Web] is the only medium in which most people are truly able to become 'authors,' presenting their suppressed or misrepresented selves to audi-ences around the world" (51). The flexibility and relative ease of using Web technologies allows composers to offer and shape such information about the self in a variety of ways, leading David Bell, in his *Introduction to Cybercultures*, to argue that, "Marshalling the identity-marking resources the Web confers, personal homepages present the self through a number of devices: biography, links, photographs, up-datable 'news' or 'diary' pages . . ." (117–8).

The emphasis on articulating, representing, and even constructing a sense of self online has long intrigued critics—both pro and con—of the Internet. As early as 1993, Michael Heim could summarize one of the prin-ciple questions posed by the increasingly pervasive simulation of self and experience via computer technology:

> In virtual reality, traditional philosophical questions are no longer hypo-thetical. What is existence? How do we know? What is reality? Who am I? [These questions] are certainly not remote or esoteric, given the pos-sibility of creating artificial experiences that are as compelling as the real ones. (ix)

And Sherry Turkle, alluding specifically, albeit briefly, to homepages in *Life on the Screen*, suggested that "Home pages on the Web are one recent and dramatic illustration of new notions of identity as multiple yet coher-ent" (259).

This notion of representing or even playing with "identity as multiple yet coherent" seems to be a key component of how scholars of homepages discuss and figure users' construction of self via the Web. In *An Introduction to Cybercultures*, Bell suggests that, "As a self-conscious articulation of self-identity . . . homepages make a useful starting-point for opening up the question of identity in cyberculture, bringing with them issues such as author and audience, truth and deception, fluidity and authenticity" (118). Notions of audience, truth, and fluidity are particularly salient as homepage composers can negotiate and construct their self-representations in purposeful ways. Cheung argues that, "by using the expressive resources of the personal homepage, authors can choose which aspects of their multiple and contradictory selves they wish to present" (45). As such, Cheung sees personal homepages as potentially "emancipatory" for two reasons:

> First, personal homepage production "emancipates" the author because it allows a much more polished and elaborate delivery of impression management compared with face-to-face interaction. . . . Second, the personal homepage is emancipatory for those who want to present "hidden" aspects of themselves—things they are cautious to reveal in "real life" because of fear of rejection of embarrassment. (47, 48)

For instance, extrapolating from one of Cheung's examples, we can note how a gay person might "out" him or herself "safely" online as a way of exploring a "public" gay identity via the Web before doing so "IRL," or "in real life." Randal Woodland has noted how such "staging" can be important, particularly in gay identity development among gay youth with Internet access (76–79).

Understanding homepages as emancipatory, however, raises some troubling questions about "authenticity," to borrow Bell's word. In "Personal Home Pages on the Web: A Review of Research," Nicola Döring reviews the current scholarly literature that has focused on studying the production, dissemination, and reception of personal homepages, and she notes that, "As a medium of nearly unrestricted self-presentation, the personal home page supplements our means of impression management through interpersonal and public relations communication" (http://www.ascusc.org/jcmc/vol7/issue3/doering.html). The prevalence of the psychological mechanism of impression management, the tendency to carefully sculpt one's presentation of self to meet certain perceived expectations, suggests that the "self" offered even on a personal homepage might itself be a constructed fiction, not necessarily an emancipated self revealing its "hidden aspects." Cheung himself must acknowledge that, "On our personal homepage . . . we can manipulate all the elements until we are satisfied" (47), and that "A certain degree of self-censorship must take place during homepage construction . . . as authors will always have information they are unwilling to reveal on the public Web" (50). Even a 2003 article in *The Chronicle of Higher Education*, Mary Morris Heiberger and Julia Miller Vick's "Building a Better Home Page," offers cautionary advice for professors and other higher education professionals who may be contemplating constructing homepages about their work and interests. Such pages are frequently viewed by hiring committees and potential employers, so Heiberger and Vick stress audience sensitivity. Their recommendations include being clear and organized, using readable text and backgrounds, and checking links for their continued viability. Perhaps most importantly, though, they offer the following caution: "Remember that you're addressing a professional audience. Avoid posting anything you wouldn't want a potential employer to see" (http://chronicle.com/jobs/2003/06/2003060601 c.htm).

Given the realities of impression management, personal homepages should always be consumed with a grain of salt and not necessarily read as emancipatory statements of self. Moreover, we need to be sensitive to how homepage composers are aware of the interplay of self-presentation and impression management, and many figure their performance of self on the homepage as an admittedly conscious construction. As such, the performances often include ironic touches, and Döring, in her summary of research about homepages, notes that "Self-irony is a common stylistic device found on personal home pages" (http://www.ascusc.org/jcmc/vol7/issue3/doering.html). "Self-irony" can take the form of an acute awareness of the personal homepage as an object of "self promotion," in which, to borrow Döring's example, the Web composer might say, "I guess that the best—and fastest—way to really get to know me is by discovering what I like. So here goes . . . I love to bla bla bla . . . (to be added later)." Such "self-irony" can also be used strategically to satirize and critically reflect on a number of issues, such as the "marketing" of self in a commercialized society.

What I do in the remainder of this chapter is focus on a few personal homepages, so that I can examine some of the dynamics described here against some of the actual practices of a few complex homepages. In examining these pages, one finds that self-expression and emancipation may certainly play a role in the motivations for constructing a personal homepage, but I want to draw attention to other significant uses, in several strategic ways, of irony and satire. Such irony is not only used in the service of "*self*-irony," but also in "ironizing" the position of the *viewer* of the homepage. In many ways, such irony, satire, and even parody are used to problematize our expectation of the personal homepage as a genre of self-expression, and to provoke us into understanding how the self is often fashioned and constructed as a commodity for public consumption via Web spaces. The Web composers I examine often seek to trouble our generic expectations about the homepage in order to open up a space for fairly complex articulations of self and representational experimentation.

To frame this discussion, I begin with an example from Charles Cheung's discussion of the function of personal homepages. I then move on to a few contrasting examples, concluding with a section on how some young queer homepage authors deploy satire and irony as key components of their Web literacies.

SPACEGIRL: MARKETING THE SELF

One of the pages that Cheung highlights is "Spacegirl's [http://www.space-girl.org/] stylish homepage, with her art, photos, journal, and more" (47). Although Cheung doesn't spend much time discussing the page (it's featured in a "textbox"), the site is one of the few he mentions that is written by a younger person, and, although it is perhaps a bit more sophisticated in design than the majority of personal homepages on the Web, it performs many of the same functions of the genre discussed previously. As such, it seems indicative of a "typical" personal homepage.

The page, designed and maintained by Angela Martin (born in 1972), offers readers a brief bio, recommendations for good books, a presentation of Angela's work as an illustrator (under "illogirl"), an opportunity to purchase some of her work, and a "funbox," with little amusing games, such as an Angela "dress-up doll":

> That's right! You can dress spacegirl up in clothes she actually wears! Dig around in her closet for some crazy stuff even she can't believe she used to wear.

The most prominent feature of Spacegirl's homepage, however, is her online journal, which you can read in archived form, seemingly organized around different themes or topics. Much of the writing is humorous and engaging, as Spacegirl tells us about her life, its foibles and triumphs. You can also choose a "random" journal entry, to surprise yourself. Spacegirl also has a Weblog, a more recent journaling format, at http://www.trip-pyswell.com/, through which she updates visitors every few days on various aspects of her life, including sales of her artwork.

Is this site emancipatory for Spacegirl? Well, that's harder to say. Certainly, the site disseminates quite a bit of information about Angela— or, at least, information that Angela wants to present us. The site also serves as a marketing tool for her illustrations and artwork, and you can purchase her work via a prominently linked Web site, http://angelamarti-ni.com/. The site also offers a bit of "self-irony" in the "teen angst" section, which presents readers with excerpts from the journal that Spacegirl kept as a teen, along with commentary from the young adult Spacegirl:

> It's here—the journal that started it all. 1989 was a scary time, especially out on Long Island. Read the actual tortured writings of my teenaged self, along with witty repartee from the sensible grown-up I am now (HA!)

The opening page for this journal and retrospective commentary— http://spacegirl.com/teenangst/journal/—is cleverly divided into "then" and "now" sections, and the emphasis throughout is on poking fun at

Screen shot of http://www.spacegirl.com/

Spacegirl's melodramatic teen life. A similar vein runs through another section, "fifteen" (http://spacegirl.com/teenangst/fifteen/), which Spacegirl describes as follows:

> Way back in 1995 it occurred to me that it might be fun to write about some of the weird things I did and felt when I was fifteen. I wrote mainly for my enjoyment, and I also sent copies of my reminiscents to my best friend from those days, Kathy. She seemed to get as big a kick out of "fifteen" as I did. When I started spacegirl in 1996, I needed content, so I typed up "fifteen" and posted it. I soon found that other people thought it was worth reading, too. So here it is, my life at fifteen.

In these ways, and with cleverly written, self-mocking prose, Spacegirl ironically reflects not only on her own angst-ridden past, but also on the humor latent in revealing that past through such a public forum as the WWW.

As a homepage, Spacegirl's slick pages may be an example of "high-end" homepage construction. Döring identifies several "dimensions" of homepage composition that could be used to describe Spacegirl's work. Such dimensions include the "reasons for the construction of the personal homepage," its "themes," its "presentational styles," and its "technological characteristics." Using these categories, we could interpret Spacegirl's pages as arising out of a dual motivation to present (if self-ironically at times) a bit about her life and to market herself as an artist and illustrator; as using online journals and blogging as prominent tools to compose her life online; and as deploying a fairly competent set of technological skills to create and maintain her site. She's obviously no "newbie." And although we cannot determine, just by examining the page, if Spacegirl is consequently "emancipated" by her site, we can nonetheless appreciate this site as a textually rich and graphically interesting representation of a "self"—which is the primary purpose of the personal homepage genre.

ASITSHOULD: "PUTTING YOUR PERSONALITY ON DISPLAY..."

I would like now to contrast Spacegirl's fairly "standard" homepage with another that plays with irony in even more powerful ways. The site, asitshould.com, is composed by Dave Myers, a student at the University of Cincinnati. Dave eagerly shows his site to many people, and it wasn't long after joining one of my classes that he introduced me to his work on the site. To capture some of Dave's own self-understanding of his aims and purposes with the site, I interviewed him about asitshould, and his comments throughout are revealing, particularly as they show Dave very consciously manipulating set expectations for homepage construction and consumption.

For example, some textbooks, aimed at college students who may be composing for the Web, offer advice on personal homepage construction, and the authors couch their comments in the rhetoric of promoting clarity of purpose, working within familiar genres, and acknowledging sensitivity to potential audiences. Margaret W. Batschelet, in the textbook *Web Writing/Web Designing*, suggests that a Web author, in composing a homepage, should "Make the identity of the person and/or organization behind the site obvious immediately" and "Project the right image for the site and the person and/or organization behind it" (151). Victor J. Vitanza, in *Writing for the World Wide Web*, also stresses the importance of audience and working within conventions that visitors are likely to understand: "Undergraduate [home page composers] . . . for the most part tend to stick to personal things such as hobbies, favorite links, photos of themselves with friends, and in some cases collaborative work" (68).

Dave's site, however, torques these genres and conventions in some clever, purposeful ways. Upon entering the site, you notice immediately that the site's structure is a bit different than most homepages. The main menu item, from which you must choose to access content, includes an intriguing, if obscure set of choices: rant, laugh, enlighten, adventure, buy. The contrast with Spacegirl's page is immediately noticeable: whereas Spacegirl offers us an array of ways to learn about her as a person, including a journal, a Web log, and a bio, Dave's site is a bit cagier about its contents, and perhaps by extension about the "person" being presented, or constructed, in these pages.

Given this, I asked Dave if he looked upon asitshould as his personal homepage, and his response which follows, is intriguing:

> Yes. That would be my personal home page. Well, actually I had an identity crisis with this a while back. I was trying to decide if it was a personal website or if it was like a humor website. I do write things in first person so it *is* my personal website but I don't want it to be like, here is a picture of my cat and here are my vacation photos. Or here is a poem I wrote. I want it to have a wider appeal to a certain group of people, which would be, I guess, people around my age that are pretty open in their humor. Not everything is appropriate and on the front

page of the site I have a little thing that explains it. I've changed it a lot but right now it says that you should leave if you are easily offended or if you are a small child.

However, if someone shows up at the site that I don't know they probably won't get the impression that it's a personal site right away.

As Dave explains, he wants the site to be distinguished from the vast number of personal homepages on the Web, which, in his view, offer rather bland snapshots (such as vacation photos) of the composer's life. Dave's view is further developed in response to the question, "What makes a good homepage?":

I would say first and foremost that it should be a reflection of the person that makes it. That's the person's website. For me a successful site is one that's not "normal." If I said to a stranger that my personal website is asitshould.com, they would go to asitshould.com and it doesn't strike you as being a personal website, which some people may not like because they just may want to see pictures of my cat or something but they are not going to get that.

I have a slogan too. I have a logo and a slogan. The slogan is, "I'm not a moron. I just have decentralized thought processes."

Dave is consciously playing with and manipulating our expectations of what a homepage normally is—a way to, in Batschelet's words, "Make the identity of the person and/or organization behind the site obvious immediately." Rather, as Dave puts it, he offers us a particular kind of personal homepage, one that he consciously constructs to appeal to other youth who are "pretty open in their humor."

Put another way, Dave says, "I tell people a lot that it's a reflection of the odd side of my personality." Is this Cheung's "emancipation"? Has Dave designed this site to present a "hidden aspect" of his personality? Certainly, part of the site, upon investigation, serves as a forum for Dave to talk about some of his odd, provocative, and at times socially deviant "adventures." Indeed, the section entitled "adventure" present us with a series of amusingly written anecdotes, often illustrated with either pictures or even video clips, about some of the stunts that Dave and his friends have pulled in their search for a good time, even a good "odd" time, such as throwing old computers out of the back of a moving van. In a way, one could interpret such pages and narrations as allowing Dave to emancipate the comedian, or social deviant, within. In his narration, he refers to smashing the computers as an idea in (at least partial) imitation of the movie *Office Space*, so he's both connecting to youth with Internet access through a film that other young readers might have seen *and* he's attempting to provide content that might appeal to a late teen or young adult audience.

"I'm not trying to change anyone's life..."

I think the situation, however, is a bit more complex, as revealed both by a closer look at the site and by Dave's own comments. For instance, the emphasis on humor often turns to the satirical. For instance, the sections "rant" and "laugh" contain short meditations and anecdotes that show a more sophisticated side to Dave's humor. He explains "rant" this way:

> [Rant is] full of odd stuff and jokes. For example, I have recurrent themes where I make fun of a certain company over and over again. McDonald's is one that I do, which is pretty easy to make fun of. They had a slogan or advertising campaign a while ago—we love to see you smile. I just thought that was the stupidest thing in the world because why don't they make it, we love to *make* you smile instead of we love to *see* you smile.

The short narrative on the site explains in greater detail:

MCDONALD'S REVEALED

I just don't get it! How could McDonald's be so dumb? To me, when I hear, "We love to see you smile," I interpret this as, "We don't want to take the time to make you smile because we'd rather go have sex with each other in the back and then put the *used condoms* on our customers' food."

Say to yourself in your head, "We love to see you smile." Now say to yourself, "We love to make you smile." They both flow just fine, and there's no reason they shouldn't've used "make" unless they truly don't want to make us smile.

The manipulated ad is more than just a case of what Henry Jenkins' calls "textual poaching," the appropriation of pop icons or images in the service of self-expression (3). Rather, such work reminds me of some of the "spoof ads" displayed on the Adbusters Web site (http://www.adbusters.com/). The ads satirize corporate products, pointing out contradictions, insincerities, or even deceptions in the marketing of various goods. Dave's "spoof ad" is in a similar vein, displaying a willingness to deploy the language and literacies of advertisement against itself. The spoof ad also shows Dave's understanding of the uses of visual literacy and rhetoric, as well as a willingness to repurpose advertisements.

Dave's penchant for such repurposement isn't limited to print advertisements. While explaining what he means by "odd humor," Dave described another example of spoofing:

Dave: Odd humor is a good thing for people.

Jonathan: What does odd mean? You've used the word odd several times...

Dave: It's kind of hard to define exactly what it is but it's kind of like mocking things. It would be fair to say that one of the themes on the site is where I take a theme and make fun of it. For example, one of the transcript things I did in the "laugh" and "read" section is a transcript of a conversation between me and this person who is trying to sell me a membership to this porn site. Every once in a while you'll get someone who is trying to lure you with online sex. It is beyond me why people do that. They don't really tell you they are trying to sell you something and I kind of knew. Ten seconds into the conversation I knew what it was all about but I wanted to post it on my Web site. I was trying to play along and make them look dumb and stuff like that.

The transcript is available on the site, and it's a wonderful, if periodically lewd, example of resistance to advertising, as Dave demonstrates both an awareness of how the "salesperson" is attempting to manipulate him and how he deftly eludes being sucked into purchasing a porno pass. The creators of Adbusters might call such work "culture jamming," or questioning how advertisers make something seem "cool" as a way to entice you to purchase a product or service (Lasn, 139–146).

In other ways, Dave's creativity on asitshould vis-à-vis advertising images and tactics also reminds me of the discussion of alternative arguments in Jeff Rice's 2003 *CCC* article, "The 1963 Hip-Hop Machine: Hip-Hop Pedagogy As Composition," which explores how the digital sampling of hip-hop music can be used as an "alternative invention strategy for research-based argumentative writing" (453). Rice contends that such sampling, which involves "saving snippets of prerecorded music and sound into a computer memory" and then re-mixing and juxtaposing these sounds, drawn from nearly any source available to create dense "texts," can create exciting sites of learning and invention (454):

> The student finds a common pattern or element that binds these moments and then understands how to form a claim out of research and investigation. The student juxtaposes these moments in one of a variety of ways and thus learns about organizations. And through the process of juxtaposing the samples, the student locates her own position within the various cultural, ideological, economic, racial, gendered, etc., discussions consistently taking place around her. The student as sampler creates an argument. (468)

Dave accomplishes such sampling, mixing, remixing, and argument creation throughout his site, and he does so through a variety of media, including textual narrations, transcripts of chat room exchanges, images, and video clips.

But what is the argument forwarded? Certainly, the advertising world seems to bear the brunt of Dave's humor, which seems to satirize how advertisements assume ignorance or thoughtlessness on the part of consumers. He explained what kinds of things prompt his satirical creativity in the following exchange:

Jonathan: What makes something the object of your attention?

Dave: That's a good question. I'd just say stupidity. If I see something that's really stupid—where it has to be kind of stupid, but you also have to be able to write something about it or do something with it that's humorous.

Jonathan: Example?

Dave: The other McDonald's thing that is on there is when
             I was out to California and ate at a McDonald's
             Express. I saw a whole bunch of them actually.
             McDonald's Express. That's express fast food. It
             seems sort of redundant to me and I don't think it
             made that much of a difference anyway. In that situ-
             ation it's just kind of stupid but not really a *bad* stu-
             pid kind of thing.

But Dave is modest about the effect of such satire. He says that "The attention of the site is to humor people not to make them stop the way they act."
More pointedly, he once told me that "I'm not trying to change anyone's
life..."; rather, his stated intent is in creating "odd humor" through questioning stupidity, largely through spoofing ads. For instance, Dave will mock
a McDonald's Express, but he'll still drive up to one and place an order.

In some ways, Dave's position reminds me of the many teenager and
young adult responses to the Frontline documentary, "The Merchants of
Cool." Frontline's producers describe the documentary as a "report on the
creators and marketers of popular culture for teenagers," and, after airing
the show, they asked a group of teens to comment on the program. Their
discussion was transcribed for publication on the Web, and can be found
at http://www.pbs.org/wgbh/pages/frontline/shows/cool/teens/. The docu-
mentarians' goal was clearly to question the extent to which marketers and
advertisers shape teen purchasing power by selling them images of "coolness." Ironically, teens know this, but their comments reveal a certain grim
fatality in accepting the situation and not being able to escape it. As one of
them puts it,

> I think one of the main problems is that with all of this constant influx
> of information and also collapse of morals, it ends up creating an apa-
> thy. I don't think people are as happy as they would be if they were
> able to do things of their own—as opposed to being told what to do
> and having, in a lot of ways, no minds of their own because they have
> no way of expressing themselves. Everything is forced into them.

I am not sure Dave would articulate his position as addressing or pointing
out a "collapse of morals," but the comments above seem to resonate at
least somewhat with his views. And, despite the satiric edge present
throughout Dave's site, this shouldn't be surprising. After all, asitshould is

a personal homepage, not a manifesto for changing social attitudes or transforming our culture.

"My personality at your convenience..."

Given the simultaneous deployment of satire and the disavowal of its effectiveness in transforming attitudes, I asked Dave why he spends so much time developing his site. Our exchange was revealing:

> Jonathan: So you're not making any money off the site, and you only get a couple of hits a day. What keeps it going, expanding and constantly changing? What drives that?
>
> Dave: I just want to have and develop the skills. I just want to improve my skills. It's kind of a two-prong thing. I want to improve my designing skills on the Web. I kind of have a little artistic side to myself. It's not big but it's there. It's just like programming, because I'm adding a lot more programming into it where you don't really see it but it makes it a lot easier to edit and stuff like that.
>
> It's just kind of fun. I may not find it fun at some point in time in the future and say to hell with this.
>
> Jonathan: It seems like half, if not even two thirds of your enjoyment of this is learning the technology.
>
> Dave: Yeah. It's very slick.

Dave knows what "sells" to many teens and young adults—quirky, sarcastic, mildly satiric oddball humor. And he also knows, in the information age, what skills he needs to "sell" himself as an employee.

I can't help but think, however, that the *net* effect of such a homepage is, in some ways, to mock the entire notion of the homepage as a self-marketing tool, as the transformation of self into a consumable on the Web. As such, asitshould becomes an *anti-homepage*, calling into question the homepage *as it should* be. For instance, in terms of "self-marketing," Dave seems well aware that homepages are often not just personal, but also pseudo-commercial ventures, in that they are "selling" a particular representation of self. He has a particular brand and a logo that permeates the site, with the brand serving as a background for nearly every page. Furthermore, he uses a service available through CafePress.com, which allows you to put your logo or brand on a variety of items, such as t-shirts and coffee mugs, and sell them through your site. For instance, visitors to asitshould's "buy" section can purchase asitshould.com t-shirts and mugs with the asitshould logo on them. Amusingly, Dave even offers a thong with his logo on it. In discussion with him, Dave revealed that he knows no one is going to buy his merchandise, and that's part of the humor of making it available. As such, "buy" is Dave's satire turned on himself in an outrageous bit of self-irony. But I would argue that this isn't just *self-deprecating* self-irony, as we saw in the earlier quotation: "I guess that the best—and fastest—way to really get to know me is by discovering what I like. So here goes . . . I love to bla bla bla. . . (to be added later)." Rather, Dave's self-irony potentially ironizes and satirizes the *genre* of the personal homepage itself.

Perhaps we can see such satire and irony at play the most in the "enlighten" section, which is curiously the portion of the site that is most like a homepage, in that it offers the most personal insights into Dave and his group of friends. Dave's friend, Sean, explains the history of the "enlighten" section:

> Somewhere around the summer of 2000, my friends and I (Sean) purchased a little black book with blank pages. Such books are generally used for diaries, sketches, or phone numbers, but we had different plans for our little black book. Though it would contain stories about things that happened in our lives and pictures would be drawn in it, our intent was to make it much more than just a diary. It was purchased because we as a group wanted a convenient way to record and document our adventures, activities, funny lines, and anything else that tickled our collective fancy and a little black book seemed the perfect solution. It would be kept with us at all times and whenever anything funny or entertaining happened that was worth remembering, it would be put in the book. . . .

On this site you will see various items that have been transcribed from the book and put in a more orderly form, along with pictures of the pages in the book if you want a slightly more organic experience. There are also quite a few things that don't really lend themselves to being typed up, so those may be viewed in their original and untouched forms as well.

Visitors to the site can view transcribed excerpts from the book, including quotations, anecdotes, and lists of things deemed pleasant ("it's the little things") or annoying ("annoyances"). You can also see a photo of each page of the "book," reproduced online from the inside front cover onward.

How can we understand such painstaking detail and the expenditure of effort to reproduce the physical book in the virtual space of the homepage? For one, the elaborate nature of this presentation seems, in many ways, fetishistic. In "Reading the Web as Fetish," Christy Desmet offers a challenging understanding of how some read (and write) Web spaces as fetish objects:

> Although both fans and opponents of electronic media have focused on the sensual pleasure afforded by the Web as a visual medium and on the propensity of its products to become mere commodities, its effect on readers and writers has not yet been discussed in terms of the fetish as a rhetorical site. The Web-page-as fetish is best compared, I would suggest, to the figure of the improvisational or homemade altar, another spiritual item enjoying popularity in post New-Age culture. The improvisational, home altar works as a fetish because it transforms ordinary objects into artifacts of special significance and because it exploits the tension between metaphor and metonymy within . . . a hybrid space. (61)

Dave's "book," an "ordinary object" is transformed into a fetish, an artifact of "special significance." This is not simply consumer fetishism, a la Marx; this is, rather, an honoring of the everyday insights and wisdom that Dave and his friends collect, encounter, and produce. It's also hyperbolic, as fetishes tend to be. Dave reproduces not just snippets and excerpts, but the book itself, one page after another.

Dave's online "book" can also be understood as both metonym and metaphor, creating a "hybrid space" on his site. Desmet suggests that the Internet "participates in both ordinary and symbolic realities," with metonymy figuring ordinary associations between objects and entities (the crown to the king, the White House to the Presidency) and metaphor figuring possible symbolic realities (a rose like my love). The Web-as-fetish and as a hybrid space, combining words and images in new configurations, confuses the distinction between metaphor and metonymy. Read this way, Dave's book is metaphorical in that it seems like, but isn't, an actual book, whereas its relationship to the actual book is also clearly metonymical, in that the online book is an extension of the actual paper book.

The hybridity is significant in that it parallels the hybridity of the homepage itself, which is simultaneously metaphorical and metonymical as a representation of self. On one hand, the site can only ever stand in a symbolic relationship to the original author or authors; on the other hand, however, the site is an extension of the individual's (or group's) attitudes and way of being in the world. In fact, one could argue that a personal homepage participates actively not only in extending one's sense of self into the world, but in constructing—both consciously and unconsciously—one's sense of self as it grapples with issues of public performance of the self.

asitshould is lodged clearly in this hybrid space—and self-consciously so. And one could argue that this hybridity is characteristic of many home-pages, although the degree to which Dave plays with it is perhaps a little less usual. Indeed, the virtual reproduction of an entire book, to the point where you can "flip" digitally through each page, seems to me not only to suggest fetishistic hybridity, but also acute self-parody. This is a virtual memory book full of jokes, strange anecdotes, and nonsense. Dave and his friends are simultaneously making fun of their antics *and* of their fetishis-tic recording, and savoring, of them. But isn't this making fun of and par-odying what homepages do in general—record what a self finds most intriguing, interesting, and valuable?

If we look back at Vitanza's list of items on the personal homepage—"personal things such as hobbies, favorite links, photos of themselves with friends, and in some cases collaborative work"—we see that asitshould has all of these, but it's either constantly using these items, these generic tags, to mock the surrounding world of representations and media constructions or to hold up the self for mockery and self-irony. The literacy practices deployed here are not only satire, irony, and self irony, but a meta-critical consciousness of how staged and constructed the representation of the self always already is, particularly in the performative spaces of cyberspace. Put another way, David Bell suggests that, "As a self-conscious articulation of self-identity . . . homepages make a useful starting-point for opening up the question of identity in cyberculture, bringing with them issues such as author and audience, truth and deception, fluidity and authenticity" (118). For Dave, these are tropes to play with and manipulate to reveal the con-structedness of self as Web commodity.

Dave's ultimate goal, then, might be to satirize the entire genre of the personal homepage. Note his comments about the "future" of "asitshould":

Jonathan: What about the content? What about the content are
            you really impressed with yourself?

Dave: I kind of like the "laugh" section. When I read back
            I laugh at them myself. Sometimes I'll write things,
            and I like to write (obviously) and I enjoy it, but I
            don't think of myself as a good writer. When I write
            certain things, it's just kind of the insanity of some

of the stuff I do. I don't know if you've seen this because it was on the market for a while. There is an animation that I did that is in the move section. I took my logo, which is kind of a weird looking question mark and animated that into a flash animation of a guy giving a girl a tit fuck.

Jonathan: Okay.

Dave: You know what I mean?

Jonathan: Yes.

Dave: I had this idea and I themed it around—well, I called it the future of as it should.

Jonathan: Okay.

Dave: It starts off with something like porn music. These things kind of like flow in and it says the future of as it should is here.... And then the next thing is the hard-core stuff.

Jonathan: Just kind of like most of the Internet. Porn is taking over the Internet!

Dave: That's what I was kind of mocking. It goes into the animation. I can show it to you if you'd like.

Jonathan: Well maybe we better not bring that up on my school computer. We'll have to see it some other time.

Dave: I'm kind of proud of that. It's not really appropriate but I was impressed that I came up with the idea and also that I created it. It wasn't easy to do.

Riffing off the prevalence of pornography on the Internet, Dave has as-it-should momentarily collapse the distinction between the personal home-page and a porn site: One can't escape the sense that, at some level, both are about selling the self, with the personal homepage, like pornography's proximity to prostitution, a form of "whoring" the self for others' view and pleasure.

And Dave is well aware that he's playing with boundaries and problematizing generic distinctions. The ambiguity of the site—is it a personal homepage or not?—is part of the point:

I originally got asitshould because I originally wasn't sure what I was going to do with it at first. I didn't know whether it was going to be a personal thing or a slightly professional thing.

asitshould was a pretty ambiguous term. It could mean pretty much anything I want because it's a new word. I kind of go for the whole ambiguity thing and the name of it and also in the logo of it, which actually—I found that logo because I wanted to make it on the same theme as ambiguity. I went and checked out the fonts for all these different question marks and I found this one that I just kind of slanted to the side a little bit and made it flat on the bottom. It's actually a question mark slanted in a weird font but people thought that the logo was a question mark or an explanation mark or a weird swoopy thing with a dot. It's all kind of ambiguous.

Such comments should be filtered through Gunther Kress' argument about design in "Visual and Verbal Modes of Representation in Electronically Mediated Communication: The Potentials of New Forms of Text":

Design takes for granted competence in the use of resources, but beyond that it requires the orchestration and remaking of these resources in the services of frameworks and models that express the maker's intentions in shaping the social and cultural environment. While critique looks at the present through the means of past production, design shapes the future through deliberate deployment of representational resources in the designer's interest. (77)

Dave's "deliberate deployment of representational resources" serves, despite his periodic disavowals, specific purposes and interests in "shaping the social and cultural environment." His purpose, however, is not purely emancipated self-expression. Rather, it may be to emancipate the viewers of his site both from their expectations of what a personal homepage is supposed to do and to provoke their awareness of how easily we construct ourselves through personal homepages as Web commodities for other surfers' "consumption."

SOME QUEER HOMEPAGES: QUESTIONING THE ONLINE MARKETING OF QUEER SELVES

Certainly, as I discuss more full in Chapter 5, and as Cheung suggests in his article on homepages, the Web has allowed many gays, lesbians, bisexuals, and the transgendered (LGBT) a space to craft and perform a variety of online identities, many of which are still proscribed in the culture at large or that LGBT people might not feel safe revealing "in real life." Indeed, queers can—and often do—highlight on their personal homepages their sexuality and its importance to their lives in ways that are more difficult to do IRL, without seeming potentially inappropriate or politically grating. The personal homepage thus seems an ideal forum for the individual wishing to explore a queer identification but fearing personal and political reprisals for doing so in the "real" world. As such, the Web, and the personal homepage in particular, offers an opportunity for queers to experiment with crafting a "public" queer identity, and thus the homepage serves an "emancipatory" function for many. Here too, however, satire, self-irony, and even parody abound, and much of the satire is focused on the generic nature of many gay and lesbian homepages. As seen here, several young queer homepage composers share sentiments comparable to Dave's in that they parody fairly generic representations of queers and queerness via the Web.

For instance, the queer author of Planet Soma (http://www.planetsoma.com/) has often been inventive—and biting—in his critique of gay identity and its representation on the Web. For April Fool's Day 1999, the author set up a temporary welcome page that parodied, with extreme hyperbole, the content and style of many personal homepages of gays and lesbians. For a few days, Planet Soma became "The GAYEST planet in the GAY Solar System!!!"—replete with affirmative slogans ("Celebrate, Don't Denigrate!") and an irritatingly assertive and graphically gaudy rainbow motif. Part of the page's mimicry—and implicit critique—targeted how many "homo-pages" articulate a gay identity, marked with bright rainbow colors and coming-out stories, as the core or central aspect of the Web author's life. For Planet Soma, such articulations seem, at best, reductive representations of the complexity of one's identity.

To show further how such pages relate all aspects of a composer's life to his or her gayness, Planet Soma created the following list of items, with corresponding hypertext links, seemingly piled on top of each other as the viewer read down the page:

- I've realized lately that I should take more seriously my status as a role model and a spokesman for the GAY COMMUNITY. According to my email, I should "set a good example" for all GAY PEOPLE. Here's how I plan to do it!
- The GAYEST Links on the Web

- Check out these links to our GAY COMMUNITY. Each of them tells you a little more about the GAY CULTURE and GAY PRIDE I live for.
- About My GAY Life
- Find out about some of the GAY things which make my GAY life worth living!
- San Francisco The GAYEST place on earth!
- Send me GAY-MALE!
- You're the 337,326th GAY visitor since 2 March 1996.

Each item refers the reader back to the author's gayness, as though no other part of the author's identity were significant. In a way, Planet Soma is not far off the mark in parodying many "homo-pages," which often do emphasize the author's gayness and deploy traditional symbolic markers of that gayness, such as rainbow flags and pink triangles. In a way, this is the *genre* of the "homo-page."

Planet Soma's parody, however, seems almost cutting—and the author has, indeed, a sharp criticism to make. In a way, the hyperbolic mimicry of Planet Soma's April Fool's page allows this Web author to critique the pressures he has felt to "affirm" gay life by a community looking for affirmative role models—or, put another way, a community that may be looking for its own story to be articulated, replicated, and affirmed on the Web. With that affirmation, though, comes the imposition of boundaries, including some unfortunate bigotries within the gay community itself; for instance, you can "gay male" Soma, but "No fats, femmes, fish, or trolls, please!"—a biting reminder that in-group membership status within the gay male community often comes at a certain price, extracted on the body of those seeking inclusion.

This page starkly contrasts with the "regular" Planet Soma site, whose welcome page is a slick and sleek portal to the Web author's life, which is narrated in often graphically interesting hypertext, including embedded links in the site's various narrations. The pages interweave Soma's queerness as part of an on-going narrative thread, not a central organizing plot item; you can link to pages on west coast cities and *The Simpsons* as easily as to pages with substantial queer content. The site author explains his position thusly:

> First and foremost, Planet SOMA is NOT a "gay website," a "leather website," nor a "sex site." For the record, I am homosexual, not gay. I am not "into leather," and I find the whole scene rather comical. I no

longer go to sex clubs, cruise tearooms, nor lurk in backrooms. If that's
what you're looking for, please go someplace else.

Planet SOMA was born in January 1996 as a site dedicated to my
formerly exiting (and increasingly generic and boring) neighborhood,
San Francisco's South of Market Area, and to a sort of non-mainstream
view of queerdom and of life in general. (http://www.planetsoma.com
/admin/aboutthesite.html)

As such, there is no need for a rainbow flag or a pink triangle; in fact, as
we can tell from the critique of the April Fool's page, such visual rhetoric
would not be welcome there.[1] Put another way, if Dave's page functions at
times as an anti-homepage, mocking the entire process of commodifying
oneself for publication on the Web, then Planet Soma mocks the formation
and replication of specific genres through which gays represent themselves
on the Web. The parody also raises questions about impression management through generic configuration of self-representation. Writing specifically about considerations of audience, Nicola Döring notes that,

While impression management in synchronous communication (face-
to-face, telephone, chat) can respond with flexibility and nuance to the
addressee's reactions, Web authors are confronted with a chronic
shortage of information regarding both the composition of their audience as well as the audience's expectations and assessments of the
home page (although some have access to log files or employ feedback
forms and counters to monitor the activity of visitors to their pages).
(http://www.ascusc.org/jcmc/vol7/issue3/doering.html)

If anything, Planet Soma is responding to a perceived surfeit of information
regarding his understanding of viewers' expectations for personal homepages about queers. He doesn't want visitors to assume that his homosexuality should be conflated with an appreciation for contemporary gay community or an acceptance of its values, which he seems to think are too consumerist and even shallow.

Planet Soma's critiques may seem harsh, but others, including scholars, have noted the similarities in homo-page construction, and they have
attempted to question what such similarities mean. In his two online

---

[1] Certainly, part of the de-emphasis of gay identity markers stems from a *queer* critique—and David very much orients his site around that critique; in fact, this site
epitomizes the "queer revolt" against "gay."

essays, "Closetspace in Cyberspace" (http://www.english.udel.edu/ gweight /prof/web/closet/index.html) and "queer wide web?" (http://www. english. udel.edu/gweight/prof/web/queer/index.html), Gregory Weight asks how "queer" the Web truly is from a queer theoretical perspective that privileges the constructedness and fluidity of identity over static essentialism. On one hand, he suggests that "the homeless and nomadic desire of queer theory seems suited to use the Web as a stage for all of its varied performances." On the other hand, however, he concludes that most queer Web sites "are not very queer at all," primarily because of their use of "fixed symbols, systems, and identities" in their representation of queer lives, as well as their similarity to "straight" homepages in design and form (http://www.english.udel.edu/gweight/prof/web/queer/left.html). Weight also, however offers the following qualification:

> [I would not] say that the current content of queer Web pages is not valuable or valid, but what has emerged on the Web are pages which conform to a particular concept of what one should put on a Web page. (http://www.english.udel.edu/gweight/prof/web/queer/content1.html)

And that conformity is telling—and politically significant. Writing about sexual stories in general, Ken Plummer suggests that "Stories are often, if not usually, conservative and preservative—tapping into [a] dominant worldview" (178). And the conservatism of such stories may be bolstered by the chaotic postmodern flux of our age:

> At both millennium and century's end, when a strong sense of massive and rapid social change is in the air, stories take on a crucial symbolic role—uniting groups against common enemies, establishing new concerns, mapping the social order to come. Stories mark out identities; identities mark out differences; differences define "the other"; and "the other" helps structure the moral life of culture, group and individual. (178)

Weight offers a slightly different critique, suggesting that the relatively small number of markers of gay identity may delimit the ways in which people can perform the stories of their sexual identities on the Web:

> [To] attain the freedom of being out of the closet, the queer subject has to perform certain symbolic and verbal acts which are recognized and codified by both heterosexuals and homosexuals. . . . Unlike the real

> world closet, the Web closet can be a relatively unconscious act: the
> choice of a lesbian not putting a rainbow flag on her Web site may just
> be based on Web style; however, because of the stylistics of queer iden-
> tity on the Web, this inaction puts that woman in the closet on the Web.
> (http://www.english.udel.edu/gweight/prof/web/closet/index2.html)

With so few ways to perform one's queerness online, the use of such markers might assume priority in the minds of many Web authors, especially if
their intent is to avoid appearing—or *being*—closeted on the Web.

Indeed, it should be noted that exceptions to the generic "homo-page"
are readily available on turf as diverse and changing as the World Wide
Web. For instance, CUMPOST: A Radical Faerie Site (www.interlog.com/~
matt634/cpost.html), may reify an essentialist understanding of homosexuality, but the site's recontextualization of it as "faerie" points to different
ways of thinking—both personally and politically—about gay sexuality.
Other Web authors intentionally forego more "traditional" markers of gay
identity (pink triangles, rainbow flags) but nonetheless clearly mark themselves as gay or queer in their content, such as Planet Soma. And still others experiment more daringly with hypertext to narrate more complex,
poly-vocal, and challenging representations of gay identity, with some setting themselves up in contradistinction—if not outright antipathy—to the
plethora of gay sites linked via The Queer Ring and Gayscape.

For instance, some queers use their personal homepages, and the multimedia formats increasingly available and enabled through developing
Web technologies, to invite visitors into the site in very intimate and challenging ways—ways that, again, question expectations about what could,
or should, be found on a "queer homepage." Let's look at one major example. "Rex's World" (at http://www.rexsworld.com/) serves as both the
homepage for Rex and for his "cams," which provide images, updated
every 30 seconds, taken at Rex's home and work. In general, the layout of
the site demonstrates high design values, which should not be surprising
since we quickly learn that Rex teaches Web design and works for
MacIntosh. The attractive welcome page offers a main menu, and from it
you can link to numerous pages within the Rex cluster—almost all of which
provide narratives with embedded links that can take you to other parts of
the site. Rainbow flags and pink pyramids are conspicuously absent, and
little exists to identify this as the homepage of a gay man, except perhaps
for the advertisement for a gay-themed CD at the bottom of the opening
page. Indeed, we only discover Rex's sexual interests once we delve into
his 'frequently asked questions' (FAQs), his "slambook" (a message board
to which you can post comments and questions), or his "rambles" (a pseu-

do-journal). Even so, at no point does Rex technically tell us his coming out story; it is as though he assumes that no one will be problematized in the least by him or his various erotic interests, which are told almost as footnotes or asides in the "rambles": Rex sees a cute guy—yeah! Rex fights with his boyfriend—yuck! Throughout, then, the relative lack of gay or queer emphasis allows us to read Rex's sexual interests as just another part of his life, not necessarily as his life's organizing core.

One unique feature to Rex's site is the presence of the RexCam, which replaces the "gallery" or "images" section found on many personal homepages, especially gay male ones.[2] Instead of the sleek, glossy, and often hyper-idealized pictures of galleries, Rex invites us to see his day-to-day life, which usually consists of Rex sitting in front of his computer staring at the screen. At other times, he's watching TV. Occasionally, you might catch Rex engaging in more "graphic" pursuits; as he explains in his FAQs:

> Although that may or may not be cool with you . . . i must stress that since this is a peek into my life and i dont script this out there may be some "adult content" . . . they! . . . it's also a peek in my house . . . sometimes i wear my underware around . . . and sometimes i pick my nose and sometimes i. . . . ummm . . . well . . . NO KIDS allowed . . . !!! ok? . . there's lot of cool content in reX.s world they can look at though . . . so i default my splash page to that . . . notice the warning? . . . thanks . . . (http://www.rexsworld.com/rexxfiles/index.html)

Rex offers the opportunity for us to see his life, but not necessarily just his *gay* life. His comment, "i dont script this," is revealing about the kind of queer story he wants to tell: If you see some queer "content," then that is just part of Rex's life; if not, then that *too* is part of Rex's life.

In fact, Rex's rationale for putting up his pages with cams speaks to an interesting critique of other digitalized gays and their homo-pages. In response to the question, "why the reX.cam?" he replies:

> Basically a peek into my life . . . personal . . . work . . . and interests . . . The rexcam gives the visitors of reX.s world the chance to see that

---

[2]The use of such cams is becoming more frequent on the Web, and several "pay sites" (for which you have to pay an entrance fee) allow the viewer to watch both men and women, sometimes in their own homes, performing a wide-range of activities, from doing laundry to having sex. In a sense, web cams are the Internet's cross between *Candid Camera* and *The Truman Show*.

there is a person behind webpages. I really dug the William Gibson books . . . think we are in the primative ages right now though . . . will be very interesting to see how this all develops. (http://www.rexs-world.com/rexxfiles/index.html)

Rex suggests that the virtuality of web pages, and the stories they tell about people's lives, can actually eclipse or elide the lived realities of the individuals writing them. Besides referencing the remove of any mediated reality from the reality it is mediating, Rex is also suggesting that web pages can be reductive ("primitive") in their representation. It is exactly this kind of reductiveness that Rex wants to avoid, and he uses his site's design and layout to do so. For instance, commenting about the various responses to his web cam, Rex says,

some of the first emails i get are . . . "nice bod" or "show me" . . . then the second emails from them are "i love your site's design" or "I have catts too" . . . The motivation has changed . . . I enjoy that . . . being able to change motivations with designs . . . that is a big challenge. (http://www.rexsworld.com/rexxfiles/index.html)

Initially, viewers respond to Rex's live pictures in much the same way they would to the gay male picture galleries on many homo-pages—in passive appreciation of the "views" offered. But then, according to Rex, comments about the site design—and about Rex's day-to-day life—replace them. Apparently, that's part of Rex's intent; as he says, "I want the viewer to get to know me . . . not what I do with my body" (http://www.rexsworld.com /rexxfiles/index.html). In a way, Rex's "web cam as gallery" subverts the typical function of such galleries, which only offer a one-dimensional view of a "gay" body; the *web cam*, however, allows a more multidimensional image of Rex to develop, both on our screens and in our minds, resulting in a neat deconstruction: Rex lets us take a peek at his body so he can undermine our interest in it. In a sense, then, sites such as Rex's, which move beyond hypertext to hypermedia, might offer both more diverse and more complex self-representations.

Some critics, however, have questioned critically the function of web cams as authentic glimpses into someone's life. In *The Virtual*, Rob Shields offers the following thoughts:

Setting aside moralizing reactions, web cam sites are significant as diaries and statements of desire—wish lists of commodities rather than life goals. Cynically, we might say that these substitute for a life

defined in terms of social meaning while the camera broadens the
bandwidth of online social interaction, but allows just a one-way visual presentation of self so that one does not have to look at the fans who
remain imagined, virtual. . . . A stranger or another independent individual is unpredictable, uncontrolled. Confining such otherness to the
virtual becomes a strategy by which the terms of sociality may be set
and controlled by youth. (103)

Although Shields has a point—the cam might be just another way to objec-
tify a body, and some Web authors use cams for that purpose—I wonder if
Rex's cam is an example of "confining . . . otherness to the virtual." I tend
to think not, for Rex seems constantly striving to problematize his self-representation as static and as simply confined to the virtual. His site's slogan
is "take it to reaLity," and other components of the site, such as a chatroom, attempt to "broaden the bandwidth of social interaction" in ways
that move beyond just a "one-way visual presentation of self." Specifically,
Rex claims that his chatroom increases interactivity *and* troubles attempts
to reduce his performance of himself on his homepage as just another static or one-dimensional representation:

interactivity with webpages . . . i can talk with the folks visiting me...
and they can talk with me . . . I can get the general comments about
my page from here. . . . It's funny cause most people will come to my
page looking for "skin" . . . after awile the motivations can change . . .
they discover my gallery . . . with myscrapbook . . . or find out that I
have a lot of webpages out there . . . they discover that there is more
than just showing off a little booty . . . (heh!... which mine is small!
true!) . . . it's not about showing off or performing it's about taking a
peek into my life . . . (http://www.rexsworld.com/rexxfiles/index.html)

Rex uses all of his various hypertext links to craft a life story that moves the
viewer beyond a unidirectional understanding of Rex as "gay" into a more
complex, multifaceted, and even poly vocal collage of a life, especially as
others are invited to contribute to the chatroom and message board, to
which Rex always responds. One might say that Rex's homepage uses multiple Web genres to trouble any generic understanding of his life as just a
"gay man."

If anything, by leading an actual life on the Web, Rex seems to strive
to collapse the boundary between, on one hand, a "performance" of a gay
life on his Web page and, on the other hand, the realities of day-to-day living. In the process, he indirectly "queeries" the various Web "performanc-

es" of gay lives on the homo-pages by showing up the univocality of the story they tell about gay identity. Indeed, the most striking feature of this site, its layout, reflects—and enables—a radical shift in the story about queers told here. Rainbows and triangles, markers of queer identity, disappear in favor of a sleeker layout that emphasizes interactivity. In a way, this Webbed articulation of self promotes a more active engagement with the (hyper)text, as opposed to the rather passive mode prompted by many web sites, where you look and read more frequently, only to return again and again to the main menu. Furthermore, because the various uses of hypertext allow for greater interactivity, the boundaries between Web author and Web reader are crossed and re-crossed, along with the boundaries between the personal and public: You, as a visitor, are invited to join your voice with others collaboratively in telling a multifaceted and multivocal life story/ies.

WORSE THAN QUEER . . .

Whereas Rex's site represents perhaps one of the most multidimensional homepages on the Web, other homepage builders streamline their sites to particular genres or venues of communication and to specific literacy practices, but their goals and aims in doing so are just as challenging and provocative as anything we have seen so far, particularly in their "queerying" of the expected functions and dimensions of a personal homepage. For instance, in contrast to asitshould, Planet Soma, and Rex's site, Worse Than Queer (http://www.worsethanqueer.com/) is almost exclusively an online journal. Constructed and maintained by Mimi Nguyen, who describes herself as "a PhD candidate in Comparative Ethnic Studies at the University of California, Berkeley, with a Designated Emphasis on Women, Gender, and Sexuality," the site is relatively "simple" in layout and design, with just a few key sections:

mission | archive | word | links | contact

You would expect—and would find—the usual suspects by following each link: "mission" takes you to an "about this site" section; "archive" stores a list of Mimi's musings, by date; "word" collects links to Mimi's writings, available online; "link" is a well-organized link list; and "contact" evokes an e-mail message to Mimi. No surprises here.

I think this simple approach is meant to highlight the *content* of the site, which is generally never less than fascinating. Her "mission" statement, which is titled "Manifesto for My Revolution," is worth quoting at length, not just to appreciate the writerly skills deployed in this little bit of self-narration, but as an introduction to the many different interests that Mimi engages and explores in her writing throughout the rest of the site:

> I'm bi-queer (currently boyfriended, sorry girls) and lucky for you, I'm also devoted to poststructuralist, feminist, and queer theorizing, with a dash of the postcolonial. (Ask me about the heteronormative dyad that defines gendered representations of the national and historical relationship of Viet Nam to the United States.) I teach and give papers at conferences.
>
> I was born in Saigon, Viet Nam, between cannon-blasts. Ten months later I spent three days in a sling, wrapped around my mother, while we waited for squatting space on a gutted U.S. cargo plane. (The third time is always a charm.) I was raised in a small town in Minnesota where I learned how to fight.
>
> My first crush was on a blonde tomboy named Snow.
>
> In my academic work, Viet Nam is again a point of departure as I attempt to weave mad theorizing 'round the politics of citizenship, nation-making, cultural imaginaries, the heterosexual matrix, performativity, paranoid patriotisms, melancholy (dis)identifications, ambivalence, and live sex acts.
>
> I'm not the punk I used to be. Once bedecked in black military surplus, a no-nonsense anarchist tomboy with a spray-can tucked under sweatshirt, I'm now the geek grrrl in lip gloss, prone toward plastics and thrift-store cottons, dropping words like "epistemological" toward stunning effect.

Given Mimi's work in cultural studies and the academy in general, her emphasis on the written word is perhaps not surprising. She often deploys the language of textual analysis, of scholarly investigation. Even when her interests are visual, as in her willingness to perform in "lo-fi queer guerilla pop music videos," she narrates and unpacks her interests as an academic might, "dropping words like 'epistemological' toward stunning effect."

But, as you can tell from self-narration her writing is not just academic. It's also nearly irresistibly playful, and Mimi is not beyond a bit of pastiche herself, dropping a provocative line—"My first crush was on a blonde tomboy named Snow"—into the middle of an otherwise standard enumeration and discussion of one's interests. This is the language of periodic interruptions and disruptions that characterize a bit more postmodern play as opposed to modern linearity. This may be a journal, which implies a chronology of events described and analyzed, but it is a journal with a pomo edge.

In fact, Mimi herself locates her online journal in a history of work with zines and popular culture, a history that she describes in terms of "fetish":

> I've done fanzines since fifteen and I'm well-versed in popular culture. I do a zine called *slander*, once *slant*. I write for *Punk Planet* as a columnist, and the occasional article for *Maximumrocknroll*, plus zine reviews and the news. I'd like to freelance more often but I don't seem to have the time, but ask anyway.
>
>   I do this site as an extension of my *fanzine fetish*. Because cultural critique is a part of my everyday, this is what my *journal* consists of (mostly). This is me, keeping my critical tongue sharp and making my brain go. This is not me laying myself out to you, like it's some kind of confession.

In some senses, to borrow from Christy Desmet, Mimi's "fanzine fetish" is showing us the spectacular, perhaps even the "sacred" in the everyday, in the artifacts of popular culture. We see this throughout her writings ("word") and journal entries ("archive"), in which she sharply and humorously critiques any number of cultural, usually pop cultural, phenomena. For instance, in a recent writing about not wanting to attend a high school reunion, Mimi offers the following complex analysis:

> Does a journal become dangerous if you find yourself reviewing your life for narrative structure, resolution, or consistent character development? I used to spend caffeinated nights with the boys, playing punk rock and pranks into the late hours of the morning. Later I walked along the Hudson River piers, arm in arm with a girl long gone, past meatpacking plants and drowsy prostitutes trailing johns behind them like kites. These days are a whirlwind of airports and layovers, restless naps snatched in uncomfortable chairs (vinyl and upholstered) and far too many details (a rainbow of neon tubes above a moving sidewalk, the empty chatter and cliched speech of businessmen, a swell of academics glad-handing around the room). Two summers ago I saw my first subterranean show in a dank basement (different than house shows, which I have been to in abundance) in Bloomington, Indiana. But of course it was a band from the Mission, their van with California plates parked on the gravel driveway, the pungent stink of unwashed punks smelling of a once-familiar sense of home.

> In the end I think I didn't go to the reunion because it seemed like
> an arbitrary anniversary, because it seemed like resolution—how does
> so-and-so get from point A to B? I would have been disappointed.
> Could I really plot the points along this linear trajectory to illustrate how
> I got here from there? How do you tell someone the story of your life
> in five awkward minutes, when it makes no sense still?[3]

Interestingly, Mimi seems simultaneously to fetishize the genre of the journal, a staple of many personal homepages, as she critiques and attacks it.
On one hand, her interest in self-examination is self-evident, but she also
clearly wants to resist the generic imposition of "narrative structure, resolution, or consistent character development," a trap of journal writing
itself, a form that seems to encourage making connections and suggesting
"character developing" across a linear expanse of time. Mimi's near sole
reliance of the form in her homepage suggests that she is trying to ironize
the form, complicate the telling of her life story, and perhaps "queer" the
form (in many senses) that such stories usually take.

A significant portion of Mimi's critical insight comes from her ability
to view cultural artifacts through the multiple lens of perspectives and
interests, which she lists in her "mission" statement: "the politics of race
and sex in reproductive rights discourse, sex-positive feminisms, digital
technologies, riot grrrl, drag and other spaces of performance and perfor-
mativity." As you can see in the previous passage, for instance, her interests are not just in sexual queerness, but also in crossing boundaries of
scholarly study. She regularly tells us in her journal what she's reading and
listening to, and the mix is always a hodge-podge of the highbrow and
lowbrow:

| reading: | *Imagine Otherwise*, Kandice Chuh; *The Healer's Keep*, Victoria Hanley; *Race and Resistance: Literature and Politics in Asian America*, Viet Thanh Nguyen |
| listening: | The Kills' *Keep on Your Mean Side* LP, Feelings on a Grid demo CD |

Mimi is just as likely to talk—and to talk both knowingly and critically—
about Harry Potter as she is to quote from the works of Sigmund Freud.

---

[3]The larger piece from which these paragraphs come was published in *Punk Planet*,
to which Mimi contributes as a columnist.

Complicating all of this boundary-crossing even further is Mimi's dedication to troubling racial categories, particularly stereotypes of Asian-American women. Michele Knobel and Colin Lankshear, in "Cut, Paste, Publish: The Production and Consumption of Zines," describe Mimi's work in terms of expanding the literacies through which we understand, articulate, and communicate issues of race and ethnicity:

> Nguyen is producing a new literacy in her zine *Slander* (and elsewhere) that is rewriting traditional conceptions of and roles for Asian American women. This literacy concerns finding ways to draw attention to assumptions and stereotypes of Asian and Asian American women that are currently at work in popular media. . . . She also carries her message in the strong, line-drawn images she creates herself for her zine. (180–1)

In all of this work, then, Mimi plays with and writes about complex issues, and she refuses to allow us to think of any of them separately: they are all together—race, sexuality, gender—a part of her identity, performance, and self-construction on the Web.

What's really striking, however, specifically in terms of Web literacy, is that the complexity of issues tackled is embedded in an intriguingly "simple" site. Whereas other personal homepage composers we've examined have moved toward greater technical sophistication and multimedia formats to query how they are viewed and how we understand the purpose of the homepage itself, Mimi seems to have eschewed technical complexity. She openly acknowledges her interests and investments in hybridity, in crossing distinct lines, in "queering it up," even while her site, her online representation of self, offers us this articulation of hybridity in a fairly traditional personal homepage format—and one relatively devoid of multimedia hybridity:

> So I wear heels and lip-gloss while I theorize, boots and cuffed jeans while I play pinball. (I like Monster Bash the best.) I climb trees and fences in anything. I like to take road trips and visit those small attractions by the wayside, go to Vegas and revel in the gross artifice.
> And you know what? I don't think there's really any going home, of recovering things called "roots" or "tradition," or authentic selves or organic community, as if these were just waiting to be found, hermetically-sealed and otherwise pure, untainted by the violence of war, imperialisms of all kinds, and more. Still, *you can try.*

A similar sentiment is expressed just a few paragraphs above this:

> I don't believe in safe spaces or authenticity. (They elude me.) I don't
> believe in the transparency of photography, autobiography, or any of
> the other methods by which we fashion ourselves. Instead, I'll gladly
> tell you about power, hegemony and the labor of representation.

The tension here, I think, is between Mimi's fairly complex sense of self-
construction, with no possibility of "recovering things called 'roots' or 'tradition,'" and its delivery in a strikingly simple, even traditional Web format.
Although the technological representation *might* be an indication of specific skills limitations (but I don't think so), it also suggests a layer of self-irony
comparable to that seen in Dave's pages about himself or Planet Soma's
pages about queer identity. The self's articulation of its complexity is perhaps best experienced on the personal homepage, not through technical
complexities, metaphoric (or metonymic?) extensions of the self's complexities into cyberspace, but rather through troubling the standard forms
and genres through which our experiences are often rendered and mediated. For instance, as described earlier, Mimi takes the form of the journal
and complicates it, making it self-reflexively reveal the limitations of its
own form and thus opening up a space for articulating new complexities of
identity construction and performance.

Moreover, Worse Than Queer suggests that the self is composed, or
constructed, or re-constructed, or even deconstructed, of too many inter-
secting interests and forces—race, national origin, class, sexuality, gender,
desire—to be rooted in a particular place or space. So why try? In fact, the
link from "you can try" takes you back to the entrance page for Worse Than
Queer. You look for a "root," a way to recover a sense of "tradition" perhaps, and when you try—that is, when you click "you can try"—you are
taken to the site's entrance page; in other words, you are taken "home," to
the origin of your displacement. A simple link reminds us of this complex
reality.

THE LIMITS OF THE HOMEPAGE: CRITIQUES AND CONCLUSIONS

Taken together, Planet Soma, Rex's, and Mimi's homepages emphasize
crossing boundaries and questioning identities. And in recognizing and cel-

ebrating this multiplicity of self, this diversity of selves within the self, such sites seem to enact the nearly utopian dreams of "cyborg theory." In one of the now classic, early studies of identity representation on the Internet, *Life on the Screen: Identity in the Age of the Internet*, Sherry Turkle provides interesting analyses of the use of computer networks to explore gender, gender differences, and gender-swapping. Turkle concludes that computer technologies might call forth "Multiple viewpoints . . . [which] call forth a new moral discourse. . . . The culture of simulation may help us achieve a vision of multiple but integrated identity whose flexibility, resilience, and capacity for joy comes from having access to our many selves" (168). In this way, Turkle picks up on the rhetoric of cyborg theory already made famous by Donna Haraway in *Simians, Cyborgs, and Women: The Reinvention of Nature*. In this book, Haraway unpacks her notion of the "knowing self," which is "partial in all its guises, never finished, whole, simply there and original; it is always constructed and stitched together imperfectly, and *therefore* able to join with another, to see together without claiming to be another" (193). For Haraway, the image of the cyborg, which straddles the line between the human and the machine, is just such a "knowing self" in that it recognizes—and *uses*—its multiplicity of identities to create new modes of being and knowing unbounded by older, more static and constraining forms of identity. The use of the cyborg imagery also underscores how our new communications technologies might foster this meeting of "human" and "machine" to redirect our attention to the uses and pleasures of multiplicity and, in Turkle's terms, our concommitant "flexibility, resilience, and capacity for joy [which] comes from having access to our many selves."

It is worth keeping in mind, however, that as some representations— as some portions, aspects, and parts of our multiple selves—are put forward, others are left behind and critical silences are created—silences that reveal assumptions, values, and omissions that call for interrogation. For instance, bisexuality and transgenderism sometimes garner a mention on the sites we've examined, as well as many other gay-themed homepages, but they are seldom explored directly despite their being clustered under the LGBT/queer umbrella. Moreover, directory documents such as Gayscape (http://www.gayscape.com/), which many queers use to find homepages and other information, usually separate bisexuality and trans issues out into their own category (http://www.jwpublishing.com/gayscape/bs.html). Furthermore, other alternative kinds of sexual practices and identities are generally festishized and fixed into their own category with corresponding (and seemingly separate and ghettoized) Webrings, such as the Gay S/M Ring, the Gay Bowlers Ring, or the Lesbian Feminist Ring. Granted, a gay man searching the Web may not feel that "Portland Lesbian Avengers" is necessarily his cup of tea, but the captions announcing content specific to men or women would not encourage his interest; instead, they reify boundaries between lesbian and gay—not to mention the division between gay and straight. Indeed, there are few pages about supportive straights, beyond sites such as Parents, Families, and Friends of Lesbians and Gays (PFLAG) at < http://www.pflag.org/ >. There seems to be a "gay Web" housed within the larger, seemingly "straight Web." Furthermore, in my on-going search for queer sites, I have come across few sites by women that are similar to Planet Soma or Rex's. This is not to say that they are not out there, but it *is* to say that this "queer" site design seems to appeal more to men than women. To explain this, a Women's Studies colleague at the University of Cincinnati commented that the sites I have identified as "queer" seem almost narcissistic in their self-display (such as Rex's web cam). Her comment is suggestive: Perhaps queer-identifying women, who traditionally also identify as feminists, would not be interested in the kinds of potentially objectifying bodily display that Rex's site, for instance, seems to engage in.

Such distinctions point to the question of ghettoization on the Web, a question that has drawn some critical commentary. In "Writing in the Body: Gender (Re)production in Online Interaction," Jodi O'Brien asks, "Is there considerable crossover [between queer/straight spaces and their users], in which case variations in forms and the dynamics of interaction found in queer spaces might be transported into straight spaces? Or are the traditional ghettos being reproduced in emerging online communities" (103).[4] The sheer volume of material on the Web, as well as the massive number of daily communications sent over the Internet, makes answering such questions difficult, but they point to a concern that the replication of

---

[4]For more specifically on gender and the Internet: *CyberReader* by Victor J. Vitanza offers numerous short articles on cyberspace as it intersects gender and sexual politics, including: "Men, Women, and Computers" by Barbara Kantrowitz; "Gender Gap in Cyberspace" by Deborah Tannen; "Cyber-Gender Stereotypes Just Don't Compute" by David Nicholson; "Bringing Familiar Baggage to the New Frontier: Gender Differences in Computer-mediated Communication" by Susan Herring. Collectively, these pieces tell a mixed story of sexist stereotypes both brought to the Internet and troubled by it. And for more critical insight on the ways in which technology might change sexual behavior, if not sexuality, see *Escape Velocity: Cyberculture at the End of the Century* by Mark Dery, particularly Chapter 5, "Robocopulation: Sex Times Technology Equals the Future."

ghettos in online spaces may serve only to reinforce differences as opposed
to fostering communication across those differences.

Other potentially unforeseen boundaries may be cropping up as well.
First, the attitude exuded by sites such as Planet Soma suggests little tolerance for traditional gay styles of representation or storytelling. Second,
some queer site authors resist "normalization by commodification"[5] in
that they refuse to mark/market their Web pages as *only* gay sites. In a
way, however, they risk re-commodifying themselves as Internet savants.
For instance, the Web authors of the queer-inflected e-zine, *Sneerzine*, now
defunct, once bemoaned the paucity of hypertextual creativity on the
Internet, suggesting that queers have not taken full advantage of the narrative possibilities afforded by hypertext. And, in contrast to the "clone-
ishness" of the homo-pages, *Sneerzine's* designers want pages with "content"—which is understood as originality of content and layout. To promote this creativity, the *Sneerzine* designers have established a set of rules
for participation in their Web ring, among which include the following:

1. Under no condition will a . . . site contain a rainbow flag, pink
   triangle, or any mainstream gay symbol unless used for humor
   purposes. If site has those horrible pink triangle/rainbow ring
   logos that people are so fond of, they must be on a separate
   page.

and

4. Standards of good design must be upheld. No QBD site will contain tons of animated gifs, large image/sound files inhibiting
   download times, blink tags, or gigantic text so blind people can
   read it. (http://www.sneerzine.com/qbd/rules.html)

Interestingly, the "standards of good design" are probably a matter of perspective and personal taste, and the expressed value seems less on presenting oneself as queer and more on presenting oneself as technically
savvy, hypertextually astute, and graphically interesting. One has to wonder, however, if the cool hypertext graphics have replaced the affirmations,
coming out stories, and nude galleries as the principle markers—the foun-

---

[5] I am indebted to David Halperin (1995) for this phrase, which appear in his *Saint-Foucault*, 112.

dational acts of self-narration—of queer Internet identity. Moreover, are not the slick graphics a new criterion for the "hip" and the queer "in-crowd," replacing perhaps "No fats, femmes, and trolls"? The end result is that, in the crossing of boundaries into, through, and with hypertext, other boundary lines are being drawn. According to Plummer, this should not be surprising, for, "The first, and in my view the most dangerous and pessimistic response to the problem of conflicting stories, is the reassertion of *tribalism, fundamentalism,* and *separatism*" (162).

As techno-hip queers tell their own, highly individualistic stories, they may be marking their separation from others—their own identity—with an assertion of cyber-tribalism. Thus, they deploy hypertext both to create new modes and genres of self-narration *and* to erect new identity boundaries.

With such critiques in mind, then, it's worth problematizing personal homepages—for queers and straights alike—as "emancipatory," or even revelatory of the construction and narration of identity in any simple or straightforward manner. Indeed, the youth whose sites we've been examining are quite powerfully conscious of the complexities of self-representation and articulation via the Web, and their sites seem to call meta-critical attention and consciousness to those complexities themselves. Such a consciousness problematizes other assumptions about personal homepages as well. In 1997, Janet H. Murray wrote the following near the end of *Hamlet on the Holodeck: The Future of Narrative in Cyberspace*:

> As more and more people are growing as facile with digital environments as they are with pen and pencil, the World Wide Web is becoming a global autobiography project, a giant illustrated magazine of public opinion. Independent digital artists are using the Web as a global distribution system of underground art, including illustrated stories, animations, hypertext novels, and even short digital films. . . . [T]he documentary elements of the Web—the family albums, travel diaries, and visual autobiographies of the current environments—are pushing digital narrative closer to the mainstream. (251–2)

As I read through this passage, I repeatedly stumble over the phrases "global autobiography project," "pushing digital narrative closer to the mainstream." For some reason, this seems exactly to be what the young composers discussed in this chapter are working against. Each one of them has shown how she or he is questioning the construction, representation, and performance of self via the personal homepage, resisting its commodification into just another Web consumable or challenging stereotypes and reductive understandings of sexuality, race, or gender. Hybridity is used again and again—in both textual narrations and in the use of a variety of multimedia formats—to problematize any simple understanding of identity or its construction in cyberspace through the homepage.

Such challenges and problematizations are often accomplished through torquing expectations for the personal homepage as a genre, as a site for self-expression and emancipation. And such torquing is frequently undertaken mixing and matching various genres and media, creating sites that are hybrid in a variety of ways. In *Hypertext 2.0: The Convergence of Contemporary Critical Theory and Technology*, George P. Landow suggested that some characteristics of Webbed writing and composition are a "tendency to exploit electronic collage for purposes of interpretive juxtaposition and comparison" and the "joining [of] what one might consider academic and so-called creative writing, that is, poetry and fiction" (257). Although I think he was correct in pointing this out, and while we have seen examples throughout of such "electronic collage" and "interpretive juxtaposition," the personal homepages discussed in this chapter use such collage and juxtaposition, even the juxtaposition of different media, as in Rex's case, for particular purposes—primarily to ironize the production and consumption of self as a known or even knowable commodity on the WWW.

It is also worth keeping in mind that the personal homepage is seldom just a lone page on the Internet. Links on the pages are often designed to collect like-minded souls together, and Web rings assemble a variety of homepages together along the lines of shared interests, ideas, and values. Indeed, several of the pages discussed here seem designed to articulate a sense of self in the hopes of building, or at least attracting, friendly community—such as Dave's collaborative writing with his friends, Rex's discussion boards and chatrooms, and Mimi's sharing of her work with zines and other publications.

Ultimately, Dave's, Rex's, and Mimi's move toward constructing community via their sites, however odd, leads us to question how some digital youth use the Web to represent their communities, and the next few chapters discuss how such youth might write *community* via the Web. First, I examine what some youth do with the genre of the e-zine in an attempt to create socially minded communities of youth with Internet access. Then, I look at how some *queer* digital youth use the Web to construct and disseminate their notions of queer community, often in contradistinction to that of older generations of gays and lesbians. In each case, I note how these youth deploy a number of striking literacy and technological practices to author and articulate their concerns—practices that themselves reflect these youths' ideologies and investments.

INTERVIEW WITH DAVE MYERS: "ASITSHOULD.COM"

Dave Myers was among my brightest and most engaging first-year writing students during the 2002–2003 academic year. Early in the year, Dave began showing me the Web sites he was creating, and I was impressed with both his technical skill and the thoughtfulness with which he composed his sites. His personal homepage, asitshould.com, is an intriguing example of how a young person (Dave was 19 at the time of this interview) can take an established Web genre and torque is for his or her own purposes.

Jonathan: We are talking with Dave Myers this afternoon. Dave, why don't you start by telling us a little about yourself.

Dave: I'm 19 years old, and this is my first year at UC [the University of Cincinnati]. I'm currently doing pre-business administration, which is a 2-year program that will transfer me into the College of Business Administration. After 2 more years, I will get a 4-year degree.

Jonathan: How long have you been writing Web sites?

Dave: Before asitshould.com, which is my current site, I had two or three smaller sites. I remember making a site called Dave's Drums. I used to be a percussionist in high school. It was just for fun, something I put up on GeoCities.com.

Jonathan: Got it. How old were you when you started putting up sites on GeoCities?

Dave: I was probably in my early teens. Thirteen maybe. I did a few sites for my high school drama department. We put pictures and stuff up and programs from the plays we performed. I used the GeoCities site for that. I think that's when I started to get serious about stuff. Shortly after that I transferred my sites to our own server, because my dad is a computer geek too. It allowed me to play around and experiment. It was fun.

Jonathan: So it was a family affair then?

Dave: Yeah. My dad is a computer geek. He's always been around computers. He's always had my brother and me around computers. He used to give us these computer classes at home. He would pay us five dollars and we had to spend the money on something related to computers. That kind of died off after a while, but I would always ask him for help and stuff.

Jonathan: So did your siblings pursue this as well, or just you?

Dave: It's mainly just me. I have a brother and he's competent in computers but he really isn't as interested.

Jonathan: How long have you had asitshould.com, which is your current main site?

Dave: I'd say just close to 2 years. It's been changing a lot since I started it.

Jonathan: Is it the site you have had the longest?

Dave: Yeah. The other significant site that I've made, I guess you could say it's a professional site, is the site for my scout group, which is www.troop3.net.

Jonathan: Okay. I've seen you wear a t-shirt with that URL on it.

Dave: We just got those t-shirts by the way.

Jonathan: Let me ask you this, would you call "asitshould" your personal homepage?

Dave: Yes. That would be my personal homepage. Well, actually I had an identity crisis with this a while back. I was trying to decide if it was a personal Web site or if it was like a humor Web site. I do write things in first person so it *is* my personal Web site but I don't want it to be like, here is a picture of my cat and here is my vacation photos. Or here is a poem I wrote. I want it to have a wider appeal to a certain group of people, which would be, I guess, people around my age that are pretty open in their humor. Not everything is appropriate for all audiences and on the front page of the site I have a little thing that explains it. I've changed it a lot but right now it says that you should leave if you are easily offended or if you are a small child. I used to have that on every page but for the past few weeks I've been really trying to streamline the site a lot.

Jonathan: I have a couple of questions for you about that. What's the "point" of your site, and how does your "identity crisis" figure into what you want the site to accomplish—if anything?

Dave: Well I tell people a lot that it's a reflection of the odd side of my personality. That's kind of the general way to say it. Some of the stuff on there is what people would consider gross, and some of the things are just corny. It's also more personal than not. A lot of that stuff is about my friends and me but I try to take those and make them kind of humorous too. I have pictures from my New Zealand trip on there and I have pictures of myself on there just because I wanted to try and take pictures of myself almost every day so I can do a . . .

Jonathan: You don't mean every day on the trip—you just mean every day period?

Dave: Yeah. Every day period. I did it at first but I do it like every week now. I just thought 10 years from now it would be cool to have pictures. There are types of things like the pictures of myself and the pictures of my New Zealand trip and stuff like that. However, if someone shows up at the site that I don't know they probably won't get the impression that it's a personal site right away.

Jonathan: Okay. How do you organize the site then, because you said that you don't put stuff in obvious categories? For instance, you don't have a trips or vacation page within your site . . .

Dave: Right. It's organized into five main parts, which has changed a lot. Currently, the five parts are entitled "rant," "laugh," "enlighten," "adventure" and "buy." If you notice all of those are verbs [sic], and for some reason I just wanted to make them all verbs instead of doing pictures or something. Then in addition, I don't know how to explain this, but the "rant" section I rant about stuff. It's also full of odd stuff and jokes. For example, have recurrent themes where I make fun of a certain company over and over again. McDonald's is one that I do, which is pretty easy to make fun of. They had a slogan or advertising campaign a while ago—"We love to see you smile." I just thought that was the stupidest thing in the world because why don't they make it, "We love to make you smile." I took their logo of the smiley faces and turned it upside down and wrote a caption for it . . .

Jonathan: So, you're saying that the company doesn't want to have to work too hard to make their customers smile?

Dave: Yeah. The next section, "laugh," has four subsections. That would be "see," "hear," "move," and "read." Those are all verbs again. "See" is just like amusing pictures I found or amusing things I see and it's basically centered around the picture. A lot of times it will have a title and a picture. Sometimes you'll have a title picture and a small explanation. Then there is the "hear" section, which has audio recordings that I've recorded with my MP3 player or recordings I've made of my funny voicemail messages. Sometimes people knew they were being recorded and sometimes they didn't know they were being recorded but it's just amusing stuff; nothing real personal or inflammatory. It depends on your sense of humor obviously. Then there is the "move" part, which are video clips and animations along the same lines. Then there is the "read" part, which is the newest one that I've done. It has a heavy emphasis on text but there might be a picture or two along with it. For some of them, I kind of had a theme going of transcripts of conversations I've had with people, like online conversations. I'm online a lot so people chat with me . . .

Jonathan: You've done more than that. I understand, from previous conversations with you, that you've actually passed yourself off as someone very different.

Dave: Yeah. I was going to get to that.

Jonathan: Okay. We'll get back to that. What about the "enlighten" section?

Dave: That is actually a section I had earlier on but I got rid of that. I just brought it back. Enlighten is based around stuff my friends and I keep in a book, which is an *actual book*. It's like a diary almost. It's a little black book. There is an intro page to that. In the book we keep quotes, humorous things that happen to us, but it kind of developed to where there are different parts of the book that could easily be transferred to Web. One of these sections is called "Things you need to know, but no one ever talks about." An example of one of these "things" would be when you see someone, but you're not sure you want to say hello, break eye contact and seriously think about it. It's far better to just say you didn't see someone than have an acquaintance that you have to say 'hello' to for the rest of your natural life (which is a true form of hell.)

Jonathan: Okay.

Dave: It's just small things like that. Other things along those lines are "Things you need to know, but no one ever talks about," "Annoyances," "It's the little things," and we've also included some quotes and just small little things that make your day. So in the "enlighten" section you can actually look at pages of the book because I've taken pictures of each page. Then there are the parts that I transferred to Web text. There is a page for each one of those. Then from each item on each one of these pages is a link to the actual page of the book so you can just see it.

Jonathan: So, is the whole book online?

Dave: Yeah. I got every page in the book online. I just took a picture of each page that's been used so far. There is some stuff that's in the book that couldn't really be typed up. For example, when my friend Sean and I flew down to see our friend Tim in Florida 2 years ago, we had the house all to ourselves for 4 days. The first night we went out grocery shopping to buy stuff for 4 days. If you looked at the receipt and looked at what we bought for 4 days, it's really absurd stuff. We bought frozen Popsicles, a jar of pickles, some batteries, and ice cream.

Jonathan: Teen food.

Dave: Yeah. Then we pasted that in the book and wrote a little note that this should be enough for 4 days. Another example of something like that was when my friend Sean and I were flying to New Zealand, we took a plane from Dayton to Cincinnati on Continental Airlines. It was one of those real short flights. The magazine on board had a letter from the CEO and they had an English version and a Spanish version; well they were almost identical. They had the same form and the same feel and the same picture of the guy. On the Spanish version they took the picture of the CEO and put a yellow tint to it to make him look more Hispanic, or at least that was the impression we got . . .

Jonathan: So you've got a copy of that in the book and you were able to get that online?

Dave: Yeah. That is online. You can look at the pictures and see that. If you want to get the whole effect of the book you've got to look at both pages.

Jonathan: What about the section "adventure"?

Dave: "Adventure" is about stupid things my friends and I do. [Laughter.]

Dave: So it's kind of stories. Everything has a story to it on the site, but these are longer things. Some recent additions are about

how I was hiking and fell 50 feet off of a cliff and messed my
arm. That was one, and then there was one about the Florida
trip that I told you about but this was actually the year after. We
basically posted a bunch of photos with a humorous caption
for each one. The captions were written by my friend Sean.

Jonathan: That seems pretty collaborative. Sean is not necessarily coding
the site, but he's at least in creating the content with you.

Dave: Exactly. My friend Sean is the main person and then some
other people. Actually, I had this idea of having a part of the
site as a little bio page for each of my friends. It would be real
humorous stuff like having funny pictures and then little tidbits of why they want to rule the world or something. I haven't
really got around to that but that could be future stuff. There is
the Florida trip, and one night we took out some old computers and threw them out the back of a van while we were driving down the highway. On that one, we have pictures and a
video clip, which is pretty humorous. Then another one was
when Sean, Tim, and I participated in something called the
confluence project. A confluence point is a geographic point
where every solid degree of longitude and latitude meet all
over the planet. This online group is trying to document every
confluence point. They are getting people to go out and take
pictures and write stories and stuff. We had heard about this
and on the spur of the moment we went out to Kentucky; it
was about a 2 1/2 hour drive, and we did this. We went
through hell just to see this one tree. It was this imaginary spot
on the planet and it wasn't really about finding the thing, it
was about the journey. It was just amazing how weird and
screwed up the situation can get. We did that one night and
then 2 days later we did another one in Ohio where we were
detained by federal officials. In both of those we had pictures
and video clips, too. I just recently put that online even though
it was about 2 years ago because we technically broke the law
in several ways to do that.

Jonathan: How so?

Dave: We hitchhiked, we trespassed on private property, and we kind
of lied to government officials. Also, we were recording with
our camera when all these security people were around us,
and they didn't want us to take pictures or anything.

Jonathan: The statute of limitations hasn't expired yet, I'm sure! So, is "buy" the last section?

Dave: Yeah. It's been up there for maybe 6 months or so. You can go through a company called Cafépress.com. Anyone can go make a design and put it on t-shirts or glasses. Cafépress has their base price and I could have raised the price on the stuff if I chose to, but I don't really care. I just kind of think it's humorous. I recently added the "asitshould" thong.

Jonathan: Why?

Dave: I thought it would be cool to say that I sell thongs.

Jonathan: I see more and more home pages that offer merchandise, where people can buy things made by the people who have the homepage.

Dave: Cafépress is the only significant company I know that does that. They have economies scale. It's a neat service. Recently, I used it to help my friend buy a personalized thong for his girl-friend.

Jonathan: What's interesting is you have people who create their own logos and their own brands, and they want to sell stuff with that on it. You have a slightly different take on it. You have stuff with your brand on it, but you are not interested in mak-ing money. It's almost as if you are mocking the whole thing.

Dave: That's not my intention. It's not that I'm trying to poke fun at people. I know that if I tried to turn it out into a commercial thing it would just be dumb. I know there is no real way to make cash off of it. I'm not even going to try. I only get a few hits to the site a day. I don't really see a substantial opportuni-ty to make any cash off of it.

Jonathan: So you're not making any money off the site, and you only get a couple of hits a day. What keeps it going, expanding and constantly changing? What drives that?

Dave: I want to improve my design skills and creativity. I have a lit-tle artistic side to myself. It's not big but it's there. This is essentially my hobby and it's a hobby I find challenging, fun, and something that will help me in life.

Jonathan: Okay. What kind of skills do you think people are going to have to have if they want to communicate successfully on the Web?

Dave: Well, when you say communicate on the Web, what do you
             mean?

Jonathan: Develop their own sites.

Dave: You basically just have to have something to say. The Internet
             is only a different medium that can be used for communica-
             tion. When you think about it, most things on the Internet
             (including my sites) can be communicated just as effectively in
             a different medium, just not on such a large scale. As soon as
             you have something to say, learning to skills to create a Web
             site is pretty routine.

Jonathan: You said that you try to put content on your site in such a way
             that it's appealing to people your age.

Dave: Yeah.

Jonathan: What appeals to people your age in terms of content and also
             in terms of layout, do you think?

Dave: In terms of content, I would say that kids are attracted to stuff
             they know they "shouldn't" look at, like text full of the words
             fuck and crap. I used to kind of try to censor the site a little bit.
             I actually used to have a password area in the site. I just kind
             of eventually said, screw that. I just put it all out there, and if
             people don't want to look at it they don't have to.

Jonathan: What else?

Dave: Odd humor is a good thing for people.

Jonathan: What does odd mean? You've used the word odd several
             times...

Dave: It's kind of hard to define exactly what it is, but it's kind of like
             mocking things. It would be fair to say that one of the themes
             on the site is where I take a theme and make fun of it. For
             example, one of the transcript things I did in "read" section is
             a transcript of a conversation between me and this person who
             is trying to sell me a membership to this porn site. Every once
             in a while you'll get someone who is trying to lure you with
             online sex. It is beyond me why people do that. They don't
             really tell you they are trying to sell you something and I kind
             of knew. Ten seconds into the conversation I knew what it was
             all about but I wanted to post it on my website. I was trying to
             play along and make them look dumb and stuff like that.

Jonathan: Okay.

Dave: I tried to lead them on a little bit, but eventually I just gave up. Pretty much all of the transcripts I have made fun of people. There is the one about the text-messaging thing. This gal was trying to get me to hang out with her and "hang out" was in quotes. We dated once previously, like 3 years ago. I kind of know what she's like and I guess she was trying to hook up with me or something. She is a friend of my brother's or something like that. The sole intention of putting that on there was to have a laugh at her expense.

Jonathan: So you use the site to exercise little personal vendettas?

Dave: Yeah.

Jonathan: You also make fun of other kinds of things. You mentioned McDonald's earlier. What makes something the object of your attention?

Dave: That's a good question. I'd just say stupidity. If I see something that's really stupid—where it has to be kind of stupid, but you also have to be able to write something about it or do something with it that's humorous.

Jonathan: Example?

Dave: The other McDonald's thing that is on there is when I was out to California and ate at a McDonald's Express. I saw a whole bunch of them actually. McDonald's Express. That's express fast food. It seems sort of redundant to me and I don't think it made that much of a difference anyway. In that situation it's just kind of stupid but not really a *bad* stupid kind of thing.

Jonathan: Okay . . .

Dave: I don't want to make fun of people like terrorists. The people who have definitely done really bad things associated with them—I avoid that. Instead, I want someone to go and read my site and say, "yeah that's kind of dumb". The intention of the site is to humor people not to make them stop the way they act. For example, I don't honestly expect someone to stop going to McDonald's because of something I said.

Jonathan: Tell me about the multimedia aspect of the site. How do you work that to appeal to people?

Dave: The layout is predominately blue. I like dark backgrounds with all white text. It might just be a personal thing, but a lot of times it just gives the impression that it's not CNN.com. CNN is a white background and black text. It's a standard site. My site kind of a bold site but that in itself communicates that this is not a normal site.

Something I have been working on a lot is trying to get most of the content in a column on the page. It's 500 pixels wide (roughly half the screen). The average amount of characters on a line is supposed to be pleasant to read, where the line isn't too long but you are not switching to the other side and back and forth all the time.

Pictures and stuff are edited in Photoshop. I use something called auto contrast. A lot of times, the pictures I take with my camera look fine, but then they look even nicer after you apply this contrast. It really kind of makes it a richer color. It's higher quality. If you look at it before and after, before kind of looks gray and hazy compared to afterward.

Then the video aspect of it—I'm not real good with that stuff because to do serious editing you have to have a good computer. I don't really have a high quality machine, so I'm kind of restricted by my resources.

Jonathan: Is video something you want to experiment more with?

Dave: Right. I don't really have a good camera. When I record something for video, I use a HI-8 tape, and then I have to put the plug in the camera to the computer and it's not really that good.

Jonathan: Do you think people are increasingly expecting to see videos on Web sites?

Dave: Not really, because even though it's kind of nice in some circumstances, it's almost over the top in some ways. The videos, except for the actual section where it's all videos—I don't try to make it so they have to watch the thing to get in on it. It's the same with the pictures. They can kind of get some of the idea by just looking at the pictures and a small explanation from me. They can get it and not have to read it because some of them are kind of long but there is a lot of interesting stuff if they chose to read it.

Jonathan: What would make a good Web site then? What would make a good personal homepage, in your opinion?

Dave: I would say first and foremost that it should be a reflection of the person that makes it. That's the person's Web site. For me, a successful site is one that's not "normal." If I said to a stranger that my personal Web site is asitshould.com, they would go to asitshould.com and it doesn't strike you as being a personal Web site, which some people may not like because they just may want to see pictures of my cat or something but they are not going to get that.

Jonathan: All right. What Web sites inspire you?

Dave: Not a whole lot really. Believe it or not, I don't just go and search different sites. A lot of the stuff I came up with from my own ideas.

Jonathan: Okay. What's a "normal" site then?

Dave: A normal *personal* site?

Jonathan: It doesn't matter, just a normal site that your site would con-trast with. You already mentioned CNN.com.

Dave: Yeah. Something like CNN or Yahoo! but Yahoo! is kind of more of a…well, it's too big to compare. People have actually told me my site is like other sites such as Rotten.com. I've been there once but I'm not really sure what that is to tell you the truth.

Jonathan: Okay.

Dave: There is another one; I forget the name of it. They gave me a link to a site that was pretty much like mine. It had random humorous stuff. That was kind of nice—to see that they consid-ered that like mine. It was kind of on the same level as mine but it had a little more content. That was a compliment. I don't always add content on a regular basis. I've gone for months without touching the site so it's kind of stagnated a little. For three months I would collect pictures and keep them on my computer to the point where I would go and edit them. This past time around I put a lot more effort into it. I streamlined the editing process a whole lot so it's a lot easier for me to change things and to keep the look on all of the pages consistent.

Jonathan: Okay.

Dave: If I didn't have that file on there all you would see would be a white background and black text and just standard links. They would all be on the left side of the page.

Jonathan: What are you most proud of on your site? What's the part that you are the most proud of or that you like the most?

Dave: I would say that I'm most proud of how the site kind of keeps on changing. Every time I write a new JavaScript code—I really just kind of surprise myself with that. That's when I'm most proud. I learn a lot of stuff then go back and work on another site and implement the stuff I've learned.

Jonathan: What about the content? What about the content are you really impressed with yourself?

Dave: I kind of like the "laugh" section. When I read back I laugh at them myself. Sometimes I'll write things, and I like to write (obviously) and I enjoy it, but I don't think of myself as a good writer. When I write certain things, it's just kind of the insanity of some of the stuff I do. I don't know if you've seen this because it was offline for a while. There is an animation that I did that is in the move section. I took my logo, which is kind of a weird looking question mark and animated that into a flash animation of a guy giving a girl a tit fuck.

Jonathan: Okay.

Dave: You know what I mean?

Jonathan: Yes.

Dave: I had this idea and I themed it around—well, I called it the future of asitshould.

Jonathan: Okay.

Dave: It starts off with 1970s porn music. Parts of my logo flow in and then "the future of asitshould" appears. . . . After a few seconds, the words "hardcore porn" replaces all of the text on the screen. From that point on you see the animation of the tit fuck. (http://asitshould.com/laugh/move/titfuck/)

Jonathan: Just kind of like most of the Internet. Porn is taking over the Internet!

Dave: That's what I was kind of mocking. It goes into the animation. I can show it to you if you'd like.

Jonathan: Well maybe we better not bring that up on my school computer. We'll have to see it some other time.

Dave: I'm kind of proud of that. It's not really appropriate but I was impressed that I came up with the idea and also that I created it. It wasn't easy to do.

Jonathan: It seems like half, if not even two thirds of your enjoyment of this is learning the technology.

Dave: Yeah. It's very slick.

Jonathan: You obviously want to Web design professionally, at some level.

Dave: Well…

Jonathan: You do to some extent, no?

Dave: I do. I really don't want to go much further than I am now. People like my dad say I should try to get an intern job at a design place, but my real career goals are to do more business stuff and do this more as a hobby.

Jonathan: Okay. To communicate successfully on a Web page what do people need to be able to learn to do?

Dave: You have to know what people want to see. You have to understand the philosophy that less is more.

Jonathan: Okay.

Dave: That's something that I'm trying to implement on the site, where it's just stripping out the unnecessary crap. Just having it lean and mean. Just have something to say and, you know, say it effectively and quickly. In my case, you can make people laugh too.

Jonathan: Yeah.

Dave: A lot of people don't like to read stuff online. I don't particularly like to read something online. If I have to read something, then I'll print it out. You've got to understand that people don't want to spend more time than they need to to get something out of it. Recently, when you asked me about the different sections of the website, I used to have a sectioned called "shout." I still have that on there but that was just a way for people to e-mail me or send me a message. It was its own page and the navigation links, and I thought to myself that's not really that important. I put a small link at the bottom of each page.

Jonathan: So people could still get in touch with you?

Dave: Yeah. Exactly. I had a section called "come," which was a section for links to other sites. I had some pretty humorous stuff. I had links to pretty interesting sites and I would give them interesting titles, like one was "take your sex life to the next level."

Jonathan: Level?

Dave: It was a link to an adult fortune cookie store.

Jonathan: Okay.

Dave: Then there was *rich person hell* and that linked to a site that was dedicated to posting pictures of exotic cars that had been totaled. I found myself not updating it very often. A lot of time I would put a link that I found from another person who had a similar page that said you should go here. A lot of them I didn't really find myself because I don't really surf the web a lot, although I do spend a lot of time online.

Jonathan: The link list is a staple of homepages, isn't it?

Dave: Yeah.

Jonathan: You streamlined yours away?

Dave: Yeah. I got rid of that because I just didn't want it to stagnate very often and the fact that I didn't find a lot of them myself. I just cut it down. Just a week ago I got rid of "shout." I got rid of "come" and I used to have something called "etceterise," which is a word I created for my miscellaneous page; it's supposed to be the verb form of et cetera. I had a link to my New Zealand pictures, but I ended up putting that in my "adventure" section at the bottom. But I figured I should just take those things in "Etceterise" and drop them or make them into something more and put them in a different section. I've been doing it with the navigation lately and just trying to get it real smooth.

One of the things I've learned is that you want to be really good have to do everything by hand coding. I used to just point and click but I've graduated to the next level. What was the question that you asked that got me talking about that?

Jonathan: I forgot.

Dave: That's okay.

Jonathan: Oh well. What else do you want to say about your site?

Dave: I have a slogan too. I have a logo and a slogan. The slogan is, "I'm not a moron. I just have decentralized thought processes.

"I kind of call that my personal slogan and that's a para-phrased quote I said once. Actually, the name of the site came for a quote I said too. I was eating out with some friends and one of my friends said I was in "Daveland mode.""

Jonathan: Daveland mode?

Dave: Yeah. It was kind of like insanity mode. I was sitting at the dinner table like 5 minutes and for some reason I was really enjoying my food a lot. I sat there and thought about something I could say that was humorous. I eventually said, "Okay everyone, I know what I'm going to say now," and they stopped. I said, "As it should, this food is good." It's just a really stupid quote but everyone really laughed.

Jonathan: All right.

Dave: It was one of those "you had to be there" kind of things.

Jonathan: So why didn't you call the site "this food is good"?

Dave: Maybe I'll get another site.

Jonathan: Maybe you will. I worry sometimes that I will appear on your site.

Dave: People have actually said that to me.

Jonathan: I'm not surprised.

Dave: I was recently kicked out of [a local chili parlor] where I used to work because of things my friends and I have been involved with that are on the website. Scenes we've created there, and I knew I got kicked out because they didn't want all of us back. They just kicked me out just to get us all to leave. We had another thing in the works.

Jonathan: Another prank?

Dave: It's going to be related, but I won't be there in person, but I may be there as a blow up doll.

Jonathan: As a blow up doll. You are very creative. That reminds me that you've said that that you have some very bizarre sexual humor on your site, which is really not surprising since that is obviously going to appeal to some extent to young people. Tell me real quick about your masquerading as someone else.

Dave: I went to a site called "Hot or Not." It's a site where you go to rate other people about whether they are attractive or not. It also has a link you can click, and it asks you if you want to meet this person. If Person A says they want to meet Person B, then Person B will be told that Person A wants to meet them and then ask if they want to meet Person A, and if they both say yes, they will be able to communicate with each other. They can do what they want from there. I had a thing on there. I have a profile.

Jonathan: You have a profile?

Dave: Yes. It's a normal one.

Jonathan: So it's actually you?

Dave: Yes. I have an actual profile.

Jonathan: Okay.

Dave: Yes I have an actual profile.

Jonathan: Were you deemed hot—or not?

Dave: I was deemed hot but I have a suspicion the site isn't totally honest.

Jonathan: Oh okay.

Dave: It's on a scale of 1 to 10 and I have a friend that has a profile on there too and it's a girl. Girls get a lot more interest than guys do. She told me that it's kind of annoying to have all these people asking to meet her, and so I just thought I'd do a little social experiment. I pretended to be someone else. I had this fake profile and I think the girl I pretended to be is really hot. People request to meet this person and every few days I go and check on the requests. I just click yes to all of them so I have like 200 people on my list of people.

Jonathan: Good God.

Dave: Actually it happened. I turned this into a big thing because the first person who wrote me—I was shocked at what they wrote. They had no idea who I was or anything, and they wrote this four-paragraph paper on why they wanted to meet this fake person. That really kind of inspired me to expand.

Jonathan: Did they spill their guts out to you, er, your fake person?

Dave: Yeah. I never contact them back. I just ignore them. I never email them back. I draw the line. I don't chat with them and pretend to be someone else. That's just extreme.

Jonathan: Extremely cruel. It's okay to be a little cruel—is that what you're saying?

Dave: Yeah. People on this site—it's not like this fake profile is the only profile that ever interested them. I recorded the e-mails that they sent me, not all of them but just a few of the humorous ones. It was probably about 10% of them, and I put them on my Web site, asitshould, with a little story about this social experiment.

Jonathan: All right. This is the final question. What *is* the future of asitshould.com, besides hard core porn?
[Laugher.]

Dave: That is totally on a day-to-day basis. Can I add a few other things?

Jonathan: Sure.

Dave: I originally tried to get the domain with daveland.com and there was actually another Dave who had that domain. I contacted the person and he said that he turned down $10,000 offers for this one domain.

Jonathan: Wow.

Dave: Yeah. People were really trying to get this domain.

Jonathan: Impressive.

Dave: I originally got asitshould because I originally wasn't sure what I was going to do with it at first. I didn't know whether it was going to be a personal thing or a slightly professional thing.

Jonathan: Okay.

Dave: asitshould was a pretty ambiguous term. It could mean pretty much anything I want because it's a new word. I kind of go for the whole ambiguity thing and the name of it and also in the logo of it, which actually—I found that logo because I wanted to make it on the same theme as ambiguity. I went and checked out the fonts for all these different question marks and I found this one that I just kind of slanted to the side a little bit and made it flat on the bottom. It's actually a question mark slanted in a weird font but people thought that the logo was a question mark or an explanation mark or a weird swoopy thing with a dot. It's all kind of ambiguous. The other

	thing is that I have a site called "pothole people." Did I tell you about the pothole people thing?
Jonathan:	"Pothole people"? No.
Dave:	That's another idea. I haven't done a lot to the site but you can go to potholepeople.com and download these pictures.
Jonathan:	potholepeople.com?
Dave:	Yeah.
Jonathan:	Okay.
Dave:	When Sean and I were in New Zealand, we were going through the country and trying to get souvenirs for people back in the States. We were half way through our trip and we were in this town called Christchurch, New Zealand, about 300,000 people. It was kind of like Cincinnati. There was this construction site, and Pothole People was the name of this company that was doing work for them. Our friend, Tim, is a kleptomaniac, kind of. He steals little signs from stores and stuff. He doesn't steal anything like of great value, but he likes to steal little signs. We decided to steal this sign from this construction site, and there was like eight of them so it's not like it was the only one. It was like a corrugated plastic sign. I don't know if you know what I mean by that.
Jonathan:	Yeah.
Dave:	It's about 3 feet wide and 6 inches tall and it was yellow and said "Pothole People." We got that and then we held onto it, and when these people we were staying with down in this other town in New Zealand, they suggested that instead of just taking it back to him we should just take pictures of people or of ourselves holding this pothole people sign in our pictures.
Jonathan:	Okay.
Dave:	We did that but then we decided to have other people hold the pictures and then we'd take pictures of them. That's really kind of where it made the big jump.
Jonathan:	Got it.
Dave:	You know we were not only taking pictures; it was kind of whole social interaction thing when people would ask to hold a sign to take a picture. It started on our New Zealand trip, and then the intention is that every time we go on a trip, we

	take the sign with us and ask people at gas stations to hold the pictures.
Jonathan:	That's pretty cool, in a weird sort of way.
Dave:	We haven't really done much with this site but I intend to and I probably will soon. It would probably be organized for different trips. There could potentially be a commercial thing out of it. It wouldn't be able to make a lot of money but the theory behind it is good.
Jonathan:	The theory?
Dave:	You go around—well, say, travel all the time, and you go around and you give someone the sign and you have them hold the sign and take the picture. Then you would give them a little card that says, "Your picture will be available at pot-holepeople.com in two days," or something like that. Then through the Cafépress thing, you could like have a "pothole people" t-shirt with their picture on the back of it. People will have all kinds of different signs.
Jonathan:	Sure.
Dave:	So that's an idea, but it's just kind of fun. I still actually have the original sign. I actually contacted the company about inquired about other signs, and actually I tried to contact some people from New Zealand and get them to steal another sign for me.
Jonathan:	Cool, I guess.
Dave:	I didn't want them to pursue it that much but then another site—well, another domain I just bought is actually savethe-dave.com. There isn't anything up there yet. I just felt like getting another site and kind of starting the process all over again. Putting something up and kind of seeing where it goes.
Jonathan:	What would you do differently from the very beginning? You obviously have greater technological ability, or technical skill.
Dave:	I think I would keep the site so that it could be a professional site and more about being smaller, but I don't have any plans right now. I was going to get one of my art friends to draw a cartoon logo version of my face so they can kind of do a retro feel to it.

Jonathan: Let me ask you, when you say professional, what do you
            mean? What would a professional site be for you?

Dave: A site that has it's own domain name, is ad-free, and a site that
            anyone can go to and not get a bad impression. You know
            what I mean?

Jonathan: They wouldn't get a bad impression . . . ?

Dave: It could be essentially, you know, whatever I could to offer
            graphic arts services and things like that. Just go and make it
            a contact page, and you put on your card savethedave.com
            and people will remember. When you were asking me how
            can we effectively communicate through the Internet—that's
            probably another way. You can have a resumé. Even if it's real
            small but it looks really nice and if someone goes to it after
            you apply for a job. They might get a good impression.

Jonathan: Sure. You would send them to savethedave but not asitshould?

Dave: Right. asitshould has progressed beyond the point…

Jonathan: Where it could serve as a professional site?

Dave: Yeah, it's fallen too far into the abyss of absurdity. I could
            potentially just change the name of asitshould. I could just
            change and load the content onto a different site and keep the
            logo but I would feel bad. It does kind of have a small brand
            to it.

Jonathan: It's taken on a life of its own.

Dave: Yeah. Sort of—yeah.

4

THE PERSONAL
AND THE POLITICAL

E-ZINES, COMMUNITY, AND THE POLITICS
OF ONLINE PUBLICATION

Besides personal homepages, which were discussed in the preceding chapter, e-zines, or "electronic magazines," have been a significant genre through which some digital youth represent and write about their lives and engage in substantive critique of the world around them. The first youth-oriented e-zine I encountered was *Gettingit* at www.gettingit.com, which, in its heyday, offered reports from the frontlines of popular culture. All of the pieces, surrounded by the site's eye-catching lime green background, addressed a pop-literate audience with essays that simultaneously lionized and ironized celebrities, television, the movies, underground cultures, and the politics of fame. The subjects were catchy, and my students and I generally appreciated the authors' adoption of a critical stance toward what they were writing about, as well as their willingness to risk a different perspective on the stories of fame, celebrity, and identity circulating around us. In general, the presentation of material on the site, as well as the content, suggested a willingness to play with Web literacies and to take advantage of the Web as a forum for attracting a particular kind of readership—a community of readers, if you will.

Some scholarly attention has been paid to *print*-based zines written by youth with an interest in writing. For instance, talking specifically about the contribution of zines to youth literacies in "Cut, Paste, Publish: The Production and Consumption of Zines," Michele Knobel and Colin Lankshear note that

> zines exemplify in varying degrees diverse forms of spiritedness (gustiness); a DIY ["do-it-yourself"] mindset; ability to seek, gain and build attention; alternative . . . perspectives; street smarts; originality and being off-beat; acute appreciation of subjectivity; tactical sense; self-belief; enterprise, and a will to build and sustain communities of shared interest and solidarity. These are the kinds of themes that will arise in our account of zines as a characteristically contemporary literacy. (165)

The remainder of Knobel and Lankshear's chapter traces these themes and characteristics through a number of youth-produced zines, some published on the Web, and the authors argue that zines represent a "characteristically contemporary literacy" practice that writing instructors can—and should—use pedagogically to engage students, help them cultivate their own voices, and instill in them an awareness of basic literacy practices. Such practices could include the aforementioned "ability to seek, gain and build attention," an "acute appreciation of subjectivity," and a "will to build and sustain communities of shared interest and solidarity" through writing.

Writing in 1998 in *Growing Up Digital: The Rise of the Net Generation*, Don Tapscott saw similar literacy tactics, sensibilities, and skills being deployed and developed as some young writers experimented with crafting zines for Web publication:

> The introduction of youth zines to the Internet is a quantum leap forward in the democratization of the media for kids. There has always been some media that looked at the world through youthful eyes, such as campus newspapers and student radio, but in the overall media scheme these were insignificant. Their audiences were minuscule.
>   Zines challenge the one-to-many dictates of conventional print media by parodying the relationships between editorial and advertising content. . . . The electronic zine provides information through articles, accepts feedback and original submissions that turn readers into authors, and provides the communicative opportunity that strengthens the feedback loop. (84)

In the online zines examined later in this chapter, we see that Tapscott's original assertions are still, for the most part, correct: Many e-zines not only provide information to youth with Internet access, but they also foster a sense of the "authorial reader," and they frequently promote active collaboration between e-savvy youth, as well as encouraging other youth to submit their writing and creative work, including art, for potential publication. As Tapscott puts it, "Overall, they provide a portrait of the culture of interaction—the antithesis of broadcast culture. This N-Gen culture foreshadows the new culture of work, consumption, and social life and it is leading to a change in the psychology of young people" (84).

Although I think that Tapscott has useful insights, I must admit that these are pretty substantial, even hyperbolic statements to make about the potential effects of Internet-based communications on literacy practices, not to mention the "psychology of young people." Others, such as Derek Foster, have written a bit more tentatively about the effects of the Web and the Internet on notions of identity and community. In "Community and Identity in the Electronic Village," published in 1996, Foster argued that, "As more people gravitate to this new means of communication, concomitant changes in the conception of both community and identity will inevitably change" (24). Given the time that has passed since Tapscott's and Foster's early theorizing, it's worth asking what kinds of effects the Web has had, if any, on digital youths' "conception of both community and identity." Certainly, in many ways, such a question is impossible to answer; its focus is *so* large that we could only gesture toward the most generalized ways in which the new communications technologies are altering how some digital youth think of themselves, both individually and collectively. At the same time, what I propose is that examining e-zines, which frequently address issues of both identity and community, as well as the place of the individual within larger communities, might offer a few insights into how some digital youth are using this particular Web genre to explore, understand, and revision notions of identity and community. In the process, we can catch a glimpse of the kinds of literacy practices that some youth deploy in e-zines to undertake this work.

The remainder of this chapter, then, focuses attention on a few youth-oriented and youth-developed e-zines, as they are developing in some urban American centers, with an eye toward answering the following questions: What literacies *are* used in the creation of online zines, and what do such literacy practices say—broadly—about these particular youths' conception of identity and community? We'll begin with a youth-oriented e-zine that Don Tapscott identifies as among the first, *Spank!*, and we'll look at it through his eyes, to explore some of the major themes and literacy practices that he sees as emerging in the construction of youth-driven e-zines. Tapscott tells us what he thinks is "typical" about how some digital youth create and use e-zines on the Web, and examples such as *Spank!* and even MTV.com offer us many textual and visual images of youth community online. At the same time, we'll also see how *Spank!* and MTV.com have substantial corporate interests—interests that problematize some of the qualities and characteristics Tapscott forwards as indicative of how some youth build community online through e-zines. Given this, we'll take a step back and look at a few less "corporate" enterprises to compare some of the broader claims that Tapscott suggests about emerging literacies with ways other digital youth are actually using and composing e-zines. Doing so will allow us to think a bit more specifically about what kinds of literacy practices these particular youth are engaging in and developing when they create and publish e-zines, and it will prompt us to critique some of Tapscott's broader generalizations.

SPANK!—THE ORIGINAL YOUTH E-ZINE

Tapscott reports that the "first youth culture online magazine by and for young people is *Spank!* Robin Thompson is the cofounder and publisher of *Spank!*, and she sold her car to fund the venture that now boasts readers and writers from five continents" (83). The site, located at http://www.spankmag.com/, has been in transition in the last few years, and its current "about" section details its more recent focus:

> **Spank! Youth Culture Online** is a worldwide, online community for 14 to 24 year olds. *Spank!* launched 01 October 1995 and has changed a great deal since, moving from a traditional magazine format to a multifaceted online community.
> Focusing on youth issues, interests, and life, *Spank!* is an ever-evolving centre for youth. For some, *Spank!* is a soapbox, for others, a place to meet friends from across North America and around the world. *Spank* is a music critic, a fashion reviewer, a political activist, an overall youth culture expert, and is never afraid to voice an opinion. (http://www.spankmag.com/content/about.cfm/cc.2/p.htm)

The current formats for participating at *Spank!* include two venues, "youth forums" and "youth news," which, according to the site authors are "features in the site to ever match the changes in youth and technology":

Youth Forums

Spank!'s forums are extremely active! With over 14,000 new posts a week, and a huge amount archived, almost any issue regarding youth can be found—from the totally frivolous to the absolutely serious. We have sections on dating, fashion, homework, religion, sexuality, poetry, art, music, happiness, and more!

Youth News

Spank!'s youth news links are suggested by our users, and link to relevant issues, events, and stories that impact them. It's a collection of current events that have relevance to them and their peers. (http://www.spankmag.com/content/about.cfm/cc.2/p.htm)

On the surface, the intent here certainly seems to be to give youth with Internet access a voice, a chance to interact, to share information and ideas that are of concern *to youth.*

Testimonials from youth who participate in *Spank!*'s forums suggest lively interest and engagement:

> *This is more than just a youth forum. You form friendships, learn about global cultures and ideals, and sharpen your arguing skills. This is all done without the regular limits and boundaries of your location.—*Smurf19

> *I have met some of the coolest people ever on this site—it's more than just a chatroom or something. People actually know each other. Most Spanklers who have been on Spank! for more than a month have talked to if not met other Spanklers. . . . So yes—that's pretty much it. More than just a website—the epitome of youth culture."—* ~ ~eV~ ~
> (http://www.spankmag.com/content/about.cfm/cc.2/p.htm)

According to Tapscott, such sentiments are in line with changing attitudes—and abilities—enabled by the new communications technologies. For Tapscott, "N-Geners," those growing up in an era of increasing use of computer networks as communications tools, embrace and exemplify the following 10 "themes":

1. Fierce Independence
2. Emotional and Intellectual Openness
3. Inclusion
4. Free Expression and Strong Views

5. Innovation
6. Preoccupation with Maturity
7. Investigation
8. Immediacy
9. Sensitivity to Corporate Interest
10. Authentication and Trust (68-77)

The comments from the two *Spank!*ers above suggest a delight in immediacy, in inclusion, and in the "free expression" of "strong views." Moreover, the willingness to "learn about global cultures and ideals" seems in line with Tapscott's assertion that "Many N-Geners believe that their global awareness will lead to a population that is more tolerant" (69-70).

Indeed, Tapscott's characteristics for what he calls the "N-Gen Mind," or the favorable qualities seemingly enabled by Internet culture and interaction, suggest both a growing awareness and acceptance of a complex and diverse world:

1. Acceptance of diversity
2. Assertiveness and self-reliance
3. Contrarian
4. Embracing "multiple selves"
5. Spatially oriented

In particular, Tapscott draws our attention to the greater open-mindedness of digital youth to social and cultural differences. As he puts it,

> In the school yard or streets, racism, sexism, discrimination based on socio-economic status, and the cult of beauty have historically been a physical basis for identifying those to be ostracized or brutalized. Does the Net eliminate this, leading to a new era of cooperation among children? . . . It's not as easy to make prejudiced comments about someone online when you cannot physically see them. (111)

Put more pointedly, Tapscott writes that "The *Growing Up Digital Kids* were unanimous . . . that in cyberspace it is harder for one child to isolate another"(113). Tapscott also uses the work of Sherry Turkle to argue that N-Geners embrace "some important new thinking regarding the self away from a view that stresses oneness, or as Turkle critiques, 'a personality for all seasons.' Rather, through the Internet, the N-Gen may be the first generation to accept and effectively manage the many selves that flourish within us" (97). As such, these youths' acceptance of diversity is tuned not just to the diversity of people in the world, but the diversity of selves and often contradictory interests and investments inhabiting each of us.

We would have to spend much time in *Spank!*'s chatrooms and forums to see if such attitudes and characteristics are playing themselves out in accompanying literacies, what the *Spank!*ers above describe as a simultaneous openness to others and a "sharpen[ing of] your arguing skills." Both skills—openness and arguing skills—are often needed to understand and negotiate differences, perhaps even just to convince others not like you that significant differences in experience can manifest in very different worldviews and political investments. In lieu of an analysis of *Spank!*'s chatrooms, and given the comments from users like those quoted above, we can assume that, *Spank!* provides many youth ("over 14,000 new posts a week") a forum for meeting other youth with Internet access and potentially learning about world cultures. As such, *Spank!* most likely offers some youth the kinds of world-expanding appreciation of difference that Tapscott suggests characterizes the "N-Gen mind."

At the same time, however, the site's "News" forums reveal a slightly more limited range of interests and literacies available for exploration. Specifically, the news items seem weighted toward the entertainment world, with features about pop icons and album and film reviews. In fact, the chat forums themselves seem organized around such lines as well. Visitors can choose from the following sample categories: "Angst & Advice," in which you can talk about "body & health," "dating & relationship," and "fashion & style"; "MusicWordsFilm," in which you can discuss recent entertainment media; and a horoscopes section. Granted, I may be looking at *Spank!* with a jaded eye, focused on the presence of corporate interests. But the corporate interest in *Spank!* seems strong, and from many pages, you can click a link such as *"Advertise on Spank! The source for high traffic, vetted, youth market exposure. Click for our Media Kit!"* The site itself is run by a group called "Lopedia, a company focused on collaboration and knowledge management through community" (http://www.spankmag.com/content/about.cfm/cc.2/p.htm). Lopedia's primary work seems to be with helping a range of businesses solve communications problems through a better use of technology. Interestingly, Lopedia is "led by Stephen R. Cassady," one of the apparent co-founders of *Spank!* (http://www.lopedia.com/content/company/leadership.cfm), so Cassady's early work with community-building seems to have led him to profitable work in the technology and business industries.

As such, I think we can say that *Spank!* represents an interesting coexistence between business interests and youth interests. On one hand, the forums, however weighted toward the entertainment world, offer youth with access a chance to communicate with one another. Other forums for submitting original creative work and discussing "general" topics, which could include anything participants want to talk about, are also actively used on the site. Furthermore, some news features directly address political issues and allow youth with access the chance to air views and explore opinions about topics as diverse as homosexuality, cigarette usage, and pollution. On the other hand, however, all news forums are "moderated," so one wonders how "authentic" the voices are of youth represented on the site.

Given this mix of the corporate and youth voices, I'm reminded of MTV's Web presence at http://www.mtv.com. There is perhaps no more widespread or pervasively watched televised representation of youth and youth culture than MTV and its various subsets, such as VH1. The popularity of MTV continues to amaze me, and my students regularly refer to and quote from MTV's videos and programs, both in conversation, in class discussion, and even in their writing. The MTV site seems primarily to exist as a venue for advertising the many programs, ranging from reality shows and cartoons to videos and celebrity documentaries, airing on the various MTV televised formats, as well as to sell MTV-related merchandise. But some sense of "community" is cultivated on the site as well. There are chatrooms and message boards for youth with access to communicate with one another, even if the primary focus of these seems to be to discuss MTV's programs and videos. As such, it's hard not to see these as continued forums for advertising MTV's many wares, and for creating and maintaining a consumer base invested in staying on top of what's "latest" and "hippest."

Again, as with *Spank!*, I hate to sound *too* harsh, especially because MTV is admittedly a commercial venture: The *point* is to sell product. But the point is *also* to sell a sense of culture, even a sense of self, *with* that product. Perhaps the ultimate goal is to sell a culture that can only really be appreciated, enjoyed, and actively participated in by purchasing certain products. Moreover, many youth are deeply invested in what MTV, and *Spank!* for that matter, has to offer. The world of entertainment speaks powerfully to the feelings and interests of many youth.

At the same time, we must acknowledge that both *Spank!* and MTV.com realize the many significant political investments that many youth have. Whereas MTV's "news" features may be dominated by stories of famous rappers and pop icons, the site (and televised programs) has at times hosted forums and features on a number of important social issues, such as homophobia, the killing of Wyoming gay college student Matthew Shephard, voter apathy among American youth, presidential elections, and the spread of sexually transmitted infections and the concurrent clampdown on comprehensive sex education programs in public schools. On the MTV Web site, such discussions can be found in the "FFYR: Protect Yourself" section (http://www.mtv.com/onair/ffyr/protect/), which focuses specifically on sexuality education. Although such sections are wonderful opportunities for youth with Internet access to learn about sexually transmitted infections and to talk with other youth about sensitive and difficult topics, the FFYR section is particularly difficult to find. It's clearly not highlighted on the main pages of MTV's site, and its significance to the MTV project is thus diminished.

What literacies are supported and encouraged here? Certainly, MTV, and *Spank!* to a lesser extent, are fully willing to use the communications technologies enabled by the Web to promote particular products, especially those aimed at youth, such as popular music and entertainment. MTV uses a host of multimedia formats, including downloadable audio and visual clips, to hawk its wares. A pop-culture literacy is privileged, and there is no doubt in my mind that such is both appreciated and enjoyed by many youth. If we return for a moment to Tapscott's lists of characteristics and themes supposedly promoted by such online youth-oriented communities, we see perhaps an interest in acceptance and diversity; MTV's willingness to engage issues of sexuality is one powerful example. But it's harder to see "free expression and strong views," "preoccupation with maturity," and "innovation," much less "sensitivity to corporate interest." Moreover, the embracing of "multiple selves" seems organized more along the axes of multiple entertainment venues and genres—pop rock, rap, videos, movies, and television shows. As such, the representation of youth offered by MTV.com, and to a lesser extent by *Spank!,* is one of pop-culture and entertainment-obsessed youth.

Granted, I think that, for many American youth to communicate with one another, being able to navigate the many forms of musical and entertainment expression, and to be able to talk with other youth about a variety of popular culture icons and artifacts, is an important literacy skill. These are, after all, the images, sound bytes, and stories that surround many youth in the Western world, and many youth regularly borrow from this pool of cultural tidbits to craft their own interactions with, and even understanding of, the world around them. However, as I have explored other youth forums and communities on the Web, I can't help but think that other, more complex literacies are at play in the representations that *digital* youth craft *of themselves in their own e-zines and Web spaces.* What I want to do now, then, is shift our focus from some largely corporate products to some smaller ventures and Web-based forums controlled a bit more directly by groups of digital youth. Doing so will help us explore how other youth use the Web to explore identity, community, and literacy via e-zines. In the process, we'll see some of Tapscott's characteristics and themes played out on these sites, as well as a few other surprising innovations on what it means to be literate on the Web.

GETTING UNDERGROUND: SOME INDEPENDENT E-ZINES

In contrast to the marketing slickness of MTV, Get Underground, at http://www.getunderground.com/, is a community-building e-zine designed to promote cultural and artistic work by youth *not* produced by the entertainment mainstream. According to Get Underground's "about" section,

> Underground culture is the visionary vanguard that propels us towards creative possibilities. It is a fusion of art, music, dance, writing, photography, and poetry in perpetual renaissance. Strip away the marketed gloss of the mainstream and it is there—the substance underneath—simple, yet progressive, drawing bold strokes of creative resistance designed for the emancipation of the human spirit.—Shlomo Sher (Publisher)
>
> Get Underground is a sub-mainstream arts and culture community dedicated to the free expression of the creative global underground. We are a robust professional-level community in design, consistency and content featuring new articles, columnists, art, music, and poetry on a consistent biweekly basis. Our "HotSpots" section is the only continuously updated national database of performance poetry venues in the United States. (http://www.getunderground.com/underground/about index.cfm)

Featuring a range of poets and artists, *Get Underground* solicits contributions with a particular political mission—to "connect sub-mainstream communities across the globe. Our focus is on the impact of the political and social on the personal. We are interested in experimental writings and arts related to personal impressions and experimental visions/techniques as well as political and social investigations." One could argue that MTV has a slightly similar mission, particularly in its FFYR section, as well as in its promotion of hip-hop, which often contentiously raises thorny questions about issues of race and class. But, in another way, the distinction between the literacies supported by MTV and *Get Underground* could not be clearer: *Get Underground* posits and promotes a direct relationship between popular culture/art and politics, between the personal and the political, in a way infrequently seen on MTV.com. For instance, a recently featured article, "Black Men, White Women, Mixed Emotions" (http://www.getunderground.com/underground/features/article.cfm?Article_ID = 1291), uses the arrest of basketball star Kobe Bryant on charges of sexual assault of a White woman to explore lingering cultural prejudices about interracial dating. A link from "alt headlines" takes us to the American Prospect, which features an article entitled "Paranormal Progressivism" on the political usefulness of the Harry Potter phenomenon: "the eerie similarities between Harry Potter's politics and ours. Good thing, as Harry Potter might just be the kind of brain food needed to grow a new generation of little liberals" (see http://www.prospect.org/webfeatures/2003/08/glacel-a-08-22.html). Such interconnectedness between pop culture and politics is seldom found on MTV.com and rarely, if ever, discussed on *Spank!*. One gets the sense that *Get Underground* wants to promote a sense of youth as actively engaged in understanding the ideological and political ramifications of the arts and popular cultures surrounding us, and this suggests a different sense of digital youth's literacy abilities and literacy investments than that gleaned from MTV.

To forward this agenda, there's room for satire, parody, and self-irony, comparable to the kind seen in some of the personal homepages discussed in Chapter 3. For instance, Jen Ambrose's column, "Reactive Personality Disorder," offers an array of innovative writing, including humorous excerpts from her prepubescent diary, cast in a delightfully self-mocking retrospective light; satiric reviews of bands such as The Smiths, mixed with self-ironic comments about the writer's obsession with the band; and scathing, nearly self-lacerating narrations of sexual encounters turned to awkward silences:

> I am no essentialist, shit, I'm all into feminist theory about socially constructed gender roles, but I can not deny that, so often, a thick steel and concrete seemingly impenetrable wall stands between women and men when it comes to communicating. Especially, and most horribly frustrating, when it comes dating! Why is it that a man and a woman will meet up, have no problem getting intimate with each other— whether it be just getting naked and fooling around some, or actually Going All the Way—but then encounter extreme difficulty talking to each other about it later on?

The title of the column itself parodies the categorization of personality into discreet categories. What are you if you're primarily *reacting* to things, as opposed to inhabiting a definable, documentable category? If anything, such a stance suggests the need for the questioning of categories, as opposed to allowing oneself to be classed in a definable "type." We're more than just the marketing genres given us by corporations, and questioning those types, genres, and categories is a key critical literacy practice promoted here.

In support of this, the range of creative expression featured on *Get Underground* is even more diverse than that on MTV. In addition to articles about music, the site offers poetry and graphic art, as well as a list of events and interactive forums for discussing happenings and anything else on visitors' minds. Furthermore, readers are encouraged to respond directly to featured articles, and their comments are posted beneath the article. Such interactivity, as Tapscott might point out, fosters collective argument, not about pop music and entertainment, but about the political dimensions, ramifications, and consequences or the pop art we consume.

A similar, perhaps even harder-edged sensibility, can be found at a Friction Magazine online at http://www.frictionmagazine.com/index.asp. The editors' stated mission is deceptively simple:

> FrictionMagazine.com was started on the principle of free-thinkers creating their own media. Tired of the pretentious and uninspiring content found on the web and in print, creators Allen Harrison and Melissa Hostetler set off to create a home for independent culture and thought on the web.
>
> Hailing from the midwest of all places, FrictionMagazine.com attempts to bring you all that is great and DIY ["do it yourself"] in music, art, literature, culture, politics, and sports. The site is updated three times a month with interviews, articles, reviews, and commentary written by people like you—people who can't stand mainstream culture and the zombies it creates. (http://www.frictionmagazine.com/aboutus.asp)

Such aims set *Friction Magazine* in direct opposition to online ventures such as MTV.com, perhaps even *Spank!*. The emphasis is on "independent" art and what I would call activist literacies—a combined aesthetic and political engagement that seeks to ask critical questions and that is not afraid to use satire to note how "mainstream culture," represented by MTV, for instance, may be more invested in financial gain than asking tough questions about contemporary sociocultural and political issues. Indeed, as with

Get Underground, a decidedly political bent permeates the features and art highlighted and discussed. One link takes you to an off-site article that tantalizingly asks, "Can Better Orgasms Thwart the BushCo [*sic*] Idiocy?"

Actually, perhaps one of the most significant contributions these e-zines make to digital youth literacy is connecting readers to a variety of other material on the Web—material, including writing, art, and music, that pushes the boundaries of the conventional, of the norm, and of the entertainment industry's taste-makers. Although one could argue that this is a fairly closed community, one that only ever links you to sites of interest to people who are already reading a site with this kind of content on it, I think that that view is fairly limited. For instance, the contentiousness in the postings and responses to articles often demonstrates a diversity of views and opinions—not always politely stated. This is very much a digital youth culture in development, still figuring out its sociopolitical investments—and dreams.

Alternative print magazines are catching on to the ability of the Web not only to disseminate views but to invite interaction among young people with access. For instance, *Other*, a new print-based, small press magazine, has a companion Web site at http://www.othermag.org/, which encourages readers to comment about particular articles and post their views. The "about" section describes the kind of readership it seeks to cultivate:

Are you bringing contraband thoughts and experiences into our society?

Please answer yes or no to the following questions:

- Are your political opinions "unacceptable"?
- Do people claim you're a member of a group you don't feel part of?
- Has your body ever clashed with social expectations?
- Have you ever had to censor yourself in a conversation about your life?
- Do you celebrate occasions that have no Hallmark card?
- Do you see something wrong when other people don't?
- Do you laugh during the serious parts of art movies?
- Are you fascinated by things people consider strange or confusing?

If you answered yes to any of the questions above, then you need *Other* magazine and we need you!

Other magazine is for people who defy categories. We print everything from genre-busting fiction, journalism, and essays, to cartoons, artwork, and innovative graphic design. Every four months, our writers bring you challenging ideas, wild tales, rebel futurism, global media, pop criticism, and indie idealism. (http://www.othermag.org/about.php)

You probably noted that a subtext of the questions posed is a critique of mainstream culture, both high and low:

- Do you celebrate occasions that have no Hallmark card?
- Do you laugh during the serious parts of art movies?

What *Other*, both in print and online, seeks to address is perceptions of identity and culture that fall *outside* those more frequently represented in the mainstream media. Topics such as transgender identity or cross-racial identity are often featured in articles and columns. This is the literacy of troubling categories, of thinking outside traditional notions of identity representation. In some ways, these zines and e-zines underscore Tapscott's assertion that the Internet can be used to promote greater tolerance of diversity. I might argue, however, that beyond promoting tolerance, these e-zines embrace diversity to *problematize* a perceived political and social order invested in corporate interests and the creation of a bland "mainstream culture." Tapscott got part of the story right; what he missed is the acutely *political* sensisbility that these youth bring to their work and writing on the Web.

Such political investments are shared by many digital youth who write for Web publication and who create e-zines, but some, even those who use the Web for such purposes, are aware of the limitations of the medium in promoting a politically aware community. Some youth attuned me to *their* awareness of the Web's limitations, and I learned much from talking with the creators of Definition Hip Hop at http://www.definitionhiphop.com, which is the Web site of a group of young Cincinnati hip-hop artists, who primarily use their site to promote their work, to direct visitors to places where their CDs can be purchased, and to offer samples of the group's music. I spoke with Ryan Welch, one of the designers of the site (Ryan's interview is included in its entirety following this chapter), and he shared with me some of the reasons why he and his friends set up their Web site. Primarily, Ryan and his group are interested in using the Web's multimedia components to offer not just text and images of Definition Hip Hop, but sound clips as well. Different short audio clips of the group's music play on each page of the site, offering visitors an auditory glimpse of the group. The site also has interactive components, so that visitors can share opinions, chat with others, and form friendships. According to Ryan, the message boards are particularly important as both sources of information about hip-hop and as ways to connect with others interested in this often politically charged music.

At the same time, however, Ryan, a young African-American man studying English at the University of Cincinnati, and himself a rapper and performing artist, sees potential dangers in relying too heavily on the Web—not just for information but for developing a sense of community around shared interests, goals, or views, Ryan complained that he's seen some youth, particularly Black youth, sitting side by side surfing the Web, when they could—and, in his view, should—be talking to one another:

> I see that a lot up at UC [the University of Cincinnati] in the computer labs. There will be a guy and a girl sitting next to each other and they are on Black Planet. They could be talking to each other instead of doing that.

For Ryan, the Web is useful, but only in so far as it *promotes* community and interchanges between people, as opposed to potentially distracting surfers from real-world interactions. The Web is powerful when it connects people, but the sense I get from Ryan's interview is that he believes that virtual connection constitutes only a *partial* connection with others; real-world interactions are needed—not just to promote hip-hop and the messages it forwards, but to create and sustain community around shared sociopolitical insights and views.

In many ways, the work in *Other*, *Friction Magazine*, and *Get Underground*, and even Definition Hip Hop, provide challenging insights about some youth's mistrust of corporate interests and their desire to carve out spaces so *they* can communicate and explore their own cultural and sociopolitical interests and investments. Dominant motifs in the creation of such spaces include a critique of the "mainstream culture" offered by large corporations, such as MTV, and a willingness to explore the complexities of cultural diversity, and appreciation of difference. Interestingly, both the personal homepages discussed in the previous chapter and the e-zines featured in this chapter seem to move toward collapsing any separation between the personal and the political. For instance, Worse Than Queer and Other online are both studies in resisting dominant identity types and categories—gay/straight, man/woman, White/of color—in order to open up spaces for understanding alternative identity, even hybrid identity constructions. In both cases, the emphasis seems on understanding identity not as a strictly personal issue, but as one influenced by media, politics, and other social forces. Perhaps this is a stretch, but I think that the communities forming to put together the e-zines we've been discussing in this chapter seem to be operating under similar assumptions and orientations as the authors of the personal homepages we've seen, particularly the queer ones. More specifically, by pitching their efforts *against* the mainstream, they are performing their own form of "queerness," in much the same way that queer activists have agitated against a normalizing, increasingly consumerist and consumer-oriented gay identity.

In terms of specific literacy practices, satire and parody are frequently deployed, as they are on the personal homepages we've seen. But on the Web, we also see a willingness to create spaces for readers and visitors to respond, a desire to open up the discussion to whomever wants to—and technologically *can*—participate. As such, the Web helps these youth put into practice one of their core values—the opening up of spaces to encourage writing and literacy practices among youth with access. This openness and nearly pervasive use of the Web to invite interactivity, on the sites we've seen at least, is not just an indicator of one of Tapscott's "N-Gen" characteristics, such as "inclusion" or "acceptance of diversity." It's more often than not a *critique* of the often streamlined and homogenized representation of youth offered by the mainstream media, such as MTV.

Moreover, the sites frequently serve as supports for other literacy practices, such as promoting an awareness of hip-hop, or altering visitors to print-based media. This is not an insignificant dimension of Web writing; early proponents of hypertext and Web literacies only imagined the use of hypertext to link different Webbed documents, not link readers to music, performances, and print-based media *outside* the Web. But, increasingly as is seen here, Web authors are doing just this. We can see these and other uses of the Web, interacting in a fairly sophisticated and complex fashion, in one final example, explored in the next section.

XRAY ON THE "CRACKS" IN PUBLISHING: A CASE STUDY

In many ways, relatively simple and affordable desktop publication has greatly enhanced the ability of a variety of people, especially young adults, to publish and disseminate their work and experiment with a diversity of textual and even visual literacies. *XRay* is a Cincinnati-based "indie" publication that, for the last 2 years, has served as one of the few alternative venues in the Cincinnati metropolitan area for young people interested in writing to publish their work, debate ideas, and offer their particular insights about society, culture, and politics. Recently, the print-based magazine's editors have been exploring a Web presence as a way to facilitate their ideas about what a literate youth populace is, and to forward their own notions of youth literacies.[1]

Indeed, the editorial staff of *XRay* prides itself on being the "alternative" newspaper/magazine in town. The XRay Web site, GoXray.com, offers a succinct description about the project, which began in December 2000: "*XRay* is Cincinnati's progessive magazine. Every month we explore local arts, culture and news with a hip, edgy style" (http://www.goxray.com /index.php?xray = about). In the past few years, *XRay* has published a variety of articles on diverse topics and using a number of genres, and, like the previously discussed e-zines, this more local magazine covers much ground in terms of content, much of which is fairly controversial. For instance, the editors of *XRay* have published articles and columns on environmental issues, sexual relations, and racial tensions. The 30th issue of the magazine, entitled "The Best of *XRay*," includes articles with titles such as "Cincinnati, a queer man's paradise," "Silencing dissent: City council muzzles local media," and an article on interracial dating, "The Phoenix and the resurrection of love: Love transcends race." Columns by environmental activist and former third-party presidential candidate, Ralph Nader, are also frequently included.

Editor and publisher, Steve Novotoni, contrasts *XRay*'s mission with that of other independent publications in the Cincinnati area, particularly *Everybody's News*, now defunct:

> At *Everybody's News*, I think they did a lot of coverage on porn and pot. There were quite a number of stories on Larry Flynt and legalizing drugs and that sort of thing. Those are both worthy topics of stories, but I always thought they focused way too much on that. There is a lot more to being independent and progressive in that.
>
> . . . I guess kind of my beef with that alternative media is that they do things that look like they are for the edification of the readership when in fact often they are not. Our [*XRay*'s] City Guide . . . is something that we created to provide information that was factually accurate and information that was for the edification of the readership, such as how to buy their first home, why they should get involved in the political process, activist resources and things like that. I think that if you kind

---

[1] I spoke at length with the editorial staff of *XRay*, and our edited interview transcript is included at the end of this chapter.

of look at what the other guys are doing and compare it to ours, you'll
see that ours is sort of a their listings *re-formed* into a different shape.

The activist tone is intentional, and, in many ways, much contemporary
independent journalism seems inspired by political activism. For instance,
XRay's staff draws inspiration, moral support, and ideas from the
Independent Media Center (IMC) *(http://www.indymedia.org/)*, which,
according to its Web site, has the following mission:

> The Independent Media Center is a network of collectively run media
> outlets for the creation of radical, accurate, and passionate tellings of
> the truth. We work out of a love and inspiration for people who contin-
> ue to work for a better world, despite corporate media's distortions and
> unwillingness to cover the efforts to free humanity. (http://www.indy-
> media.org/about.php3)

According to Steve, "The IMC is one of 30 outlets internationally that began
with the WTO [World Trade Organization] protest. . . . Essentially it was a
group that used the resources of the Web to go around traditional media
outlets to work together. Originally it was to bring people there to protest
the WTO."

Although the mission seems simple and straightforward, the *process* of
reporting and disseminating "radical, accurate, and passionate tellings of
the truth" is a bit more complicated. During the interview, the editorial staff
questioned and debated the definition of alternative or independent
media. For instance, within the larger alternative press community, debates
rage about whether ventures such as *XRay* should be for profit or strictly
not for profit. Other issues debated are a bit more theoretical, with splits
along ideological lines. Steve offered the following commentary:

> There are two types of folks in the independent media scene that we
> know of. There are those that are activists first and journalists second,
> most of which we met at the UPC [Underground Publishing
> Conference]. Then there are those who are journalists first and activists
> second. We fit into that category I believe.

I asked Stacey, "So what does it mean to be a journalist first?" Her reply is
worth quoting at length:

> I would say that we all come to this project because of our fierce belief
> in the First Amendment. It's our desire to write and our desire to report

on events accurately. I think as an activist your aim is to portray a certain idea and to find things that are around that, which is not to say they don't portray things accurately. At the same time, we never pretend to be *completely objective*, and we don't think that's a good goal to have—to be objective. We try to instruct our writers that you are going to go out there and you are going to have an idea and a pre-conceived notion, so don't be blind to it, but also be completely opened to what you might find. I had a writer who said to me, "Stacey, I went to go and look for this story and it was interviewing people on their religious beliefs in regards to Halloween. They said most people were like, I just want to get candy and have fun." The reporter found something completely different than what she was looking for. So I told her to write what she found. When you go out to see the story, one of the great things about being a journalist is that you do find new things and you almost never find what you think you'll find. I think an activist-*first* mission is, you know, what you seek to find and you look everywhere to find it. Whereas our mission is, we don't know what the hell we are going to find. We know it's going to be scary and exciting and weird and fun. We are going to be open to it.

A bit later in the interview, Stacey summarized her stance by defining journalism as "Truthful but not objective." Two aspects of these comments are worth further exploration. First, the understanding of journalism as truthful but not necessarily objective reminds me of Tapscott's assertion that "N-Geners" are invested in "investigation" but are also "contrarian" and open to an "acceptance of diversity." The willingness to emphasize—and value—perspective, which I think is at the heart of Stacey's comments, seems to capture and combine some of the characteristics that Tapscott highlights as indicative of a younger generation's attitudes—and literacy practices. The reconfiguring of "truth" to include an active, probing awareness of one's own perspective plays itself out in *XRay*'s articles in a number of ways. Specifically, many of the pieces are highly narrative in content, and the narrative often structures the pieces, lending them a "story-like" organization. Furthermore, nothing is stated "objectively"; everything is qualified, and biases, even those of the author, are always pointed out. In general, one could call this the literacy of self-reflection, or a heightened attention to how one's perceptions shape our understanding of the world around us and a willingness to incorporate an acknowledgment of those perceptions into our writing.

Second, concurrent with these editors' activist mission to report on and provide alternative views is a decided focus on "opening up" what "news" is, as well as who gets to report on that news. According to Steve,

"A lot of what *XRay* is, or at least what it started out to be, was a merger of the ideas behind alternative press and community press. . . . We are focused primarily on media for and by regular people. . . . We try to include people who are not necessarily career journalists in the creation of the media." In a way, this follows up on the first aspect previously discussed. Journalists do not need to be trained, objective reporters; rather, reportage can come from "regular people" with an eye toward critically examining the interplay of their perceptions and "reality." And there are many signs that *XRay*'s editors are committed to their goal to expand our notions of what journalism is and who journalists are. In the fall of 2002, *XRay* hosted a "DIY," or "Do It Yourself," media workshop for local Cincinnatians who were interested in creating their own independent publications, with additional conferences scheduled annually for subsequent years.

Of course, "doing it yourself" is not with its own complications—for producers *and consumers* of information. Thomas S. Valovic, writing in *Digital Mythologies: The Hidden Complexities of the Internet*, suggests that the denizens of "digital culture justify their disdain for traditional media by declaring that they are owned and controlled by large media empires and are based on the outdated one-to-many broadcast model instead of the Internet's many-to-many model. . . . In digital culture, information from the broadcast media is generally held suspect because it is filtered by editors and other information managers rather than pure, undiluted, and aboriginal, as it is on the Internet" (160). I think we can see some of this disdain at play in the comments of the *XRay* editors, who seem to figure mass media as either elitist or in the service of potentially un-democratic, self-appointed organizations, such as the WTO. At the same time, Valovic offers a caution against putting too much faith in Internet-based news: "That information on the Net is often spurious, disingenuously framed, deliberately falsified, or spin-doctored does not seem to be taken into account in this mode of thinking" (160). Valovic's point is well-taken, but I have a hard time thinking that it applies directly to the reporting and editorial processes of *XRay*. Certainly, anyone with technical know-how can post up a Web page with practically any kind of content imaginable, so the presence of "falsified" or "spin-doctored" information should be assumed and taken into consideration when reading anything on the Web. But *XRay*'s editorial policies, particularly the editors' meta-conscious considerations of objectivity and truth, reveal that *these* youth writers are very much aware of how information can be ideologically constructed, and they have made such an awareness a part of their editorial and compositional processes. In many ways, I think such a policy is in direct response *to* the glut of information, often uncritically disseminated and uncritically consumed, on the Web. Put another way, if these editors and writers are going to contribute to composing and publishing the news on the Web, then they will do so in full acknowledgment and interrogation of their biases, sociopolitical investments, and agendas. Indeed, awareness and acknowledgment of such is part of their understanding of what constitutes "information" and "news."

Another significant part of the process of producing such a publication is the mechanics of publication itself, such as the technology necessary to produce the magazine. The staff, particularly Steve, is well aware that they are able to accomplish their goals and produce *XRay* because of contemporary desktop publishing technologies. Steve spoke about this at length:

> If you look at what we are doing now with this publication on a shoestring budget, it's something that really was not possible to do 20 or 30 years ago. *The Independent Eye* is testimony to that, coming out in the 60s, but it was much more difficult and much more costly than it is now. Layouts and design and computer equipment make it so that anyone with proper training and study, even if it's independent training that some of us have had, can put together a publication that looks just as good as any other thing that's out there on the street.

Steve also made an immediate connection between what the staff of *XRay* is able to do *now*, and what future writers, journalists, and media activists will be able to do (and, in fact, have begun doing) with the Internet and the Web:

> I think, right now, Internet radio and Internet video are really in their infancy, but there is going to come a time where those tools will be just as cheap and just as easy to use and just as effective as the tools in desktop publishing, so that any person can create a film or a newscast or whatever that looks just as good as anything produced by CBS, CNN or whoever. As long as there is a way to get that to the people, there is a chance for real cultural evolution with this sort of democratization of tools.

Steve offers us a hefty, heady claim—"cultural evolution," perhaps revolution, coming with the "democratization of tools" for media and information shaping and dissemination. Given such hopes for the impact of technology on the use and spread of information, I asked the *XRay* how they were using *their* Web site—and if it was living up to their expectations. We turn to this issue now.

XRAY ON THE WEB: BENDING TIME AND SPACE AS A TOOL FOR DEMOCRATIZATION?

Given the editorial and publishing commitment of the *XRay* staff to an open, alternative, even activist journalism, I asked the group what their plans were for the companion Web site, at http://www.goxray.com/. Their answers build on and extend many of the comments about e-zines just made, so we will spend a little bit of time here unpacking and discussing them, particularly as they offer us insights into how some digital youth view the Web as a literacy tool.

The Potential—and Peril—of Archiving. At a rudimentary level, the staff, especially Stacey, who was largely responsible for the site, viewed their Web presence as a "support" for the print publication, and as a way to disseminate a wider variety of information, such as that from news wire agencies, that couldn't make it into print publication due to space limitations. Stacey explains the situation as follows:

> What we do with the Web site is almost entirely different from the [print] publication. We want it to be in support of the publication, but also most of the content we use comes from that Dry Erase wire [a news wire service for independent publications]. We use the Web site. That's a way we can get new content and also helps the Dry Erase people get their names out there in other cities.

The Web site can also serve powerfully as an archival tool—again, offering access to material printed in past volumes or to material that, for whatever reason, doesn't make it into print:

> We are going to go back as far as the publication goes back. We have every story that's ever been written for *XRay* on a disk somewhere. Theoretically, we will be able to bend time and space. We can put them on there with an automated program. I hope to be able to but as it is right now it takes me 5 to 10 minutes to put up any one story. If you also added coding and editing—because when an error goes to print it

doesn't have to go to the Web. It's a way to cover our butts in some sorts. It's also inevitable [that] there are stories that don't make it into the print publication because of finite dollars and space. We don't have that on the Web. If someone writes us a 10,000-page letter to the editor, well, we can put that on the Web site and we wouldn't take up the space in the magazine.

On the surface, such comments don't hold out much promise for the Web site as a transformative tool, one that will itself alter how people communicate with one another, shape information, and create new, dynamic literacy practices. Storage of information is necessary, and the Web provides a relatively cheap way to house material. But this seems a very utilitarian use of the Web—until an issue of *content* comes along.

Knowing the tensions surrounding race relations in Cincinnati, the staff of *XRay* has sought ways to address productively in its pages issues of race, racism, and prejudice. When the magazine received a submission entitled "Welcome to Niggertown," the staff faced a quandary: Would they publish a piece, written by a White man using an "exaggerated affectation of ebonics encouraging Black people to tear up the suburbs rather than their own neighborhoods when they riot"? (http://www.goxray.com/27/mediacrit.html). The piece was certainly controversial, on a number of fronts. Although it seemed intended to support awareness of the plight of many urban African Americans in Cincinnati, its *style* was provocative and raised a number of questions for the editorial staff. Would readers appreciate its message? Would they find the author's use of ebonics creative and useful in making a critical point? Or would they be offended by the use of terms such as "nigger," or by the affectation of ebonics itself, potentially viewed as yet another White man performing in Black face? The tensions surrounding such questions was heightened given recent (2001) race riots in the city.

Steve decided to have his staff vote on whether to publish the piece, and it was rejected. One contributing writer resigned over the issue, and many letters were written to *XRay* in protest of this perceived "censorship." Steve, in a column about the staff's struggle, entitled "More Than Just Black and White: Behind the Scenes of *XRay*'s Struggle to be Progressive," notes that the piece was rejected democratically, after serious discussion and consideration. One can tell, though, that the decision was not easy:

Looking back, I question the decision of *XRay* as a whole not to feature the essay. The writing was incendiary, discomforting and at times shocking. The incitements to violence and the vast criticisms of Cincinnati's Black population make the piece difficult to justify.

Nonetheless, [the author] posed some new, outrageous ideas that
deserve public attention and—yes—criticism. (http://www.goxray.
com/27/mediacrit.html)

Given this desire to further the debate about race relations in Cincinnati,
XRay's editors published the piece online, including with it letters to the
editor about the refusal to publish the piece in print, one contributing
writer's resignation following the issue, and Steve's own reflections on the
process of refusing to publish the piece and then the decision to post it on
the Web.

This strikes me a wonderful, if pained instance of how the Web can
help a print publication "follow up" on a story or continue a significant
debate, and it pushes our understanding of the Web as a medium of "support" for other media sources. Specifically, the editors were willing to use
Web publication to continue the debate—and even expand it to include
provocative discussions of censorship and the difficulties of using democratic processes to determine what goes into print and what does not. Such
discussions could not have been held efficiently in print, and the editors
relied on GoXRay.com to help them further their own, and their readers',
interrogation of this important issue.

From Information Storage to Community-Building. As we continued our conversation, the staff revealed their sense of some of the other possibilities of
the Web—possibilities that the staff is just now exploring. For instance, in
listening to Steve talk about his plans and hopes for the Web site, I could
distinctly hear his desire for GoXRay.com to play a role in community-
building:

> I think what we've done on the projects is that we kind of go through
> phases where an aspect of the project moves from one level to anoth-
> er. I mean the magazine that you have now is much different than the
> print magazine twelve months ago in terms of the capabilities and the
> content. Even the quality of writing has improved. The Web site also
> contains more and newer content now than it did in the past. It used
> to be just the work that was in the issue mirrored on the site. I know
> some things that I'd like to see on the Web is the "City Guide" that we
> just produced. I want the Website to be a continuing, growing resource
> for people in the city, to link to everything that is Cincinnati. I'd like us
> to be a central hub for activist groups and a central source for finding
> information on other Cincinnati media.

Steve also has a particular kind of community building in mind; he would like to create a networked community for writers, journalists, and media activists, and he sees the Web as playing a crucial role in the development of that community:

> We list the publications, phone numbers, addresses, who is in charge there [at other alternative or independent publications], a description of the publications, where you can get them, how much, Web links and all these sorts of things. Also what we think of it. I'd like that to continue to grow, which is something that we are working on right now. Also I'd like fresh and new content. I think the ultimate would be a daily. That's not something we have the capabilities to do right now, but perhaps with the automated program that Stacey is working on we could do more straight-up reporting than we have done in the past.

Clearly, one of the principle aims here is to expand readership by offering additional content, both in print and on the Web. But, like other e-zines or print magazines with a Web presence, such as *Other*, the goal is also to invite a broader range of participants in the construction and reportage of "news," of the media:

Stacey: One of the things I want to do at *XRay* is make us as *XRay* approachable and accessible, which is why our office is open for people like you to come in and use our resources. We wanted the Web site to be the same thing. We want it to be interactive. We want it to foster the base between users and us. In kind of an academic sense, our mission is to destroy the boundaries that separate editors, writers and readers. I don't know if you've read the latest issue but in my column, I argue that the readers of *XRay* are journalists. Simply by picking up an *XRay* magazine, reading it and thinking about it and maybe changing your mind or acting on what you read, I feel that makes you a journalist. That's what I kind of wanted to do with the Web site—to reach a broader audience, get the points of views of our artists and writers out there, and get Quincy's artwork out there so people can see it. Quincy has a beautiful Web site by the way.

Steve: It got tore up though.

Stacey: I think that what we want to do with the Web site is
              create an online community where we are destroy-
              ing that structure of, well, I'm the editor and I tell
              you what to write. I am the writer and I tell you what
              to read. You know? It's sort of the hierarchy of the
              traditional media. I feel like having the web site
              working with us goes right along with our mission.

In many ways, the understanding of the reportage of the "news" itself *as* a
community effort is a striking literacy value—and practice. The staff seem
to believe that the impact of their writing on changing a reader's views—
on having that reader rewrite or revise his or her understanding of the
world—is a profound engagement with literacy. But also, the concomitant
erasure of difference between writers and readers signals a potential shift
in these youths' understanding of literacy. Writing is not viewed as a soli-
tary act, but as an effort actively engaged with a readership and its concerns, ideas, and potential feedback. In this context, the Web is a powerful
medium for not only disseminating writers' views, but for helping create
the community that will both receive and respond to them. Furthermore,
with the Web, readers *can* potentially and generally easily contribute,
becoming writers themselves.

Style As a Literacy Value.   Part of expanding *XRay*'s editors desire to expand
coverage of events involves enhancing their ability to provide immediate
reportage. Our discussion of the value of immediacy revealed an aspect of
literacy practice worth exploring in greater depth—the value of style. My
thoughts have been prompted by Steve's commentary on *XRay*'s reportage
about the 2001 race riots in Cincinnati:

> When we had the [race] riots in 2001, I remember being shocked at
> the poverty of information there was. There was a riot going on down-
> town, and you could turn on all three or four television stations and not
> see what was going on. I couldn't believe no one was having a full-time
> report on the site or on television or radio. I remember wanting a Web
> site at that time. We existed at that time but we didn't have these capa-
> bilities yet to do this. I wanted to have a Web site that would have con-
> tinual updates.

In a way, Steve's desire to have had "on the spot" Web coverage of
Cincinnati's 2001 race riots reminds me of CNN's coverage of "breaking
events," with live reportage. On one hand, the goal is immediacy, provid-

ing up-to-date information. On the other hand, the goal might also be to mimic some of the perceived "slickness" of such coverage.

Steve spoke further about the value of such "slickness" in discussing *XRay*'s coverage of a visit President George W. Bush made to Cincinnati to rally support for the war in Iraq:

> In some ways it's changed a lot of things and in some ways it's changed very little. The world is still run by individuals and groups that operate on base motives instead of altruistic ones. I still believe that a world where people operate off of, well, where the majority of people operate off of altruistic motives *first* is possible and attainable. I think what has to be done is you have to change people's mythology in a way. There is a cultural set of ideas that we all walk around with and believe. People buy into them. When we went down to that protest and I came back the next day to work and one of my co-workers said to me, "I can't believe you were down there protesting President Bush!" it was an affront to his idea about what the myth of patriotism is, that it's blind allegiance. That's one that has been pushed. It's like when you tell a story enough times. The one that's told enough is the one that sinks in. One of the reasons we tried to package things in a very slick manner is because we are hoping that people will pay attention and we can change the story. We are also merging art with politics, with music and culture and religion and sexuality and all these things. We do that because it's interesting to us and we are interested in all of those areas, but also because putting in things that are candy in with the medicine and mixing that all up is a way to make a progressive culture accessible to many different people. If things are too "academic," they are distasteful to many people.

The connections among "changing the story," altering the "myths" that people live by, and the need to present material in an eye-catching, slick fashion is fascinating. Steve's comments also remind me of what Stuart Hall has said about the "colonization" of culture by the media:

> As social groups and classes live, if not in their productive then in their "social" relations, increasingly fragmented and sectionally differentiated lives, the mass media are more and more responsible (a) for providing the basis on which groups and classes construct an image of the lives, meanings, practices and values of *other* groups and classes; (b) for providing the images, representations and ideas around which the social totality composed of all these separate and fragmented pieces can be coherently grasped. (qtd. in Hebdige, "Posing," 448–9)

XRay's editors want a bit more control over how they, as youth, are represented to the larger society via the mass media, and they believe that contemporary communications technologies, such as desktop publishing and the Web, offer them an opportunity to participate a bit more actively in how "groups and classes construct an image of the lives, meanings, practices and values of other groups and classes."

But more than this, the editors and writers seem willing to use the *style* of the mass media to disseminate their stories. Following Hall, Dick Hebdige suggests that

> It is primarily through the press, television, film etc. that experience is organized, interpreted and made to *cohere in contradiction* as it were. It should hardly surprise us then, to discover that much of what finds itself encoded in subculture has already been subjected to a certain amount of prior handling by the media. ("Posing," 448)

To my mind, what has been handled "by the media" that is finding itself "encoded" in the subculture of youth that *XRay* represents is the very slick

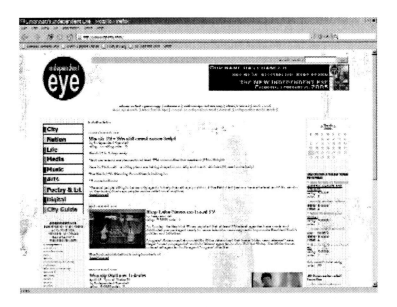

Screen Shot of http://www.goxray.com/

style of news reportage and event coverage of the major news media, such as CNN. The editors of *XRay* know what they're "up against." Hi-tech televised media and snazzy Web sites (such as MTV.com) are going to "hook" attention quickly. To compete, and to introduce their views and provide alternative readings on society, culture, and politics, ventures such as *XRay* need some of the same snazziness. As such, it seems as though the editors of GoXRay.com have attempted to design their site in a visually appealing fashion, and there is some modeling of format, however small, based on major new agency Web sites, such as CNN. You'll notice, for instance, the sparing but careful use of visuals, clear text, columns, and interactive features, such as a search function and a poll (e.g., "What's the worst thing about Cincinnati?"). All are common to a site such as CNN.com.

Such formatting prompt visitors to "read" this site as a news source, and I think this attention to style is in itself is a literacy value, a key component of how these youth are shaping their literacies—and their understanding of literacy—to participate in an increasingly media-saturated environment. The key difference in their deployment of such media styles, however, is their desire to vary the kind and number of stories offered about the world around us; by actively inviting reader and visitor participation, by attempting to shift our understanding of how "news" is reported, and by questioning the supposed "objectivity" of that "news," *XRay*'s editors use the Web less to disseminate information (a la CNN.com) than to create a community of writers and other artists who will contribute to that community's understanding of itself and the world.

Finally, I asked the staff of *XRay* to comment on their ultimate goals, and they responded succinctly and poignantly:

> We want to live in a world that is progressive. We want to live in a world where ideas are progressive and where there is no culture mythology that holds people to a certain identity.

That they are willing to use a variety of literacy practices, and that they seek to fulfill their goals primarily via text, is both heartening to those who value writing in general and a useful reminder—and counter—to those who think that many youth are increasingly illiterate and disengaged from a variety of important literacy practices. That some e-savvy youth, such as *XRay*'s writers and editors, focus on technology as a key component of their literacy practices is a sign of how technology can aid and abet the loftiest of goals for promoting critical thinking and critical engagement with the world around us.

Still, I would be remiss if I didn't comment on—and allow my interviewees to comment on—some of the pitfalls of relying on technology to promote literacy and alternative understandings of the world. Here is a telling
exchange:

> Stacey: *XRay* does that too. *XRay* finds the cracks, seeps in,
> occupies the biggest space, and tries to speak to the
> biggest audience about the most important issues
> regardless of who is out there trying to plug up the
> many holes in their own societal system.
>
> Steve: I was just going to say, and I don't know if we've
> already made this point but it's not only the
> Internet, it's the actual hardware and the actual abil-
> ity to use a computer in your home that's a revolu-
> tion. It's not just the Internet but all of the technolo-
> gies put together is really what's creating, I think,
> the revolution as far as putting media in the hands
> of the people.
>
> Stacey: And a new generation that is more and more digital-
> ly savvy.
>
> Steve: Although, one of the things that I think should be
> said about this technology is that it still is primarily
> limited to, you know, a middle-class and wealthier
> White folks.

Certainly race and class are significant "cracks" in the digital divide, and I
am increasingly convinced that only time and the liberal expenditure of
resources earmarked for bringing technology to a wider spectrum of our
population can effectively address this issue.

CONCLUSIONS

As I conclude this chapter, I highlight four literacy practices that I think are
salient in our consideration of some youth's use of e-zines. Certainly, many
of Tapscott's qualities and characteristics of the "Net generation" mind are
represented in the e-zines and online companion sites discussed here. In
particular, an openness to diversity, a willingness to be contrarian, and a
desire to be inclusive seem to shape the literacy values and practices of

nearly all of these writers and editors. But so are some others, particularly some intriguing literacy skills that push us beyond some of Tapscott's
generalities.

First, I think that the Stacey's comments about *XRay*'s attempt to
redefine the relationship between truth and objectivity is probably a significant goal of most of the e-zine writers and editors discussed here. At
the very least, most of these e-zines do *not* assume that the mass media
report "objectively" on "reality." In fact, the rhetoric deployed in the
majority of these e-zines' "about" sections on their Web sites reveals that
they are both skeptical and critical of (a) the ability of the mass media to
offer "truth" about the world around us and (b) the ability of *any* reportage
to "objectively" communicate. Instead, these writers suggest that literate
practice *requires* us to be aware of our perceptions, biases, and ideological
investments.

Second, and concomitant with this view, is a desire to expand the number of those participating in reporting on, interpreting, and constructing
our sense of the "news." Attempting to breakdown the traditional (and hierarchical) division between writer and reader signals a desire to open up a
space for greater interactivity in constructing views and representations of
the world, particularly of some *digital youth's* view of the world. The interactive features of Web technologies are often put to use to further this end.
Others have noted similar trends, especially vis-à-vis the increasing use of
the Web to "report" news. In "Journalism Online: Exploring the Impact of
New Media on News and Society," John V. Pavlik and Steven S. Ross argue
the following:

> For the most part, news organizations gathered information from news
> sources . . . then packaged that information in a manner palatable to
> the public, who consumed the news in linear format (i.e., as stories told
> sequentially with a beginning, middle and end), as delivered via a vari-
> ety of traditional analog media. . . . By empowering the public and
> redefining the reporter-source relationship in an age of direct public
> access to primary news sources, the Internet and WWW have chal-
> lenged journalistic organizations to reinvent their role in this relation-
> ship. (131)

This is exactly what a magazine such as *XRay*, both in print and online, is
doing, and the editors envision the Web as vital to assisting with their rede-
finition of journalism.

Third, we've seen a literacy value, what we might call the literacy of
slickness, that Tapscott does *not* address as an "impact" of technology on

e-savvy youths' attitudes and literacies. Throughout the e-zines under discussion is an appreciation of corporate smarts and media savvy, and a willingness to use such savvy to claim a share of Web readership. Carla Freccero, in her study of popular culture, noted similar trends in some youths' ability to understand culture as filtered through the mass media, and she recommends using such skills pedagogically to teach other young adult students about critical thinking and to help them value their own developing skills as critical consumers of mass-mediated culture:

> What students have learned outside the classroom are the techniques of acquiring information from media, the technological processes that inform their production, and how to go about obtaining access to the technologies themselves—how to "consume" them. This is what advanced capitalist culture successfully teaches. What the cultural studies approach to popular culture in the classroom can provide, then, is an approach to technological cultures that seeks to understand the social meanings of the representations produced by those cultures: a way, in other words, to analyze these products. The result will be not only an "informed consumer" but someone who may be able to intervene to produce meanings in the language of the medium itself and intervene politically when those representations are used to support particular agendas. (4)

My analysis of the e-zines in this chapter suggests that some digital youth are already "interven[ing] to produce meanings in the language of the medium itself," and they are doing so to re-represent themselves as youth concerned about significant issues in society, culture, and politics. The increasing ease of creating such compositions via the Web is a significant factor, I believe, in helping these youth create images and texts that can compete with the slick media images of CNN or MTV.

Fourth, along with this desire and ability to produce such e-zines comes a realization that they are not ends in and of themselves. In fact, if we speak in terms specifically of *Web* literacies, one of the striking things I've noted is that many of these youth think of the Web as a "support" for other literacy projects. This is particularly true for *XRay*, Definition Hip Hop, and even *Friction Magazine*, which has been developing a print publication. In "Community and Identity in the Electronic Village," Derek Foster (1996) points out that "Any sense of community found on the Internet must, I contend, necessarily be virtual, but may not be sufficiently communal" (24). Indeed, the Web authors I interviewed understand the Web as a support or companion projects for pre-existing communities or communities in the initial stages of coalescing. The Web is *not* a community in and of itself, and we'll encounter additional examples of this in the following chapters.

Finally, I think there is in the e-zines examined here an unstated critique of global culture and global community. Although none of the writers address this directly, a *lack* of discussion of or perception of their projects as "global" is telling. Granted, the editors of *XRay* pride themselves on having readers overseas and in even receiving contributions from "foreign correspondents." But, for the most part, all of the Web e-zines discussed here seem focused on *local* projects and issues and on fostering local literacies and literate interventions. In a way, this seems to fly in the face of some of the more "utopian" dreams for the Internet—such as its vaunted ability to foster global networking, communication, and eventual understanding, ushering in newfound tolerance for and acceptance of diversity.

Scholars and critics of the Internet have debated such issues far and wide, and I only bring up a couple of related points here to suggest that we should hardly be surprised that the *World* Wide Web is probably frequently used less to support global literacies than it is to foster *local* literacy practices. In their article, "The Projection of Geographical Communities into Cyberspace," Duncan Sanderson and Andree Fortin argue the following:

> A public communication space in which a society debates its orientations and concerns has always existed. With the Internet, a new form of public space has appeared, one which is at the same time interpersonal (for example, e-mail) and mediated (Web pages). It is a communication space which allows new relationships between self, physical space, and others. (190)

The question is, of course, how? What kinds of "new relationships" are allowed and enabled? Sanderson and Fortin contend that "one of the conditions for these relationships is a common culture"—a notion giving rise to "two contradictory tendencies":

> On the one hand, sociability seems to be reduced to the metaphorical, in the sense that people have no shared relationship to actual geographical place. Thus some identities are not based on place, but rather on personal and cultural characteristics, such as sex, age, tastes and lifestyles. . . . On the other hand, this medium can also be used to reinforce identities based on geographical space, and then it becomes a medium in which local identities can be projected and expressed, heard and recognized. (190)

What we are seeing with e-zines, I think, is the creation of affinity groups, such as like-minded youth getting together to publish e-zines on topics of import to them, and a preoccupation with how such publications can impact the geographic localities in which they originate. This seems particularly true for ventures like *XRay* and Definition Hip Hop, both of which are (justifiably) focused on issues relevant to Cincinnati, their home community.

Other scholars have noted similar movements from the global to local in how users and composers understand and figure the Web and the Internet. In "The World is Quite Enough: Young Danes, Media and Identity in the Crossing between the Global and the Local," Gitte Staid of the University of Copenhagen analyzes reactions of young Danes and their experiences on the Internet with an eye toward understanding how their sense of themselves as global citizens might be developing vis-à-vis their access to technology. Her discussion is enlightening, and she concludes, in part:

> In spite of the intriguing prospects of travels in virtual reality and in spite of the extensive use of the Internet as a medium of cultural and social exchange, my informants did not "buy" the arguments and slogans. Some would not reject the idea that in a distant future . . . we would all primarily travel and socialise in cyberspace but the thought was not appealing. Many argued from their experience of meetings with foreign cultures, people, locations, climates, and added their thoughts on the need for sense impressions on location in order to fully comprehend and experience cultural diversities. (144)

Such statements query our understanding of the global reach of the Web and its ability to reconfigure our understanding of literacy along global lines. Marshall McLuhan, writing in *The Medium is the Message*, suggested that the increasing quickness of media, providing an immediacy of information, would foster the creation of the "global village." Barry Vacker summarizes McLuhan's views as follows: "McLuhan observed that the electronic mass media were collapsing the space-time barriers of traditional human communication, thus creating a 'global village' in which events are known and/or experienced simultaneously around the world" (212). For Vacker, and for others, however, the actuality of Web usage—both in consumption and in production, I might add—seems less a "global village" and more a "world bazaar":

> Rather than globally unifying persons, the hypermedia make possible a greater range of cultural diversity and individual expressions as cul-

tures chaotically cooperate, coexist, compete, and combine into new forms. The computer and the World Wide Web represent a new style of media that is transforming the substance of culture; the result is a chaotic landscape populated by industrial global villagers amidst an emergent postindustrial "world bazaar." (236)

Thus, *XRay, Friction Magazine,* and Definition Hip Hop, no matter how appealing their content is to a variety of readers, even worldwide visitors to their sites, remain predominantly products of—and concerned with—literacy issues in Ohio, their home state. And this is not a criticism. It is just an awareness of how literacy practices still survive, thrive, and develop in local contexts, even when enabled by networking technologies such as the Web.

In the following chapter, I continue my discussion of Web-based communal literacies by focusing attention on how another group of youth—queer youth with Internet access, or *queer digital youth*—are using the Web to experiment with community-building sites. Examining these will provide further examples of how some other youth deploy a variety of literacy practices to help us understand both themselves and the uses to which they are putting the new communications technologies.

INTERVIEW WITH THE EDITORIAL STAFF OF XRAY

XRay is a Cincinnati-based alternative press publication with a companion Web site, GoXRay.com, that tackles a variety of cultural, social, and political issues. The publication is run by a group of young adults, most in their early to mid-20s, who challenge the notions of what both print and Web-based news reportage can—and should—be. I discussed these and other issues with several members of the *XRay* staff, including Steve Novotoni (editor and publisher) and his editorial assistants, Stacey Recht, Becky Carter, and Quincy Robinson.

Jonathan: How would you classify your work? Is *XRay* a magazine or newspaper?

Steve: Magazine.

Jonathan: Okay. Magazine. The local magazine/weekly that I was familiar with, and it was right before you started coming out with *XRay,* was *Everybody's News.*

Steve: You probably caught *Everybody's News* actually in decline.

Jonathan: Yes.

Steve: That was actually where I got my start in 1995. *Everybody's* probably peaked around '93 through '96 in terms of the quality of content and distribution. I think it went out of business in 1999 due to financial problems. I think that at the time and since then there are a number of people who had been associated with that project and some who had not and blamed their demise on *City Beat* [another local news-magazine/ weekly, published in Cincinnati]. But I really think this town is big enough to support more than just one "alternative" publication.

Jonathan: Sure.

Steve: Some ideas for *XRay* came out of that and my work for *Everybody's News.* I also worked at the *Clermont Sun* newspaper in Batavia for 2 years as a reporter. A lot of what *XRay* is, or at least what it started out to be, was a merger of the ideas behind alternative press and community press.

Jonathan: Now, in terms of *Everybody's News*—would you characterize that as an alternative publication?

Steve: Yes.

Jonathan: As opposed to *City Beat*? Most large cites have something like *City Beat*, which strikes me as kind of the mouthpiece of official culture in the city.

Steve: Right.

Jonathan: *Everybody's News* and, I think, now *XRay* occupies that space of alternative *beyond* the official culture or sanctioned culture. What do you think?

Steve: Right. I agree with you. I think that a lot of people have made comparisons between us and *Everybody's News.* I've been a little bit careful about that in how I respond publicly. *Everybody's News* was known as the area's first alternative news weekly. It really wasn't. There was a publication called the *Independent Eye* and it was produced in the late 1960s. It was produced for 12 years from the late '60s to the mid '70s. That's actually where the idea for our photo spread comes from. That was more independent than *Everybody's News* was. There was also the *Queen's Jester*—that was another one locally. There were a few others like *The Ink Wire*. They got into a legal dispute with the *Enquirer* [one of Cincinnati's two major daily newspapers] over that.

Jonathan: Interesting.

Steve: It was meant to do that. They would call people up and say they were with *The Ink Wire*. I've actually seen some copies of the *Independent Eye* and I've been able to read some of those at the Bowling Green Pop Culture Library. *Everybody's* was something that was more "indie" than *City Beat* is now. We are definitely more indie in terms of the way we do things. We are focused primarily on media for and by regular people.

Jonathan: Okay.

Steve: We try to include people who are not necessarily career journalists in the creation of the media. Some people are schooled journalists, as Stacey is. Some are journalists who just came to be so just through circumstance, just like I am. I kind of just happened in to it because there was a rock concert I wanted to sneak in to. A buddy of mine suggested I pretend to be a reporter to get in. I called *Everybody's News* and they told me they would go ahead and get me in because they thought it was kind of cool that I was going to sneak into a concert. I did my first story like that and that's how I got into journalism, through that avenue. Quincy is studying at the art academy, as is Nathan, who is also on our team. I guess I'm kind of answering the question in a round about way.

Jonathan: No. That's okay.

Steve: At *Everybody's News*, I think they did a lot of coverage on porn and pot. There were quite a number of stories on Larry Flynt and legalizing drugs and that sort of thing. Those are both worthy topics of stories, but I always thought they focused way too much on that. There is a lot more to being independent and progressive than that.

           Many of the ideas that were at *Everybody's News* went on to *City Beat*. The reason that *City Beat* has been tremendously successful is because they market themselves very very well. They do a lot of things like their annual manual . . .

Jonathan: "The Best of Cincinnati" manual . . .

Steve: Yes. The "Best of" issue. The shopping guide and the health and wellness directory. I guess kind of my beef with that alternative media is that they do things that look like they are for the edification of the readership when in fact often they are not. Our [*XRay*'s] City Guide that is out now is something that we created to provide information that was factually accurate and information that was for the edification of the readership, such as how to buy their first home, why they should get involved in the political process, activist resources and things like that. I think that if you kind of look at what the other guys are doing and compare it to ours, you'll see that ours is sort of their listings *re-formed* into a different shape.

Jonathan: What's striking is the number of consumer listings and ads in *City Beat* . . .

Steve: It's very consumer focused because they are the number two publication in town. They outdo the *Post* [the other daily Cincinnati newspaper] in circulation and I believe in ad rates as well as in revenue. They are also an AAN affiliate. The Association of Alternative Newsweeklies has a formula. It's not dissimilar from the way we work with the IPA, The Independent Press Association. The IPA is dedicated to keeping member publications independent. It's also dedicated to promoting diversity. It works for now and they may change one day. But you know how that goes. It seems that all things move from being, you know, cutting edge and independent to being mainstream conservative if they last long enough.

Jonathan: Right.

Steve: I don't know if that has to be true. We'd like to prove that it is not.

Jonathan: I was going to ask you about that because you identify yourself and your publication as "indie." Tell me about that. What does "indie" mean?

Steve: It depends on which conferences you go to I guess. It depends on who you are listening to. These are something that I was going to give you if you'd like to take them . . .

Jonathan: [Taking a bundle of papers] Okay.

Steve: That's *Indypendent*. [Hands Jonathan a newspaper.] It's from New York city and it's produced by the Independent Media Center there [http://www.indymedia.org/]. The IMC is one of 30 outlets internationally that began with the WTO [World Trade Organization] protest.

Jonathan: Okay.

Steve: Seattle in 1999, I believe, or maybe it was 2000.

Jonathan: 2000, I think.

Steve: Maybe 2000. Essentially it was a group that used the resources of the Web to go around traditional media outlets to work together. Originally, it was to bring people there to protest the WTO.

Jonathan: Right.

Steve: That was done successfully and they established their own media network system. The *Indypendent* is what I know to be the flagship of their publications that they put out. Most all of them are online.

Jonathan: Right.

Steve: There are many people in the independent media scene that I'm aware of that believe that you have to be non-profit in order to be legitimate or even sustainable. To give you a for instance—like when we, Quincy, Stacey, Becky and our friend Amanda went to the UPC, which is the Underground Publishing Conference, in Bowling Green [OH]. It's now known as The Allied Media Conference.

Jonathan: Okay.

Steve: I think they've changed the name a little bit so they don't scare certain people off from the independent media scene.

Jonathan: Okay.

Steve: They can make it more inclusive. This conference includes everybody, including people just making photocopy zines. *Clamor Magazine* held the conference, which is an arts-culture-news magazine out of Bowling Green and *XRay* was there, too. There were about 500 to 700 people there.

Jonathan: Wow.

Steve: They had a structure of workshops and discussions. One of them was on fundraising and grant writing. In this meeting they were talking about money and how you raise money. The woman who was holding the discussion asked everyone in the room, "What do you think when you hear the word money?" I said it's a tool and that was as positive as it got. There was a lot of talk of pain, suffering, bills, the government, and the evils of capitalism.

At the conference, we also met with a discussion group about how to produce a radical weekly or something like that. In the midst of the discussion, a group called Dry Erase Board [now at http://www.allied-press.org/] was formed by the Asheville Global Report, which was holding the meeting. They are at www.agrnews.org. There were probably about maybe five to seven different publications. There are about 30 groups now involved with the Dry Erase Board. The Dry Erase Board is a news wire service that was created at this conference kind of quickly. When were discussing this there at the UPC, I said I think we should talk a little bit about compensation. We should talk about how we are going to—well I know none of us are making any money right now, but when we do, we should pay a contributor to the Dry Erase Board the same thing we would pay one of our normal team members for producing that. The money would go back to that publication of the team member who created that media or whatever. The fellow who started the discussion was, "Well I didn't bring this up to talk about making money. I brought this up to get the word out." He started going into the evils of capitalism and the evils of the democratic system of government. There are some people who are anarchists in the independent media scene.

Stacey: They had a high faith in humanity. They think we can all exist without protection from the government.

Steve: Right. Not a road warrior type thing but more like . . .

Stacey: More like, let's do it for love.

Steve: They believe in groups functioning as collectives only.

Stacey: Yeah.

Steve: No higher up systems. Another letter in the same publication was criticizing the magazine for including magazines that do it for profit or even sell their publications. That was something that we learned that was really important and that really took us by surprise when we were there.

Stacey: There was such antipathy toward trying to achieve a profit. I find it interesting, after going to the underground publishing conference, to see the difference between "publishing activists" versus another activist team. I feel like, and I don't know if it was that particular group, but within independent publishing they all seemed to fit in the "activist stereotype" and the "young grungy type."

Steve: I think we should add this in too. Let me just jump in for a moment. There are two types of folks in the independent media scene that we know of. There are those that are activists first and journalists second, most of which we met at the UPC. Then there are those who are journalists first and activists second. We fit into that category I believe. I believe the folks that we will be meeting with at the IPA convention fit under that category as well.

Jonathan: So what does it mean to be a journalist first?

Stacey: I would say that we all come to this project because of our fierce belief in the First Amendment. It's our desire to write and our desire to report on events accurately. I think as an activist your aim is to portray a certain idea and to find things that are around that, which is not to say they don't portray things accurately. At the same time, we never pretend to be *completely objective*, and we don't think that's a good goal to have—to be objective. We try to instruct our writers that you are going to go out there and you are going to have an idea and a pre-conceived notion, so don't be blind to it, but also be completely opened to what you might find. I had a writer who said to me, "Stacey, I went to go and look for this story and it was interviewing people on their religious beliefs in regards to Halloween. They said most people were like, I just want to get candy and have fun." The reporter found something completely different than what she was looking for. So I told her to write what she found. When you go out to see the story, one of the great things about being a journalist is that you do find new things and you almost never find what you think you'll find. I think an activist-*first* mission is, you know, what you seek to find and you look everywhere to find it. Whereas our mission is, we don't know what the hell we are going to find. We know it's going to be scary and exciting and weird and fun. We are going to be open to it.

Jonathan: You can certainly see that in the diversity of subjects that you covered even in the last year or so. It makes for very interesting reading.

Stacey: Thank you.

Jonathan: I'm particularly interested in the way the younger journalists
              and media savvy folks want to use the Web. Now you've got
              already a Web site. Can you tell me a little bit about it and
              what you envision it doing and what you are going to do in the
              future? How does it fit into your overall goals for *XRay*?

Steve: Stacey is doing the reengineering on that.

Stacey: We look at the Web site as a separate publication of the mag-
              azine. The nature of the media is such that it is a 24-hour dead-
              line publication. But we are a 30-day deadline publication as a
              magazine.

Jonathan: Okay, which means what?

Stacey: It means that we have a new issue every 30 days.

Jonathan: A new issue every 30 days.

Stacey: Or so. Sometimes it's 35 days and sometimes it's 27 days but
              generally speaking the magazine is a one-check deal, and once
              it's out there it's out there. It is unchangeable, but the Web, on
              the other hand, is very changeable and what we do with the
              Web site is almost entirely different from the publication. We
              want it to be in support of the publication, but also most of the
              content we use comes from that Dry Erase wire that Steve was
              talking about earlier. We use the Web site. That's a way we can
              get new content and also helps the Dry Erase people get their
              names out there in other cities.

              What we are planning to do with the Web site in the future is
              kind of toss up. I'm exploring some kinds of automated pro-
              grams that will allow any staff member to update stories, links,
              pictures and whatever. We are exploring many diverse Web
              advertising possibilities, too.

Jonathan: Okay.

Stacey: We are working on getting our archives in complete working
              order and a consistent site, which we don't have.

Jonathan: What will the archives contain?

Stacey: We are going to go back as far as the publication goes back.
              We have every story that's ever been written for *XRay* on a
              disk somewhere. Theoretically, we will be able to bend time
              and space. We can put them on there with an automated pro-

gram. I hope to be able to do that soon, but as it is right now, it takes me 5 to 10 minutes to put up any one story. More, if you also add in coding and editing—because when an error goes to print it doesn't have to go to the Web. It's a way to cover our butts in some sorts. It's also inevitable [that] there are stories that don't make it into the print publication because of finite dollars and space. We don't have that on the Web. If someone writes us a 10,000 page letter to the editor, well, we can put that on the Web site and we wouldn't take up the space in the magazine.

Steve: I think what we've done on the projects is that we kind of go through phases where an aspect of the project moves from one level to another. I mean the magazine that you have now is much different than the print magazine 12 months ago in terms of the capabilities and the content. Even the quality of writing has approved. The Web site also contains more and newer content now than it did in the past. It used to be just the work that was in the issue mirrored on the site. I know some things that I'd like to see on the Web is the City Guide that we just produced. I want the Web site to be a continuing, growing resource for people in the city, to link to everything that is Cincinnati. I'd like us to be a central hub for activist groups and a central source for finding information on other Cincinnati media. Right now, we have the most comprehensive media guide that is available right now in the city.

Stacey: Okay. When you say covering local media . . .

Steve: We list the publications, phone numbers, addresses, who is in charge there, a description of the publications, where you can get them, how much, Web links and all these sorts of things. Also what we think of it. I'd like that to continue to grow, which is something that we are working on right now. Also I'd like fresh and new content. I think the ultimate would be a daily. That's not something we have the capabilities to do right now, but perhaps the automated program with that Stacey is working on we could do more straight-up reporting than we have done in the past. When we had the [race] riots in 2001, I remember being shocked at the poverty of information there was. There was a riot going on downtown, and you could turn on all three or four television stations and not see what was going on. I couldn't believe no one was having a full-time report on the site or on television or radio. I remember wanting a Web site at that time. We existed at that time but we didn't have these capabilities yet to do this. I wanted to have a Web site that would have continual updates.

Jonathan: Right.

Steve: I wanted to know what was going on in a discussion board so people could have a real-time chat on what was going on. I would like more avenues to empower citizens to be journalists.

Stacey: Do you mind if I address that?

Steve: Sure.

Stacey: When George Bush came to speak in Cincinnati in support of the war, I think he didn't expect a lot of opposition, and if you look at the media locally or nationwide you didn't see a lot of opportunity either. But there were dozens of people downtown protesting his speech, his being here. The protestors said, essentially, that they were going to show them a peaceful demonstration as a front to their belligerent warring presentation. That's my very objective point of view. *XRay* was present, and Steve actually did all the reporting for this, because I told him I was only going as a protestor and not at all as a reporter. He did all the reporting. He took pictures. He got video and wrote stories and did interviews with people. They were all on the site within 24 hours. Well, you know, you look at the local news and it was like George Bush spoke to these rich people and some people were upset about it. They would show one person, just one protestor, with a sign.

Jonathan: It was very evident when you watched the news. You would see a few protestors *for* and a few protestors *against* the war. It looked like there were only 10 people who showed up at the Museum Center.

Stacey: Yes. Exactly. But there were maybe only 50 people for Bush. Lots, *lots* more against Bush.

Jonathan: It was very frustrating news coverage.

Steve: The video is something that we did not get up.

Stacey: We took video.

Steve: We have that, but it was something that we had technical difficulties with, and something that I'd also like to move toward that at one point is having video coverage of that. One of the things that . . .

Stacey: Do you mind if I finish one thing?

Steve: Oh. I'm sorry.

Stacey: When Steve was talking about trying to empower citizens to become journalists—that is essentially our mission. One thing that we all did when we were down there, Beck was with us, Steve, and I. I think it was just the three of us, and we were passing out business cards to people with information about our media workshop. We were telling people where they could send pictures that they had taken and accounts that they had written. We didn't get a lot of response on that. I think we could have gotten more if people understood what we were trying to do. That's the kind of thing that we are about: just going out into the community and saying we want to hear what you have to say.

Jonathan: Did you tell them that you would put their stuff up on the Web?

Stacey: Yeah.

Jonathan: Okay.

Steve: Yeah, but I think we should have had it on a piece of paper and handed it to them saying we are this and we are doing this, and if you send us this, we will do this.

Stacey: Yeah. We had like 2 days notice of Bush's coming too.

Steve: Right. Again this is the infrastructure we have yet to build.

Jonathan: It sounds like you want it to be a real core part of what you do, the Web site, that is.

Steve: Yeah. Oh for sure. Actually, Stacey is doing that almost primarily this month and, you know, normally she would be doing a lot more reporting. I've been trying to do a lot of those responsibilities so she can do a lot on the Web site. She wants to really clean it up.

Stacey: I was just going to say we have gotten more hits than ever this month. I believe it was 3,500.

Steve: The most unique visitors that we've ever done is 3,400, last month. Right now we are the 14th day of the month and we are up to about 1,500 unique visitors on the site.

Stacey:	Is that per day?
Steve:	No. It's per month. Yeah. If it were per day, we would be fine. To give you some scope last year we were probably attracting anywhere from 1,000 to 1,500 unique visitors a month, so it's gone up quite considerably, especially accelerated at about 150 new visitors a month in the past 3 months or so.
Jonathan:	Okay. I have a broader theoretical question based on what you've said. Is the Web a tool for democracy?
Steve:	Oh yeah.
Quincy:	Absolutely.
Steve:	It's a tool for democracy if it's used properly. If you look at what we are doing now with this publication on a shoestring budget, it's something that really was not possible to do 20 or 30 years ago. *The Independent Eye* is testimony to that, coming out in the 60s, but it was much more difficult and much more costly than it is now. Layouts and design and computer equipment make it so that anyone with proper training and study, even if it's independent training that some of us have had, can put together a publication that looks just as good as any other thing that's out there on the street.
Quincy:	Better.
Steve:	Or better. I think, right now, Internet radio and Internet video are really in their infancy, but there is going to come a time where those tools will be just as cheap and just as easy to use and just as effective as the tools in desktop publishing, so that any person can create a film or a newscast or whatever that looks just as good as anything produced by CBS, CNN, or whoever. As long as there is a way to get that to the people, there is a chance for real cultural evolution with this sort of democratization of tools.
Quincy:	When the Web first started to expand with graphics and images and even sound, the government didn't know how to regulate it or whether they should regulate it. So here they come along with the Telecommunications Act in 1996 and the Communication Decency Act that was a part of that, and trying to regulate what goes on on the Internet. And now we have Clear Channel and whatever else there is that's out there that's controlling our media outlets, and they're also trying to put a

stranglehold on the Internet, but they can't. I'll give you an example. In Germany, they have this restriction against Neo Nazis and Neo Nazi propaganda on the Internet. You are not allowed to be a Nazi in Germany on the Internet. You are just not. What do Germans who are Neo Nazi do? They go through an American ISP or Dutch ISP or wherever they can go. That's why the Internet can never be taken away from us because they [the government?] won't find it. There are always other channels around it. The Internet is kind of like water. You can put it into a bowl with a hole in it and try to plug up the hole but it will find another hole and it will seep out into where there is a space that it can occupy. It's fluid and that's what the Internet is and that's kind of what the progressive revolution is. Revolution is not the word, but the progressive movement is.

Steve: Right.

Quincy: And that we are a part of. *XRay* does that too. *XRay* finds the cracks, seeps in, occupies the biggest space, and tries to speak to the biggest audience about the most important issues regardless of who is out there trying to plug up the many holes in their own societal system.

Steve: I was just going to say, and I don't know if we've already made this point, but it's not only the Internet, it's the actual hardware and the actual ability to use a computer in your home that's a revolution. It's not just the Internet but all of the technologies put together is really what's creating, I think, the revolution as far as putting media in the hands of the people.

Quincy: And a new generation that is more and more digitally savvy.

Steve: Although, one of the things that I think should be said about this technology is that it still is primarily limited to, you know, a middle class and wealthier White folks. You don't find a lot of, you know you find . . .

Quincy: Access is limited.

Steve: Even being cheap—if you are a Black kid growing up in Over-the-Rhine and you don't have the best education going on and no one has put you in front of a computer so you can play games on it from a young age and then learn why you use it as a tool—you have a serious disadvantage compared to a White kid in the suburbs.

Quincy: Well, on the other hand, I'd like to mention where you were talking about the digital divide in access to technology—there is a definite digital divide. On the other hand, where it used to be that to publish a very slick, well-designed, and well-researched, and sexy-looking publication would take you thousands of dollars each month—we can do that on the Internet with a singular investment of about $1,000. So there is a digital divide with access but as far as publishing goes, you can do it cheaper, faster, and better than ever before on the Internet. Look at Yahoo!—it's the biggest Web site ever.

Steve: But it's still so . . .

Quincy: It's big with college kids.

Steve: It's still so culturally limited, however, to what's "white," many times.

Stacey: It's becoming less and less however. It's faster than television and print ever could be.

Steve: Right, but . . .

Stacey: It's more diverse.

Steve: I'm just saying it's still . . .

Stacey: I'm the optimist here.

Steve: I don't know that I'm a pessimist. . . . A lot of times, I mean from what I've read in different journals and magazines and what I've seen from some of my Black neighbors, many of the folks who are Black are discouraged from doing certain things, which are identified as "White." We have a friend of ours and a neighbor who is going to school at Cincinnati State, and she is trying to get her first degree at 26 or 27 years old, and her neighbors in the building that she lives in are all Black, the same way that she is. They tell her she is not going to do it and that they don't even know why she's trying to get her degree. Or they ask her why she is trying to be White. There is a *cultural* gap as well as a money gap. It's where the motivation is too. I really think it's all about proper education . . .

Stacey: *Community* education. Everybody says if you just educate everybody more, everything will be great. Well yeah, but no. It's the belief that education will change society. It's kind of like that trickle-down economic stuff. Well, if you do this one thing, it will be dominoes and all this other stuff. You know what, society is so complex, it just doesn't work that way. It is lack of education that started all the crime and poverty. There were so many other factors you know. I feel like that is one major way media can help and must help.

Jonathan: Let me ask you a question about that because you raised an interesting point. I would agree education is probably insufficient alone. There has to be kind of a critical willingness to instigate and follow through with change. People have said similar things about the Web. All right, so we've got all this information out there, and anybody who can, can slap up a Web page. Does that change anything?

Stacey: Has it yet?

Jonathan: Has it? Could it?

Steve: In some ways it's changed a lot of things and in some ways it's changed very little. The world is still run by individuals and groups that operate on base motives instead of altruistic ones. I still believe that a world where people operate off of, well, where the majority of people operate off of altruistic motives *first* is possible and attainable. I think what has to be done is you have to change people's mythology in a way. There is a cultural set of ideas that we all walk around with and believe. People buy into them. When we went down to that protest and I came back the next day to work and one of my co-workers said to me, "I can't believe you were down there protesting President Bush!" It was an affront to his idea about what the myth of patriotism is, that it's blind allegiance. That's one that has been pushed. It's like when you tell a story enough times. The one that's told enough is the one that sinks in. One of the reasons we tried to package things in a very slick manner is because we are hoping that people will pay attention and we can change the story. We are also merging art with politics, with music and culture and religion and sexuality and all these things. We do that because it's interesting to us and we are interested in all of those areas, but also because putting in things that are candy in with the medicine and mixing that all up is a way to make a progressive culture accessible to many different people. If things are too "academic," they are distasteful to many people.

Stacey: They are boring.

Steve: Right. The reason I became a journalist is because there was a rock concert that I wanted to go to. It was a base motive that led me there in a way.

Stacey: Do you think so? A base motive to go to a rock concert to appreciate music and to watch someone express themselves artistically? I'm sorry but I totally disagree with you, and I disagree that what we are doing is primarily all twisted. We want to live in a world that is progressive. We want to live in a world where ideas are progressive and where there is no culture mythology that holds people to a certain identity. In fact that's why we are doing this. I would hardly say that it's altruistic because we are trying to build a world that *we* want to live in. We are doing this for ourselves in the grand scheme of things. When we say we are doing this for ourselves, I think that is where the altruism comes in. Are we doing this for ourselves *only*, or we doing for ourselves in the grand sense—society and the guy standing on the corner banging on the plastic bucket?

Steve: When I say "base motives" I'm not using that as a necessarily negative term. I'm just saying if people have an interest in something because it's just unusual or they are curious about the sexuality article or they are kind of turned on by the imagery and the piece of art or maybe they just think the cover's really hip. . . . This month's cover is based off of a Grand Theft Auto [a popular computer game] cover. We did that on our City Guide to kind of portray Cincinnati in the way that we see it as opposed to the way that others see it. We are trying to access different kinds of things, and when I say "base things" I mean a base attraction or just a hunger-based motive, and that if you follow your nose, you know, it can take you to some pretty interesting and some pretty lofty places sometimes, too. I guess what I'm saying, in my opinion, and this is also something that should be said about the group—*XRay* isn't my *XRay* or Stacey's *XRay* or Becky's or Quincy's. It's a group of different people who have different ideas on different things. Sometimes we . . .

Stacey: We're sort of a comical . . .

Steve: Yeah. But we do individualistic journalism, which is coming at it from a truthful prospective.

Stacey:　Truthful but not objective.

I think it's a matter of semantics. What you are calling "base" is what I consider, like, when I hear the word "base," I think of good stuff. Like including an article on sex, which is a "base" thing and yet it's something that our society is afraid to address. I think that where we get in trouble is, say for example, a corporate interest that is only after profits and doesn't care what the heck they to do to anyone else, like the environment, people, human rights, or whatever. I think our goal is more lofty in a way.

I think that what we [Stacey and Steve] are saying is essentially the same thing, which is basically that maybe we have different motives than what other people have fallen into. Ironically enough, the only thing I think differently on is that we are following our instincts more than maybe we realize, and other people, what they are doing is following more social constructs. Such as, you are powerful if you have money. I see that as being a social construct that most people follow. Well, money is not speech. Money is money. It's the equivalent of what you can buy. It's a bartering tool. That's what it is. Speech is speech. Speech is, if I have something to say, then I'm going to say it, and I have the right to say it because it's a First Amendment right. That's the difference. The culture of mythology out there is that money is power and power is money.

Steve:　Often the reality.

Stacey:　It is a reality because those who have money have the biggest space and time to speak.

Steve:　They are allowed.

Stacey:　They have the biggest voice and the biggest audience.

Steve:　Right.

Stacey:　Well that's a structure that we are just trying to turn on its head. We are trying to give all that time space and audience to a larger base I think. Does that make sense?

Jonathan:　Yes, it does. I wanted to ask, though, why you went with GoXRay.*com*, as opposed to .net, or .org.

Stacey:　One of the things I want to do at *XRay* is make us as *XRay* approachable and accessible, which is why our office is open for people like you to come in and use our resources. We wanted the Web site to be the same thing. We want it to be interactive. We want it to foster the base between users and us. In kind of an academic sense, our mission is to destroy the boundaries that separate editors, writers, and readers. I don't know if you've read the latest issue but in my column, I argue that the readers of *XRay* are journalists. Simply by picking up an *XRay* magazine, reading it and thinking about it and maybe changing your mind or acting on what you read, I feel that makes you a journalist. That's what I kind of wanted to do with the Web site—to reach a broader audience, get the points of views of our artists and writers out there, and get Quincy's artwork out there so people can see it. Quincy has a beautiful Web site by the way.

Steve: It got tore up though.

Stacey: I think that what we want to do with the Web site is create an online community where we are destroying that structure of, well, I'm the editor and I tell you what to write. I am the writer and I tell you what to read. You know? It's sort of the hierarchy of the traditional media. I feel like having the Web site working with us goes right along with our mission.

Steve: I agree. I think it says a lot.

Stacey: If I could add something about the Web site. Another aspect that we can provide with the Web site is that, with the magazine, we are really limited about the audiences that we reach. On one hand, anytime anybody is out anywhere and doesn't have a computer or even if they do, they just pick us up and read us and take us with them. We print an average of 7,000 copies a month so that means that once those 7,000 are gone, and we usually keep about 500 maybe . . .

Steve: Maybe . . .

Stacey: We usually keep about 500 so, so once those 500 issues are gone, they are gone. The Web site reaches 3,500 a month so you know we getting a different audience. We are also getting users who are outside the urban core, where we distribute. We distribute to 250 locations, and the copies are gone within 2 weeks, so if you don't make it downtown and you are like some kid who is trapped in suburbs and you don't have a car or whatever and you don't have access to that urban culture, then you may not be able to make it down to Kaldi's [a popular downtown coffeeshop].

Steve: Or Aaron Ansel, for instance.

Stacey: Right.

Steve: Aaron Ansel is a Cincinnatian who found us online and right now he is living in the Netherlands and he's been sitting in on the Slobodan Milosevic trial, and so he asked us if we would like a story on it. We said sure, cover it for us. So we got an exclusive from the Hague. I know we've got another reader who is living in Germany who is originally from Cincy. We also have another reader from New Orleans. I mean we try to invite people on the Web site to contact us and submit their content and that sort of thing. It's not like a wide open door. That's been tried locally, to allow people to do instant posting. But it *has* been something that is pretty open unless they are saying something that is really despicable. We will work with you toward getting your stuff online.

Stacey: I think that also ties into our mission—the fact that we have an editorial review of things for quality. It's a quality control issue and that does kind of make us seem like we have a more traditional, hierarchical media model, but what we are trying to do is take the power that we have, and the power that we have is to get 7,000 or more of our magazines out to the people in Cincinnati. We are trying to take that power that we have and make it the best and purest that it can be. One month we ran a little ad that said, you know, send us a letter and we'll publish every letter that we get. It was probably a mistake, but I want to be an open door. I'm not going to say, "Well shoot, you don't have a degree from Ohio University or from Indiana University—well then, you can't write for us. So you don't have a degree from Columbia? Well then, screw you. We don't want your stuff."

The thing is that we want to work with writers, and maybe that's an activist mission of ours. If people have something to say and it's interesting and it's a good way to say it, then it's part of our mission as educators and as people who are involved in their communities to get their word out and help them to become better writers, because in a way we consider ourselves good writers. Maybe that is a false egotistical kind of claim but I feel that we are. We are trained and we do it every single day. Also I feel like anybody who comes to me and says, "I want to become a better writer. How do I become a better writer?" All I can say is, "Read whatever you get your hands on. Don't read books about writing, but just read books or comic books or the newspaper circulars for Kroger. Just read and keep reading and you're spelling will improve, your diction will improve, your understanding of grammar will improve, and your own voice will get better because you'll get to make it more unique."

Jonathan: OK, final questions. Let me get your names again, just for clarity's sake, your favorite Web site, and why.

Steve: My name is Stephen Novotoni and I'm the editor, publisher, and founder of *XRay*. I use Google.com more than anything else on the Web. When I'm reading I'll go to indypress.org, or I'll go to aan.org, which is the Association of Alternative Newsweeklies' Web site because they actually do some good stuff. I also go to the Independent Media Center, which is indymedia.org. Oh. Can I have one more?

Jonathan: Sure.

Steve: About.com. About uses regular people as site editors or subsite editors, and I like that a lot—that they use people to create the media and it's for profit. The people who are the editors are not necessarily beholden, as far as I know, to the interest of the advertisers on this site. I don't think they know who the advertisers are.

Jonathan: Who's next?

Becky: I'll go. Becky Carter.

Jonathan: Is that C-K-Y

Becky: C-K-Y. Yes. I do school, I do *XRay*, and I have a part-time job.

Jonathan: Office manager is your title?

Becky: I am office manager of *XRay*. I would say Yahoo! is a big one. I check my e-mail about three times a day now. I have so many files for school, *XRay*, an activist group that I'm a member of. I keep folders and I keep them all organized. I'm on there a lot. Google is an important search engine that I use on a regular basis. I would say I'm at my school's Web site a lot, doing stuff like registration, dropping, and adding classes, and all that good stuff. When I do research for *XRay* I often find myself going to a lot of arts and the venue Web sites.

Quincy: My name is Quincy Robinson it's Q-U-I-N-C-Y. I am the art director for *XRay*. When I'm on the Internet, I pretty much stick to Google and an image-searching engine. That's pretty much all the resources that I really need to do. Journalistically, I just stick with GoXRay.com because I really don't research stories too much myself. It's just more based on the images.

Jonathan: Besides GoXRay.com, your favorite site is . . . ?

Quincy: That's the one I stick with. Image-wise I'm searching Workforcevisuals.com, which you find a lot of work by Shepherd Fairy and some other street artist. Then you've got the regulars like Hotmail. That's about it. I just usually use those searching engines.

Jonathan: Anything for fun?

Quincy: Well yeah there is. If I'm doing something casual. This is just a passing interest of mine and that is Transformers. I go to this great Web site called Tformers.com, and they have a great rumors section for upcoming Transformers . . .

Stephen: Theforce.net also, for *Star Wars*.

Quincy: Another good one that I think has been shut down is Extremepassive.com.

Jonathan: Passive?

Stacey: Yeah. I think that has been shut down.

Quincy: I've been trying to get to that one.

Stacey: What's that one?

Quincy: It has hacked Web sites. It's an adult Web site and it's great.

Stacey: Hi, this is Stacey. You [Quincy] know porn sites better than I would, so what's a good porn site to go to get some images that I can use for the magazine? You know what, I do have to say something about porn. Just like with VHS, the Internet could never be profitable without porn and thank goodness for it, because what the Internet does with porn is, although it has all the disgusting sick and horrifying images that you could find, it also allows for the kind of artistic porn that Quincy is talking about. The idea that pornography is by its nature like bad and horrible and something to be hidden really stems from the fact that porn has been so poorly made in the past. If we were able to artistically portray sex in a dignified way—which I think the Internet is beginning to do more and more. For kids like us, who like sex, it isn't a bad thing, it's a good thing, so why are we like, you know, kind of trying to hide it and not celebrating the very human, very wonderful thing that is sex with art.

Jonathan: Could that also be celebrating the indignities of sex?

Stacey: Sure absolutely.

Jonathan: But you said "dignified" portrayal of sex.

Stacey: Dignified in the sense that I'm not going to tease my hair up and wear like high heels and pearls when I'm having sex kind of thing.

Jonathan: I'm just envisioning people over other people's knees getting spankings. There is nothing really dignified about that.

Stacey: Well, exactly, but you can portray it artistically with sensitivity and emotion . . .

Jonathan: Ok, Stacey, you've avoided your favorite Web site.

Stacey: Oh, my name is Stacey and don't forget the E because everybody does. I will kill you if you do. R-E-C-H-T. I am 24 and . . .

Becky: My favorite color is . . .

Stacey: My favorite color is red. I'm the managing editor of *XRay*, which sounds like a really specific title for what is really a very fluid list of duties. The Web site that I like to visit for research is the Ohio Public Libraries database site, which isn't so much a Web site as it is a resource. When you go to any of your local libraries' Web site, and you have a library card with a number on the back of it, you can just find your library on the list and type in the number on the library card, and you get access to database that can search magazine articles as far back as they have them. It's really amazing and it's completely free if you have your library card. I highly recommend it to anybody who is doing any research. Then, of course, Google is an amazing resource and I suggest to anybody who is doing any research to learn how to do advanced searches with Web sites like

Google. I feel like with Google and things like that out there, our searching is going to be improved. For Web construction resources Webmonkey.com does it the best, and they've done it the longest. They've got real people, and they talk about technology and doing technology in a fun, accessible way for people like me, who is a bit of a technophobe. I'm trying to do all this tech stuff, and you throw a couple of acronyms at me and I'm just completely stupid. I feel Webmonkey tries to make things really accessible at whatever level you are, like beginner or intermediate or completely geeked out or whatever. You can go on there and find new things, and they have tons of resources. I love it. Every time I do something on the Web I go there. For news, I don't have a lot of time to read news, unfortunately, though I'm reporting on it. I like to go to Fark.com. F-A-R-K. They present news from an incredible variety of sources, and a lot of times it's really funny. They have a way of specifying what kind of headline you are going to get into with one that has a little graphic of boobs and it says "boobies." It's not safe for work so you don't want to click on that link. Then there are other things. They are taking stories from all over the place. Of course, with more of a liberal vent than anything, but that's really what I look for.

Jonathan: Okay.

Stacey: Honestly, I look at the local news Web sites too. I look at Cincinnati.com. I really do. I look at Citybeat.com.

Steve: Don't forget Thislife.org.

Stacey: Thislife does real work. Steve and I have become major lovers of this. I turned Steve onto This American Life a while back, so now, whenever we are in the office, we turn it on, just a random show, and just get information. It's produced by NPR.

Steve: NPR.

Stacey: It's regular stories by regular people. It's so fascinating.

Steve: It's PRI actually isn't it?

Stacey: It's PRI [Public Radio International]. You're right. It is PRI. Sorry. Thislife.org. I would recommend to anybody. It's fun. For audio files, it's really great.

Stacey: It's so real. It's just like every time you listen to it, and I think what Ira Glass [the host] does, I think it's some kind of independent media that's really, really strong. What Ira Glass does, or what the show does, is they take an idea or concept or movement and they find stories that are completely unrelated to each other. They are completely unrelated to each other but they have might have one thing in common. One was about "do gooders." You know people who try to do good things. It's every kind do human idiosyncrasy they explore to the utmost with these scary American stories. It's so funny. Have you ever listened to it?

Jonathan: I've heard of it but I've never listened to it.

Stacey: Thislife.org. It's on at 10 a.m. on Sundays if you are up that early.

Steve: May I add something in?

Jonathan: Please do.

Steve: I feel this would be a great omission if I did not. One of the most important things that we use on the Web is Topica.com. It's a listserv.

Jonathan: Can you spell that?

Steve: Sure. It's T-O-P-I-C-A dot com. Listservs are the backbone of independent press networks in the United States. Whether it's the one the Dry Erase Board uses (and I don't remember what that URL is, but I could give it to you) or whether it's the IPA listserv or the *XRay* Scanner, which is our team.

Stacey: We have one for all of the Cincinnati media. We've invited all the local publications to participate.

Steve: Right.

Jonathan: Did you set that up during the "Do It Yourself" workshop?

Steve: Right. It hasn't gone very far yet.

Stacey: Right.

Steve: We are working on it. It has allowed us through the IPA to connect with about 400 other independent publishers, editors and sales people all over the U.S.

Stacey: On a daily basis.

Steve: On a daily basis, and we get answers to our questions from everything to how much is a street box [box stands holding newspapers and magazines] to where do I get them.

Stacey:	It also helps with advertising.
Steve:	We've covered ethical questions, technical questions, and all sorts of things on the listservs. As a team it's allowed us to discuss things and decide on things democratically even when we can't be in the same place at the same time.
Stacey:	It's such a powerful tool.
Steve:	That's the thing that we use most often. Really the two Web sites I use most are our e-mail site at Yahoo! and Topica. I'm constantly going there for consultation, and I'm trying to answer other people's questions.
Stacey:	It's like a consulting tool.
Becky:	It's a vehicle of communication for the publication, and it's so integral to what we do. Otherwise, how do we discuss what topics we cover?
Stacey:	Deadlines. When we are going to be in the office.
Becky:	Getting to know each other on a personal level so we can work together.
Stacey:	It has a real social aspect to it. It's a party line kind of thing. A lot of people aren't comfortable with that, but you know whatever *XRay* is—Becky said when I first signed on for the project, I remember her saying to me that *XRay* is very social. It's true.
Becky:	I'm being quoted. That's exciting.
Jonathan:	No I'm very glad you mentioned that. That actually is really key.
Stacey:	Integral.
Becky:	I wouldn't say more important than the Web site.
Steve:	It allows us to build community and do everything from plan parties to plan issues.
Becky:	It helps us run the magazine. For example, here are five things that need to be done around the office. We need street boxes painted, we need the papers organized, we need someone to go shopping, or whatever. We put that up there and the idea, theoretically, is that people volunteer to do it.
Stacey:	I tried to get instant messaging going in the office so people wouldn't shout at people across the room. It didn't really pick up.

Jonathan:	I think instant messaging survives better in business.
Stacey:	Yeah. I think you're right.
Jonathan:	From what I've seen, a lot of companies are using instant messaging. Rapid fire businesses need people to communicate like that—quickly.
	Any final comments.
Everyone:	No.
Stacey:	We've really enjoyed this.
Jonathan:	I appreciate it.
Steve:	It's part of our mission.
Stacey:	It is part of our mission. This is how we are building media—through this dialogue. Whether it be through the magazine or talking to a person.
Becky:	This is how we clarify how we feel about the new projects to each other as well.
Stacey:	Literally it's like performing. They say, if you are a musician, you don't really know your piece until you've performed it about six times.
Steve:	Sure.
Stacey:	Each time we are in a session like this talking out our views we are performing them.
Becky:	We are clarifying the mission of the magazine and the goals of the magazine and ourselves as individuals because we are collective but we each have a goal.
Jonathan:	Sure.
Stacey:	I wouldn't be doing this if I didn't love it. I wouldn't be here during the day if I didn't absolutely relish every minute I spend on a story. It isn't primarily all choice. It's a very selfish thing and I'm happy to say that.
Becky:	I agree. You get a sense of personal satisfaction. When we did the DYI ["Do It Yourself" media] workshop, I felt like this is something that we've done that has really helped the community or has been a positive thing in the community. I don't know how many people knew about it, but I think it was about 60. I really feel like we worked one more step to accomplishing a strong mission.

INTERVIEW WITH RYAN WELCH:
DEFINITIONHIPHOP.COM

Ryan Welch was a first-year writing student of mine during the 2001–2002 academic year. An English major, Ryan also has a rich "hidden literacy" life in his engagement with hip-hop music, spoken-word, and performance poetry—a life he only fleetingly brings into the classroom. I met Ryan one Friday in early August, after he got off work at a local branch of the city's library. Ryan works in the library, where he's also hosted spoken-word performances.

Jonathan: Hi Ryan. As you know, I'm really interested in Web sites and how young people use Web sites to communicate their interests and talk about their lives. You've shown me the Definition Hip Hop Web site [http://www.definitionhiphop.com/]. Tell me a little bit about your involvement in that and where that comes from and how that got started.

Ryan: Basically, it was just some kids that I knew who also rapped and they wanted a Web site. They asked another friend of ours to help them do the Web site, and I basically just did some music for it and coded a little basic HTML. I also helped them do some set up for the message board forms.

Jonathan: Okay. Who do you think goes to the site, besides you and your friends?

Ryan: Mostly people around the town and people who are into local hip-hop. Maybe people from upstate Ohio as well. I would say that would be the majority, and also a couple of people from Canada.

Jonathan: And what, exactly, is the purpose of the site?

Ryan: The purpose of the site is to help the local group, Definition Hip Hop, get their music out and let you know where you can get their music and where you can read reviews about them and their music. You can also hear some of their music, and you can post on the online community and network with them and things like that.

Jonathan: Do a lot of people post on that community? I noticed there were a few different discussion boards.

Ryan: Yeah. There are probably about 50 or so. There is not that
             many compared to other bigger hip-hop sites like Hip-Hop
             Infinity [http://www.hiphopinfinity.com/], which has like thou-
             sands and thousands of people posting on it.

Jonathan: Hip-Hop Infinity? That makes me wonder, when you and your
             friends were designing the site, did you use another site as a
             model, or did you get any ideas from other sites?

Ryan: Well, I couldn't really say for sure just because I was involved
             in the latter aspects and not so much the designs. I'm sure
             they did, though. Just like having an entrance page before you
             get to the main site. I'm sure they got that from some other
             Web site.

Jonathan: What are some of your favorite Web sites?

Ryan: My favorite Web sites are Hip-Hop Infinity, The Onion online,
             Newyorktimes.com, and Eye.net.

Jonathan: What was the last one?

Ryan: E-Y-E dot net. [http://www.eye.net]

Jonathan: What is that one?

Ryan: It's like some Canadian alternative paper. It's kind of like *City
             Beat*, I guess. There's this like these two people that write arti-
             cles for them, and I just really like to read their articles.

Jonathan: So you like some alternative sites. Onion is really "alternative"
             news . . .

Ryan: Yeah. It's pretty funny.

Jonathan: Satire and stuff like that.

Ryan: Yeah.

Jonathan: Has the Web been good for promoting hip-hop music and
             culture?

Ryan: Yeah. It's been really good. As far as independent hip-hop, the
             Web just enabled people to network. Now, we just had the
             Scribble Jam here, and a lot of people came because they saw
             it advertised on Hip-Hop Infinity, which is a Web site that a lot
             of people who would attend Scribble Jam would go to. Before
             that Web site, the attendance at Scribble Jam was so much
             lower than it is now. Before, I mean, when it first started, there
             were 50 graffiti writers, I think. The guy who started said there

were 50, and it was just a party to celebrate the birth of this magazine. Now it's like there is almost 10,000 people who come to it.

Jonathan: Where is Scribble Jam?

Ryan: Scribble Jam is held every year in Cincinnati.

Jonathan: It's in Cincinnati?

Ryan: Mostly at Annie's or Top Cats in Clifton on Short Vine, well actually that would be Coryville.

Jonathan: What is Scribble Jam, exactly?

Ryan: Scribble Jam, as far as independent hip-hop goes, it's the biggest event of the year. It's pretty much grown to become a really big thing.

Jonathan: Is there a Web site for Scribble Jam?

Ryan: Yeah. It's scribblemagazine.com [http://scribblemagazine.com/].

Jonathan: So essentially the print magazine moved online. . . .

Ryan: Well there is nothing really on the Web site except an advertisement for the event.

Jonathan: Oh. Okay.

Ryan: It just tells you when Scribble Jam is and stuff like that.

Jonathan: Okay. That still obviously gets the word out and lets people know.

Ryan: Yeah.

Jonathan: You said that it also advertised through Hip-Hop Infinity.

Ryan: Yeah.

Jonathan: Do you participate in Scribble Jam?

Ryan: I participated in it. I was in it last year and I was actually going to be in it this year, but we had to do a concert up at Bogart's.

Jonathan: Who is we?

Ryan: I have a band.

Jonathan: Okay.

Ryan: Renaissance Establishment.

Jonathan: Oh so that's *your* poster I saw in the library.

Ryan:	Yeah.
Jonathan:	That's your band. Is it hip-hop?
Ryan:	Yeah. It's hip-hop. It's a live band with drums, bass, violin, keyboard and classical guitar.
Jonathan:	That's fascinating. What do you do?
Ryan:	I rap.
Jonathan:	Do you write all of your own material?
Ryan:	Yes.
Jonathan:	Okay. Have you thought about making your own Web site to promote the stuff that you do? I notice you have flyers all over the library.
Ryan:	Right.
Jonathan:	Would the Web help you out in any way?
Ryan:	Yeah. Well, since we don't have any recorded material as of yet, I was pretty much waiting until that happened. You know, how you have all the promotion but with no music . . .
Jonathan:	I noticed that one thing on the Definition Hip Hop site that's really key is each page within the site seems to have a slightly different sample of the music. Did you do that?
Ryan:	Yeah. I pretty much selected it and put the music up. It wasn't too hard.
Jonathan:	Why was that important to do?
Ryan:	Well, I did it because they asked me to, but I imagine it's important because nobody wants to buy something they don't know about, especially when it comes to the music. There is so much stuff out there that you don't want to get ripped off and feel like you just wasted your money. It's good to be able to hear a sample of it before you get it.
Jonathan:	Tell me just a little bit more about the Hip-Hop Infinity site, which I'm definitely going to visit. I want to know why you like that site so much. What does it do for you?
Ryan:	Well, because it has the message board. For the most part, the discussion about hip-hop is usually kept pretty intelligent. People know and are pretty knowledgeable about hip-hop, and they help me to learn more. Plus, in the other different

forums, there is so much crazy stuff discussed and it's pretty funny.

Jonathan: Okay. So it sounds like as if it's almost a community-building tool.

Ryan: Yeah.

Jonathan: How many people participate on it? Is it from all over the country?

Ryan: It's from all over the world.

Jonathan: Oh. All over the world.

Ryan: It's a lot. I don't know for sure, but I would guess it's somewhere between 5 and 7,000 people. A lot of people are registered to that site.

Jonathan: Wow. That's pretty good.

Ryan: It's a pretty good site.

Jonathan: That's pretty cool. Would you say most of the people on it, well, if it's worldwide, they are probably drawing on people from all different races. I noticed that Definition Hip Hop is a duo, a White guy and a Black guy, right?

Ryan: Yeah.

Jonathan: Okay. Is that common or uncommon in hip-hop?

Ryan: It depends. There are a lot more White rappers in mainstream hip-hop. As far as different elements, you will definitely notice that there are a lot of Asian DJs. There are a lot of Asian and Hispanic break-dancers. A lot of graffiti writers are White. I don't know. Hispanics have always been a major part. Hip-hop started off as Black and Hispanic.

Jonathan: I'm thinking about some people, some critics of the Internet, who have said, in some ways, that African Americans have been among the last people in the States to have access to the Web. Do you think that's true?

Ryan: Yeah. Just in this library system, we just got new computers, but as far as that goes, they gave 10 extra computers to the place I used to work at in Hyde Park, which is White middle-class to upper-class people. They gave 10 extra computers to them before they gave us one. We only have three. Most of the people there [in Hyde Park] already have computers.

Jonathan: Fascinating. Do you think it's changing any?

Ryan: Yeah. I see a lot of Black kids coming in here every day getting on the computer. Then again, I don't know if they are necessarily utilizing it in a good way.

Jonathan: What do you mean?

Ryan: Not to say the way they use it is bad, but it's just going in and looking online and looking at cute boys and girls. That's not really productive.

Jonathan: OK.

Ryan: It seems like it's isolating them from each other. I see that a lot up at UC [the University of Cincinnati] in the computer labs. There will be a guy and a girl sitting next to each other and they are on Black Planet. They could be talking to each other instead of doing that.

Jonathan: Do you ever direct the kids in the library to hip-hop sites?

Ryan: No.

Jonathan: I mean, it's not part of your job duty, of course.
             [Laugher]

Ryan: Yeah, of course, but I don't. I don't see how that's really productive either.

Jonathan: Even as involved as you are in hip-hop scene or the MC battle scene?

Ryan: Yeah. I'm involved in the hip-hop scene, but that's not really involving yourself in the hip-hop scene. That's just observing.

Jonathan: Ok. What would involvement be?

Ryan: Involvement would be throwing out the shows and writing rhymes or free styling or practicing your dance moves or getting up and writing some graffiti or practicing your scratchin' or whatever. Just throwing shows and trying to meet and connect with people. That message board could help you meet somebody and connect with them, if you use it right, but most people just go in there to talk about hip-hop.

Jonathan: Is there anything else you want to say about your use of the Web or what you think is important about the Web?

Ryan: I think one good thing about the Web is that it would enable you to come across people and things that you may not have had access to otherwise.

Jonathan: Can you give me an example?

Ryan: For example, I was telling you the I go to that eye.net site, and the reason I always go to that site is because I was looking for something on graffiti, and I was looking up some specific graffiti writing and this guy's name just kept popping up, so I typed in his name and found out he was a film producer. I watched his movies, but some of them were kind of extreme. They were all interesting, though. I read one of his columns and I enjoyed what he had to say. I thought he had a good viewpoint.

Jonathan: Who is it?

Ryan: Bruce LaBruce. Have you heard of him?

Jonathan: Oh yeah. He is very entertaining.

Ryan: Yeah. He's a pretty entertaining guy.

Jonathan: Do you have any final words?

Ryan: No. Jonathan Alexander is a great English professor.

Jonathan: You are very kind.

5

WRITING QUEER DIGITAL YOUTH

A CASE OF IDENTITY AND COMMUNITY
ON THE WEB

The explosion of images of gays in the mass media, from popular television shows such as *Queer Eye for the Straight Guy* and *Will & Grace*, to an ever growing spate of alternative films and magazines, suggests that the larger culture is increasingly comfortable with gayness. Or, if it's not exactly comfortable, it's at least willing to entertain—and be entertained by—greater gay visibility. Moreover, recent research studies commissioned by the Gay and Lesbian Alliance Against Defamation (GLAAD) have underscored the personal, social, and potentially political effects of the ever increasing diversity of images of LGBT folk in media, ranging from television shows to computer games. For instance, in "How Youth Media Can Help Combat Homophobia Among American Teenagers," Rodger Streitmatter "identifies the specific types of characters and storylines that are most successful in increasing what he defines as the 'gay comfort level' among non-LGBT youth" (http://www.glaad.org/programs/csms/initiatives. php?PHPSESSID = 5d5 acde4f3cfe1e3983643aacb2bfae7). As Streitmatter concludes, "Youth media have impact." As such, studying the ways in which a variety of youth interact with media should be a central component of understanding changing attitudes and views about homosexuality of any number of youth, both queer and straight.

Part of this mass media explosion has occurred via the Internet, as some "digital queers" have used listservs, chatrooms, discussion boards, and Web sites, among other Internet-based communications platforms, to communicate with one another about their lives and loves. Popular portals such as Gay.com and PlanetOut boast monthly visitor counts in the millions, and the number of personal queer-themed homepages, or "homopages," seems nearly countless. For instance, in 2001, Gay.com and PlanetOut claimed 4 million visitors per month (Gamson 265).

As seen in preceding chapters, however, one of the salient differences between Internet-based and non-Internet-based mass media is that, despite the presence and popularity of many commercial sites (such as Gay.com or PlanetOut), the Internet hosts a variety of Web sites that are created, maintained, and built by people without overt commercial interests. Unlike representations provided through television and in major motion pictures, representations on the Web are often more "home grown" in that they are not constructed and disseminated with corporate and advertiser interests in mind, even if they are influenced in part by commercially produced and distributed representations. As such, the Internet and the Web provide a wealth of opportunities for exploring how a variety of queers construct, represent, and articulate their own understanding of sexuality, sexual orientation, and sexual politics. Consequently, examining noncommercial sites might afford us a glimpse into how many queer people throughout the country wish to represent themselves and their interests, engage in debate about relevant issues, and express their ideas and insights about culture, society, and politics.

Of all of the groups that have taken to the Internet and the Web as venues of self-expression, some queers with access, and some queer youth in particular, have been among the most ardent users, especially in the construction of Web spaces designed specifically for other queers. Joanne Addison and Michelle Comstock, in "Virtually Out: The Emergence of a Lesbian, Bisexual and Gay Youth Cyberculture" (1998), suggest that "more and more les-bi-gay youth have begun to employ technology in order to understand and express their experiences and demand that they be considered culturally significant members of society" (368). The authors make a good point for studying some queer youths' use of the Web, particularly youth-written sites, as an opportunity for understanding what *queer digital youth* think about sexuality, gay culture, and politics. As they put it, many such queer digital youth are "establishing cyberzines, discussion groups, and support services through the Internet. In studying these public sites, we can gain insight into an emerging les-bi-gay youth cyberculture that we would not otherwise be able to engage" (371). The Web, then, offers a nearly unparalleled opportunity to explore what young people, particularly young queer people, think about sexuality, both its personal and its political dimensions.

At the same time, the Web is increasingly a commercial space, and much of the advertising energy expended on the Web is aimed at many youth, including queer youth. Homo-erotic images of young men and women on the sites of clothing vendors and sexualized images of young people on pornographic sites all use images of the young to encourage visitors to make a purchase. And some sites run by queer people themselves, such as Gay.com, advertise a variety of goods, from clothing and music to travel and vacation opportunities; the imagery used in ads for these products and services are inevitably of young people, enjoying the life their purchases can bring them. The advertising lessons are simple: Youth—*sexy* youth—sells.

Given the presence of both commercial and "home-grown" sites on the Web, with many clamoring for the attention of queer digital youth, it is worth asking what kinds of images and representations are created *for* queer youth and what kinds are created *by* queer youth. Are the images and representations comparable, or do they offer us different understandings of queer digital youth and *their* interests, ideas, and sociopolitical investments with regard to queer sexuality?

To approach these questions, I first review some of the scholarly literature that has already laid out some of the dominant themes tracing how queer digital youth use the Web. Then, I examine prominent sites largely maintained by adults (in this case, those over 30) to serve the personal, social, and commercial interests of queer digital youth. And finally, I trace some of the dominant trends emerging in how such youth *themselves* represent and articulate their personal, social, cultural, and political concerns on sites that *they* largely compose and maintain themselves. In general, to borrow from Rodger Streitmatter's assertion, I explore what kind of "impact" these e-savvy queer youth and their writing on the Web might be having on how such youth configure and construct themselves as queer and sexual. Put another way, we can catch a glimpse of the contours and dimensions of their emerging *sexual literacy*. Ultimately, I believe we have much to learn from a younger, queer generation's strategies of digital representation about the way they are rethinking and reconfiguring their relationship to queer politics, identity, and community.

STUDYING QUEER YOUTH ON THE INTERNET:
SOME BACKGROUND

Nina Wakeford's 1997 article, "Cyberqueer," reviewed the work up to that point that analyzed how queers use and experience the Internet. As part of her summary and analysis of the extant research, Wakeford asks a probing question: "What is queer cyberspace?" (404). Through 1997, two answers seemed to dominate both the use of and research about queer cyberspaces. First, "Cyberqueer spaces are constantly reconstituted as points of resistance against the dominant assumption of the normality of heterosexuality in ways which are familiar to activists engaged in other struggles against heterosexism" (408). Second, "Cyberqueer spaces are framed as new places within which lesbian, gay, transgender or queer experiences can take place, with a particular focus on the advantages compared to 'real' physically-located space" (410).[1] What were some of those perceived advantages? Specifically, "The importance of a new space is viewed not as an end in itself, but rather as a contextual feature for the creation of new versions of the self" (411).

In many ways, Wakeford's early categorizations of how queers were using the Internet in general and the Web in particular hold true today, particularly for many young queers. Some youth, for instance, have taken up the mantra, "We're Teen, We're Queer, and We've Got E-Mail," the title of a frequently anthologized piece by Steve Silberman on the power of the Internet to dispense information and foster contacts about subjects about the still largely taboo subject of homosexuality. According to Silberman,

---

[1]Some examples of research that might have prompted Wakeford to make these claims include the following. In "Queer 'n' Asian Virtual Sex," Daniel C. Tsang notes that, in cyberspace, "For once, you are in total control of your sexual identity, or identities, or at least what you decide to show the outside world" (433). David F. Shaw's "Gay Men and Computer Communication: A Discourse of Sex and Identity in Cyberspace" analyzes 12 interviews the author conducted with gay men who use Internet Relay Chart (IRC). Based on his observations as a participant-observer, Shaw concluded that, "while the playground potential of the IRC inarguably exists and people will . . . try on different personalities, the uniqueness of gaysex lies in the fact that it presents an opportunity for gay men, who often go through life hiding the most vital aspect of their identity, to try on this real identity" (144). Specifically addressing how queers use the Web, Gregory M. Weight noted in "queer wide web?" how gay authors can use the hypertextual possibili-

young Internet-savvy teens can "follow dispatches from queer activists worldwide, hone [their] writing, flirt, try on disposable identities, and battle bigots—all from [their] home screen[s]" (59). Indeed, gay chatrooms, queer Web rings, homo-themed synchronous and asynchronous communications platforms, and LGBT Usenet groups abound, as queers of all ages "come out" on the Infobahn to tell their stories and make contact with one another.

Another more recent article is even more suggestive about the connection between cyberspace, queerness, and identity. In "Lonely Gay Teen Seeking Same," Jennifer Egan notes that more and more gay teens are using the Web to make contact with others, to find role models for their fledgling lives as gay people, and even to establish romantic and sexual relationships. Many of these kids are in rather isolated areas, and they want to know that they are not alone in the world:

> For homosexual teenagers with computer access, the Internet has, quite simply, revolutionized the experience of growing up gay. Isolation and shame persist among gay teenagers, of course, but now, along with the inhospitable families and towns in which many find themselves marooned, there exists a parallel online community—real people like them in cyberspace with whom they can chat, exchange messages and even engage in (online) sex. (113)

Egan also quotes experts who cite studies that suggest that gay teens are coming out at younger and younger ages, perhaps due to the availability of information, and interactivity, offered by the Internet. Some scholarship

---

ties of the Web to craft their own unique, poly-vocal narratives of identity and experience:

> [T]he Web, if it is anything, is a space of nomadic travel, which constantly subverts paradigms of dominance, especially two key binaries: author/reader and text/image. With often unlimited choices of how to create their own narrative by using links to other sites, Web viewers become their own authors, using bits and pieces of what the "original" Web authors provide and discarding others. The authority of the author is thus destabilized, with the author and viewer being able to construct narratives that are never stable, and often unable to be recalled. (http://www.english.udel.edu/gweight/prof/web/queer/form1.html)

The emphasis throughout such studies is on lauding the seeming ability of the Internet to provide spaces for both self-expression and self-exploration, particularly for people, such as queers, who might find such expression and exploration either constrained by or even threatened "in real life."

has undertaken an investigation of such assertions. Randal Woodland's 1995 article, "Queer Spaces, Modem Boys and Pagan Statues," examines four "queer spaces": ModemBoy, America Online, ISCA BBS, and LambdaMOO. Woodland calls cyberspace a "distinctive kind of 'third place' for many gay and lesbian people": "These on-line 'queer spaces'. . . are 'third places' in . . . combining the connected sociality of public space with the anonymity of the closet" (418). As such, they are relatively "safe" spaces to encounter and experiment with a queer identity—an experimentation that might carry over into real life. Randal Woodland, writing a few years later in 1999, again argued that online communities or modes of communication provide "safer spaces" for queers to explore, test, and experiment with identities. In an article published in *Computers & Composition*, "'I plan to be a 10': Online Literacy and Lesbian, Gay, Bisexual, and Transgender Students," Woodland is hopeful when he suggests that, "Through gathering information, testing identities, and finding supportive communities, many can move from these safer spaces into the more threatening world of IRL ['in real life']" (79). Those working in the field, helping to maintain Web sites to assist a variety of queer youth with Web access, for instance, corroborate Woodland's analysis. Mike Glatze, the founder of the Website Young Gay America (YGA), offered the following comments about the significance of the Web site for some queer youth:

> Gay youth use the Web like no other subset of the population. It has single-handedly revolutionized the entire LGBT youth movement. What exists today was completely unheard-of even 10 years ago. The Internet has brought access to life-saving and life-affirming information to kids everywhere, and that information can be gained without having to identify yourself. Ten years ago a kid too afraid to go to a gay bookstore and unable to see any positive depictions of gayness or meet a single gay peer might have resorted to suicide out of a sense of hopelessness.
>
> Today, because of the Internet, LGBT youth can see others like them, find information that supports them (and contradicts the hate they hear in their small towns), and gain a sense of hope and promise. It's a revolutionary thing and very important. LGBT youth have huge networks of friends and supporters online. They are able to formulate a community of other young gays even when in their physical location they might be the only LGBT youth they know of.

Viewed from this perspective, the Web seems to offer both a sense of identity *and* community to many queer youth who might not otherwise have access to such IRL. Such articles and comments reinforce what Nina Wakeford pointed out in her research summary: "The construction of identity is the key thematic which unites almost all cyberqueer studies" (31),[2] and a significant aspect of that identity construction has been in providing a space for queers to "come out," as can be seen in the list of coming-out stories at "All Things Queer" (http://www.rslevinson.com/ gaylesissues/ comingout stories/blcoming_youth.htm).

One of the few studies focusing specifically on queer digital *youth* has been Joanne Addison and Michelle Comstock's "Virtually Out: The Emergence of a Lesbian, Bisexual and Gay Youth Cyberculture" (1998), in which the authors turn their attention to youth cyber-queer spaces, in part, to problematize an understanding of queer Internet spaces as ghettoized, and also to argue that queer digital youth are using such spaces to articulate fairly complex self-representations. To do this, Addison and Comstock examined four cyberzines, an IRC, and one "on-line les-bi-gay youth services site" (372). Their study of the "emerging cyberculture" represented by

---

[2]Of course, identity in cyberspace is a troubled, troubling, and contested concept, particularly when considering the potential diversity of Internet users. In "Homopages and Queer Sites: Studying the Construction and Representation of Queer Identities on the World Wide Web," I attempted to summarize some major concerns that some authors have pinpointed when thinking about the seeming "global" reach of the Internet and the potential erasure of social and cultural differences that occurs on the Internet:

> Rainbows aside, the reality envisioned and performed is invariably a White one, with little crossing of the racial divide so present IRL ("in real life"), for both gays and straights. And the ramifications of such divides are drawing increasing critical attention. By the mid-nineties, Daniel C. Tsang (1996), in "Notes on Queer 'n' Asian Virtual Sex," could note how Asian-Americans would often hide their ethnicity on Internet Bulletin Board Services in order to be more attractive to Caucasians. Further, Max Padilla (1998) asserts in "Affirmative Access: A Gay Chicano Lost in Cyberspace," "The World Wide Web has turned out to be nowhere near as diverse as the number 7 train I ride home every night. . . . Netizens post about themselves, and I don't see myself in there" (122). For Padilla and others like him, the relative lack of racial and ethnic diversity on the Internet problematizes some of the assertions made by the medium's more enthusiastic supporters: "I still use the Internet, but I'm wary of its claims. This is no Netopia, but an all-too-painful reflection of the real world. American online [sic] resembles America, all right. Majority rules" (122).

such venues "focuses on two broad aspects . . . : (1) how its members articulate and situate themselves politically in relation to heterosexist mainstream adult cultures and other youth subcultures . . . ; and (2) how the
sites represent and actualize a variety of gendered, raced, classed, and sexualized subjectivities and/or identities" (372).

Some of Addison and Comstock's conclusions echo other discussions
of the usefulness of the Internet for young queers. For instance, they point
out that "Many of the online youth participants describe the Internet as a
virtual stage—a space and time to safely rehearse the coming-out process"
(374). This observation is supported by Woodland's 1999 essay, "'I plan to
be a 10.'" In that article, Woodland discusses a national, online survey he
conducted to discover why some LGBT youth go online. Several respondents noted that they found both mentors and audiences to listen to them
"draft" a self. Woodland writes of one subject that "[b]y rehearsing his new
identity via email, he was able to communicate more openly with his parents" (83). Beyond this, however, Addison and Comstock wanted to demonstrate how

> representing cyberspace, particularly the les-bi-gay youth cyberculture,
> as dialectical . . . challenges early efforts to map or partition off lesbian
> and gay subcultures. These often racist and homophobic mappings
> argued for the existence of "gay ghettos," where lesbian and gay men
> led "lifestyles" that were distinct and separate from more mainstream
> lifestyles. Our mapping not only resists ghettoizing les-bi-gay youth,
> but works to take into account the complexity of their lives—their par-
> ticipation in a variety of on- and off-line mainstream and countercul-
> tural activities. (370)

In fact, the sites the authors examined reveal a complex articulation of identity and community, one willing to cross lines of race and gender. For
instance, Addison and Comstock note that "an aspect that stands out in
many of these sites is the express attempt at constructing an inclusive community, despite the reality of exclusiveness based on gender, race, class, and
sexuality" (375–6). For instance, Oasis, an online community, boasts many
discussions of the intersections between race, gender, and sexuality.

Ultimately, a key goal of Addison and Comstock's study is to demonstrate how "Positioning the les-bi-gay cyberculture in dialogue with and in
relationship to other cultures challenges claims that the Internet is purely a
bourgeois space controlled by the military-industrial establishment" (370).
Addison and Comstock suggest that we should view queer youth sites as
"important sites for resistance, reproduction, and pleasure." In particular,

they argue that many queer youth sites "provide powerful opportunities for resistance and political organization" (371). For instance, the authors examine Youth Action Online (YAO) and note that the site, in providing a "safe space" for queer digital youth so they can "reach a point where they can 'accept' their own sexuality." As such, YAO's work is "just as much political as personal in its resistance to homophobia and ageism" (372).[3]

Indeed, as these studies suggest, large amounts of material on the Web attempt to appeal to queer digital youth or claim to represent such youth and their interests. Such sites include a variety of informational, agency, and commercial sites. What's missing in this research, it seems to me, is a sharper understanding of the *diversity* of sites depicting, representing, and appealing to queer youth—both those created *for* queer youth and those created *by* queer youth. Indeed, I believe what's needed is a sustained study and analysis of *queer digital youths'* self-representations on the Web—a gap I am hoping to begin to fill in the following pages. Addison and Comstock take us part of the way toward such an analysis, focusing on a handful of youth-oriented sites. But even they, writing in 1998, noted that, "While there are a number of sites that deal with issues affecting les-bi-gay youth, very few of these were founded and are being maintained *by* les-bi-gay youth" (372). Since the publication of their article, however, other sites have surfaced that *are* largely created by queer digital youth; examining those sites can help update Addison and Comstock's research.

Moreover, much of the research so far has focused on whether or not the Web in particular and the Internet in general provide safe (or safer) spaces for queers (both youth and adults) to experiment with and explore a queer identity. Although this is an important realm of inquiry, I suggest that recent Web authoring by young queers demonstrates that their interests and concerns, expressed on the Web, encompass a wider variety of

---

[3]And, as time has passed, I think the continued proliferation of Web sites and other forums for electronically enabled communication and dialogue have demonstrated that many different digital queers, from a diversity of backgrounds and identity positions, are using the Internet to experiment with identity and construct a sense of community, even political efficacy. My own work in my article, "Homo-pages and Queer Sites: Studying the Construction and Representation of Queer Identities on the World Wide Web," for a special issue of *The International Journal of Sexuality and Gender Studies*, offers thoughts on the varieties of representations and Web-based platforms that queers use to represent themselves, and I have argued that studying that *variety* provides significant insights into how different members of the larger LGBT/queer community think about, understand, and define—often in contentious ways—their sexuality.

issues, many of which reveal a complex and sophisticated grappling with issues of sexuality, sexual identity, and the constitution of the "gay community." For instance, Addison and Comstock do not consider transgender issues, just "les-bi-gay" content, but, as we shall see, transgender issues are increasingly important to many queer digital youth, and they are widely discussed via queer digital youth Web sites. Much discussion in these sites revolves around how such want to be represented—usually in contradistinction to their representation by sites *not* authored by them, such as commercial sites, or sites that may be youth-*oriented*, but not necessarily *composed* by queer digital youth themselves.

With these thoughts in mind, then, this chapter attempts to extend the understanding of how some queer digital youth use the Web to communicate information about their lives, interests, and sociocultural investments. To find sites for analysis, I used major search engines (Google and Yahoo!), polled three queer studies listservs and asked for potential sites to examine, and surveyed queer digital youth at my home institution, the University of Cincinnati, to provide URLs for appropriate sites. To manage the overwhelming number of sites found, I focused my attention on the following kinds of sites:

- Sites that serve as community-building Web spaces, where a number of youth can post thoughts, ideas, and insights;
- Sites created by, largely composed by, or primarily maintained by some youth (under 30 years of age);
- Sites in English.

Working with such sites, I concentrated on those that seem more prominent (in terms of visitors), and I collected and categorized about 40 such sites. Sites were categorized based on primary purpose, intended audience, and variety of content. I also attempted to conduct interviews with site authors or editors via e-mail, and many of those e-mailed responded generously with comments and insights.

After collecting and categorizing the sites, I began my analysis by looking at some major queer-themed Web sites that many queer digital youth use to find information about queerness, as well as some of the prominent sites that claim to represent such youth and their concerns. Then, I compared such sites to the ones that are designed, authored, and maintained *by queer digital youth themselves*. In the process, I discovered that queer digital youth certainly use the Web in ways similar to those described Woodland, Addison, and Comstock (among others), but I also noted more sites that attempt to create "virtual community," specifically a digital youth community organized around helping such youth not only become comfortable with their sexuality, but also to explore complex social, cultural, and even political dimensions of being queer. In general, the sites suggest a developing and increasingly complex sense of *sexual literacy*—of understanding the connections between personal, social, cultural, and political forces as they intersect with and impact one's sense of sexuality and sexual intimacy. Based on this information, I have highlighted some of the dominant trends I found on these sites, using specific examples and comments from site authors, editors, and contributors.

At this point, however, I enter two important qualifications into this discussion—qualifications that have helped me delimit the scope of my study of the Internet and Web spaces throughout this book. First, I have focused primarily on Web sites because, unlike postings on discussion boards, to listservs, or in chatrooms, Web pages provide a somewhat "stable" form of writing on the Internet that we can examine. Nonetheless, queer digital youth use a variety of chat and discussion forums extensively, such as those offered by various MSN "communities" and Yahoo! groups, which have queer-focused groups, or Outminds (http://www.outminds.com/) to which visitors can log in and participate. Although I touch on such Web-based projects here, a separate study should be undertaken to analyze the content and style of communication in those forums. Second, I am only offering here a glimpse into some of the main issues that some LGBT/queer youth are grappling with *as revealed on the World Wide Web*. Put another way, I am attempting to answer the following question: What are some queer digital youth telling us about their lives and interests by the way they write—and use—Web space? Answering such a question is necessarily interpretive, and, given the scope of the Web, hardly exhaustive. I return to potential limitations of this approach in the conclusion.

SOME QUEER CYBERTYPES: SITES COMPOSED FOR QUEER DIGITAL YOUTH

Young queer Web surfers are likely to see a variety of different types of sites clamoring for their attention—sites ranging from commercial ventures to informational sites to sites written and maintained primarily by queer digital youth, for queer digital youth. We can catch a glimpse of the diversity of queer and queer youth-oriented content on the Web by examining Web portals, such as the popular Yahoo!. Such portals provide useful guides to the glut of information on the Web, and they frequently use categories that help surfers navigate the wide array of information available on the Web. As such, they generally offer a valuable service, linking info searchers to material quickly. At the same time, as some critics have pointed out, such portals and their categories can be a bit *too* reductive or limiting in the kind, quality, and diversity of information presented. Moreover, their reductions and categorizations can also carry with them ideological valences and assumptions.

One of the largest and oldest gay-specific portals, or what I call "organized link lists," is Gayscape.com, which boasts "over 68,000 indexed sites" and claims to "provide the specialized search tool that's fast, easy, and fun" (http://www.gayscape.com/). Gayscape organizes information into a set of easy-to-navigate categories—Products, Topics, Services, the United States, and the World, with an "Adults Only" section boxed off to the side. "Youth" appears as the last (in alphabetical order) entry under "Topics," and clicking it leads to a further subdivision: "by location in the United States," "by country," and "by sub topic," which contains only two categories: "Parents, Family and Friends of Lesbians and Gays" and "Support Groups."

"Support Groups" is organized geographically, and "Parents, Family and Friends of Lesbians and Gays" takes you to a one-page listing or prominent PFLAG sites on the Web. What picture is offered here? Although Gayscape provides an abundance of information about a multitude of queer subjects, its offers for young queer Web searchers seem scanty and limited primarily to issues of support. No writing or pages *by* queer digital youth are readily available.

Ironically, when the search is expanded to a general interest portal, such as Yahoo!, a bit more diversity is found in the kind of links offered. Using Yahoo!, I searched the phrase "gay youth" and came up with a variety of hits, of which it's instructive to view the first 20:[4] The Web results, out of 790,000, yielded an initial page with the following "hits":

1. **Youth** Resources
    information, support, and resources for lesbian **gay**, bisexual, and transgender **youth**.

---

[4] I conducted this search on Wednesday, August 13, 2003, and it is worth keeping in mind that such searches will, of course, yield different results on different days, depending on how the search is configured and reflecting the changing popularity of the pages that Yahoo! accesses to "rank" them.

www.youthresource.com/ cached | more results from this site
More sites about: Lesbian, Gay, and Bisexual **Youth**

2. OutProud
    national coalition for **gay**, lesbian, and bisexual **youth**.
    www.outproud.org/ cached | more results from this site
    More sites about: Lesbian, Gay, and Bisexual **Youth**
    Organizations

3. Elight!
    a Web ezine created by and for **gay youth** and young adults.
    www.elight.org/ cached | more results from this site
    More sites about: Lesbian, Gay, and Bisexual **Youth** Magazines

4. **Youth** Action Online
    support center and resource for GLB and questioning **youth**.
    www.youth.org/ cached | more results from this site
    More sites about: Lesbian, Gay, and Bisexual **Youth**

5. Oasis Queer **Youth** Monthly Webzine
    for queer and questioning **youth** featuring celebrity interviews,
    profiles and personal writings.
    www.oasismag.com/ cached
    More sites about: Lesbian, Gay, and Bisexual **Youth** Magazines

6. **Gay** Bisexual **Youth** Suicide Studies
    www.virtualcity.com/youthsuicide/ cached | more results from
    this site
    More sites about: Lesbian, Gay, and Bisexual **Youth** Suicide

7. **Gay Youth** UK : Home
    Gay Youth UK - Information, Resources, help, discussion, per-
    sonals, competitions and much more! ... Information, Resources
    and Support for **Gay Youth** Nationwide! ...
    www.gayyouthuk.org.uk/ cached | more results from this site

8. Australian **Gay Youth** Resources Homepage
    Australian **Gay Youth** Resources Homepage. Welcome to the
    Australian **Gay Youth** Resources Homepage This is a resource
    designed for same-sex attracted **youth**. ...
    www.dogwomble.worfie.net/ cached | more results from this
    site

9. Mogenic
    news, information, and entertainment for **gay** and lesbian
    youth.
    www.mogenic.com/ cached
    More sites about: Australia > Lesbian, Gay, and Bisexual **Youth**
    Magazines

10. DavePD.co.uk
     Updates: May 2003, Again I'm pondering with the new design -
     Just gotta keep your fingers crossed that I get it completed in
     May.
     www.davepd.co.uk/ cached
11. Lesbian **Gay** Bi **Youth** Line
     provides safe, supportive and confidential place for young l/g/b
     youth to talk about their concerns. Toll free number across
     Ontario.
     www.icomm.ca/lgbline/ cached
     More sites about: Canada > Lesbian, **Gay**, and Bisexual **Youth**
12. Memphis Area **Gay Youth** Automatic Re-Direct Page
     This page should automatically redirect you to the MAGY home-
     page according to your current resolution, and browser type.
     This is ...
     www.gaymemphis.com/magy/ cached
13. Bonus Round's **Gay Youth** Page
     ... ELIGHT at http://www.elight.org is an ezine and community
     run by Jason Seymour a **gay youth** who took matters into his
     own hands and created this safe place for ...
     www.bonusround.com/gayyouth/ cached | more results from
     this site
14. Young **Gay** America - **Gay** and Lesbian **Youth** Resource
     ... Gallery Show, you. **Gay** in America's Heartland Meet LGBT
     youth on our trip through Texas, Nebraska, & Oklahoma. yga,
     YGA international photo exhibit. ...
     www.younggayamerica.com/ cached | more results from this
     site
15. Long Island **Gay** And Lesbian **Youth**, Inc.
     providing counseling, support groups, drop-in community cen-
     ter, campus leadership network, activities and other cool stuff.
     www.ligaly.com/ cached | more results from this site
     More sites about: New York State > Bay Shore > Lesbians,
     Gays, and Bisexuals > Community Centers
16. Amazon.com: Listmania! **Gay Youth** Classics
     Listmania! **Gay Youth** Classics by Brad, **gay**-friendly gym teacher
     ... 8. **Gay** and Lesbian **Youth** by Gilbert Herdt (Editor)
     (Paperback - July 1989) List Price: $19.95. ...
     www.amazon.com/exec/obidos/tg/listmania/list-browse/-
     /FUQ589Z7IT96/qid = 1059525261/sr = lmlf-10/ref = br_
     lmlf__10/ cached | more results from this site

17. QueerAmerica - Find Your Way.
     QueerAmerica is a database published by OutProud, The
     National Coalition for **Gay**, Lesbian, Bisexual and Transgender
     Youth. With ...
     www.queeramerica.com/ cached
18. : : : bgiok : : :
     A support and advice website for **gay youth**. bgiok! aims to
     answer questions about sex, coming out and dealing with
     homosexual feelings.
     www.bgiok.org.uk/ cached
19. Resource for Parents of Gays, Lesbians, Bisexuals, Transgenders
     support and advice for parents of **gay youth**. Includes questions
     and statements.
     www.bidstrup.com/parents.htm cached | more results from this
     site
     More sites about: Lesbian, **Gay**, and Bisexual **Youth**
20. Tremblay 10/95
     The Homosexuality Factor in the **Youth** Suicide Problem. Pierre
     J. Tremblay B.Sc., BA, B.Ed. Presented at the Sixth Annual
     Conference ...
     www.qrd.org/qrd/www/youth/tremblay/ cached | more results
     from this site

After spending some time at each site, I organized the list into the following categories, based on what the primary purpose of the site *seemed* to be.
Of the 20 listed, five were organization-based sites, providing helpful information and support, generally for youth just coming out or realizing they
might be queer, and two dealt specifically with suicide among queer teens:

OutProud: www.outproud.org/
Youth Action Online: www.youth.org/
Memphis Area Gay Youth: www.gaymemphis.com/magy/
Long Island Gay and Lesbian Youth: www.ligaly.com/
Resources for Parents of Gays, Lesbians, Bisexuals, Transgenders:
    www.bidstrup.com/parents.htm

Gay Bisexual Youth Suicide Studies: www.virtualcity.com/youthsui-
    cide/
The Homosexuality Factor in the *Youth* Suicide Problem. Pierre J.
    Tremblay B.Sc., BA, B.Ed: www.qrd.org/qrd/www/youth/trem-
    blay/

Besides these sites, there was also one link list, offering additional information about a variety of queer related topics, and one database-driven site:

Bonus Rounds Gay Youth Page: www.bonusround.com/gayyouth/
Queer America – Find Your Way: www.queeramerica.com/

Queer America, associated with OutProud, offers a database of searchable resources and support agencies, such as local PFLAG groups. When I visited the site and typed in my area code and the first three digits of my postal code, I was given 41 entries of local LGBT/queer supportive groups, many of which I knew.

The remaining sites can be divided into those written specifically by digital youth and a grab-bag of assorted sites, which included a commercial site, Amazon.com: Listmania! Gay Youth; a personals site, Gay Youth UK; a dead link, Lesbian Gay Bi Youth Line; and two homepages, which also seem to serve as information clearinghouses, offering support and advice for young queers: Dave PD at www.davepd.co.uk/, and :::bgiok::: ["Being Gay Is OK"]: www.bgiok.org.uk/. The author of :::bgiok::: writes, "I'm 27 years old, live in Farnham, Surrey in the UK, in a gay house-share. I currently work in I.T." The purpose of his site is comparable to that of many of the sites that listed:

> You might have heard negative attitudes about homosexuality. Maybe you're having a tough time coming to terms with being gay or with other peoples intolerance toward you. Whatever your situation, I hope that you will find the information and reassurance on this website that you're looking for.

The other six sites included five that seem specifically written *by* queer digital youth, at least in part, and one site that *may* be written by queer digital youth, but whose authorship is a bit unclear:

Youth Resources: www.youthresource.com/
Elight!: www.elight.org/ —defunct, redirect to Mogenic and Oasis
Oasis Queer Youth Monthly Magazine: www.oasismag.com/
Mogenic: www.mogenic.com/
Young Gay America: www.younggayamerica.com/
Australian Gay Youth Resources Homepage: www.dogwomble.wor-
fie.net

Elight (http://www.elight.org/) is one of the sites discussed by Addison and Comstock, but it unfortunately seems defunct and the page simply redirects one to other pages and a list of recommended sites: "Youth that wish to publish their writings online should check out **Oasis**. For youth personals, check out **Mogenic**." Both of these two prominently recommended sites are composed mostly by queer digital youth themselves, and I return to a discussion of them later in this chapter.[5]

The search engine also suggests some "recommended categories" for further searching: "Lesbian, Gay, and Bisexual Youth," "Lesbian, Gay, and Bisexual Youth Suicide," and "Internet Relay Chat (IRC) > Youth." Clicking on the first category yields much the same in terms of results, including a mixture of additional categories and a selection of "most popular" sites:

- Coming-out resources (4)
- Events (2)
- Internet relay chat (IRC)
- Magazines (10)
- Organizations (51)
- Suicide
- Web directories (1)
- Usenet (1)

The most popular site listings included the following:

- <u>Youth Action Online</u>—a support center and resource for GLB and questioning youth.
- <u>Youth Resources</u>—information, support, and resources for LGBT youth.
- <u>Resource for Parents of Gays, Lesbians, Bisexuals, Transgenders</u>—support and advice for parents of gay youth. Includes questions and statements.

---

[5]Yahoo! also provides "sponsor results," which, according to the site, are "are paid listings provided by Overture Services, Inc. that appear on Yahoo! Search results pages. This program uses a performance-based model in which businesses bid for enhanced placement in search results on terms that are relevant to their business, and pay on a per-click basis" (http://help.yahoo.com/help/us/ysearch/sponsor/sponsor-01.html). The two "sponsor results" for my search seemed similar to those for the general search on the phrase "gay youth":

- <u>Huge Selection of Videos and DVDs</u>—Amazon's extensive online catalog has almost any movie you're looking for, including "**Gay Youth**." www.amazon.com
- <u>Cathedral of Hope Proclaiming God's Love</u>—**Gay** and lesbian Christian church in Dallas, Texas. Proclaiming God's inclusive love via Internet worship, online sermons and many other Christian homosexual resources. www.cathedralof hope.com

- <u>Cool Page for Queer Teens</u>—resource page for LGBT youth.
- <u>FAQ—Soc.support.youth.gay-lesbian-bi</u>

These sites can be broken down into much the same categories as those just listed, with some offering organization-based support, advice, or other "resources," some supporting parents of queer youth, and at least one, Youth Resources, providing information written by queer digital youth themselves. It shouldn't be surprising that the "sponsor sites" include at least one commercial site and one religious-based site; the commercialization of the Internet and the Web is at least partially responsible for the maintenance of much information on the Internet, and credit must be given to some religious organizations across the country that have taken a sincere interest in helping young queers, especially when so many parents, guardians, and other religious institutions abandon queer children.

In *Cybertypes: Race, Ethnicity, and Identity on the Internet*, cyberstudies scholar Lisa Nakamura has analyzed how comparable Web portals for those seeking information about race and ethnicity are double-edged in terms of their depictions and representations; specifically, they provide information about different races and ethnicities, but at a cost:

> Web portals function in a . . . double way; they encourage tolerance by acknowledging "diverse" identities, yet create ambiguities about identities that fall between the cracks of hierarchical lists, those sites or "no-places" of hybrid being that seem to hover phantasmatically between the fine strands of the portaled Web. What if you just don't fit into any of the categories available on the list, or do not consider any one of them *dominant* but are nonetheless required by the interface to choose one first? (112)

Nakamura suggests that many portals "cybertype" races and ethnicities, reductively foreclosing on articulating and representing some of the complexities of living as a particular race or racial mix. It's worth asking if similar dynamics are at play on some prominent *queer* portals, or on general portals that queer digital youth use to find information and representations of themselves.

When I consider Nakamura's thinking in relation to what we find with even just a cursory search of Web portals, I am tempted to think that the situation regarding information available to queer e-savvy youth may not be as dire as Nakamura suggests it is for comparable information about race and ethnicity. In general, the diversity of sites accessible through such a search is impressive, and the presence of international sites, even if they are all English-based, points perhaps to a serious consideration of queer issues across the globe. Young queers can at least read about experiences of queerness from different parts of the world. If we "lump" the Australian Gay Youth Resources home page with the support and organization-based sites listed earlier from the original search of 20 sites, then that leaves us with five sites (not including the one defunct site, Elight!) with content specifically written by queer digital youth, not just *for* such youth—about 25%.

Although this seems to suggest that queer digital youth control at least *part* of the information that is offered on the Web about them, I couldn't help but wonder what content was being filtered out, or, to borrow Nakamura's phrase, "what's missing." When I used the "advanced search" options, I noted that the default for the "mature content filter" was on "moderate," set to exclude "mature images only." This leads me to believe that, potentially, *textual* information discussing sexuality, and issues such as safer sex, are probably not being excluded.

Mature Content Filter   ☐ **Strict**–Filter out mature images and Web content

☐ **Moderate**–Filter out mature images only

☐ **Off**–Do not filter search results

Advisory–The mature content filter is designed to filter out explicit, adult-oriented content from Yahoo! Search results. However, Yahoo! cannot guarantee that all explicit content will be filtered out.

Nakamura says, pointedly, that "Cyberspace's interfaces are perfectly hegemonic, in the sense that they are enforced and informed by dominant ideologies, however unconscious, as well as, to a much lesser extent, infrastructure and design limitations" (135). As I look at the variety of youth-oriented sites listed via Yahoo! and even Gayscape, I have a hard time pinpointing a particular dominant ideology, beyond the sense that queer youth are in need of support and assistance—which they often are. The diversity of sites speaks to a range of interests, and the presence of a number of sites written specifically by queer digital youth attests to the "colonization" of at least some part of cyberspace by those youth.

However, when we take a closer look at some of the more prominent sites listed, I think we do see quite a bit more "cybertyping" and consequent reductive foreclosing on acknowledging the complexity of young queer lives. This is especially the case in some frequently visited and high-profile organization-based and commercial sites.

Some .com sites style themselves as community-building ventures, with relatively small commercial interests; such sites include PlanetOut and Gay.com (which merged in 2001), both of which have subsections targeting youth with Internet access, and both of which are frequently used by some queer youth looking for information; one person I interviewed online reported that "Tons of people I know use the net to link up in numerous ways, from PlanetOut.com to Gay.com and have since they were young." Commercial sites certainly help promote visibility of LGBT peoples, but it is worth asking what kinds of marketing "stereotypes" or "cybertypes" are disseminated in the process of attracting buyers and visitors. Given the impact of the media on helping many youth construct a sense of self and community, we should pay attention to the ways in which marketers, even seemingly "queer-friendly" ones, are representing youth and queerness as conceptual categories.

For instance, on a very popular site such as "PlanetOut" (http://www.planetout.com/pno/splash.html), visitors can search through a number of links to find information on health issues, romance, entertainment, and money. The primary emphasis, however, seems to be on entertainment, with many links to reviews of movies, commentaries on stars, and gossip about celebrities. When I visited on August 15, 2003, a feature link declared that "You haven't earned your gay card until you've seen every one of the movies on this list." The youth- or teen-oriented pages of this site feature similar venues and material, including chat rooms, message boards, information about movies, celebrities, and music, advice about "Coming Out," a "School survival kit," and a series of questions and answers: Could I be gay?, Am I a lesbian?, What about bisexual?, and Am I transgender? Advertisements abound.

Certainly, the presence of message boards and chatrooms allow digital youth to communicate with one another, but most of the content of these pages seem to "type" queer youth as either looking for support or interested in entertainment media. And although many youth may be looking for information along such lines, this strikes me as a very limited representation of queer youth interests and lives. Gay.com seems configured along similar lines, with links to stories about the entertainment world highlighted, as well as links to information on business, finance, health, fitness, and headline news. Again, a limited range of links suggests a "type"—a gay person interested in media, wanting to be updated on news from the entertainment world and informed about some sociopolitical events. Such emphases are not necessarily surprising because these *are* commercial sites, so their funneling of visitors to other commercial ventures, such as the entertainment industry, is to be expected.

Cybersocket, at http://www.cybersocket.com/, is a bit glitzier than Gayscape, and its menu of categories is (perhaps concomitantly) a bit more commercially, even sexually oriented. Links to African-American and Asian-American queer interests foreclose on representing, as Nakamura might point out, hybrid identities, and, in general, the list seems to privilege those looking to make purchases, as the majority of categories link to products. The final category, listed alphabetically, is "youth resources," and it links to a mix of porn sites and resource sites, with *some* written and maintained by queer digital youth. Typical listings, however, include Gay College Party (http://www.gaycollegeparty.com/) and Red Dog Sportswear (http://www.reddogsportswear.com), with one promoting various gay clubs and night venues and the other serving as a clothing vendor. Perhaps the dominant "cybertype" here is that you are as queer as your purchases.

In "Gay Media, Inc.: Media Structures, the New Gay Conglomerates, and Collective Sexual Identities," Joshua Gamson suggests that these large gay-themed online business ventures, such as Gay.com and PlanetOut, are increasingly created out of mergers between and among various smaller enterprises, such as the merger in 2001 between Gay.com and PlanetOut. In the process, however, these business mergers result in a weakening of these gay media's relation to activist causes and institutions, and they turn more toward business ventures and modes to expand. At one point, gay activism and media were tightly intertwined, with activists, reporters, columnists, and other artists cocreating messages, information, and publications to get the word out about queer life, to increase queer visibility in the public consciousness. Now, according to Gamson, with increased visibility and the "commodification-of-homosexuality," we are seeing greater "distancing of gay media from LGBT-activist movements" (272). For instance, in Gamson's view, PlanetOut Partners is a business venture, not necessarily accountable to the community that it seeks to reach (263). Thus, a particular cybertype—the purchasing queer—is forwarded and disseminated via such sites.

At the same time, Gamson acknowledges that commercial sites *do* present a spectrum of issues, ranging from transgender concerns to discussions of "alternative" sexual practices, such as sado-masochism. However, sites such as "PlanetOut and Gay.com must also be presentable to advertisers and investors, and as a result the sex talk, the insistent and complicated mixes of racial and gender and sexual (and sometimes class) identities, the confident perversions—the things that might remind advertisers and investors of the dissident parts of gayness—are pushed below the rainbow-flaggy, advice-from-Ellen's-mother, celebrity-profile, shop-til-you-drop front pages" (269). For Gamson, the end result has been a strange mix of marketers promoting a certain kind of respectability while, at the same time, attempting to appeal to a diversity of queers: "The transformation of the lesbian, gay, bisexual, and transgender movement into a market, which requires narrow and palatable versions of identity and community, is taking place through businesses with a particular interest in casting the identity net very wide" (Gamson 274). Perhaps the simple truth to be gleaned from this is that, although certain images and types are fostered on the Web by marketers, the Web is large enough to provide a diversity of representations—with most generally just a few clicks away.

Beyond the plethora of commercial sites, other Web-based ventures provide a different cybertype for queer digital youth. For instance, less commercially driven and more community-oriented sites focus on information that site sponsors perceive LGBT youth need and want. For instance, OutProud (http://www.outproud.org/) is sponsored by the National Coalition for Gay, Lesbian, Bisexual & Transgender Youth, and it offers a "wide range of resources available for youth and educators," including coming-out stories, information about "community role models," school resources, book recommendations, and a forum for "correspond[ing] with other queer youth on issues affecting our community."

> We provide outreach and support to queer teens just coming to terms with their sexual orientation and to those contemplating coming out. We let them know they're not alone by helping them find local sources of friendship and support.
>
> We believe in effecting change at a grass-roots level by catalyzing and fostering the development of a new generation of queer youth activists who will take positions at the forefront of our civil rights and social movements.

Chris Kryzan, in an e-mail interview about OutProud, suggests that "The primary topic we address could probably best be summed up in this statement 'Help. I've just begun to understand (or deal with, or accept) that I am gay. Where do I go from here?'"

A similar site, Youth.org (http://www.youth.org/), has a comparable mission:

> YOUTH.ORG is a service run by volunteers, created to help self-identi-
> fying gay, lesbian, bisexual and questioning youth. YOUTH.ORG exists
> to provide young people with a safe space online to be themselves.

> YOUTH.ORG was formed to provide for the needs of GLBT youth; the
> need for a rare opportunity to express themselves, to know they are
> not alone, and to interact with others who have already accepted their
> sexuality.

Any number of other organization-based sites provide information compa-
rable to that found on both of these sites—ranging from safer sex advice at
It's Your (Sex) Life, http://www.itsyoursexlife.com/, sponsored by the Kaiser
Family Foundation; to discussions of educational settings at the Gay,
Lesbian, Straight Education Network, http://www.glsen.org/; to more local
resources, such as Atlanta-based Youthpride (www.youthpride.org) and
Kaleidoscope (http://www.kaleidoscope.org/) in Columbus, Ohio.

Such sites certainly provide queer youth Web users with often much-
needed information and support. In the process, such sites construct a different "cybertype" of queer youth: Queer youth are youth who need to
know they are not alone, who need models for healthy sexuality and sexual identity development, and who need safe forums for asking questions
and talking to one another. "Safety," however, may be determined by the
organizations themselves, not necessarily by the queer youth visiting those
sites. For instance, one reviewer of this project suggests that such sites
"offer a message board, but appears to be closely refereed. How does such
mediation—presumably non-youth mediation since the underlying motivations would most likely be legal—figure into . . . issues of representation,
interactivity, community, and Web literacies?" Let me be clear: In no way
am I disparaging the value of these sites; it is clear that they provide much
needed information and points of contact for queer youth accessing them.
But it's also worth asking if such sites are providing youth visitors with the
information and resources that *they* want themselves. Certainly, many of
the organization-based sites are monitored by boards and other evaluation
committees that include at least *some* queer youth.

But I wonder what sites that are specifically designed and written *by*
LGBT digital youth tell us about those youth that commercially or organiza-
tionally sponsored sites do not. Put another way, what do more "home
grown" LGBT youth sites tell us about the interests, concerns, and values
of those e-savvy youth? To approach some answers to these questions, let's
look at some of the more prominent ways in which queer digital youth
contribute to and compose their thoughts, ideas, and insights via Web
texts—many of which can actually be found via links from sites such as

OutProud or Gay.com. This discussion encompasses analysis of some fairly high-profile queer-themed e-zines, other sites that promote queer digital youth writing and Web texts, and interviews with representative authors of such Web texts.

QUEER WRITING YOUTH ON THE WEB: SITES COMPOSED BY QUEER YOUTH

In the previous section, I examined some of the major cybertypes to be found on a variety of large-scale sites, including commercial and information vendors. In this section, however, I ask a different question: What kinds of representations, images, and depictions do queer digital youth foster of themselves when *they* control the content of Web spaces designed for them? To approach this question, I have searched for a variety of sites with content largely or even exclusively generated by queer digital youth, and I discuss some of the more prominent of these sites here. In general, there are a few distinct trends emerging on these sites—trends often in contradistinction to the cybertypes just outlined. Specifically, queer youth composing for Web publications seem invested in discussing political issues surrounding queerness, exploring the diversity of identity and sexual expression in the queer community, and in having frank discussions about sexual practices and safer sex education.

One of the most prominent and frequently referenced youth-oriented and largely youth-run Webzines is the Australian-based Mogenic: Gay & Lesbian Youth Magazine at http://mogenic.com/index.asp. A close runner-up is XYmag.com, at http://www.xymag.com/, which serves as the Web site for the popular glossy magazine aimed at gay youth. Mogenic, which is touted as "the world's leading gay, lesbian, bisexual and transgendered youth Web site," has a simply stated mission:

> Mogenic is a special place on the net where gay and lesbian youth have the freedom to exchange ideas, share experiences, discuss coming out, make friends, read interesting content and most importantly: *make contact.*

> Literally millions of young people around the world are making Mogenic a daily ritual. We are seeking your support to develop and grow Mogenic to cater to the overwhelming demand for increased services.

> We invite you to help Mogenic help gay, lesbian, bisexual and transgender youth (GLBT) know that they are not alone, that there is a community of acceptance, vibrancy, support, beauty and pride.
>
> A community that cares for the positive advancement of its young people—*like any community should.*
> (http://mogenic.com/about/default.asp)

In some ways, the mission seems reminiscent of many of the organizations discussed above, such as OutProud. Its uniqueness, however, stems from its origin, as the brainchild of a young queer man. The *Sidney Star Observer* reported the following in 2001:

> Its arrival has been spectacular: a 19-year-old Sydneysider with the vision to create Australia's first gay and lesbian youth website has become an international hit. Given the name Angel by users of his site, his vision–Mogenic.com–has grown in one year to become the world's most popular site for lesbian and gay youth.
>
> "Before Mogenic there weren't many alternative Australian-based websites for young people to meet, except for sites offering really clinical, dry information about homosexuality," Angel told *Sydney Star Observer*. "I think those sites were written by really scared people that are worried about negative feedback, whereas I don't give a shit—I knew more had to be said for young people so I went ahead and set up Mogenic." (linked from Mogenic to http://www.ssonet.com.au/show article.asp?ArticleID = 992)

Another news source, linked from Mogenic, *Fridae: Asia's Gay & Lesbian Network*, records much the same story, highlighting the popularity and extensive audience the site has:

> Barely an adult, Sebastian is the creator and managing director of the world's most popular gay and lesbian youth website, *Mogenic.com*, attracting about 230,000 readers each month. Some 60 % are from the US, the rest from Australasia and Europe.
>
> By day, the 20-year-old works as the production manager of Australian gay site *Outbiz.com*. He also volunteers as the Co-Chair of the Twenty 10 Association, a gay and lesbian youth support group. (http://www.fridae.com/magazine/ep20011205_1_1.php)

What distinguishes Mogenic from other "support group," organization-based sites? The primary difference is that Mogenic emphasizes, highlights, and features *digital youth writing* in ways that few organization-based or commercial sites do. Various sections—"Hot Advice," "Columns," "My Story," and "Expressions"—present writing and other "expressions," such as art work, from queer digital youth themselves, and readers are invited to contribute their own work, to link up with the "army of mogenic" and "join the revolution" (http://mogenic.com/about/joinus.asp).

The layout of this site emphasizes a youth focus, with glossy pictures of young people abounding, and it also signals that the site is *not* primarily a support site, but a site designed, first and foremost, to offer queer digital youth an opportunity to write about and represent their own lives. For instance, the menu emphasizes venues of *expression* rather than information resources—a striking difference from many organization-based sites. Menu items highlight chatrooms, columns, and "My Stories," suggesting that digital youth voices are emphasized throughout the site.

The "Columns" section (http://mogenic.com/columns/default.asp) is quite interesting in that it reveals a diversity of topics largely missing on any site examined so far. The expected discussions and stories about life in the closet and coming out are set side by side with stories about civil rights struggles, bi-phobia, and the battle to represent homo-eroticism fairly and equitably in sex education. In general, the site feels much more "radical," even more activist than the organization-based sites. Indeed, one senses that there *is* a "revolution" and an "army" here.

XY online, at http://www.xymag.com/, offers a comparable feel—to an extent. The menu "about XY," "XY articles," "bois," "places guide," "survival," "sex," "contribute," "XY shop" reflects the mission statement in its attempt to bring a diversity of queer digital youth issues to its readers. And although the site is fairly commercial and related to other gay business ventures—in 2000, PlanetOut bought the digital rights to XY (Gamson 262)—XY online seems to attempt to publish work not just *for* youth with e-access but *by* youth such access:

> **xy**.com is the online home of *xyMagazine*, the only national magazine dedicated solely to the interests and needs of young gay men, in print since 1996.
>
> **xy** is a glossy, color magazine, published bi-monthly, and known best for its original photography, brazenly honest commentary on politics and culture, review of film, music and literature, reader contributions, advice on surviving young and gay, and a rather dark sense of humor.
>
> **xy** (http://www.xymag.com/index.php?t = 3)

Also, clicking on the menu heading "bois," also you to "peep" at personals and profiles or "chat" with others, and you are invited to contribute your own writing if you so desire.

XY online differs from Mogenic a bit in its treatment of sex. Based in the United States, the site offers a "warning" about potentially sexually explicit content before allowing you to click through to it:

> WARNING: The Sex section contains sexually-explicit and erotic material. Do not continue if this will offend you. If accessing this content causes you to break local laws, please leave now.
>
> By viewing any content you implicitly declare and affirm that you are not a minor or in the company of a minor and are entitled to have access to material intended for adults. (http://www.xymag.com/index.php?t = 10)

You can then "proceed" or "run away," but if you click through you might find just a spattering of articles on sex, such as the following

The highschool boy's guide to getting laid
Sex is not bad for you—take a stand, and get some lovin'.

Kinky sex
Sometimes all you need is a bit of kink. Feel good about your fantasies.

Rethinking virginity
Escape from the Planet of the SortaVirgins.

In terms of articles, the choice is limited (http://www.xymag.com/index.php?t = 4):

"The Abercrombie Boy"
"Why do they hate us?"
"Nuke Your Closet"
"Why do I lust for a boy?"
"Age of Dissent"—takes you to an article on why the drinking age should be 18
"Peter is a Slut"
"Non Scene"
"Altruism"

But the titles alone suggest an activist mindset, even a militancy ("Nuke Your Closet") not always found, if ever, in organization-based sites. There is also evidence of acute awareness of generational differences among gays. In the article "Non Scene," for instance, the author states unequivocally that

> The generation now coming up needs to be very careful to switch its values from the connection-negative values of the 1990s to the love-connection values I hope are coming up in the 2000s. In the meantime, I am going to go and walk on the beach again—which is almost as good as a shag—and I'll continue to be one of those reclusive non-scene people whom everyone wants to meet.
> I hope someone fixes our value system soon, so I can come back. (http://www.xymag.com/index.php?t = 4&b = 1 &image_set = b&a = arti cles/mag/xy28 % 20non % 20scene)

This is a poignant statement, attesting not only to generational differences, but to a need to self-define, to assert a sense of self against both older queers' expectations for younger queers *and* against any perceived communal expectations or values. We can see perhaps a bit of this in Mogenic as well. The relative lack of traditional gay signifiers and visual rhetoric, such as rainbow flags and pink triangles, suggests a move away from "older" representations and articulations of gay sexuality.

As such, XY online and Mogenic show us queer digital youth writing their lives with much more political and social awareness than we often see on the organization-based or commercial sites. Although there is certainly some emphasis on creating a "safe space" for queer digital youth to express themselves, there is also quite a bit material that promotes a more political understanding or interrogation of sexuality. Articles on sex education, for instance, question of the status quo in its treatment—or frequent dismissal—of queer issues in the classroom. Furthermore, the ease of Web publication is used to expand the number of voices, and thus potential topics, that the sites present and discuss. This has the initial net effect, as it were, of problematizing any cybertyping of queer youth; diversity of topics and interests, particularly in Mogenic, seems prioritized over providing advice on how best to adapt and assimilate into the larger culture as a young gay person.

Comparing these two particular sites, however, reveals some curious international differences. Mogenic seems pitched at both men and women, whereas XY is, as its title suggests, a "boi" zine. In general, I have found non-American-based sites to be a bit more willing to speak to people of both (or many) genders than their American counterparts. Also, XY online is fairly "skittish" about its sexual content, providing "warnings," whereas references to sex and sexuality are sprinkled throughout Mogenic's many pages. Still, both sites grapple with "thorny" sexuality issues, such as kinky sex and bisexuality. There seems to be a willingness here not only to explore traditionally touchy or taboo subjects, but to delight in them as well.

Ultimately, both of these large-scale sites suggest that queer digital youth are willing to use the Web to discuss a variety of tricky and thorny issues, and we can see the same interest in developing a language of *sexual literacy* in a variety of other, smaller online queer youth zines and community-building sites. *Oasismag* (http://www.oasismag.com/) is a frequently referenced site, by both search engines and respondents to surveys, as a forum for featuring queer digital youth writing, and it's one of the sites (with Mogenic) recommended by the now defunct Elight!. Indeed, the site is subtitled "a writing community for queer and questioning youth," the main menu highlights digital youth writing, particularly the Web-based journaling venue, blogging:

"home," "archives," "user blogs," "forum," "photo gallery," "polls," "user account"

As with Mogenic, and to a lesser extent XY, a political emphasis is prominent. The opening page in August 2003 highlighted the Supreme Court decision that overturned Texas' sodomy laws and President Bush's interest in a constitutional amendment to define marriage as a relationship only between men and women. Blogs allowed visitors to discuss the issue and air their ideas, insights, and aggravations. Indeed, the presence of blogs, a Web-based forum for written contributions, allows a diversity of users to contribute to the site, and prominent blogging topics include gay characters on television, being out, writing poetry, meeting people, having crushes, and navigating relationships. The site also includes polls (on topics such as how much do parents know about users' sexuality) and forums (with topics such as songs with special personal significance).

Two smaller-scale e-zines, offering a range of articles instead of postings, include *Tenpercentbent* (http://www.tenpercentbent.com/) and *Can't Think Str8* (http://www20.brinkster.com/str8/). *Tenpercentbent* is, according to the site,

> a bi-weekly ezine, composed of GLBT youth under the age of 26, who write on all topics under the sun. Created to give GLBT youth a forum to express their thoughts and opinions, we're here to show the world

that we do exist and we're proud of who we are! (http://www.tenper-
centbent.com/)

The diversity of topics covered in the articles reflects the trends in other
comparable forums, such as Mogenic, to address socially and politically
important topics. For instance, in addition to articles about relationships and
entertainment, a section on "queer issues" highlights a variety of topics:

[Queer and Disabled] **by Chris**
"Confessions of a Chat Whore"

[Religion Corner] **by Krystal Quinn**
"Young gay christian.. Looking for answers."

[School life] **by Emily Wright**
"Words from a teenage dirtbag"

[Coming Out] **by Elyse Lattanzio**
"it's all about me, kids."

[Activist at Heart] **by C.J. Griffiths**
"An outrage"

[Trannies] **by Frances Farmer**
"Liberated at last"

There seems to be a willingness here to address a wide range of diversity
within the queer youth community, as well as to consider activist issues. In
"Activist at Heart," C. J. Griffiths features an angry letter written to the
American Red Cross about that organization's refusal to accept blood dona-
tions from gay men. The author queries the fundamental unfairness (and
perhaps bigotry) that he feels is implicit in such a policy.

According to Pelle Nyren, age 24 and the Web master for Can't Think
Str8, the importance of such sites lies in how young queer visitors are the
ones generating such content:

> For the visitors the benefit over other sites is that this one actually has
> some content (and no gif-anims of rainbows). Making the visitors
> make the content is important, for it's close to impossible for any web-
> master to keep a hobby site feel fresh if he's to produce the content
> himself.

As with Tenpercentbent, topics include a mix of the personal and the political, including addressing issues such as coming out, homophobia, love,
and identity. The key, as the site suggests, is that the issues are addressed

by youth themselves: "Can't think STR8 is a non-pornografic non-commercial site for young gay guys made by young gay guys! The idea of this site is that the people surfing in here (yes, that means *you*) will share experiences and advice!"

A slightly more ambitious queer digital youth writing project is offered by YGA (http://www.younggayamerica.com/), whose mission statement says:

> Young Gay America is a long-term research project/road trip adventure dedicated to improving the lives of LGBTQ youth. We aim to educate and inform LGBTQ youth about their importance in society by placing their individual stories in an international forum; to foster and encourage the exchange of ideas by queer youth on issues pertinent to queer youth (to allow their voices to be heard); and to promote positive self-image and sense of belonging. (http://www.younggayamerica.com /about.shtml)[6]

To accomplish this mission, the site authors invite queer youth with Web access to email in their stories, and the site authors are also willing to con-

---

[6]In an e-mail interview, Mike Glatze offered the following comments about YGA's work: "We are friends with Chris Kryzan from OutProud and our goals are similar. We support each others' projects. We are a non-profit volunteer organization created by Benjie Nycum and me in 2001, supported by high school senior/web designer Andy Brown, Adobe Systems Inc. Designer Ted McGuire, and production assistant Scott MacPhee. Benjie and I were formerly Associate Publisher and Managing Editor, respectively, of *XY Magazine* and author/editor of The *XY Survival Guide: Everything You Need to Know About Being Young and Gay*. We were also volunteers for the Stop AIDS Project, San Francisco and the Gay and Lesbian National Hotline. We left XY in 2001 to start Young Gay America with the goal of providing a different method of media outreach to LGBT youth across America, especially youth in rural locations, and to reach out to a more diverse crowd of LGBT youth (*XY* is only a male publication). Our mission is to educate and inform LGBTQ youth about their importance in society by placing their individual stories in an international forum; to foster and encourage the exchange of ideas by queer youth on issues pertinent to queer youth (to allow their voices to be heard); and to promote positive self-image and sense of belonging. We have now visited 41 states and 4 Canadian provinces and interviewed around 1,000 LGBT youth. Our project is funded solely from out-of-pocket income we save from working regular jobs in architecture and marketing in our hometown of Halifax, Nova Scotia. The YGA crew volunteers evenings, weekends, and unpaid vacation time to the success of the project. We also have many strategic alliances with individuals and organizations such as Dr. Ritch C Savin-Williams, developmental psychologist who has written many books on LGBT youth, the Gay and Lesbian National Hotline, and Equality Forum in Philadelphia."

duct face-to-face interviews. Detailed information about how such interviews are conducted, as well as permissions forms, is all readily available for download. As such, you can read a variety of stories written by youth with Internet access. Moreover, the menu items—"home," "articles," "closet," "sex," "advice," "reviews," and "links"—suggest consideration of topics similar to those found on organization-based sites, but the range of articles on the site is more comparable to that on Mogenic or Tenpercentbent, particularly in the willingness to grapple with difficult topics. For instance, articles and interviews discuss coming out and crushes on straight friends, but more challenging topics abound, such as transsexuality and how to have safer sex.

Indeed, addressing transgenderism is a frequent topic on these sites, and one that queer digital youth seem to be willing to approach and discuss with an open mind. Christina, a young person I interviewed via e-mail, offered *Butch Dyke Boy* (http://www.butchdykeboy.com/) as her favorite site. While the site doesn't have a particular youth focus, many of the articles do address the interests and concerns of queer or transgendered youth. For instance, discussions of racism, domestic violence, and negotiating a place within the larger LGBT/queer community are all issues tackled on queer digital youth-oriented sites. Gunner, the site founder, says that he started Butch Dyke Boy Productions in 1999 because "I saw a need for more events serving the Trans, Queer, Gender Queer, Bi, Dyke, and other marginalized communities. Since then, Butch Dyke Boy Productions has diversified into a variety of fields" (http://www.butchdykeboy.com /bdb/us). The site lives up to its mission by offering a variety of articles, book reviews, announcements, and pictures and comics. Indeed, the photos and comics of and about queer and transgendered people are a key ingredient of the visual appeal—and rhetoric—of the site, in that sighted visitors receive a visual representation of transgendered existence—a depiction often left out of the mass media with the exception of the occasional drag queer and talk-show spectacles about transsexuality, a rare few of which are particularly flattering, understanding, or sympathetic. As such, these images go some way to correcting mistaken assumptions about queer/transgendered people, representing a broader spectrum of queer/transgendered experience, and, more provocatively, provoking in the visitor a reconsideration of how many in our society experience gender oppression. For instance, the comic, "Welcome to Sunny Camp Trans," discusses in an engaging and enlightening format how many transwomyn have been excluded from many women-only festivals or events, such as the Michigan Women's Festival, because some women and feminists believe that transwomyn are really men in drag. The comic, however, proposes the need for different spaces, a "Camp Trans":

Raising such issues, and depicting them with images of the young engaged in such debate, suggests that these are important concerns of young queers—concerns that query the supposedly "safe spaces," such as the Michigan Festival, which claim to create safe spaces for queers, but in practice exclude members of the queer community.

These are fundamentally sociopolitical issues, and Young Gay America also addresses a smattering of other topics that suggests a willingness on the part of many queer digital youth to engage in political debate, about gay marriage for instance, and to consider the particular needs of those occupying multiple minority or marginzalized identities, such as being both African American and gay. Comparable topics include the following:

To Hell With Manners, It's Time to Take Charge!!!
"I myself am not your typical stereotype of a dyke. I am loud, outspoken, friends with a multitude of gay and straight men alike, affectionate toward them and just plain myself..." an essay by **Alicia Yowell**

We've Come a Long Way, But We Still Have Farther To Go
An essay about reviving our civil rights movement. By **Ryan McWilliams**

The Same Thing Happened to the Blacks
"No matter what happens to this society, there will still be me, a 20 year-old black gay male who is tired of his people deserting him and others in need..." A statement by **Eddie Peterson**

Is Gay Marriage Worth It?
According to **Chris Kaufman**, Direct Services Coordinator at Outright Vermont, the answer might very well be NO. He has had some frustrating times with Outright, VT, in the wake of the battle for Civil Union legislation. That battle had some devastating effects on queer youth and Outright is still trying to pick up the pieces from the whole.

Personally, I think that questioning the value of "gay marriage" is a fascinating topic for these youth to be discussing. The question alone does not assume that assimilating into the mainstream culture is the primary goal, or *should* be the primary goal, of young queers. In fact, another article suggests that gays are "luckier" than straights, particularly regarding issues of gender conformity: "When I think of all those straight boys who have to watch themselves to make sure they don't say anything too affectionate, I get sad for them. Every time they glance at each other in the locker room it has to be turned into a joke."

In general, I have found the digital youth-driven sites to be a bit more frank in their discussions of sexuality, a tad more politically minded, and more embracing of bi-sexual and transgendered issues than either the commercial or organization-based sites examined earlier. Making a direct comparison between a digital youth-composed and an organizational site written *for* such youth might clarify some of these differences—particularly the emphasis on sex and sexual practices.

In an e-mail interview, Mike Glatze, founder of YGA, reported that YGA's goals and aims were comparable to those of OutProud, and that he and a colleague had actually worked for *XY* magazine, as "Associate Publisher and Managing Editor, respectively, of *XY* magazine and author/editor of *The XY Survival Guide: Everything You Need to Know About Being Young and Gay.*" Although I appreciate their support of OutProud's work and can certainly see some similarities between the two projects, I am not entirely convinced that the effect, or even the tone, is the same. For instance, OutProud highlights in its link lists "coming-out stories" and "community role models," designed to help gay youth "be yourself." The tone is inviting and informational. In contrast, the lead article at YGA, written by a 16-year-old lesbian, is much more confrontational, encouraging queer youth with Internet access to "take charge," particularly when it comes to harassment at school:

> It's time for us queer youth to stand up and shout that we are sick of being under-rated behind adults just because we haven't reached 18 or 21! Straight youth, gay youth, I do not care! It's time for us to stand up and take charge of matters that affect us in our growing up and our thoughts of the future. Do not let people think wrong of you. Retaliate when people harm you. Take charge of the common goal that we deserve to attend school without being worried that we might be killed, beat, or verbally abused just because. (http://www.younggayamerica. com/streettalk31.shtml)

This seems much more, to me at least, the language of political confrontation than the calmer tones of information dissemination.

We can also see some intriguing differences in how content is organized and laid out. For example, OutProud's main menu offers a new link for transgendered youth, "a special resource and support area for transgender youth." The link takes visitors to very useful information, including an FAQ section, articles on the Web, and links to relevant and helpful sites. In contrast, YGA does not seem to have a separate section for transgendered people, although transgendered youth with Internet access are encouraged to write in about their lives and share their stories. Rather, dominant menu items are "articles," "in the closet?," "sex," "advice," and "reviews." The organization itself suggests a different approach—one perhaps a bit more invested in exploring common ground across the varieties of queerness and the diversity of queer digital youth potentially visiting the site (despite the use of the word gay in the site's title). The prominence of the menu item "sex"—and the relative invisibility of "sex" on the front page of OutProud—signals a different awareness of what youth with Internet access want, and need, to read about. Queer digital youth know they need reliable information about sex and sexually transmitted diseases. Highlighting "sex" as a main menu item, as opposed to a category of identity, such as "transgender," indicates, I believe, a different approach to issues of sexuality and sexual orientation; specifically, identities are important to queer digital youth, but perhaps more important is information necessary for the safe *practicing* of one's queerness. The emphasis thus shifts from pride in an *identity* to responsibility in *sexual expression*.

In the preceding pages in this section, I contrasted organization-based sites providing information *for* queer digital youth with community-building sites composed *by* such youth, and some intriguing differences in both approach and content have been seen. Other sites, however, offer content by both digital youth and adults, and I think of such sites as "hybrid" in that they combine writing by digital youth with material by adults. One such site is *YouthResource* (http://www.youthresource.com/), whose mission statement offers an eloquent attempt to bring together some youth and adults to foster respect for young queers and to provide them the information they want and need:

> YouthResource, a Web site created by and for gay, lesbian, bisexual, transgender, and questioning (GLBTQ) young people 13 to 24 years old, takes a holistic approach to sexual health by offering support, community, resources, and peer-to-peer education about issues of concern to GLBTQ young people. YouthResource has four focus areas: health, advocacy, community, and issues in our lives.
>
> YouthResource is a project of *Advocates for Youth*. Advocates for Youth is dedicated to creating programs and advocating for policies that help young people make informed and responsible decisions about their reproductive and sexual health. Advocates provides information, training, and strategic assistance to youth-serving organizations, policy makers, youth activists, and the media in the United States and in developing countries.
>
> Advocates believes that:
>
> - Adolescents have the right to balanced, accurate, and realistic sexuality education, confidential and affordable sexual health services, and a secure stake in the future.
> - Youth deserve respect. Today, they are perceived only as part of the problem. Valuing young people means they are part of the solution and are included in the development of programs and policies that affect their well-being.
> - Society has the responsibility to provide young people with the tools they need to safeguard their sexual health and young people have the responsibility to protect themselves from too early childbearing and sexually transmitted infections, including HIV. (http://www.youthresource.com/about/index.cfm)

To accomplish these goals, the site is packed with information; this is not a glitzy, glossy e-zine, but rather an informational site that boasts as much, if not more, information than the organization-based sites discussed previously. Moreover, this project aims to incorporate digital youth voices as much as possible. According to Jessie Gilliam, Advocates for Youth has between 70,000 and 80,000 visitors per month and "operates the site in partnership with 15 peer educators, ages 13–24. They decide the content of the site and develop materials and articles for the site." Having e-savvy youth involved in developing the site and participating in providing information is an important part of the mission of Advocates for Youth; Gilliam says the site "has both static content and 'peer education'—where young people can write into peers for information and support on a more individual level." A host of online peer educators provides direct and appropriate education and information, as needed. Topics covered, and addressed by either peers or other digital youth, include substance abuse, sexual assault, and body image issues, as well as bi youth, women, and transgendered youth.

Although the site may not seem as overtly political as the content of articles on Mogenic, or even Oasis, a political agenda is nonetheless embraced and forwarded here. The site is just one of a host of sites set up by Advocates for Youth (http://www.advocatesforyouth.org/), which is "dedicated to creating programs and advocating for policies that help young people make informed and responsible decisions about their reproductive and sexual health. Advocates provides information, training, and strategic assistance to youth-serving organizations, policymakers, youth activists, and the media in the United States and the developing world" (http://www.advocatesforyouth.org/about/index.htm).[7] As a project that values not only youth but frank discussion of sex and sexuality, Advocates for Youth's approach to queer youth contrasts with that of even XY online, which posts "warnings" about sexual content, potentially reifying sex and sexuality as taboo, even shameful subjects.

A similar approach is seen in another prominent "hybrid" site that aims to give a voice to concerns shared by many queer digital youth, as well as to provide information about safer sex practices, in the Gaydar section of Scarleteen.com. According to the parent Web site, Scarleteen is "owned by Heather Corinna and *Scarlet Letters*. Scarleteen serves over 6,000 teens, young adults, parents and educators every day of the year, 24 hours each day. It is operated with the help of a generous handful of volunteers ranging in age from 14 to 60." The goal of the project is primarily to serve as a "far better resource for sex information for teens than adult sexuality sites, as well as a supplement to in-home and school-based sex education," in recognition of the fact that "there is every evidence that much in-school sex education is not working" (http://www.scarleteen.com/about.html). As

---

[7]More specific information about Advocates for Youth's mission and vision can be found at http://www.advocatesforyouth.org/about/vision.htm.

such, Scarleteen's mission is political—to provide the kind of safer sex education, particularly *comprehensive* sex education, that is either handled poorly in the public educational system or that is avoided due to ideological biases against frank discussion of sexuality in schools. Scarleteen's founder, Heather Corinna, is identified as a queer woman (in her 30s at this point), and a significant portion of the site is devoted to Gaydar, a subsection focused on the sexual health needs of queer youth (http://www.scarleteen. com/gaydar/). The overall site is attractive and easy to navigate, dealing with a variety of issues, from use of Viagra and condoms to breast and testicle self-exams. The Gaydar section primarily consists of coming-out advice, but the fact that a queer-identified younger person initiated the site in 1997, suggests that queers have been at the forefront of providing safer sex information—and of understanding the importance of making such information available through venues such as the Web.

A more youth-directed project has been the YOUth and AIDS Web Project (http://oz.uc.edu/~alexanj/What.html) at the University of Cincinnati (UC), which I initiated in 2001. Arising out of a class project, in which students wrote about safer sex and HIV/AIDS prevention topics for other students, the site has grown to include a variety of information written for youth with Internet access *by digital youth* about safer sex, Sexually Transmitted Disease risks involved with tattooing and piercing, and communicating about safer sex with partners. The site is not queer-focused, but its openness and frankness in dealing with sexuality is comparable to that seen on other sites predominantly written by digital youth. I discuss this site, collaboratively written by students at UC, in Chapter 7.

In general, then, the "cybertype" of queer youth depicted on sites such as Mogenic, Oasis, YGA, and even YouthResource and Scarleteens' Gayday, is one of digital youth who wish to actively participate through a variety of Web forums—chatting, blogging, and article posting—about a variety of cultural and sociopolitical issues, particularly those revolving around frank discussions of sex.

QUEER YOUTH WEB AUTHORS SPEAKING: AN INTERVIEW WITH EMILY J.

To develop a better sense of how e-savvy queer youth write the Web, I interviewed, both face-to-face and online, a few queer youth who have worked extensively with the Web. Emily, a UC student, was among the most eloquent and informative about her Web-based practices, and her comments reflect many of the others I collected from interviewees. Nineteen at the time of the interview, Emily grew up around computers and the Internet, and she described her early experiences with the words "geek" and "geekness," saying that she has had Internet access as long as she can remember. For instance, even though her parents were hardly wealthy (by her reckoning), she had a monitored AOL account, and she also had high school classes in basic Web page construction and design.

In some ways, the story that Emily told about being young, queer, and an Internet user is fairly typical. She used the Internet and the Web to make contact with other queers, and she reported that her only contact with gays as a youngster was through the media. In fact, the first lesbian she knew about was Ellen DeGeneres. Shortly after identifying with DeGeneres (and the openly gay character she played on her television show), Emily began searching for, e-mailing, and chatting with other, usually older lesbians. Eventually her parents found out about her online activities, and banned her from the Internet for a few months. Such stories are most likely not uncommon. Emily reported being the only queer person she knew at school, except for one other friend, and having to sit through abstinence-only sex education that provided her no information about queer sexuality issues. She says:

> I was very much afraid. I did get harassed a lot when I came out. The Internet was really my only resource to the outside world. I didn't know of anything beyond Norwood, the neighborhood I grew up in. I didn't know of any of the queer organizations in the city.
>
> The Internet played a vital part in my discovery. It wasn't like it was telling me that I should be gay or anything like that. I had these feelings and it just verified that what I'm doing is okay and there are other people out there who feel like this. "You are not alone and here is some information for you so that you can be safe" and stuff like that. It wasn't like, "Come to the dark side!" It wasn't saying that gays are cool and you should be gay.

Given such comments, it's hard for me not to think of Emily's use of the Internet as not only necessary, but probably life-saving.

Emily has also worked on composing and producing Web sites, building on skills she learned initially in high school. Her two main Web projects have been one for the Cincinnati Youth Summit, a yearly convocation of area LGBT and queer youth, and a site for the UC's LGBT Student Alliance. Emily explained her vision for the Youth Summit site (http://www.cincyyouthsummit.org/) this way:

> It was mainly just to get people interested in what we were doing and present the information in a very easily obtainable way so that it wasn't confusing. Have the link so that it's easy to click to the link and get something and then go back and click that and keep going through the information instead of having to jump around or whatever. Just have it laid out in front of you and really have access to it.

Her goals for the Student Alliance site (http://www.soa.uc.edu/org/algbp/) were very similar, with a focus on providing information and opportunities for networking. The site also promotes a listserv for students and other interested parties:

> This listserv will be used for all of the announcements that will not be sent through this account and meeting updates and reminders. It will also act as a forum for you all to connect to each other. Please don't abuse it. We all hate spam mail and those annoying "send this to 10 friends now" e-mails.

And, in the spirit of disseminating information, Emily has borrowed text from listservs and e-mail chains, such as a segment on "10 ways to make it through family gatherings," which offers advice, particularly for queer youth, on how survive the holidays with family members who may be less than supportive or understanding. Such "borrowings" remind me of Lisa Nakamura's commentary in *Cybertypes* about the importance of forwarded e-mail messages in helping recipients to create and share a sense of community and identity, and Emily's interest in posting such information on the Student Alliance Web site was designed, I think, to facilitate not only the sharing of important information but the creation of a shared sense of identity and community. The site, however, also pushes at the boundaries of that community by linking (and perhaps, pardon the pun, networking) to other sites, such as the Spicy Divas (http://www.spicydivas.com/). Again, as with other queer youth-driven sites, the willingness to consider transgendered issues seriously is a striking feature of these youths' articulation of queerness.

Despite her interest and involvement with the Web, Emily was skeptical about the vaunted democratizing effects of it. She presented herself as a "realist," someone who is willing to use the Web and even write for Web publication, but who has no misconceptions about the power, and limitations, of the Web. As a queer person, she has certainly benefited from the Web, and she has used it to disseminate information to other queers and their allies, but perhaps her experiences with Internet monitoring have nipped in the bud any sense that the Web will *necessarily* make the world safer for queers.

Interestingly, perhaps Emily's most concentrated use of the Web comes from participation in Live Journal (http://www.livejournal.com/), at which she reported posting regular journal entries for her friends. She claimed that many entries are "public," provided one is a member of the online service. For Emily, and for others, I would imagine, such online journaling provides an outlet for insights, gripes, and various thoughts. The primary reading audience seems to be one's friends (both online acquaintances and friends made "IRL"), so the writing is much more "localized" than global. Indeed, Emily reported that she didn't spend much time reading others' journals unless she was already acquainted with the writer. I've come across a few other queer digital youth who use such functions, including one young man who has set up his own site with accompanying journal at http://www.alienkult.com/main.html.

Such journaling is comparable to the kinds of journaling and blogging we have seen on other queer youth sites, such as Oasismag or even YGA. A newer site, Queertopia (http://queertopia.org/) aims, like Oasis, at providing a space for queer youth with Internet access to discuss issues of importance to them, as well as to share stories and build online community. What is valued in such projects is not necessarily reading the advice, columns, and coming-out stories of gay role models, but rather the ability of the Web to enable queer digital youth to communicate directly with one another in sharing a variety of ideas and insights. Indeed, I argue that the interest in such communication might mark a shift in emphasis among queer digital youth from a focus on a specific identity ("I am a gay youth") to a consideration and articulation of one's queerness within a complex context of identity, personal interests, and social investments. Establishing pride and comfort with queerness takes a back seat to interrogation of a wide variety of subjects via chat, journals, and blogs.

Ultimately, for young queers like Emily, the Web is good for disseminating information, assisting with educational endeavors, and for finding information "you wouldn't normally get in the library." Another respondent, Christina B., reported a similar sentiment: "It allows me to connect to a variety of queer individuals, organizations, and resources that I may not otherwise have access to." We can see such values at play in Emily's writing for the Web, and, moreover, her writing on Live Journal helps her create a sense of local community. Inevitably, there may be downsides. Christina pointed out that "Doing any sort of research [on the Web] inevitably involves digging through heterosexually intended pornographic and other disparaging sites. It also opens up attack from far-Right groups and individuals." Perhaps such experiences have tempered enthusiasm among queer digital youth about the potential of the Web, and in the following section, I consider how some youth have responded to the potential downsides of self-representation on the Web.

SITES OF CONTRAST: PLAYING IT SAFE

Despite Emily's enthusiasm for the Web, not all queer youth, even queer *digital* youth, can afford to be as comfortable in articulating their queerness, even online, and the willingness to have frank discussions of sexuality, for instance, should not be read as a ubiquitous commonplace among queer youth sites. As I initially drafted this chapter, the Episcopal Church in America approved the election of its first openly gay bishop, the Reverend Gene Robinson. Part of the controversy surrounding his election as bishop of New Hampshire focused on accusations that a Web site for a youth group that he had been affiliated with had links to pornographic content. According to a report on CNN.com,

> On the second allegation, involving a Web site brought to bishops' attention by a member of the American Anglican Council, which opposes Robinson's ratification, Bishop Gordon Scruton, who oversaw the investigation, said Robinson helped found a chapter of the organization Outright in 1995, and ended his involvement with the group in 1998.
>
> In 2002, the group established a Web site that linked to another site, which in turn linked to a site that included what Scruton called "graphic sexual materials."
>
> Robinson "was not aware that the organization has a Web site until this convention," Scruton said, noting that Outright's response to investigators "emphasized to me" that Robinson had no part in the creation of the Web site.
>
> Outright was founded to provide support and counseling for young people concerned about their sexuality, Scruton said. ("Episcopalians" http://www.cnn.com/2003/US/08/05/bishop/)

Of course, I couldn't resist visiting the site, http://www.outright.org/. The site's mission statement is offered near the top of the page:

> Outright's mission is to create safe, positive, and affirming environments for young gay, lesbian, bisexual, trans, and questioning people

ages 22 and under. Outright aspires to a youth-driven philosophy in which youth needs and beliefs form decisions, and a collaboration of youth and adults provides support, education, advocacy, and social activities.

The site is very simple, with links to sister groups' Web sites in Maine, New Hampshire, and Vermont, and it is clear that education and information dissemination are the primary goals of the sites listed.

A link labeled "news release," however, refers directly to the issue involving Bishop Robinson:

> On Monday, August 4, 2003 Outright in Portland removed a link from our Web site to www.allthingsbi.com, a resource for bisexual people. We were not aware that www.allthingsbi.com contains a link to an erotic Web site. We do not believe the link in question is appropriate on our Web site for the population we serve. We want to thank the media for alerting us to a link that we were unaware existed.
>
> Many autonomous and loosely affiliated gay, lesbian, bisexual, and transgender youth groups throughout Northern New England have adopted the organizational name of "Outright". Outright in Portland is the first Outright organization, founded in 1987. Outright in Portland provides Web-hosting services and links as a courtesy to other Outrights. The Web site was developed in February 2002.
>
> Bishop-elect Reverend Gene Robinson has not been involved, at any time, with our Outright organization in Portland or our Web site and its content. This is clearly an attempt to discredit his important nomination.

In so many ways, the disclaimer on the site is situated squarely in the conflicted and contested territory of the representation of queerness in our culture. In order for Outright to maintain a "safe" and, in their words, "appropriate" image for the public at large, its authors cannot link to explicitly erotic material—or link to a site that links to such material—despite the fact that the organization serves a population who are either self-identifying as or considering self-identifying with an identity based primarily on affectional and erotic attraction.

This is the double bind of queerness in a homophobic culture. How does one claim and take pride in an identity based on sexual attraction while having to disavow the *sexuality* of such attractions for sake of offending an often prudish, sex-phobic public? What's fascinating, perhaps even frightening, is that Bishop Robinson's election could be called into question because he was, at one point, affiliated with an organization that eventually put up a Web site that contained a link that contained yet another link to a site with erotic content. On one hand, I can't help but agree with the "news release" posted on the Outright Web site; the accusation seems simply an attempt to "discredit" Robinson. On the other hand, if the accusation stemmed from authentic (if conservative) concerns about Bishop Robinson, it betrays a phenomenal lack of understanding of the Web as a communications medium: all of us on the Web are separated by a just a few links.

My ultimate point, however, in referencing the situation with Bishop Robinson is that many youth organizations, despite the sites I have examined earlier, are quite aware that their representation on the Web is being scrutinized—often by people who are not particularly interested in their well-being or by people with homophobic agendas. As such, the caution with which Outright articulates its position testifies both to the continued sense of precariousness and even peril with which some youth adopt queer identities and their consciousness that *Web*-based representations can and *are* used in ways that defy authorial and compositional intention.

CONCLUSIONS: BEYOND THE SAFE SPACE

The use of the Web by queer digital youth offers a unique opportunity to understand how these youth are thinking—and writing—about their sexuality, what they find important in terms of their queerness, and how they wish to be represented and thought about in the larger, "real" world. What are some of the dominant issues of interest to these youth? In general, the following trends in discussion and self-representation seem salient:

- There is frequent discussion and consideration of the *variety* of sexual identities currently circulating in both the real and virtual worlds;
- There is often great willingness to address issues of bisexuality and transgenderism;
- There is an interest in examining and discussing sociopolitical aspects of being queer;
- There is much frankness in discussion of a sexual practices, including candid discussions of safer sex practices.

More specifically, we see queer digital youth writing their lives on the Web in ways that are fairly complex, even provocative—in ways that, in general, emphasize a developing and increasingly complex *sexual literacy*. Beyond simply using the Web as a platform or "safe space" for experimenting with a queer identity, the digital youth sites examined here show these youth composing the Web as a space for hashing out fairly complex understandings, even reconfigurations, of sexuality and sexual orientation identity. There is much interest in creating spaces for these youth voices, not just to "come out," but to share ideas, insights, and views on a variety of subjects.

Indeed, my analyses suggest that "coming out" is only one dimension of sexual orientation identity that queer digital youth are using the Web to explore. Rather, for many of these youth, the Web has perhaps played a part in opening them up to a diversity of sexual expression—and it is that diversity that they are writing about. Even the exploration of alternative, nonbinaristic (i.e., beyond the gay–straight dichotomy) terms and markers for sexuality, such as "bisexuality" and "transgenderism," show how queer digital youth are reconsidering the gay–straight binary as perhaps too limited in describing their sexual interests and investments. At the very least, the lack of "traditional" gay visual rhetoric on the youth-composed sites— rainbow flags and pink triangles—suggests that older narrations of gay sexuality and identity are not static concepts for these queer youth, but themselves items for play, contestation, and reconfiguring.

Mogenic, for instance, eschews simple identifications of gay or visual markers that signal that Mogenic is a "gay page" in an effort, it seems, to appreciate and value *varieties* of queer experience, including bisexuality and transgenderism. More strikingly, the organization of content in such sites around issues of sex or political issues, as opposed to discrete identities, signals an emphasis on *commonalities* of experience—or even potential commonalities of political investment and action. This is particularly true about discussions of specific sexual practices. After all, gays, lesbians, bisexuals, and the transgendered all face comparable problems in finding reliable information about safer sexual practices. More than anything else, perhaps this issue, which seems foregrounded on many sites, unites these different queers socially, communally, and politically.

Additionally, I suspect that queer digital youth sometimes use online representations to counter a variety of marketing stereotypes that render their queerness a bland commodity. Any number of sites, such as Gay College Party or even XY online, sometimes present a very stereotypical understanding of queer digital youths' concerns and issues, and many such sites seem most intent on selling products, such as "club gear." Although I do not want to dismiss the importance of such sites for many youth, particularly in promoting a sex-positive understanding of gay sexuality, we have seen queer youth sites that portray the interests of queer digital youth in a variety of other, far less commercial ways. Such sites often eschew glitzy graphics and glossy photos, and they focus attention instead on personal and political issues. For instance, articles by young queers on YGA grapple with issues of homophobia and even trans-phobia. Some articles suggest that it's time for queer youth to say "To Hell With Manners, It's Time to Take Charge!!!" Such a proactive attitude permeates much of the writing on the youth-composed sites.

Certainly, generational issues may be at play in such discussions and representations, and I sense that many queer digital youth are defining and articulating their senses of self via the Web in contradistinction to perceived "older" gay understandings of sexuality and sexual orientation identity. The frequent use of the word queer, for instance, might signal a configuring of sexuality that appreciates, if not fluidity, then at least *variety*, as opposed to the binary oppositionality of gay and straight. We see this frequently in the embracing of discussions about bi- and trans-youth lives. Moreover, increased attention to issues of race on these pages suggests a desire to situate queerness as one of several identity nodes in the complex network of identity. Much of this work and self-representation seems to be in the service of opening up more spaces, more points of discussion and conversation, about the social and political complexities of being young and queer. As such, an emphasis on the Web's interactive features, such as blogging and the frequent use of discussion boards, foregrounds these youths' interest in discussion and interrogation over and beyond a more static representation of identity, also reflected perhaps in the nearly pervasive lack of traditional gay visual signifiers.

Inevitably, some salient critiques need to raised, both about these queer youth-composed sites and about issues of access. As with any study of the Internet and the Web, we need here to be tentative and provisional. In her study, *Virtual Ethnography*, Christine Hine correctly notes that a "holistic understanding of the Internet seems a futile undertaking. . . . However hard the ethnographer works, she or he will only ever partially experience the Internet" (63). Content on the Web in particular shifts quickly and suddenly, so our deduction of trends from the content of the sites analyzed should be considered temporary—and in need of revision as time goes on and other content, and other sites, replace the ones studied here. In terms of access, one should bear in mind that search engines, as well as portals, might direct youth with Internet access to sites with a lot of Internet traffic, such as Gay.com or PlanetOut, in which case some youth, and others, might not find smaller sites with content more directly driven, created, and maintained by queer digital youth themselves.

How will queer youth with Internet access find such sites? Fortunately, links between sites, even between the "biggies" such as Gay.com and PlanetOut and smaller ventures such as Oasis and YGA, are easily and frequently created, linking visitors from the larger more commercial sites to smaller, home-grown projects. Joshua Gamson reminds us of this in his article on commercially oriented gay Web spaces: "Unlike in many of its print siblings, [alternative] images and voices and ideas are a click away [from commercial sites]. For all its crass commercialism—indeed, because of its crass commercialism—this is a more pluralistic cultural setting than most LGBT institutions" (269–70).

Despite these limitations, we should acknowledge both the diversity of content on the Web generated specifically *by* queer digital youth, as well as what that content has to teach us about such youths' social, cultural, personal, and political investments. Judging from these sites—and from their differences from commercial and organization-based Web spaces—queer digital youth seem to be carving out their own online space for discussion and consideration of issues that they deem are important. We would do well to pay attention, particularly if we are invested in understanding some of the possible futures of queer culture, politics, and lives.

INTERVIEW WITH EMILY JOY: THE UNIVERSITY OF CINCINNATI LGBT STUDENT ALLIANCE

Emily Joy, 19 years old at the time of the interview, was a second–year student at the University of Cincinnati's School or Design, Art, Architecture, and Planning. She also served as president of the Lesbian, Gay, Bisexual, and Transgender Student Alliance, whose Web site (http://www.sald.uc.edu/org/algbp/) she composed and maintained, and she also has several other Web projects to her credit.

Jonathan: Tell me a little bit about how you get started composing Web sites. When did you get started doing Web sites?

Emily: Actually, back in high school one of our requirements for the honors diploma [was that] we had to take a certain number of computer classes and so I decided to take one on the Internet, and in it we learned how to do basic Web page design. I picked it up really fast and learned basic HTML. My dad is a computer geek so I was already into the whole computer geekness thing. I was a really quick learner about it and I blew the class away with my Web site. I thought, "I have a knack for this." For a while, I kind of didn't do anything else. I took that class probably my junior year or senior year, and then I didn't really do anything with it. I just kind of learned it and made some demo Web sites. They didn't really get up on the Web or anything like that.

Jonathan: What kind of Web site did you do in high school that just blew the class away?

Emily: Well basically, we just had to do a Web site with a biography about ourselves or stuff that we were interested in. We had to put pictures up about our favorite bands or cars or whatever.

Jonathan: So, you had assignments to do personal homepages and things of that nature.

Emily: Yeah. Right. That kind of thing. Then I took a year off after high school and then I just started flirting around with it again. I was just practicing and that kind of thing. Eventually, I had a personal homepage through a Web site called Chick Pages.

Jonathan: Chick pages? Was that the domain?

Emily: Yeah. It was chickpages.com I think. It's not in operation anymore. It was this feminist Web site where you could subscribe for an e-mail address and you got a certain amount of space for a Web site, your homepage or whatever. I got back interested it in again with that. I never really did much with it though because I was always busy working. Then the site went down and that was that. Later, about the winter of my first year in college, I got involved with the local chapter of GLSEN [the Gay, Lesbian and Straight Education Network]. They were putting on the first Cincinnati Youth Summit for LGBT students.

Jonathan: When was that?

Emily: 2002. They were in desperate need of help and I not only provided them with a venue for the first conference but I also designed a logo and created a Web site. I basically maintain the Web site [http://www.cincyyouthsummit.org/]. That has been my responsibility ever since that first Youth Summit.

Jonathan: And there have been two Youth Summits, right?

Emily: Yes there was a second Youth Summit.

Jonathan: How about the plans for the upcoming Youth Summit? Are you doing the Web site for that as well?

Emily: I might help out a little bit with it, but my friend Shawn is going to be taking over that because he's a lot more advanced in his skills. That's actually what he's going to school for. To me it's more of a hobby and for him it's more of a degree.

Jonathan: What was the experience of doing that like? What was your vision for the Youth Summit Web site?

Emily: I don't know what my vision was. It was mainly just to get people interested in what we were doing and present the information in a very easily obtainable way so that it wasn't confusing. Have the link so that it's easy to click to the link and get something and then go back and click that and keep going through the information instead of having to jump around or whatever. Just have it laid out in front of you and really have access to it.

Jonathan: Have you done other Web sites?

Emily: I've done one and that's the UC LGBT Student Alliance Web site [http://www.soa.uc.edu/org/algbp/].

Jonathan: What's in that?

Emily: It's really simple. It basically has our office location and mail location and stuff like that. It also has our contact information and our logo on it. It has a link to our e-mail address. It also has links to an officer page where we have fliers about all the officers of the group. I put something up there called "10 ways to make it through family gatherings." Family gatherings are difficult times for gay and lesbian students.

Jonathan: Where did you get that info for "10 ways to make it through family gatherings," or is that something you wrote yourself?

Emily: No. Actually I got that from a listserv from an e-mail that I had gotten from somebody. I put that up there because I thought it was really good information. That came out around Christmas time and I thought people should know this.

Jonathan: Just in time for the holidays.

Emily: Right. I left it up because I think people should have that no matter what because it doesn't matter what kind of family gathering you go to. It could be a wedding, a funeral, or it could be anything. It happens all the time. Then the only other stuff that we have on the Web site currently is just links to other student organizations and a link to stuff about drag queens, the Spicy Divas, one of the local drag queen groups in Cincinnati [http://www.spicydivas.com/].

Jonathan: How did that happen? It's kind of a curious list of links!

Emily: Very true. Student organizations, activities, and drag queens. Basically, one of the queens e-mailed me and said, "Hey, we have shows every Thursday and if you put up a link to our Web site on your Web site we will announce your meetings at all of our performances." I was like, that's cool, so we did that.

Jonathan: Anything else?

Emily: We did have an interactive calendar on the Web site. We had it on there for a while and I was experimenting with it and it's pretty cool. You went to another page where it had the calendar, and it's basically a table and in each box there was a link and you clicked the link and a little pop up window came up with a list of events for that day. That worked pretty well. We got a lot of responses from that. A lot of people showed up to events through that, but I just got really busy so I had to take it down because I couldn't do it every month. Now I just put it up to announce the meetings. I usually have to update it every couple of weeks because we have meetings every other week.

Jonathan: I understand. Are there any other sites you've worked on or contributed to?

Emily: That's all the stuff that's actually been put on the net. I actually took an Internet class here at UC. A Media Foundations class. It was for digital artwork and stuff like that, but we also had to design Web sites. I came knowing all this HTML and what not. I was really surpassing the class.

Jonathan: Yeah.

Emily: We had to create Web sites for that and I did a feminist "herstory" Web site and I did another biography Web site. My final project was a political action Web site where I was telling people not to believe what the government told you and that kind of thing. I spent most of my time in that class working on a

CD animation for it. I actually worked on a couple of CD animations for the Web site.

Jonathan: What did they do?

Emily: Well the first one was a pyramid, an upside down pyramid. It had a Lady Liberty in a rainbow robe, and it rotated. It was really simple. Then the last one was a maze and it was 3D [three dimensional]. You enter it and you see the picture and it's like you are walking through this maze. You get to the end of it and you've reached "enlightenment." [Laughter] There is this golden sphere that you've reached and it's glowing and stuff like that and then; it's pretty cool.

Jonathan: What were you hoping to convey with that?

Emily: I don't know. It was just kind of cool. You go through this path; I called it the path to enlightenment. You go through all these tunnels, these darkened tunnels and what not, and then finally you get to enlightenment and your treasure at the end.

Jonathan: Okay. Did that maybe symbolize people slogging through the Web site?

Emily: Yeah. [Laughter]

Jonathan: I'm just picking at you. Have you put those up recently?

Emily: No.

Jonathan: Why not?

Emily: Well actually the teacher did. He put up the final Web page for the students but he takes it down every quarter. He left it up for a few weeks and then he took it down. The only reason I don't have it really up now is because I've had problems getting an account with the university because they require you to download certain programs to upload the files, and I just don't want to hassle with that.

Jonathan: That's true. I have had to do that for my own pages. It's actually very easy to operate. You do have to go through the motions, though. Let's change course just a little bit. What's been your experience of the Web?

Emily: I was one of the first kids in my neighborhood to get online, and granted, I was one of the poorest kids in my neighborhood, but I had a computer because my step-dad worked at Circuit City or something like that. We always had a computer in the house growing up because my dad is a computer geek. I've had a computer since I was probably 6 or 7, when they really first started getting marketed. I always boast to my friends that I'm the only person our age that knows how to work DOS. I can actually work DOS. They look at me and they are like, "What's DOS?" I say, "Before Windows, there was DOS."

Jonathan: Right.

Emily: People would ask me to type up their papers for them because I had a computer and they didn't. It was a nice little source of income growing up. The Internet, I can't remember when we got it and had our first access. I know it was AOL. I had an account. It was my own little account that was monitored by my parents, of course. I'd say we probably got the Internet when I was like . . . well, I really don't know. I can't remember because it's been a part of me for as long as I remember.

Jonathan: As long as you've been using computers?

Emily: Yeah.

Jonathan: You've always had access to the Internet?

Emily: I know it was at least through high school.

Jonathan: What would you look for on the Web?

Emily: When I first started using the Internet, I mostly went into chatrooms because I thought it was so cool that you could talk to people. Being a teenager at that time it was like a social connection or whatever. I was also coming to terms with my sexuality and what not. I went into the lesbian chatrooms and asked people how they knew that they were gay because I was questioning myself and I didn't know if I was gay and all those kinds of things. I would look up gay-related stuff and information on being gay and stuff like that. I wondered, "Are there people out there that are gay?"

Jonathan: Did you know other gay people at the time?

Emily: No.

Jonathan: No one?

Emily: No. Ellen [DeGeneres] made me gay.

Jonathan: Was she really the first lesbian that you encountered?

Emily: Yes. She actually was. I really think so. I was a big fan of her show right when it came out and I was a loyal fan. I watched it every night that it was on. I really identified with her totally and completely. Then she came out and it was really kind of interesting because I was like, "Wow, I really identify with her and I'm feeling the same thing that she is and I just wonder . . ." That kind of started me on the whole gay thing really.

Jonathan: Did your parents know?

Emily: Actually, due to the Internet, they found out.

Jonathan: Really?

Emily: Like I said I had a monitored account on AOL and they went in and I did not know about that little special feature called the "filing cabinet," and they essentially went in and read all of my e-mails. I thought when you deleted them they were gone. But a copy of them was stored in the filing cabinet and my parents read those e-mails that I had been writing back and forth with this older lesbian. I was just asking her for advice and questions and all of that kind of stuff. They read them and they grounded me from the Internet. We had the big "are you gay" talk. It came out okay but I was still grounded from the Internet though.

Jonathan: Really? When did you get back on?

Emily: Well, I had Internet access at school at that point because I was like 16 or 17 then. It was my junior year. It was sophomore or junior year or something like that. I had Internet access at school so it wasn't like I was completely void of the Internet, but at home I didn't have it for a good amount of time. It was probably like 6 months.

Jonathan: Were they concerned about you looking for information about lesbianism?

Emily: The big concern was me giving out my personal information.

Jonathan: Oh...

Emily: Yeah. That was mainly it. They said, "How do you know for sure that she is a lesbian? How do you know she's even a woman? She could be an 80-year-old man preying on little children and stuff like that!" That was the main concern.

Jonathan: I hear you. There are clearly a lot of sick and disgusting 80-year-old men out there.

Emily: Oh God, yes! [Laughter]

Jonathan: They are blamed for quite a lot. Well what kind of Web sites do you go to? Obviously you went to some with gay content.

Emily: Right.

Jonathan: What was your favorite Web site?

Emily: My favorite Web site. My favorite Web site was probably that chick pages site. It was feminist in nature and they just had fun articles, satirical stuff, which I enjoyed greatly.

Jonathan: Sure.

Emily: Yeah. I'd visit anything that wasn't mainstream. And research for projects.

Jonathan: Okay.

Emily: I was mainly surfing the net. Most of the time I spent it in my chat groups and stuff like that. When I surfed the net it was usually for research, to find information for projects for school or on HTML stuff. I was looking up how to learn to build Web pages and stuff.

Jonathan: How about now? What do you spend time surfing for?

Emily: Now a big chunk of my time is checking my e-mail and updating a live journal.

Jonathan: What's a live journal?

Emily: A live journal is like a diary that's all mine. It's my diary actually.

Jonathan: Is it built into a Web page?

Emily: Yeah. You go to the Web site Livejournal.com [http://www.livejournal.com/], and you have to be a member, and the way to get membership is that you have to have a friend who has joined, and then after a week after they join, they get a code. They give that code to you and then you can join and then you can generate a code so that you can pass it on.

Jonathan: You pass it on. That's fascinating.

Emily: If you don't have a code, you can't get on unless you get a paid account.

Jonathan:	The friend that gave you the code, is this an online friend or IRL [in real life] friend?
Emily:	A real life friend that I went to high school with.
Jonathan:	Okay. I imagine some people get the code through online friends.
Emily:	Yeah. That too. Once you're a member, you go to the Web site and you log in and you can post your own entries. You type them up right there on the Web page. You post them and they come up just like that. You can post it three different ways. There is "public," which everybody can see. Then there is "friends only," which you signify or you designate a certain— well, you type in your friends' screen names for that site and then they can see what you write. But only them. Then there is "private," which no one can read but you. You can go to those links to your friends' journals, and what it will do is bring up all of your friends' entries for the current day, week, or whatever.
Jonathan:	How far back do they go?
Emily:	You can keep going back but the first page is probably only 20 entries. If you go to a friend's page, it will show the first 20 [most recent] entries, in chronological order.
Jonathan:	Okay. Previous entries go to archive?
Emily:	Yeah. It's more like if you go to my friend's page right now, you'd see my friend Sara's entry and then my friend Ellen's entries and probably another one of Ellen's entries and then Pat's entry.
Jonathan:	Okay.
Emily:	It would all depend on when they posted it.
Jonathan:	What do you write about? Are yours private or friend only?
Emily:	Mine are mostly public. I refuse to censor myself. There have been a couple of times that I have censored myself just because there is some private information I don't want the general public knowing. Also with my journal I never give out anyone's actual names. I'll abbreviate with just initials or something. Mostly my posts are public and right now they have been kind of ranting just because I'm pissed off at the world and my general situation right now.

Jonathan:	Personally or politically?
Emily:	Both. All of the above.
Jonathan:	All of the above?
Emily:	Yeah.
Jonathan:	What do you rant about?
Emily:	Let's see, my most recent post was just about how some people are just, like, oh what was it. . . . It's basically how being happy was looked down upon. If you are not moody but angry and upset and whatever, people look up to you and they see you as this bigger better person because . . .
Jonathan:	You seem serious . . .
Emily:	Because you are serious. Right. If you are happy, you are not taken seriously and you are just taken lightly and made fun of and stuff like that. You get walked all over. That was my most recent rant.
Jonathan:	Do people respond to your rants?
Emily:	Yes. There is a comments feature that allows people to leave comments about your entry. Some of the comments get interesting. With all the ranting that I do and all the telling people how much they suck and telling people how much Republicans suck and stuff like that, I haven't had a lot of comments recently.
Jonathan:	What kind of comments have you gotten in the past?
Emily:	Most of my comments are from my friends saying like, "Hey, what are we doing?"—not even responding to the entry, or sometimes it's more like, "I'm sorry you feel that way. Do you need a hug?" You know it's just that kind of thing. If I post a bad thing, then they will say, "Are you okay? Do you want to hang out?"
Jonathan:	Seems like they're reading what you write.
Emily:	Yeah.
Jonathan:	You've obviously outed yourself on Live Journal.
Emily:	Of course.
Jonathan:	Any response about that?
Emily:	No. No. Most of my friends—well, everybody who reads my live journal or at least that I know of, is okay with it.

Jonathan: Has anybody been flamed at Livejournal.com? Surely there are other people who have outed themselves and taken some shit for it . . .

Emily: I don't know.

Jonathan: Really?

Emily: I really don't know because I only really operate within my circle of friends. I only read my friends' journals. I haven't really explored live journal much. I'm so busy with my own.

Jonathan: What makes a really good Web site for you then? What would you characterize as a good Web site?

Emily: Something that's not annoying. I like my Web sites without a lot of bells and whistles and what not. I do kind of like the more inventive ones where you put your mouse over something and the cursor gets a little tail behind it. Web sites with pictures *can* be good. Some type of imagery on it whether it be a simple background and not necessarily one of those repeating ones with a celebrity's face over and over again. Those get kind of annoying. Then you can't read the text. So I like something clear where you can read the text, but maybe a faint image in the background for wallpaper or whatever.

Jonathan: Okay.

Emily: The links should definitely be working and up-to-date links. I personally believe you should have a list of links on one side or up and down the top where even if you click one you can still click to another and be able to get back to where you were before and stuff like that.

Jonathan: Clear navigation.

Emily: Right. Very clear navigation. Web sites that don't take forever to download are good. I personally have a cable connection so it doesn't take me that long, but when I had dial up I was sitting there forever for some of them. I was like, what's taking up all this space on my drive for this Web site to just download?

Jonathan: Sure. Anything else?

Emily: A catchy name. The intro contained on the Web site has to be interesting. I mean, the Web site should have all different kinds of things really. It all depends on the entries that you put in. But there should be a catchy name for it. Also, I think there should be accurate information, and make it fun for the person to look at your site. Not some boring thing like scrolling through something forever.

Jonathan: Besides style, what about content?

Emily: I think it's really good for education. There is just so much information out on the Web. You learn when you are little to go to the library and look up books on things, but what you learn depends on what the library has. If the library doesn't have a certain book, then you are limited in your information and I'm not saying that the Internet isn't limited because there are Web sites where you have to pay for the domain and all of that. It is kind of limited.

Jonathan: There can only be a finite number of Web sites . . .

Emily: Right. For the most part the Internet is not really censored. You can go to Web sites for other countries and get *their* news. You can get their perspective on the war. You can compare notes of what you are seeing at home and really get a better sense of what's actually going on and not just what the media are feeding you.

Jonathan: Sure.

Emily: I'm a big advocate of education and learning as much as possible. I would say that's what the Internet is really good for.

Jonathan: Because of its ability to give us access to more information, some people say that the Web can be a great tool for democracy, for helping to inform the citizenry so we can make more informed choices. What do you think?

Emily: Yeah, I agree, but then there are limits. Is it really doing any good? I do belong to the vote.com Web site where, if you sign up for certain issues that you're interested in and the government is trying to pass a law or something pertaining to that, then they will send you an update. I will vote or sign a petition depending on my take on it, and I never know what happens with that. That's where it kind of falls through, I guess. We have these Web sites where you can sign petitions where you can get your voice heard and what not. I never know what happens to those petitions that I sign. I never know. They don't send me an update saying this passed or this failed or whatever. I'm kind of more resistant to acting on them now because you don't know what's going to happen. It's just like those emails where there is an issue, sign your name at the bottom of the email and, forward it on. It's that kind of thing.

Jonathan: Right.

Emily: I don't know how they work really or how accurate that they are or if they get anything done.

Jonathan: That's interesting. I hadn't thought about that.

Emily: But I think it does *aid* in democracy. It gives people a chance to view things that would help them and see what's actually going on politically so they can make up their own minds instead of like just being pushed into their thoughts by the media

Jonathan: How about for queer people? What has the Web done for queers?

Emily: I think it's awesome. Pretty much all of my information growing up came from the Internet. I went online and I remember being in the school computer lab printing out pages and pages. There was like 40 pages of queer resources of books and literature. It was like a queer library. I printed out all the sheets of books and whatever. I wasn't out then. I was using up all of the printer ink and paper. Other kids were waiting for their documents to be printed, and they were standing by the printer and looking at the sheets after they came out. They were like, "What's all this queer stuff, what's all this shit?" I just kind of sit at my computer like, oh I'm just going to sit here and wait until it's done to go get my papers. [Laughter]

              After they left, I went over and gathered all of the papers that they had thrown in the trash can and took them home with me. I got a lot of my information from news articles and research information and stuff like that. I downloaded it or printed it out. I actually have what I call my queer resource book. I have this big binder of information. Any magazine article I saw or anything I found online, I would put into this book. I would read through it and it was my little resource book.

Jonathan: Did you believe all of it?

Emily:	I didn't believe all of it. There was this one study where it said something queer people have longer ring fingers. The ring finger is either as long as the middle finger or longer.
Jonathan:	Okay . . .
Emily:	The same with the toe. That has something to do with your level of hormones during pregnancy. I didn't quite get that just because there are so many biological differences and genetic make-ups. My fingers obviously don't do that.
	[Laughter]
Jonathan:	Is there a downside about the Web for lesbians and gays?
Emily:	The main limitation right now is in high schools, they have the firewalls up so that you can't access certain sites. Net nannies and what nots. This is bad for young queers discovering their sexuality and not getting the right kinds of sexuality education or not even being told that there are queer people in the world. Going online and trying to find information is really hard because most gay and lesbian sites are blocked unless it's a scientific study or something like that. It's blocked from these students because gay and lesbian materials are classified as pornography even if there isn't any pornography on it.
Jonathan:	Is that true at your high school?
Emily:	Yeah. I hit a few roadblocks. Most of the stuff I was looking up was informational stuff.
Jonathan:	Did you know other queers in high school, other queer students?
Emily:	I know there are other people who went to high school with me who have come out now. Then it was just me and James, so we would have to sit through those abstinence–only sexuality education things. They didn't even talk about queer people and we'd be asking, "Well, what about us?"
Jonathan:	Right.
Emily:	We were sitting there in health class, and gays and lesbians were mentioned as deviant from normal sexuality. We were like, "Well, what's wrong? What's going on? What about us?"
Jonathan:	Did you ever ask those questions in class?

Emily: No. Too afraid. When I took my health class I was still kind of
              questioning myself and I wasn't the out loud spoken person
              that I am now.

              [Laughter]

              I was very much afraid. I did get harassed a lot when I came
              out. The Internet was really my only resource to the outside
              world. I didn't know of anything beyond Norwood, the neigh-
              borhood I grew up in. I didn't know of any of the queer organ-
              izations in the city. It wasn't until my senior year of high
              school that I attended the first "gay night" at King's Island [a
              local amusement park] and that was amazing. I walked into
              King's Island and I'm like, wow there are queer people every-
              where. Woo hoo! It was awesome. The Internet played a vital
              part in my discovery. It wasn't like it was telling me that I
              should be gay or anything like that. I had these feelings and it
              just verified that what I'm doing is okay and there are other
              people out there who feel like this. "You are not alone and here
              is some information for you so that you can be safe." and stuff
              like that. It wasn't like, "Come to the dark side!". It wasn't say-
              ing that gays are cool and you should be gay.

Jonathan: What else do you want to say about the Web? Any concluding
              remarks?

Emily: It rocks. Except all the pop up ads that bug the crap out of me.
              You try to go to a single Web site and you get five pop up ads.
              I'm like, "C'mon, I just want to look at the Web site!" I hate
              that.

Jonathan: But otherwise it rocks.

Emily: Yeah. It rocks.

Jonathan: Thanks, Emily.

Emily: No problem.

PART III
ACTIVIST LITERACIES

6

DIGITAL YOUTH ACTIVISM ONLINE

RETHINKING WEB ACTIVISM

Although an increasing amount of scholarly work has been undertaken to study the WWW as a site for the construction of online identities, the exploration of alternative communities, and the dissemination of information, which I have been discussing vis-à-vis digital youth in the preceding chapters, some scholars have been turning their attention to studying the Web as a site of activist work. Many different organizations and agencies have been using the Web not only to share information about their concerns and agendas, but to actively agitate for various forms of political change. For instance, the Funding Exchange (at http://www.fex.org /home.html), a network of community-based foundations and organizations, recently announced the creation of a "Media Justice Fund," with the following mission statement:

> A major goal of the Media Justice Fund is to reach grassroots organizations across the country that are interested in incorporating media advocacy into their social justice work. These include organizations that are concerned about the impact of media regulation on their communities, organizations that want to support or create local independent media infrastructure and those interested in developing media literacy. (http://www.fex.org/2.3.2_mediajusticefundrelease.html)

Such a fund follows on the heels of work being done by organizations such as the Center for Democracy and Technology (CDT: http://www.cdt.org/), which, according to its mission statement, works to promote democratic values and constitutional liberties in the digital age. With expertise in law, technology, and policy, CDT seeks practical solutions to enhance free expression and privacy in global communications technologies. CDT is dedicated to building consensus among all parties interested in the future of the Internet and other new communications media. (http://www.cdt.org/mission/)

Such activity recognizes both the potential usefulness of various media, particularly the Internet, in forwarding a variety of activist causes *and* the necessity of monitoring laws about the use of media, to make sure that a diversity of people have access to and can use the media in representing their ideas and contributing to public dialogue about important issues.

In many ways, belief in the possibilities and potential of online activism harkens back to a more idealistic vision of the Web, one in which the sharing of information in quickly accessible and visually exciting formats seemed sufficient itself to create communal sites of political activism and resistance. You can hear the strains of the early promise of Internet-activism in Chapter 9 of Howard Rheingold's *The Virtual Community*, "Electronic Frontiers and Online Activists":

> By 1992, there were enough online environmentalist efforts to support the publication of a popular guidebook to CMC as a tool for environmental activism, Ecolinking: Everyone's Guide to Online Environmental Organization. Ecolinking is a combination of CompuMentor-in-a-book that instructs activists in the arcana of going online, and a directory that lists the key information about different BBSs and networks that already exist. (http://www.rheingold.com/vc/book/9.html)

But even more recently, Christopher Mele has asserted that "Computer-mediated communication and networking is a useful mechanism for disadvantaged groups in their efforts at collective action and empowerment" (292). And, speaking more broadly, Marc A. Smith and Peter Kollock maintain in *Communities in Cyberspace* that "Technology has its most profound effect when it alters the ways in which people come together and communicate" (4).

The question, of course, is *how* does Web-based technology "alter" the "ways in which people come together and communicate"? How can the Web *empower* or *support* activist causes? Measuring the success of activist-oriented Web sites, as well as analyzing the various strategies and literacies deployed in writing the Web in the service of activist causes, is steadily drawing critical attention as critics try to determine how—and even if—the

Web can serve as a powerful activist tool. For instance, in their introduction to the recently published book, *Cyberactivism: Online Activism in Theory and Practice*, Martha McCaughey and Michael D. Ayers pose one of the central questions currently being addressed in this scholarship: "In terms of political opportunities, we can raise a question: To what extent does the Internet create or not create activist opportunities?" (8).

Many young activists have been experimenting with the Web "in terms of [its] political opportunities," and although I don't have sufficient time or space in this chapter to explore such questions in the depth and detail they deserve, I do highlight specifically how some youth activists have taken to the Web as a medium or tool in the promotion of various activist causes—with some intriguing qualifications and caveats deployed in their thinking of the Web as a space to "create activist opportunities." As seen in previous chapters, the utopian dreams about subcultural youth and technology that Douglas Rushkoff entertained in *Playing the Future* may not have been realized, but some digital youth *have* developed strategies for filtering information about themselves and their political concerns in useful, even provocative ways. And as is seen in this chapter, some youth activists' technological literacy may focus not on using the Web so much to build *community*, but perhaps as a tool of information *critique*. Moreover, we see a move *away* from thinking about the Web in a utopian, community-enhancing mode, and *toward* a figuring of the Web as a support system for other media serving activists' ends.

To set up the discussion of how some youth use the Web as an activist tool, let's first explore some of the critical parameters set by critics and scholars in their attempt to understand activist work on the Web and Internet; then, we follow up with an in-depth discussion of one specific project in which a group of e-savvy youth use the Web to further an activist cause. Comparing the two—the scholarly questions being raised and a case study of some digital youth Web activists at work—should highlight some of the ways in which young activists are pushing our understanding of the Web, both as an activist *and* a literacy tool.

CYBORGS AND THE KNOWING SELF: THE SCHOLARSHIP OF WEB ACTIVISM

In *Cyberactivism: Online Activism in Theory and Practice* (2003), Martha McCaughey and Michael D. Ayers suggest that "Activists have not only incorporated the Internet into their repertoire but also . . . have changed substantially what counts as activism, what counts as community, collective identity, democratic space, and political strategy" (1–2). The suggestion that the Internet is responsible for changing, or at least "substantially" affecting, not only our conceptualization of activism, but also community, identity, democratic space, and political strategy is a motif at the heart of much thinking about the potential social implications of networked communications technologies. Donna Haraway's conceptualizations have been perhaps among the earliest, and most influential, of such theorizing. In *Simians, Cyborgs, and Women: The Reinvention of Nature*, Haraway unpacks her notion of the cyborgian "knowing self," which is "partial in all its guises, never finished, whole, simply there and original; it is always constructed and stitched together imperfectly, and *therefore* able to join with another, to see together without claiming to be another" (193). Such a "knowing self" is crucial in the postmodern world, in which our knowledges are necessarily incomplete, a full understanding of self (and other) always already under erasure given the dissolution of organizing grand meta-narratives imparting meaning and stability. Given this postmodern condition, we need identities that not only recognize but value their contingency and that can create community out of such contingency.

For Haraway, the image of the cyborg, which straddles the line between the human and the machine, is just such a "knowing self" in that it recognizes—and *uses*—its multiplicity of identities to create new modes of being and knowing unbounded by older, more static and constraining forms of identity. The use of the cyborg imagery also underscores how our new communications technologies might foster this meeting of "human" and "machine" to redirect our attention to the uses of multiplicity and, in Turkle's terms, our concomitant "flexibility, resilience, and capacity for joy [which] comes from having access to our many selves" (168). For Haraway, imagery such as that of the knowing cyborg, fantastic as it may seem, is ineluctably political; as she puts it in "Fractured Identities," "It is important to note that the effort to construct revolutionary standpoints, epistemologies as achievements of people committed to changing the world, has been part of the process of showing the limits of identification" (96).

How so? How can "showing the limits of identification" in general and the cyborg in particular offer us "revolutionary standpoints"? And what ideologies, values, or politics will such a revolution serve? In his book, *Subjectivity*, Nick Mansfield summarizes these concerns by asking the critical question of Haraway's position: "what can the cyborg offer a radical politics?" Mansfield, reading Haraway's work closely, provides the following possible answer:

[The cyborg] creates a generalized "oppositional consciousness" not hung up on its own essence and truth, but ever forging new coalitions and interconnections. These alliances at the expense of essences is the positive version of the cyborg's dependence on a logic of the interface and communication. The cyborg is forever inventing new interconnections and new systems to be part of. . . . It is this invention of new and valuable interconnections that will make the cyborg (that product of the arms race and the globalization of capital) some possible vehicle for productive change. (160)

Read through Mansfield's interpretation, Haraway's cyborg politics both embraces postmodern fluidity, flux, change *and* disavows static, consumerist identities that organize senses of self into quantifiable market niches (perhaps at best) and post-industrial cogs (perhaps at worst). Instead, the cyborg privileges a fluid sense of self that recognizes and forges multiple interconnections with others, that is open to seeing the world through multiple eyes and multiple perspectives. Such a movement should, hopefully, result in a consciousness unwilling (perhaps unable) to impose its truth and its meanings on others; rather, an openness to forming connections and forging coalitions might create sites of more cooperative work, in which the needs, hopes, and desires of many are foregrounded and addressed, as opposed to being subsumed in the will to power of a ruling minority. This is not the technology of *The Matrix*, which uses human–machine interfaces to trap the self in lulling dreams, isolating us from each other and hampering our ability to work collectively; rather, it is the creation of networks that reshape our world by bringing us into closer contact with one another.

In many ways, I think, this early, political, activist cyborgian metaphor has stayed with much scholarly and critical analyses of Internet and Web activism. Let's look at some specific examples. In "'Substantive & Feminist Girlie Action': Women Online," Jacqueline Rhodes writes about how women use the Internet and the Web to explore radical feminist thinking and to make connections with others doing similar work. She argues that, "Part of the importance of these radical women's Web sites is that they serve as good examples of writers in a network linking up with other writers, creating community through text without retreating from public space. One purpose of these networked texts (and of writing them at all) is to openly challenge the seeming hegemony of the Internet, to use writing as subversion" (134–5). Along similar lines, Donna M. Kowal's "Digitizing and Globalizing Indigenous Voices: The Zapatista Movement" offers a powerful, generally positive example of how the Internet can not only further activist organizations but, in some cases, serve as one of the primary forms of activism itself. Kowal writes that "The Zapatista movement has been labeled as the world's first postmodern revolution. Scholars have marveled at how this movement on behalf of an indigenous and agricultural people, primarily Mayan Indians in the Chiapas region of southern Mexico, has successfully used the Internet as a means of promulgating global support" (105). Specifically, Kowal traces in her article how "Zapatistas have used Internet technology to mobilize their struggle, gain representation, and generate a collective voice composed of an intercontinental, decentralized, egalitarian coalition of human rights advocates" (106). Kowal writes in tones reminiscent of McCaughey and Ayers's assertion of how the Internet has fostered "substantial" changes in our concepts of not only activism, but also community, identity, social space, and political strategy. For instance, look at the following description:

> Web pages and e-mail exchanges provide firsthand accounts of their plight, disseminate it widely, and facilitate grassroots organization and action. . . . Information technology has thus enabled them to successfully overcome the obstacles typically encountered by indigenous and disenfranchised groups. In turn, they have also created an alternative public sphere, a digitized counter sphere connected electronically as well as in person—both composed of a democratically formed collective of people from diverse regions, cultures, and classes. (120)

I argue that, even several years after Haraway's formulations, the cyborg metaphor is still predominant in both Rhodes' and Kowal's understanding of the activist potential of the Web and the Internet. In this mode, the cyborg, to borrow again from Mansfield, is "this invention of new and valuable interconnections that will make the cyborg . . . some possible vehicle for productive change."

Granted, not all scholarly understandings of the Internet and its connection to activist work and "productive [social] change" are so cyborgian—or positive. For instance, at the end of her essay, Kowal herself asks some critical questions: "Will the Zapatistas' emphasis on collective identity and action on a global scale, realized through Internet communication, undermine efforts to address the specific experiences of Mayan Indians living in Chiapas? In other words, will it lead to new forms of exclusion?" (121). Although Kowal raises important questions, her critique still assumes a cyborgian point of evaluation: who will *not* be networked and thus represented appropriately?

Some scholars have attempted to be a bit more specific in analyzing the ways in which activists use the Web, as well as how their understanding of activism is affected by the possibilities of the Internet. Such analyses have often involved *classifying* forms of Web activism and literacy practice. For instance, in "Classifying Forms of Online Activism," Sandor Vegh suggests that

> At first glance, the types of Internet activism fall into three general areas: awareness/advocacy; organization/mobilization; and action/reaction. This typology emphasizes the direction of initiative—whether one sends out information or receives it, calls for action or is called upon, or initiates an action or reacts to one. These are progressive steps of online activism leading from basic information seeking and distribution to online direct action, better know as "hacktivism." (72)

Beyond using the Web to disseminate information ("awareness/advocacy") and enlisting supporters ("organization/mobilization"), "hacktivism" might involve the disruption of computer networks through the use of viruses or other forms of actual sabotage of hardware. Graham Meikle, in *Future Active: Media Activism and the Internet*, identifies three of his own types of "Internet campaigns," and these focus a bit more on the *literacy* practices involved in using the Web as a tool for activist work: interactivity, alternative media, and tactical media (5). Interactivity involves using the Web to put activists in contact with one another; using alternative media includes the creation of "independent" or "dissident" sites of information; and tactical media takes the form of "hit-and-run guerilla-media campaigns," which might include "culture jamming," such as that seen on the Adbusters site (http://www.adbusters.org) and its spoofing of commercial advertisements, or even "online sabotage," comparable to what Vegh calls "hacktivism." Besides the spoofing done on the Adbusters site, another provocative form of "hit-and-run guerilla-media campaigns" might include how some Web authors took advantage of the "I'm Feeling Lucky" search feature of Google, a prominent search engine (http://www.google.com), to protest the war in Iraq. Apparently, the composers created a site and made sure that specific searches would lead to their site. I heard about this bit of hactivism when I received an e-mail from a colleague with the following instructions:

1. go to google
2. type in "weapons of mass destruction"
3. hit "I'm feeling lucky"
4. read the 404 page closely.

The 404 "error page" read as follows:

These Weapons of Mass Destruction cannot be displayed

The weapons you are looking for are currently unavailable. The country might be experiencing technical difficulties, or you may need to adjust your weapons inspectors mandate.

Please try the following:

- Click the 📄 Regime change button, or try again later.

- If you are George Bush and typed the country's name in the address bar, make sure that it is spelled correctly. (IRAQ).

- To check your weapons inspector settings, click the **UN** menu, and then click **Weapons Inspector Options**. On the **Security Council** tab, click **Consensus**. The settings should match those provided by your government or NATO.

- If the Security Council has enabled it, The United States of America can examine your country and automatically discover Weapons of Mass Destruction.

- If you would like to use the CIA to try and discover them, click 🔍 Detect weapons

- Some countries require 128 thousand troops to liberate them. Click the **Panic** menu and then click **About US foreign policy** to determine what regime they will install.

- If you are an Old European Country trying to protect your interests, make sure your options are left wide open as long as possible. Click the **Tools** menu, and then click on **League of Nations**. On the Advanced tab, scroll to the Head in the Sand section and check settings for your exports to Iraq.

- Click the 💣 Bomb button if you are Donald Rumsfeld.

Cannot find weapons or CIA Error
Iraqi Explorer
Get the WMD 404 T-shirt.

The activists at Adbusters might call this a form of "culture jamming," in which a particular text, such as a commonly seen advertisement or other text (such as a 404 "error page") is tweaked a bit to make a point, usually highlighting inconsistencies or hypocrisies in the media. In this particular case, the online "search" for "weapons of mass destruction" yields a satirical comment about the inability of the "real world" American government to find weapons of mass destruction in a country it invaded in search of such weapons. As we've seen, such satire is hardly uncommon as a literacy practice on the Web, even as if, as in this particular case, the satirical comment leads to another site selling anti-war t-shirts.

Paying attention to such specific literacy practices allows scholars to critique, in a more tempered way, the activist possibilities of the Web and the Internet. For instance, in "The Rhetorics of Three Women Activist Groups on the Web: Building and Transforming Communities," Sibylle Gruber examines three women-focused activist groups to "show how different rhetorical strategies are used to embrace similar goals: the promotion of women's rights issues and peaceful interaction in a wide array of political, social, religious, and cultural settings" (78). All are widely accessed, frequently updated sites that provide information about the sociocultural and political status of women in a variety of nations and situations around the world. Gruber's analysis, particularly her attention to rhetorical issues, such as audience awareness and the crafting of information for specific readerships, prompts her to conclude the following:

> [the sites'] success . . . can be attributed to a number of factors. First, the virtual spaces created by the activist groups . . . and the virtual audience and participants in . . . online exchanges are not separate from the issues and concerns addressed by off-line communities. . . . Second, although the groups appeal to a global audience, many of the issues they address are anchored in local politics and local economic situations. . . . Third, the issues addressed are not part of a virtual world but they are "real" issues that influence women's everyday lives, such as violence, poverty, and other forms of oppression. Fourth, all three sites encourage participation online through discussion groups, and offline through getting involved with specific women's issues. (88–9)

Although Gruber's analysis is ultimately very positive in its assessment of the "success" of these women-focused activist sites, her approach to and appreciation of them is focused primarily on their connection to "real" life. In each of her concluding points, she emphasizes not simply the networked connections that women activists are forging, but the offline connections that will further the causes of economic, social, and political equality for women. As such, Gruber's analysis takes our understanding of the cyborg out of the hyperreal and returns it, at least in part, to the realities of the flesh. And although Gruber does not note any instances of "hacktivism," her descriptions of "awareness/advocacy" and "organization/mobilization" highlight the interconnectivity of not only different women in different places, but the need to evaluate Web activism in terms of its impact on real-world situations and circumstances.

As we turn our attention to youth-oriented and youth-created activist sites, I think that Vegh's and Meikle's classifications, as well as Gruber's analysis, offer some *starting* points in thinking critically about the various literacies used in activist Web sites, and they help us evaluate the effectiveness of such sites—in fulfilling their stated objectives *and* in prompting socially productive reconsiderations of identity, community, and political practice. We can see how this might work by taking a look at a couple of anti-war/pro-peace Web site campaigns. Indeed, the recent war in Iraq has seen the development of some fairly extensive activist sites, with sections devoted specifically to informing, even mobilizing youth with Internet access about the contemporary peace movement. For instance, the United for Peace and Justice (UFPJ) at http://www.unitedforpeace.org/ is a very large community-building site that serves as both an awareness and advocacy site and as a tool for organization and mobilization. According to UFPJ's "about" section,

> United for Peace and Justice is a coalition of more than 650 local and national groups throughout the United States who have joined together to oppose our government's policy of permanent warfare and empire-building.
>
> UFPJ began as a national campaign to bring together a broad range of organizations throughout the United States to help coordinate work against a U.S. war on Iraq. At an initial meeting in Washington, DC on October 25, 2002, more than 70 peace and justice organizations agreed to form United for Peace and Justice and coordinate efforts to oppose the war on Iraq. (http://www.unitedforpeace.org/article.php?list = type&type = 16)

UFPJ's authors use the Web site to disseminate information through "calls to action," "e-mail updates," and an online "press room," all of which are designed to help activists, most of them young people, connect with one another, network, and form coalitions across groups to protest the war in and occupation of Iraq.

Other sites, such as MoveOn.org (at http://www.moveon.org) use the Web and Internet as their primary activist tools. MoveOn's FAQs offer the following explanation of its use of network technologies to forward its agenda:

What is MoveOn all about?

MoveOn is working to bring ordinary people back into politics. With a system that today revolves around big money and big media, most citizens are left out. When it becomes clear that our "representatives" don't represent the public, the foundations of democracy are in peril. MoveOn is a catalyst for a new kind of grassroots involvement, supporting busy but concerned citizens in finding their political voice. Our international network of more than 2,000,000 online activists is one of the most effective and responsive outlets for democratic participation available today.

What does MoveOn do?

When there is a disconnect between broad public opinion and legislative action, MoveOn builds electronic advocacy groups. Examples of such issues are campaign finance, environmental and energy issues, impeachment, gun safety, and nuclear disarmament. Once a group is assembled, MoveOn provides information and tools to help each individual have the greatest possible impact. During impeachment, MoveOn's grassroots advocates generated more than 250,000 phone calls and a million emails to Congress. We helped Congress come to understand the depth of public opposition to impeachment.

Who started MoveOn?

MoveOn was started by Joan Blades and Wes Boyd, two Silicon Valley entrepreneurs, with their family and friends. Although none of us had experience in politics, all shared deep frustration with impeachment and the lack of congressional leadership toward quick resolution. We all heard this same sentiment from a diverse group of friends and colleagues. On September 18th 1998, we decided to do something. Three of us with background in Internet software worked on the website. Others have worked to put together materials and start the ball rolling through their personal contacts. We are located all over the country, but most of the web work took place in Silicon Valley.

The MoveOn Peace campaign was founded independently as "9-11Peace.org" by Eli Pariser, a Maine native and recent graduate of Simon's Rock College of Bard. In the days following September 11th, 2001, he launched an online petition calling for a peaceful response to break the cycle of violence, which was quickly signed by more than one hundred thousand people in the U.S. and almost half a million worldwide. Eli joined forces with MoveOn soon afterward, and is now our International Campaigns Director. (http://www.moveon.org/about/)

Such online activism, arising out of and reacting to real-world situations, attempts to use the Web and the Internet simultaneously to inform and mobilize citizens into action groups and coalitions that will address specific issues and promote specific changes. What's impressive about MoveOn.org in particular is that it is largely run by e-savvy youth, generally under age 30, who see the value of questioning federal policies and who feel the Web is an effective means of distributing information and informing a voting constituency of its message.

As I reflect on these two examples, both of which were prominently discussed in the major news media shortly after the launch of military operations in Iraq in March 2003, I am struck by several things. First, the goals are relatively simple—inform and mobilize. There is very much a sense of the need to "get the word out" here, and a confidence, perhaps, that forwarding enough information will prompt action, will encourage a site visitor to send an e-mail to a congressional representative, for instance. I can't help but wonder, however, if that confidence is justified. The extensive networking of UFPJ, for instance, is certainly admirable, but the occupation of Iraq (as of this writing) continues. Second, MoveOn reports fairly substantial numbers of people participating in their various Web campaigns, claiming more than 2 million "online activists" (http://www. moveon.org/about/). Although these are impressive numbers, one wonders what the diversity of political opinion is among the activists. I would imagine that the activists are similarly aligned in terms of political persuasions and ideologies. As such, the "networking" is most likely preaching to the proverbial choir, and I wonder about the effectiveness of such a site in changing opinion, opening up new avenues of discussion, and being open to the "other"—in the Donna Haraway-cyborgian sense. In other words, is a particular form of identity, clustered around leftist or left-learning politics, reified and replicated in such efforts? Are other views left out or left unconsidered?

With such questions, I do not mean at all to disparage the work being done by either UFPJ or MoveOn. Rather, my goal is to think a bit more critically about the possibilities and limitations of such online activism, and to push the scholarship about such activism into new territory. For instance, following Gruber's lead, we might note how both sites address issues of global importance, particularly wars affecting numerous nations, but we should also ask how the sites might be "anchored in local politics and local economic situations." Would their effectiveness be enhanced if they were?

My hunch is that yes, the sites' ability to mobilize people and affect political change might work better at the local level. For example, MoveOn notes the use of "flash campaigns," with the following offered as an example:

PHASE I—PRIOR TO HOUSE VOTE ON IMPEACHMENT INQUIRY

September 22—Petition site launched

September 29—100,000 mark reached

October 1—80,000 petitioners armed with their representative's phone and fax; asked to call

October 1—1,000 volunteers armed with phone and fax for all judiciary committee members

October 3—Begin daily e-mail of individual petitions to constituent's representative

October 4—Compiled petition to each Judiciary Committee member, with comments

October 5—Additional 50,000 petitioners asked to call their district's representative

October 7—Compiled petition sent to each member of the House with an e-mail address (80% of districts)

October 8—200,000 mark reached

October 8—Compiled petition hand delivered to each member of the House before vote (http://www.moveon.org/about/#s8)

Such a use of the Internet, primarily e-mail, to protest the impeachment of President Clinton seems a bit more directed and localized than more diffuse (if albeit necessary) anti-war Web sites, which are most likely only ever visited by like-minded individuals looking for information to bolster their (preformed) opinions.

As such, the question remains whether or not the Web can be used strategically in the cause of political activism. Fortunately, some youth activists are doing this work—using the Web in some startling and ingenuous ways *and* thinking critically about how they write the Web in their activist causes. In the remainder of this chapter, I take a closer look at one such effort, the International Middle East Media Center (IMEMC), which is operated largely by a group of activist-oriented, e-savvy youth. In my discussion of the site and my interview with Tim Covi, the primary Web designer for the site, I explain how this group's specific use of the Web, including a pragmatic understanding of its possibilities *and* its limitations, is telling in understanding how some youth are (re)configuring the Web as a literacy and activist tool.

RECONFIGURING WEB ACTIVISM:
THE INTERNATIONAL MIDDLE EAST MEDIA CENTER

The International Middle East Media Center IMEMC, at http://www.imemc. org, is primarily, at this point at least, a Web-based activist effort whose primary goal is to provide alternative sources of news information about the ongoing Israeli–Palestinian conflict. The "mission statement" of the IMEMC provides a detailed description of the group's aims and goals, worth quoting in full:

> In an attempt to balance the scales of representation and to bring the public a clearer picture of the realities in the region, a group of international and Palestinian journalists have joined together to create a new media center that will function as a cross roads of information for both the public and for professional journalists. The International Middle East Media Center has started a basic article print service and news wire on the internet, offering articles from 45 journalists stationed throughout the West Bank and Gaza Strip, and commentary from editors and political analysts well versed in the history of the region.
>
> The International Middle East Media Center's main objective is to provide both the public, and professional international journalists, with accurate, well investigated information regarding the current crisis in Palestine (the West Bank and Gaza Strip by 1967 boarders). After an extensive analysis of the methods of media operation in the West Bank and Gaza Strip, our team determined that news coming from international and local agencies was lacking on multiple levels, from source interviews to actual research and publication. The dramatic importance this region plays in international affairs makes accurate information about the region an absolute necessity. People in the international community need this information in order to generate realistic opinions regarding necessary courses of action toward peaceful settlement of the conflict.
>
> To further accomplish its goal, IMEMC seeks to provide a service to international journalists as a clearinghouse of information, both by way of daily articles, and by way of establishing relationships with journalists working in the region, and with international bureaus working outside the region. In our beginning stages, our news production will

be limited to print sources. As we expand, however, IMEMC seeks to generate news services for international audiences and journalists in the field of TV and radio broadcast as well. Over time IMEMC will initiate a "stringer" service, providing TV and radio stations with short interviews and small clips of video and audio from local events where international media may not have been present.

Generally speaking, IMEMC seeks to focus not only on the day-to-day problems presented by military action, but on the general effects of occupation. Issues such as the treatment of Palestinians at checkpoints, Chronic Traumatic Stress Syndrome caused by generalized military action in civilian areas, water rights and water quality, and ecological disasters caused by lack of resources and waste facilities play a large role in everyday life for most Palestinians and underscore the problems inherent in the current peace process, yet these issues are terribly under-represented in international media. Bringing these issues to light and putting them before international public opinion will help facilitate more equitable decisions regarding international diplomacy and action within the region.

The larger goal of the Middle East Media Center project is to always produce fair and accurate reporting. The nature of this project is to attempt to balance scales of reporting internationally by effectively reporting on Palestinian issues that are largely neglected by the international media. Maintaining balance in a macro perspective can only be attained by radically shifting the focus of international media, and, as regards the Middle East, this can only be done with consistent focus on Palestinian issues. (http://www.imemc.org/mission_statement.html)

This project has several dimensions that I want to discuss in and, because the project is primarily, at this point, Web-based, I focus much of my attention on its cyberspace dimension.

Tim Covi, who is largely responsible for the maintenance of the IMEMC Web site, explained in an interview that the organization's goals are, indeed, ideological. At the time I interviewed Tim, he was only 24 years old, but a model activist nonetheless—engaged, committed, even inspired. He was one of the founders of the IMEMC organization, and he explains that his own travels in Palestine were key in convincing him of the need for media activism surrounding the reportage of information from the Middle East in general and Palestine in particular:

I was in the West Bank as a freelance journalist, and I noticed pretty immediately after going out into the field and working in different refugee camps and villages for a couple of weeks getting interviews— I noticed that there wasn't a very good system of reporting by interna-

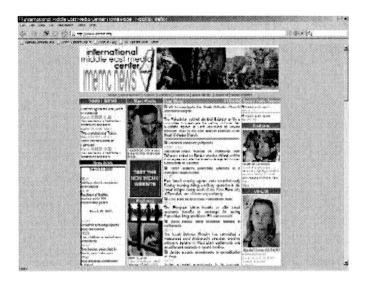

Screen shot of http://www.imemc.org/

tional journalists. There were a lot of freelancers out there, but the
mainstream media wasn't doing much to get their people into the field.
We felt that one way of shifting the focus in international media, which
is predominately focused on Israeli issues more than Palestinian perspectives, would be to create a new service that could push its way into
the eyes of the mainstream media and try to shift journalists' focus
here and see about different things.

As such, the activist aims of the IMEMC are primarily focused on (a)
expanding awareness about different points of view and perspectives vis-
à-vis the Israeli–Palestinian conflict and (b) mobilizing reporters to reconsider how they are reporting on the conflict. And for Tim, such goals are
intimately tied to issues of literacy. In an earlier e-mail to me about the
project, Tim argued the following:

> Media in this environment is critical, and the way media approaches
> both the conflict and the issue of reconciliation partially determines
> how much we actually understand about root causes regarding the new
> turns in the conflict.

The questions we ask, the stories we look at and those we exclude, the areas in which we have a field presence and those where we lack such a presence—all of this determines what type of coverage we can provide, and predetermines the kinds of relationships we can develop with both independent and mainstream associations in the West.

Media—and, more specifically, the stories shared through that media—are crucial in shaping opinion about the Israeli–Palestinian conflict, and such a view suggests that Tim is not just a political activist, but a *media* activist as well.

A Critical Approach to the Web

When I talked with Tim specifically about the IMEMC's use of the Web, a number of literacy issues dominated our discussion, such as literacy's connection to technology and the impact of the Web in particular on various aspects of literacy and rhetorical practice, such as considering and addressing audience interests and needs. As we talked, I was surprised at how very *un*-utopian his view of the Web was, despite the group's reliance on the Web as both their primary medium and, in some senses, the focal point of their media activism. But Tim was clear that he and his colleagues do not think of the Web as ideal, but rather cost-effective:

> I think the service that we are offering right now—hmmm, I don't think the Web is the ideal forum for what we are doing. It's just an unfortunate reality that the cost of production in the media has gotten so high that any independent organization that is just starting is going to be very hard pressed to be able to saturate a large portion of the market in any other way than using the Web. Even with the TV projects that we'll look to create in the future and the radio projects. The costs of those media services is just astronomical, and there is no way that as an independent organization, regardless of how much money you could possibly get, there is no way that we could do everything that we would like to. I think that is just sort of a problem that a lot of independent organizations have to deal with now.

Interestingly, Tim seems to favor more "traditional" media formats, such as television, for "getting the word out" about the plight of the Palestinians and their perspective on the situation. And he may have a point: Many people receive their news from television, not the Web, particularly because access to the Web, on a regular, daily basis, is still restricted (or nonexistent) for many, even in the population of highly developed countries such as the United States.

At the same time, Tim wanted to be positive about the IMEMC's use of the Web, although one can hear his ambivalence in his comments:

> On the other hand, what we'd like to do is be able to saturate a large international audience, and with the Web you can reach an English language audience, let's say, across the globe. We would no longer be looking at one pocket area; we can expand beyond that. There are problems that come with that too. When you consider what the media is for—it's a tool for educating and even manipulating public opinion. If you want to do that in any way that has an effect on international affairs and politics, you try to saturate one audience.
>
> The problem with the Web is ultimately it's so huge your saturation effect isn't going to be very large in one given area. It also has its downside.

Later in the interview, Tim reiterated this concern, offering examples and comparisons to clarify his thinking:

> I think that the biggest challenge is really being able to saturate a large audience because, unlike something locally, if you start a local newspaper you can advertise in a section of the city and reach a lot of people that way. On the Web, where do you even begin? From a business perspective, a lot of people say that starting a business, you don't want to go to a place where there are a lot of vacant buildings. No one is going to be going there. You want to go to a place that has a ton of happening businesses. If you don't get the right window space or you're not in the right place on this street where all these businesses are, then chances are you are not going to be found. I think the same thing goes for the Web. People want to be on the Web because there are a lot of things on the Web and a lot of people using the Web on a daily basis, but it's so massive. It's like having a shopping center that's five times the size of Cincinnati [where I conducted the interview with Tim].

With such statements, Tim directly addresses issues of the purported *global* nature of the Web. On one hand, he acknowledges that the Web is fairly extensive—in terms of reaching an "English-language audience." At the same time, it's that extensiveness that problematizes the IMEMC's use of the Web in accomplishing its goal. If its mission is educating, "even manipulating public opinion," with the goal of having an "effect on international affairs and politics," then how can Tim and his cohort be sure that the right people are viewing their site, receiving their messages, paying attention to the alternative information available?

For Tim, such a question is tied to other rhetorical concerns about attempting to reach an audience and readership via a Web site:

> Already we could tell that we were only getting a niche market and that's something that we wanted to adjust. Now what we are doing is actually looking at the way in which we are targeting an audience. We are going through a process of analyzing our site and our services to see what we can do to engineer it to try and reach more of an audience that's in the center, maybe center left, which is an audience that's actually fairly difficult to cater to. They don't consist of a very easily understood core body. It's easy to sing to the left, and it's easy to sing to the right but those extremes are very identifiable. What is center and center left is a little more difficult to identify.

Tim's dilemma has been noted by other scholars studying the use of the Internet in activist work. Jenny Pickerill, in "Weaving a Green Web: Environmental Protest and Computer-Mediated Communication in Britain," notes that "participants are still mobilized more effectively if they are within existing movement networks, rather than non-integrated individuals" (143). Such comments echo my sneaking suspicions about sites such as MoveOn.org or even the UFPJ site: They are most likely visited by the like-minded and sympathetic.

The question of reaching an audience is made even more complicated by the creation of links from *other* sites to the IMEMC site—links that the original site designers cannot control and cannot craft themselves. In an e-mail written to me shortly after the interview, Tim made the following observation:

> If you want to get an impression of how self-marketing media on the Web can be, do a quick google search of "international middle east media center." One month ago the same search would have produced five listings, now it's three pages with a number of different sources. It just keeps advertising itself. The question is, how do we control the advertising—one site actually misrepresents us by stating that we are run by Palestinian journalists and international solidarity movement volunteers—a little troubling in my opinion.

It's as though the hypertextual nature of the Web, particularly the creation and proliferation of links, complicates and potentially distorts the dissemination of information. Although hypertextual theorists, such as George Landow, might have once lauded the ability of the Web to help forge interconnections across bits of information, Tim's experience sounds a distinct cautionary note: Hyperlinks don't simply "connect" but serve themselves as possibilities for making interpretations, reinterpreting, and even evaluating and judging the content to which one is linked.

Indeed, Tim consistently critiqued the efficiency of the Web in delivering and disseminating information. Shortly after our interview, and once he had returned to Palestine, Tim wrote me the following email. In it, he refers to materials for an article that he collected from both correspondents *and* from Web sources, primarily news sources; the report concerned an incident that had just occurred and that a variety of news agencies, including IMEMC, were reporting on almost simultaneously as the event was unfolding:

> learned something new regarding web based media in times of emergency. it is extraordinarily efficient, jonathan. look at yesterday's article on the imemc site. i compiled that report over the course of 45 minutes, based on reports from our correspondents that were coming in from the street, but also based on information from various news paper's web services. within 30 minutes, reports had been posted on every major website for every major news paper in the area. the coverage is obviously constantly changing and is rarely complete, but the fact remains that it was quite effective under the circumstances. that's the good side. the down side is the potential for confusion and incomprehensive coverage that leads to misconceptions under such constraints. so it has its benefits, and, as always, there are hazards you have to be conscious of and have to try to mitigate.

Tim is clearly impressed with the speediness of the dissemination of information. But he insists that such efficiency should not tempt us to overlook significant literacy issues, such as comprehensibility of the information disseminated. One can also read between the lines of his e-mail and glean from it that he is concerned with the diversity or variety of information disseminated; too little diversity could lead to "misconceptions" or "constraints" on understanding the complexity of significant sociopolitical events.

RECONFIGURING WEB USE:
A LITERACY OF PRAGMATICS

Given his caveats and reservations about the Web, I asked Tim to define "success" vis-à-vis his project: How would he know if the IMEMC Web site was, in any way, "successful," especially given his critical appreciation of the Web as a communications tool? He answered as follows:

> I think our success is going to be the degree to which we can reshape the way the mainstream media is functioning with regards to this conflict between Israel and Palestine.

The question is—and this is a question that Tim poses, at times skeptically, to himself about the project—how *can* the Web help to "reshape" the "mainstream media"? In other words, how *do* you spread the word about a Web site, and its content, especially if you want to use it to change how people think about a topic? What's intriguing about Tim's comments is the tension between his willingness to attempt to transform situations through communication via the Web and his recognition of the limitations of the Web as a communications medium. Such a tension has led him to adopt what I call a *literacy of pragmatics*—a strategic use of the Web that simultaneously uses and acknowledges its very real limitations as a communications tool.

For instance, things will improve, Tim thinks, once the IMEMC both (a) takes advantage of more of the Web's multimedia capabilities and (b) promotes the Web as a "support" for other media, such as television or radio:

> Ultimately, when we start a TV service, what we are going to offer is a stringer service, which means small clips of video and for radio as well. We'll have small clips of audio from the field that we can put onto the Web and the TV stations. TV journalists and radio journalists can download them from the Web for a very small fee. That way, TV stations locally, let's say in Colorado or any country really that might have an interest in a story and couldn't afford to get a journalist there, can now download this stuff for a very small fee and produce a story about it. Ultimately, we are offering a service that could have a high demand, and it could make things much cheaper for some TV stations that are spending a lot of money on having journalists there like a photojournalist or a video journalist. I think ultimately that service is what's going to determine our success.

The Web, in this view, primarily functions as a conduit of information—*with a critical difference*: that information is cast in a variety of multimedia formats and delivered *for use in more traditional media.* This reminds me of what Steve Novotoni, editor and publisher of Cincinnati's independent and alternative news magazine, *XRay*, told me in an interview about the increasing ease of using multimedia: "there is going to come a time where [multimedia] tools will be just as cheap and just as easy to use and just as effective as the tools in desktop publishing, so that any person can create a film or a newscast or whatever that looks just as good as anything produced by CBS, CNN or whoever." For Tim, that ease translates not into using the Web as the primary delivery of information to visitors, but as a tool to support such delivery via other media.

Tim's comments, particularly about CNN and the use of multimedia, reminded me of Jay David Bolter and Richard Grusin's work in *Remediation: Understanding New Media*, in which the authors argue that the construction and dissemination of information via new media is characterized by "a double logic of 'remediation.'" They explain as follows: "Our culture wants both to multiply its media and to erase all traces of mediation: ideally, it wants to erase its media in the very act of multiplying them" (http://www.lcc. gatech.edu/ ~ bolter/remediation/bk_intro.html). As a powerful example, Bolter and Grusin offer an analysis of the CNN Web site and televised broadcasts, which, they claim, aim for both *hypermedia* and *immediacy*:

> The CNN Interactive site is hypermediated—arranging text, graphics, and video in multiple panes and windows and joining them with numerous hyperlinks; yet the Web site borrows its sense of immediacy from the televised CNN newscasts. At the same time the televised newcasts are coming to resemble Web pages in their hypermediacy. The team of Web editors and designers, working in the same building in Atlanta from which the television news networks are also administered, clearly do want their technology to be "television only better." (http://www.lcc.gatech.edu/ ~ bolter/remediation/bk_intro.html)

This is a compelling example of how news "composers" at one major news agency are using multiple media, both on the Web and on television, to give viewers and consumers a sense of immediacy in their perception and reception of the news. Curiously, this is also an example of how one medium, such as the Web, is being used to "re-mediate" another, older medium, such as television; that is, televised broadcasts are made to look like Web pages in the hopes perhaps of transferring some of the immediacy associated with Internet communications to the medium of television.

Although their example is compelling, I don't know that I can fully agree with Bolter and Grusin's assessment that "ideally, [our culture] wants to erase its media in the very act of multiplying them"—at least not based on some of the work I've seen and analyzed in these pages. Tim's work for IMEMC suggests a different way of thinking about the Web as a multimedia platform—one that works in *support* of other, older media, not necessarily leading to their remediation. At the same time, I don't think that this view and Bolter and Grusin's view of remediation need necessarily be in opposition; after all, Tim certainly sees benefits in using the Web: It's efficient and fairly immediate in news dissemination. But his goal is to *filter* information to those older media in the hopes of promulgating reception of different viewpoints, not necessarily to immerse television viewers in the supposed and vaunted immediacy of the Web. Granted, the quicker his agency's news items filter to and through the older media, the better. But I still sense here a distinction in *use* of the Web: Tim doesn't want to "erase all traces of mediation"; rather, he seems more focused on recognizing and using the different strengths of the various media to mediate news that he thinks is important and vital.

Tim's pragmatic thinking shows itself in other configurations of the Web as a literacy tool. For example, Tim argued that having a Web presence is significant in that it provides an "official presence" that one can then use to attract other kinds of organizations or even funding sources:

> We do need money and the Web site is really useful when you are going to get funding from a foundation, because if you have nothing to show, it is just an abstract idea on a piece of paper.

For Tim, such a presence is also tied into issues of "professionalism," such as using formats comparable to other news agencies, so users know both who you are and how to navigate your site:

> There is a fairly standard format. There may be slight variations, but the general format is already there, and it's going to be very easy to navigate through a new site. You are going to probably have a bar along the side like a navigation bar, which will list the features that you have. It will list the different services for journalists or the different services that you offer for foundations in a given area. Whatever it might be. In the center, you typically have headline news, and then you have links to other portions of your newspaper, like, if you are a huge newspaper owner you may have comics and sports and that kind of thing. The layout has become fairly standardized and what I've noticed is that a lot

of independent media organizations haven't been utilizing that format. They are trying to create their own thing, but that can become very frustrating to the average user because, when you go to the site, it's more difficult to navigate because you are so used to this format that has already been created.

When I say professional, we are trying to fit into the professional media's formats as opposed to independent media formats.

Providing news in a format that can be "read" as news, that is recognizably presented as news and is comparable to that of other news sites, is key not only in promoting the professionalism of their venture, but also in simply making their site legible as a news site to viewers and visitors—much like the editors of GoXRay.com seem to style their site on major news agency Web sites. As such, issues of layout and the use of visuals become important considerations in crafting the site so that visitors know how to "read" it.

And such a task requires constant revision. I interviewed Tim in July 2003, and by late August he had e-mailed the following update about his ongoing attempts to "professionalize" the site, to make it legible for readers as a news-oriented informational Web site:

> If you've been using the imemc site, you've probably noticed we're changing things around a bit. Last week I realized something as I was flipping through news sites—imemc fell somewhere sadly between independent news / mainstream news when it came to our image (content is another story, but i think image affects the way content is read on the Web). Presentation is critical as we're taking steps to begin the networking aspect of our project, so George and I have been re-designing the site, trying to make it appear a bit more professional, a little less half assed (it's already been pointed out by at least one person a day that we're using the colors of the Israeli flag . . .) Anyway, here's the point: I need some feedback regarding the changes we've made and the ones we'll be making in the next month. We're updating our content to include weekly feature reports which will come out every Monday; we'll probably begin weekly slide shows from different areas around the West Bank beginning a couple weeks from now; We have a set editorial schedule which in a few weeks should include regular column writers in addition to consistently produced interviews with Palestinian/Israeli political figures.

Certainly, as a writing instructor, I appreciated Tim's call for feedback. As a scholar of Web writing, I can only underscore again the extent to which certain genres of articulation, representation, and information dissemination are already common on the Web, as well as the extent to which Web-savvy youth like Tim understand that being able to replicate and manipulate such genres is a crucial Web literacy skill.

SOME CONCLUSIONS

An examination of IMEMC's site reveals for us a number of Web literacies at play in these youths' construction of activist Web space. At the most basic level, rhetorical issues, such as crafting the site so that it (a) is readable as a news site and (b) reaches its intended audience, dominate the composition of the site. By attending to these issues, Tim and others at IMEMC are consciously crafting Web space to disseminate information (Vegh's "awareness/advocacy") and enlist supporters ("organization/mobilization"). Thus, IMEMC's use of the Web is comparable in these ways to what other scholars have noted about how activists—young or old—use the Web.

More significantly, however, IMEMC's reconceptualization of the purpose and power of the Web as primarily a "support" for other media is itself a reconsideration of the Web's usefulness as a literacy tool. From this perspective, the Web seems less cyborgian, in Haraway's sense, in its creation of networks and coalitions between one person and another, from one group to another. Rather, through Tim's understanding of the Web, we see primarily its limitations in disseminating information, and its potential for creating information networks is recast in thinking of the Web as just one additional tool in furthering an activist agenda of increasing the kind, quality, and diversity of information we receive. One could argue that such a reconceptualization of the Web still casts it as part of a network of information conduits that might lead to a cyborgian sense of self and community. But IMEMC's strategic use of the Web suggests a more critical—and critically aware—approach about how information is disseminated—and of how to best use a multiplicity of mediations in crafting and disseminating their message.

This is, interestingly enough, in line with some early theorizing about how the Web might serve in activist causes. In his now classic essay, "The Temporary Autonomous Zone," Hakim Bey writes the following about the

Web and the creation of Temporary Autonomous Zones (TAZs), or the "political tactic of creating temporary space that eludes formal structures of control":[1]

> At this moment in the evolution of the Web, and considering our demands for the "face-to-face" and the sensual, we must consider the Web primarily as a support system, capable of carrying information from one TAZ to another, of defending the TAZ, rendering it "invisible" or giving it teeth, as the situation might demand. But more than that: If the TAZ is a nomad camp, then the Web helps provide the epics, songs, genealogies, and legends of the tribe; it provides the secret caravan routes and raiding trails which make up the flowlines of tribal economy; it even contains some of the very roads they will follow, some of the very dreams they will experience as signs and portents. (Ludlow, 412)

In many ways, I think Bey's metaphors can help us understand Tim's approach to the Web as an information and literacy tool. In the opening up of "TAZs," those spaces in which thinking can be reshaped and revised by new insights or the consideration of other perspectives, the Web is less the "nomad camp" itself than it is one of the "caravan routes" providing the stimulating and revision-inspiring "epics, songs, genealogies, and legends." In other words, to use Bey's words, the Web might actually work best as a "support system" for activists. And, from Tim's perspective, conceiving of the Web as such a "support system" shapes the activists' approach to it as a communications tool, as a writing environment, and as a mode of literacy.

Furthermore, it's worth noting that Tim's and the IMEMC's use of the Web is actually fairly localized, despite the desire to reach a potentially global audience. Such use is comparable to that noted by Gruber vis-à-vis the women-oriented sites she studied. Gruber suggested that, "although the groups appeal to a global audience, many of the issues they address are anchored in local politics and local economic situations" (88). I think such a description applies directly to Tim's goals for the IMEMC—a Web site disseminating information about a local issue via a—potentially, with qualifications noted—global reach.

---

[1] Bey never defines the TAZ. The definition I use comes from Wikipedia: http://www.wikipedia.org/wiki/TAZ.

In *Cybering Democracy: Public Space and the Internet*, Diana Saco argues the following:

> The electronic domain of computer networking is certainly an other space in relation to the more familiar spaces we embody daily. At the minimum, it is a space devoid of meat—of the body—and cannot therefore be fully inhabited. As that observation suggests, however, cyberspace, despite its challenges, cannot replace physical spaces and bodies; it can at best supplement and perhaps modify them. How cyberspace constitutes spaces and bodies differently is the crux of the matter for understanding its relation to politics, egalitarian or otherwise. (xxviii)

I think we have seen, particularly in analyzing the IMEMC Web site and Tim's self-understanding of his work on that Web project, that cyberspace is indeed a "supplement" to other forms of activist work, and a "supplement"—both useful and limited—in promoting an understanding of politics. And inevitably, understanding and appreciating these limitations of the Web helps us understand and appreciate its limitations—and potential—as a literacy tool. Steve Jones and Stephanie Kucker argue in "Computers, the Internet, and Virtual Cultures" that, "To study the ways the Internet allows connection and then do little else is not only an acritical approach to the study of life online but it ultimately reifies technology and subsumes human, interpretive activity to the tyranny of the Internet itself" (222). Without reservation, I can say that Tim is definitely *not* going to allow this to happen—at least not in relation to his work on the IMEMC site.

In this chapter, then, we have seen how some youth activists are reconceiving their understanding of the WWW in their efforts to use it strategically, effectively, and politically in the service of their activist causes. Their use of the Web fully acknowledges both its potential strengths and its significant limitations. In the following chapter, I discuss whether other e-savvy youth share Tim's views, as well as the hopes of other young activists, however qualified, for the potential of the Web to help them craft and disseminate sociopolitically important information. Specifically, I show how student writers attempt to create an activist site for addressing a cause that affects many youth directly—the spread of HIV and AIDS.

INTERVIEW WITH TIM COVI:
THE INTERNATIONAL MIDDLE EAST MEDIA CENTER

Tim Covi was a student of mine a few years ago when I taught at the University of Southern Colorado, now Colorado State University, Pueblo. Tim was very bright and a great writer, and he completed a degree in English at the University of Colorado, Boulder, where he became passionately involved in a variety of activist causes. In his early twenties, he traveled to Palestine as part of his activist work, and he and a group of other activists created the International Middle East Media Center, the subject of my interview with Tim. Tim was 24 at the time of the interview (Summer 2003).

Jonathan: Hi, Tim. Tell me a little bit about the work that you do, about the organization and how you got involved with it.

Tim: Okay. The organization is called the International Middle East Media Center [http://www.imemc.org]. Its primary function right now is just to provide a basic print news service on the Web. We started the project about 8 months ago as just an idea, and more recently, about 2 months ago, we actually put the Web site up and started to get enough funding to have enough people working on it on a regular basis. The Web site is managed from both the West Bank [in Palestine] and the U.S. People will post articles, and I will edit the articles on this side, morning and night, and repost the articles on the Web. The idea of the project in the long run is to try to create a space on the Internet where we can create a press wire service for TV, radio, and newsprint. We will move away from our own news reporting. We'll still have news reporting as a print service, but we'll move more away from that and create a press wire service that can be used by international media in a number of different ways. What we'd like to do is basically be able to push the envelope on what gets recorded in the international media regarding the conflict in Israel and Palestine.

Jonathan: Okay. You used the term print service. What do you mean by that?

Tim: Well, it's to differentiate between TV news service and radio news service. I guess it's kind of an ironic way of using the term because nothing is printed. We are using written articles right now as the primary service.

Jonathan: Why is the Web used in this particular case?

Tim: There are a number of reasons. I think the service that we are offering right now—hmmm, I don't think the Web is the ideal forum for what we are doing. It's just an unfortunate reality that the cost of production in the media has gotten so high that any independent organization that is just starting is going to be very hard pressed to be able to saturate a large portion of the market in any other way than using the Web. Even with the TV projects that we'll look to create in the future and the radio projects. The costs of those media services is just astronomical, and there is no way that as an independent organization, regardless of how much money you could possibly get, there is no way that we could do everything that we would like to. I think that is just sort of a problem that a lot of independent organizations have to deal with now. On the other hand, what we'd like to do is be able to saturate a large international audience, and with the Web you can reach an English language audience, let's say, across the globe. We would no longer be looking at one pocket area; we can expand beyond that. There are problems that come with that too. When you consider what the media is for—it's a tool for educating and even manipulating public opinion. If you want to do that in any way that has an effect on international affairs and politics, you try to saturate one audience.

Jonathan: What do you mean by "saturate"?

Tim: Well, you know, I'm saying like, public opinion in the United States is much different than public opinion in any European country and any South American country. So if you are trying to educate a certain population and affect a public opinion, so that public opinion can then have an effect on legislation or negotiations nationally, you ought to saturate one area to a degree that you have a high population density in that area that is reading that news and learning from it and changing their opinions.

Jonathan: Okay.

Tim: The problem with the Web is ultimately it's so huge your saturation effect isn't going to be very large in one given area. It also has its downside.

Jonathan: You can put your stuff out there, but can you track how many people are reading it?

Tim: Not very well. You can track the amount of hits you are getting, but you have no idea where they are coming from.

Jonathan: Let me back track just a bit and go back to the kind of reporting you do. Where does your info for your articles come from?

Tim: We have about 40 journalists or 44 correspondents, I should say, in the West Bank and Gaza Strip, and a team of editors and journalists who will take information from the field from these correspondents and create articles. We basically get like five to six articles ranging from political analysis to daily reporting on the Web.

Jonathan: I can tell, though, that you have an ideological purpose in posting this reporting...

Tim: Yes.

Jonathan: Tell me a little bit about that.

Tim: The idea behind the reporting is ultimately . . . the way this project started is, I was in the West Bank as a freelance journalist, and I noticed pretty immediately after going out into the field and working in different refugee camps and villages for a couple of weeks getting interviews—I noticed that there wasn't a very good system of reporting by international journalists. There were a lot of freelancers out there, but the mainstream media wasn't doing much to get their people into the field. We felt that one way of shifting the focus in international media, which is predominately focused on Israeli issues more than Palestinian perspectives, would be to create a new service that could push its way into the eyes of the mainstream media and try to shift journalists' focus here and see about different things.

Jonathan: And your use of the Web is one driven by economics?

Tim: Yeah. I think it is.

Jonathan: It's easier to post stuff up on the Web, for the time being, as opposed to using more widespread media such as television or radio?

Tim: Yeah. It is mostly an economic issue.

Jonathan: It's interesting because, while you've been here visiting us, I've actually seen you post stuff up. It seems not just economical, but it's easy as well.

Tim: Yeah.

Jonathan: It's very simple for you to momentarily recode a portion of the Web site or upload something. I'm very intrigued by that because the story you are telling about your use of the Web is one that is very different from the story that was told in the mid-90s about the possibilities of the Web, particularly in terms of its supposed ability to reach people and transform how the world communicates. You have a much more realistic understanding, or a pragmatic understanding, of the Web's possibilities—and serious limitations. Have you received commentary or feedback about your Web site from other people?

Tim: A little.

Jonathan: What has that been like?

Tim: We've received really good feedback. The feedback that we've gotten isn't anything negative. People have said that they are really happy that we are there. We got a couple immediately after we started the Web site. We got maybe five e-mails saying that people are really happy that it's out there, and they are going to bookmark this site as one of the things they are going to use for information on things that are happening in Palestine.

Jonathan: What kinds of people were those?

Tim: This is the trick; most of them are the people that were obviously involved with some type of organization that focused on Palestinian issues or human rights issues. Already we could tell that we were only getting a niche market and that's something that we wanted to adjust. Now what we are doing is actually looking at the way in which we are targeting an audience. We are going through a process of analyzing our site and our services to see what we can do to engineer it to try and reach more of an audience that's in the center, maybe center left, which is an audience that's actually fairly difficult to cater to. They don't consist of a very easily understood core body. It's easy to sing to the left, and it's easy to sing to the right but those extremes are very identifiable. What is center and center left is a little more difficult to identify. The feedback was useful in that way, in that we kind of know where we have to change.

Jonathan: Speaking about audience—how do you advertise your Web site's existence?

Tim: You know, we had thought a lot about how we were going to do that, and advertising obviously costs a lot of money, so the only thing we could think to do initially was try to contact other organizations that are interested in the mission of our project and see if we could put a banner on their Web sites. That has severe limitations as well.

Jonathan: Sure.

Tim: You are going to keep it in the same audience all the time by doing that, but it's an initial way of getting yourselves out there. That's one process that we've been going through, and the other thing I noticed about the Web is, about 3 weeks after we posted the original Web site, I did a very basic Google search and Yahoo! search and it came up that there were about five other Web sites that we hadn't contacted. They had us down as a link. There were two in Germany and one in Israel. There was also one in the States and one in Palestine. These are people that we had never contacted, so it sort of ends up growing on its own. There are people out there that we have had no contact with one way or the other. Indirectly someone found us through the Internet.

Jonathan: You never know. There could be a Web site that is a very controversial Web site, and it's completely contrary to your view and what you are trying to do, but it's linking to your site and suggesting what you're doing is "evil" or . . .

Tim: In fact, that's just about it.

Jonathan: Is there?

Tim: There is a Web site and it's one of the Israeli Web sites, and it's very pro-Zionist from what I have read, but they have a list of secondary sources that you can go to, so even though they have their own ideological beliefs, they have this list of Web sites that are from the opposite side or the opposite perspective. They just list them; they don't say anything nasty about them.

Jonathan: Do you do the same?

Tim: No, we don't.

Jonathan: What would you think would be ideal for your Web site right now? How would you be able to tell if it was successful, or do you think it's successful right now, as is?

Tim: I think that our success isn't going to be our news service, our internally produced news service. I think our success is going to be the degree to which we can reshape the way the main-stream media is functioning with regards to this conflict between Israel and Palestine. Ultimately, we are not going to be able to see that success for at least another year. It's some-thing that we have to work on. We have to work on network-ing a lot with international media.

Jonathan: Okay.

Tim: Ultimately, when we start a TV service, what we are going to offer is a stringer service, which means small clips of video and for radio as well. We'll have small clips of audio from the field that we can put onto the Web and the TV stations. TV journalists and radio journalists can download them from the Web for a very small fee. That way, TV stations locally, let's say in Colorado or any country really that might have an interest in a story and couldn't afford to get a journalist there, can now download this stuff for a very small fee and produce a story about it. Ultimately, we are offering a service that could have a high demand, and it could make things much cheaper for some TV stations that are spending a lot of money on having journalists, there like a photojournalist or a video journalist. I think ultimately that service is what's going to determine our success. That is really the goal of the project, and we won't be able to even see that for at least another year.

Jonathan: It's sounds as though you are saying that the success of the Web site will come if it is actually useful for feeding and sup-porting other media somewhat.

Tim: Yeah. Our idea with this wasn't so much to reinvent the wheel and create our own news site. Instead, we really want to push along that line, where TV services, TV stations, radio stations, and newspapers are looking at our Web site as a way to get critical information. We're approaching this from an investiga-tive journalistic model where the reports that we will create, the press wire services that we'll offer, will all be based around well investigated, detailed information that journalists know they can trust. It takes a long time to push your way into that field, but I think it can be done. The degree to which it can be done ultimately—as opposed to having to spend so much money and resources on reinventing the wheel and trying to, like, push your way into mainstream media as a huge TV station. If you push your way into the TV stations that *already exist* and try to change the format of what they are doing a little bit—that's what we're trying to do.

Jonathan: Interesting. It seems like you were suggesting that part of the reason you have a Web site is to have an official presence that you can then use to attract other kinds of organizations or even funding sources.

Tim: Yes.

Jonathan: Talk to me a little bit about that.

Tim: We *do* need funding because it's going to cost at least $100,000 to $150,000 a year to start the projects in TV and radio and to run a press wire in that way. We are going to need video cameras in the field. We are going to need mini disk recorders in the field. We are going to need to set up satellite stations that can feed the video that's been taped in one portion of the West Bank and get them back to a central office where they can be edited and distributed. We do need money and the Web site is really useful when you are going to get funding from a foundation, because if you have nothing to show, it is just an abstract idea on a piece of paper.

Jonathan: OK.

Tim: Whereas, if you can walk into a meeting with some foundation with a laptop there and say this is already what we have going and see the types of services that we are offering, you can see that we are very professional about the way we are approaching this, then these organizations are much more likely to help you and to give you money.

Jonathan: Here's a question: What is a professional-looking Web site?

Tim: Okay. I suppose at this point it is something that's very streamlined. Aesthetically speaking, I guess it would be the difference in using very basic HTML, which has become antiquated. We are using a good amount of JAVA. Either JAVA or even FLASH offer some qualities that can make things look very stream-lined. For a news Web site, I think it's much different than what would be professional for an airline ticket site. There is now a standard in news Web sites. If you go to 15 or 20 news sites on the Web, like CNN, *New York Times*, or you can look at AlAhram in Cairo . . . I'm saying different countries because there is a good reason. Each of them has a prestandard format of how things are laid out.

Jonathan: Individually or kind of comparatively?

Tim: Comparatively. There is a fairly standard format. There may be slight variations, but the general format is already there, and it's going to be very easy to navigate through a new site. You are going to probably have a bar along the side like a naviga-tion bar, which will list the features that you have. It will list the different services for journalists or the different services that you offer for foundations in a given area. Whatever it might be. In the center, you typically have headline news, and then you have links to other portions of your newspaper, like, if you are a huge newspaper owner you may have comics and sports and that kind of thing. The layout has become fairly standard-ized and what I've noticed is that a lot of independent media organizations haven't been utilizing that format. They are try-ing to create their own thing, but that can become very frus-trating to the average user because, when you go to the site, it's more difficult to navigate because you are so used to this format that has already been created.

When I say professional, we are trying to fit into the profes-sional media's formats as opposed to independent media for-mats.

Jonathan: That's very interesting. What Web sites do you find yourself going to frequently?

Tim: In terms of news or just in general?

Jonathan: In general, or both.

Tim: Okay. I guess, predominately, I do go to news sites. I don't know if you've ever heard of DMOZ [http://dmoz.org/] as a search engine. It's an open source project across the globe, and volunteers basically from everywhere will list different sites that they have found, and they are really well organized.

If you start doing a search for specific research topics that you are looking at, it's really easy to find results that are very specific to what you are dealing with. I've used DMOZ quite a bit.

Jonathan: Is that primarily a news source engine?

Tim: No. It's a general search engine and I use that quite a bit for news articles and background information that I'm looking for. Other than that, I search all types of English-language news sites from around the globe. I do use IMC, the Independent Media Center Web site, just to see what's happening. Let me think. Amnesty International, too. That's primarily the info sites I visit.

Jonathan: Okay. Is there a site that you particularly like besides your own?

Tim: Yeah. I'm not actually entirely keen on our own site right now. There are a lot of problems that need to be dealt with.

Jonathan: What's the problem?

Tim: One thing is that the editing on two sides of the globe becomes really challenging because you are in a 7- to 9-hour time difference depending on where I am in the States. That becomes really challenging. If somebody slips up and doesn't download the site before editing it, then they post errors that were there a day before and so everything gets 2 days behind schedule in terms of having the site up to date. That's one frustrating thing. And then just the layout. There are a number of things that I feel need to be changed. There are positions of things on the page and formatting issues.

Jonathan: Would those formatting changes align the site to look more like professional news sites?

Tim: Yeah.

Jonathan: So what is your favorite site right now?

Tim: The site I guess I use the most is AlAhram [http://weekly.ahram.org.eg/], which is a newspaper out of Cairo. It's a phenomenal newspaper, I guess, more than anything. If I had the print version I probably wouldn't use the site as much. It's difficult to find that newspaper here, so I end up using the Web site. In terms of, I mean my favorite site just to go to because it's fun, is called GNN.

Jonathan: Okay.

Tim: It's called Guerilla News Network [http://www.guerrillanews. com/].

Jonathan: All right.

Tim: You need a high-speed Internet connection to use this at all. There is no way you'd be using it on a 56K. It's incredible. They have these graphics that start the page and open for you, where these letters are forming out of a spinning globe that flattens out and turns into a map of the world.

Jonathan: Okay.

Tim: They have these letters that are forming out that say GNN, and then it takes you into the site, and they are a great news site as well. They have a lot of critical information. The way the put it together is really flashy.

Jonathan: I can't help but imagine that they are spooking CNN.

Tim: Yeah, they are.

Jonathan: When you say "critical information," what does that mean to you?

Tim: Well, it means that they are offer very critical investigative news stories. It's a place where you can go and get 5- and 7- minute TV newsreels, sort of like short documentaries on various political issues and social cultural issues. They are really analytical. The people who are working for them have a great understanding of the history of the topics and dealing with.

Jonathan: Okay.

Tim: It's not something where you are getting puppy dog news. It's nothing like Fox News.

Jonathan: All right. How does the site then compare to CNN in terms of form and content?

Tim: In terms of form, it's completely different.

Jonathan: Okay.

Tim: It's actually a fairly difficult site to navigate through. I don't think the people at GNN were too concerned about that. I think their audience was one that is going there because they really want to get information, so they are going to spend the time to flip through the site and its various pages to find it. I think they are sort of like a modern day subculture site, too, in the respect that, it's not like you are only going there for news service. It's almost part of a lifestyle, the way the flashiness comes out at the beginning, and it's very artistic I guess.

Jonathan: Okay.

Tim: It might also fit into an artistic subculture. Some of the documentaries they create will have a three-dimensional cube that pops out, and every time they are changing scenes from one interview to another, the cube is flipping around and changing its shape onto another side of the cube so you have another image appearing slowly but surely as an interview fades into another section of the video.

Jonathan: Okay. Why do they do that do you think?

Tim: It's like I said, they are just flashy.

Jonathan: Just flashy, okay. Ideologically, how to they compare to CNN?

Tim: Ideologically, they are really far to the left and it's very obvious.

Jonathan: Would you call CNN far to the right?

Tim: No. I'd call CNN the "liberal media."

Jonathan: Okay.

Tim: I say that with an understanding the there is a really strong myth of what the liberal media is. In the States, you have Republicans constantly harping on how liberal the media is, but ultimately liberal, I think, at this point stands for business relations.

Jonathan: Okay.

Tim: You are not going to get a lot of investigative reports or something like that on CNN. It's too expensive. TV stations and most news companies, even newspapers, which are still sort of the bastion of any kind of investigative reporting, don't want to spend more than 9 or 10% of their budget on investigative reporting. If you really want to do that kind of journalism, it takes far more than that.

Jonathan: Okay.

Tim: I would say that CNN fits more into the liberal mode. They will raise some issues, but they are not an extraordinarily critical news service.

Jonathan: For reporting or . . . ?

Tim: Yeah. It doesn't get much beyond that. Let's take a recent incident.

Jonathan: Okay.

Tim: Regarding President Bush's use of fabricated information in the lead up to the Iraq attack. The way that CNN treated that story, they were obviously critical of the Bush administration. They were critical of the Bush administration and the CIA and of Britain's intelligence service where they said the information had originated from. This is a story, which realistically should have some amount of investigation put into it. You are dealing with massive assault on another country, which stems from information that was completely false, and yet this is something that was reported on a fairly small scale. When I watched the news, they advertised this story throughout the entire program for about an hour before they finally aired it.

Jonathan: Okay.

Tim: This is something that in newsprint is called "secreting" an article and pushing it into the back lines of the paper because most people tend to go straight from the headlines on the first page, follow those headlines through and then read a couple of other stories. They are never going to find the articles that are sunk in between a lot of advertisements at the back end of the paper and the very center of it, right?

Jonathan: Okay.

Tim: So ultimately, what they did was slide this story to the back burner, which is really irritating to begin with because they had a number of stories that were just puppy dog news ultimately in the beginning, and they put this hot issue towards the end, which is one way of keeping avid viewers on advertising time for an hour. That's really frustrating. Then the follow-up on the story has really been lacking. Almost every story that has come out since the headline of this issue has been the same story repeatedly. It's just different people saying the same thing. They get different senators or different congressmen and different political analysts from Washington Hill talking about the issue, but they are all saying the same things. There hasn't been any investigative reporting about this issue.

Jonathan: Do you have investigative reporting on your site?

Tim: Yeah. It's a difficult thing to manage without funding. Fortunately, the volunteer rate in Palestine is really high. A lot of people are really interested in doing work because they have to and because most people at this point are dealing with a place that has, like, about fifty percent unemployment. People have a lot of time on their hands to do this kind of thing. We have a couple of journalists who spend a lot of time following up on certain stories. We have produced a few investigative reports and those are stories that we are going to be following up on and continuing to investigate. So far it has only been a few, and that's really a resource issue, not an interest issue.

Jonathan: Sure.

Tim: We would like to do more.

Jonathan: I'm sure you can only speculate on this, but you might have some sort of verifiable data. What is the Internet infiltration rate in Palestine? How many Palestinians use the Internet?

Tim: A lot actually. Something that has come from USAID [U.S. Agency for International Development], which is one beneficial thing that has come from U.S. support. USAID provides a lot of support for projects that are going to be useful to the U.S. in the future.

Jonathan: Okay. Explain please.

Tim: One of the things is providing the structural assistance that's needed to create good business services in the future. Actually Palestine is a place, a third-world country oddly with a lot of T-1 lines running through the country. There aren't a lot of terminals for these in the end, though. People don't have computers in their homes. In a refugee camp, they might have one computer, and that's because of the international presence, not because they can afford it. In the larger cities, you'll have Internet cafes and that kind of thing, but not everyone can afford to use those. Universities throughout the country serve a lot of the needs of Internet users. It is a place where the Internet could become broadly used because it does have the basis for it. Right now, it's mostly in bigger cities like Bethlehem, Jerusalem, Mullah, and Hebron. A lot of kids in those places and a lot of adults will have access to the Web. Otherwise, if you are in a refugee camp or something like that, it's just not sure.

Jonathan: As we wrap up, talk to me just a little about some of the biggest challenges in putting up a Web site. You can, if you want, be a bit more theoretical too, talking about the biggest challenge the Web faces in disseminating information. Up to you.

Tim: The biggest challenge, I guess, in putting up the Web site—it isn't really that hard, you know. It's fairly easy to do. Maintaining it is a little bit challenging for us because we have limited resources. There are only a couple of people with the knowledge of the Web to actually maintain it. That can get try- ing because you are just constantly working on a site that needs to be updated a lot. I think that the biggest challenge is really being able to saturate a large audience because, unlike something locally, if you start a local newspaper you can advertise in a section of the city and reach a lot of people that way. On the Web, where do you even begin? From a business perspective, a lot of people say that starting a business, you don't want to go to a place where there are a lot of vacant buildings. No one is going to be going there. You want to go to a place that has a ton of happening businesses. If you don't get the right window space or you're not in the right place on this street where all these businesses are, then chances are you are not going to be found. I think the same thing goes for the Web. People want to be on the Web because there are a lot of things on the Web and a lot of people using the Web on a daily basis, but it's so massive. It's like having a shopping center that's five times the size of Cincinnati.

Jonathan: Right. Where's your window space?

Tim: Where the *hell* is your window space?

Jonathan: Sure.

Tim: It's really challenging to find a way to attract people to your site.

Jonathan: There have been some good organizations and some good Web sites that have appeared recently to protest the war in Iraq and to rally people to protest the war. What do you think about those?

Tim: I think there is nothing wrong with it. I think that, generally speaking, it's a good idea as long as those sites are providing information. One of the real problems that I've seen in war protests, like anti-war gatherings, has been a general lack of information. People aren't sure. They know that they feel as if they should be against the war, but there is no clear understanding as to why. There is just a general sensation that, well, violence is bad and we should have peace. I think that a lot of the sites that are using the Web to get people involved in anti-war movements would do better to provide information as to how this war is particularly a nasty thing as opposed to simply using it as an advertisement mechanism to reach, you know, a population. There is another thing called Denverevolution. org [http://www.denverevolution.org/] that just started.

Jonathan: Okay.

Tim: This is a site that is trying to pull together all the leftist political organizations and social organizations in the Denver area. It's trying to pull them together, and Denverevolution wants to be the site that lists all the events that are happening in each organization to try to bridge gaps between different organizations. Ones that have a lot of public presence and ones that don't. They can cross reference them and people can find out about those things. That's a really clever idea. The fact that it could be a useful supplement for the organizer, as long as it doesn't become the sole medium organizer.

Jonathan: Is there anything that you'd like to add?

Tim: I don't think so.

Jonathan: Okay. Cool. Thanks Tim.

7

LITERACIES IN ACTION

THE YOUTH AND AIDS WEB PROJECT

In this chapter, I turn our attention, if only briefly, to a few pedagogical issues, such as how a greater awareness of digital youth literacies and writing might impact the teaching of writing and literacy. More specifically, I am interested in how some of the emerging literacy and compositional practices I've been examining in this book can be addressed and put to use in the writing classroom. As in the preceding chapters, however, I focus attention on what digital youth have to tell us about technology and literacy, even in contexts, such as the classroom, where young writers are situated as "learners," not "teachers." In the process of such discussion, it will be clear that some youth are configuring the Web, even with an awareness of its limitations, as a site for experiments in a variety of activist literacies.

First, a little bit of background.

As a writing instructor, I am keenly interested in the literacies that my students bring into the classroom, if only because I know that these literacies are the lenses through which they view, communicate with, and construct the world around them. Paying attention to those literacies might model for them, I hope, a respect both for their particular discourses and ways of being in the world *and* an openness to alternative discourses and literacies, particularly those that might seem strange or unusual (such as the world of academic discourse, about which I am authorized and obliged to instruct them).

But my interests in digital youth writing are also a little pedagogically selfish. I have often asked myself how I could capture some of the energy, creativity, and innovation of the writing I was seeing—writing that young people were doing on their own, not for a course or as part of a degree requirement. For instance, I would show and discuss with students a variety of activist-oriented Web sites, sharing with them my enthusiasm for the variety of ways in which fairly young writers are manipulating Web spaces, text, and visuals to promote substantive sociopolitical change. At the very least, I felt, and continue to feel, that such sites can model for students a sense of writing as critically engaged with important issues, as exploring alternative views and positions, as extending dialogues about significant debates. With a bit of searching one can probably find sites in your local communities that are also useful as models of not only alternative viewpoints but socially and politically engaged writing.

For instance, I've used both print and electronic versions of *XRay*, the local Cincinnati magazine discussed in Chapter 4, as an example of how young writers, almost all under age 30, are committed to thinking about their writing as an act of critical inquiry and as "interventive" in the larger community. According to the "about" section on their Web site,

> *XRay* is Cincinnati's progessive magazine. Every month we explore local arts, culture and news with a hip, edgy style. . . .
>
> *XRay* is designed to merge the concepts behind community and alternative news publications. (http://www.goxray.com/index.php?xray = about)

Such projects, both online and in print, certainly disseminate information, with a variety of viewpoints expressed and debated. As online repositories of news articles, they are nearly unparalleled resources. But they also demonstrate how factual information can be contextualized to promote various views or forward certain arguments—a strategy made particularly clear when evaluating with students a variety of different sites with different emphases and agendas. In fact, once students begin reading through these sites, many will automatically begin comparing information and views presented with more mainstream views disseminated through readily available mass media "sites," such as CNN.com, news-oriented television programs, and nation-wide print publications.

As such, in terms of studying writing with students, the sites put the *crafting* of information and viewpoints on the table, as it were, as an item for analysis. *XRay*, for instance, identifies *style* as one of the key points of differentiation between the writing its editors publish versus the writing found in other, more mainstream venues. By promoting a "hip, edgy style" among its writers, *XRay* is fostering a particular approach to culture and community—one that is not lost on students; they frequently note that different ideas are at play in *XRay*'s articles, and it's a short step from such an insight to a discussion of how differences in style can represent, even construct differences in ideology. For instance, in covering local elections, GoXray's editors update their site daily with breaking news, use a message board to invite readers to post their thoughts and discuss election-related issues, and host a continuing column, "Vigilancia Política," which serves as commentary, often barbed or satirical, on the candidates and the election process. The name alone, "Vigilancia Política," suggests an attitude, perhaps one expressing these particular youths' perceived disenfranchisement from the political process, and a desire to reinvigorate these youths' contribution to local politics.

Most significantly for college-aged students, I think, is that such sites, usually composed by recent college graduates or other young activists, model for students a sense of writing as engaged in significant public debate and community-building. For instance, *XRay*'s commitment to "merge the concepts behind community and alternative news publications" signals an approach to writing that many students have not encountered before—a sense that writing not only provides information and divergent views but can be used to create a sense of community among those who want to use acts of reading and writing to critique the worldviews given to them by the major news corporations. In tandem with this is the use of the technological innovations of *Webbed* writing to promote interactivity through message boards, leading, potentially further, to text-based community and even identity-building, as readers and contributors "try on" different ideas, social views, and political identities. Pedagogically, then, studying the work of Web-based or Web-savvy activists offers students the opportunity to explore how such activists use the multimedia capabilities of the Web to disseminate information, shape community, and construct politically aware, politically active identities via a variety of textual and visual rhetorics. As such, Webbed activist sites are often powerful, even provocative sites to use in helping students understand the potential of a critical and critically engaged literacy. They make an excellent contribution to a critical pedagogy concerned with examining both (a) the ideological and political dimensions of various discourses and (b) the increasing use of multimedia formats in the construction and dissemination of those discourses.

All of this work with students is part of facilitating their understanding of writing as potentially "interventive," as useful for engaging, critiquing, and contributing to significant issues. It's thinking about writing in an "activist" vein. In summary, I have wanted even my most recalcitrant students to be exposed to such writing, to catch a whiff of the excitement surrounding it, to be impressed by their peers' use of language, even visual "texts." I have wanted to use digital youth writing to model how many young writers are already actively engaged in constructing, critiquing, and reconstructing their worlds through the inventive, playful, and purposeful use of language, in all its many forms. I have wanted my students to be willing to take in their own writing the same sorts of risks I have seen other young writers take in theirs.

Perhaps more provocatively, I was eager to see if a "space" could be opened up in the academy for honoring innovative digital youth writing, for appreciating its critiques, and for helping writers to develop their work further. Taking seriously and adopting for myself Christopher Schroeder's commitment to "constructing literacies jointly with students, and by so doing to bring students to engage more deeply with education and society" (backcover), I have looked for ways to create spaces for student and youth writing and literacies in my writing courses. Because I have taught almost exclusively in computer-assisted environments, I have not hesitated to use technologies, such as desktop and Web publishing, to assist us in experimenting with and pushing the boundaries of literacy and writing in the academy and in our community.

My first attempts in creating such spaces were detailed in an article published in 2002 in *Computers and Composition*, entitled "Digital Spins: The Politics and Pedagogy of Student-Centered E-Zines." I had initially turned to the e-zine as a forum for encouraging students to work collaboratively on projects to publish their writing:

> In [my] course, students analyzed existing e-zines, submitted articles to those e-zines, and collaboratively assisted me in the project of creating a course e-zine, to which students were encouraged to submit their essays and writing projects. In general, these students were already pretty well versed and practiced in the basics of academic discourse, and many had had experience in using the Internet to research topics and issues, as well as in using word processors to facilitate the invention, drafting, and revision of their written work. But my hope for our course was that our work with e-zines would increase their sense of "connectedness" with their own and others' writing as they began to publish or at least prepare their work for potential publication on the Web.

I also wanted them to see how writers, frequently young writers published in online publications as diverse as Salon.com or Gettingit.com, were using writing in innovative ways to explore ideas, communicate insights, and offer critiques. As I reflect on this project, I can appreciate the initial steps I took in helping students create a space to play with their writing and experience new literacies. Unfortunately, as with any such project based on publishing student writing, the audience was ultimately fairly small. We needed another forum, another venue for reaching a readership.

I soon found one.

Our service-learning director, knowing of my interests in both promoting student writing and my work in queer theory and sexuality studies, suggested that I apply for funding for a Bridges to Healthy Communities grant, a project sponsored by the American Association of Community Colleges (AACC), working as a sub-grantee of the Centers for Disease Control (CDC). The goal of the project was to help create and sustain a "community college infrastructure that supports education and information programs to prevent HIV infection and other serious health problems in students and youth" (http://www.aacc.nche.edu/Content/NavigationMenu/ResourceCen ter/Projects_Partnerships/Current/BridgestoHealthyCommunities/Aboutthe Project/AbouttheProject.htm). A substantial component of this grant project involved fostering service-learning projects focusing on HIV and AIDS, and our active participation arose out of a strong sense, shared with AACC and the CDC, that (a) appropriate messages about sexual health were *not* reaching our students and (b) students' understanding of HIV and AIDS would benefit from active engagement with community resources seeking to address issues of sexual health and sexually transmitted infections (STIs).

Indeed, a CDC fact sheet, entitled "Young People at Risk: HIV/AIDS Among America's Youth," reported alarming rises in HIV infection and HIV-related fatalities among a range of American young people:

> In the United States, HIV-related death has the greatest impact on young and middle-aged adults, particularly racial and ethnic minorities. In 1999, HIV was the fifth leading cause of death for Americans between the ages of 25 and 44. Among African American men in this age group, HIV infection has been the leading cause of death since 1991. In 1999, among black women 25-44 years old, HIV infection was the third leading cause of death. Many of these young adults likely were infected in their teens and twenties. It has been estimated that at least half of all new HIV infections in the United States are among peo-

ple under 25, and the majority of young people are infected sexually. (http://www.cdc.gov/hiv/pubs/facts/youth.htm)

More broadly, the need for accurate information about HIV—information that can reach specific groups or, to use the CDC term, populations—seems urgent: according to a report released by the National Institute of Allergy and Infectious Diseases (NIAID) on May 15, 2003,

> Many Americans wrongly believe that a preventive vaccine for HIV/AIDS has already been developed, according to surveys recently conducted by the National Institute of Allergy and Infectious Diseases (NIAID). Nearly half of African Americans surveyed (48 percent) and more than a quarter of Hispanics (28 percent) believe that an HIV vaccine already exists and is being kept a secret. Twenty percent of adults in the general population share that belief. (http://www.nih.gov/news/pr/may2003 /niaid-15.htm)

The increase in infections and the continued circulation of misinformation about HIV have been so dramatic that the CDC has sponsored a number of national campaigns and funded numerous colleges and universities, through programs like Bridges to Healthy Communities, to promote HIV education, awareness, and prevention. One such project resulted in a joint collaboration between the American AACC, the American College Health Association, and the Bacchus and Gamma Peer Education Network to produce a resource and strategy guide for college faculty and staff, *Campus HIV Prevention Strategies: Planning for Success* (Hoban et al. 2003).

Our particular "Bridges" project began in a series of first-year composition courses, marketed as a writing-intensive service-learning course about HIV/AIDS and its personal, cultural, and political dimensions. This series of courses was offered in University College, a 2-year, open-access unit located on the main campus of the University of Cincinnati. As in many other colleges and universities, our sequence of first-year writing courses focused on expository, argumentative, persuasive, and research writing. At University College, such courses were generally populated by young adults (ages 18–25) from a variety of racial and class backgrounds, and I taught all sections of this sequence in a computerized classroom, in which each student had access to a personal e-mail account, a Web browser, a word processor, and (via the Web) a Blackboard site, which contained the syllabus, other course documents and handouts, teacher contact information, and access to several message boards. Students frequently used the Web as a research tool, and we discussed assignments and issues surrounding sexuality and youth, both in class discussions and via Blackboard message boards set up specifically for this course.

The primary writing assignments evolved as service-learning opportunities, in which students would negotiate with area AIDS service organizations (ASOs) to work with them on a variety of writing projects, such as writing newsletter articles, composing content or articles for Web sites, creating brochures, drafting reports about grant-funding possibilities, and writing proposals for or helping to develop sexual-health curricula. As I worked with colleagues, local HIV experts and educators, and a group of students on developing such materials, and a host of others including flyers, posters, bookmarks, presentations, and workshop outlines, it occurred to us that a Web site might be a good way to speak to students on campus about HIV and AIDS, particularly if the content of the site was generated by students themselves. Moreover, as I've shown in previous chapters, I was inspired by the work that I had seen my students do with Web-based compositions on their own, and I wanted to see if we could capture some of their energy and creativity for this educational project.

The Web site was initially supposed to serve as a "clearinghouse" for the campus by providing information about ASOs in the local area. Pedagogically, I thought of the Web project as an assignment in audience analysis and discourse communities, a project in which students would both learn about a deadly disease *and* develop skills in connecting with and conveying information to specific audiences; for instance, I was very interested in thinking with students about how they could craft important information about HIV so that it appealed to their peers, other young college-aged students. Essentially, my thinking revolved around questions that are comparable to ones addressed throughout this book: How are *digital youth* talking to one another about "touchy" topics or about topics of interest and import to them, and how are they using the compositional possibilities of the Web to craft messages that they think will appeal to other youth?

As such, beyond addressing a particular sexual health need, I also wanted to enliven my students' sense of the possibilities of writing for their peers, for their community. In "Community Literacy," Wayne Campbell Peck, Linda Flower, and Lorraine Higgins argue that some projects, such as service-learning and other community writing-based projects, can enable "college students and community teens to create a hybrid discourse in order to address local political and social issues" (x). Specifically, they maintain that

> community literacy occurs wherever there are bridging discourses invented and enacted by writers trying to solve a community problem. Community literacy is intercultural and multi-vocal. It is practiced as people cross boundaries, share various perspectives, and move into action. (587)

This was the model of literacy with which I initiated the project, and the Web seemed a particularly good forum for publishing student writing and disseminating it across campus. Unlike earlier e-zine projects that my students and I had undertaken, this health-focused Web publication had the potential to gain a wide audience and readership, particularly if units across campus, such as our Wellness Center or Student Health Center, would link to it from their pages. Rhetorically, students could also experiment with "electric literacies" or what Gregory Ulmer has called "electracy," or the transformation of literacy when we begin thinking about communicating in digital spaces (http://www.nwe.ufl.edu/elf/electracy.html).

Although my mission, and my students' ultimate acceptance *and reconfiguration* of that mission for their own agenda, might seem to partake of a utopian view of the Web, the remainder of this chapter also takes a critical look at the work we've done—as teacher and students— in creating what has come to be known as the "YOUth and AIDS Web Project." In particular, I discuss how that project has, pedagogically, left my hands and transformed in some interesting ways into a venue for some pretty provocative writing. Indeed, in key ways, the YOUth and AIDS Web Project moved from being a purely pedagogical endeavor to an experience in digital youth activist writing. In general, then, this chapter begins to unpack the pedagogical efficacy of using Web-based/Web-savvy activist sites, particularly those related to sexuality issues, and discusses how students developed critical literacy skills, involving both Web and visual literacies, as they attempted to create their own multimedia activist site.

First, however, to understand how we envisioned this site as both a creative and a potentialy interventive project, let's take a look at some of the writing *contexts* surrounding this work, particularly the representation of youth and sexuality in the media, and the use of the Web as a tool to promote, disseminate, and construct information about health. Examining such will set the stage, as it were, for understanding the media milieu in which students approached, conceived, and reconceived the YOUth and AIDS Web Project.

A WRITING CONTEXT:
YOUTH, SEX, THE MEDIA, AND THE WEB

As I undertook with my students the YOUth and AIDS Web Project, I was frequently reminded by my students themselves that images of youth and sexuality surround us everywhere in the media—on television, in the movies, and on the Web. One Web site, "Sexuality in the Mass Media: How to View the Media Critically," offers some useful commentary on the "sexual content" of television shows. The page is housed within a site called SexInfo, which "is run by students doing advanced research on sexuality through the Sociology Department at the University of California, Santa Barbara" (http://www.soc.ucsb.edu/sexinfo/). The researchers note that "Nearly 50% of adolescents report getting information about birth control from the mass media" and that "Four out of ten teens (40%) report that they have gained ideas for how to talk to a boyfriend or girlfriend about sex directly from media portrayals. . . . The mass media was the source of information about sexuality and relationships that was most frequently mentioned in a survey of youth ages ten to fifteen." Given such data, the site authors pose some questions to prompt students to think critically about such sexually loaded content:

- Who has created the sexual images?
- Who is engaging in the sexual behavior?
- Whose viewpoint is not heard?
- From whose perspective does the camera frame the events?
- How would your parents, girlfriend or boyfriend talk about the story you just saw?
- What is our role as spectators in identifying with, or questioning what we see and hear?
- Who owns the medium? How much do the owners profit from showing sexual content? (http://www.soc.ucsb.edu/sexinfo/?article = activity&refid = 026)

An example of how such questions work is instructive in how students themselves are noting what "viewpoints" are and are *not* heard—and how such affect their understanding, reception, and critique of the representation of images of both sexuality and youth in the media. As I've worked with college-aged writing students over the last few years, one film seems cited and referenced more than any other, both in my students' writing and in their conversations about popular culture: *American Pie*. This isn't surprising because the film depicts American youth similar in age, class, and background to many of the midwestern college students I teach. Although I, personally, like many of my colleagues, have found the antics depicted in the film both juvenile and somewhat less than charming, other scholars have noted some intriguing pedagogical dimensions of the film. In "'As Wholesome As...': *American Pie* as a New Millennium Sex Manual," Sharyn Pearce argues that the popular teen and young adult film actually serves as a "manual for self-formation, as a means whereby young men can progress relatively smoothly toward adulthood with particular reference to the management of sexual conduct" (70).

Pearce's analysis is intriguing, as she examines the film's sometimes boundary-pushing depictions of sexuality, such as masturbation and intergenerational sex, and the often complex (and occasionally amusing) negotiations of the characters as they seek sexual intimacy with one another. And I think she has a salient point in that *American Pie* ultimately serves up a fairly "wholesome" depiction of maleness—a sensitive and approachable maleness couched in discussions "about being nice to girls, by treating them equally, and not using them, and by letting them take the initiative to accept or reject sexual advances" (78). My students and I, however, noted some curious lacunae in the film's discussion of sexuality—some gaps that even Pearce fails to address in her analysis. Namely, the films do not grapple substantively, if at all, with issues of sexually transmitted diseases (STDs) and STI. Given this, the film raises some interesting questions for students, such as how do college-aged American youth want to be represented (and to represent themselves) as *sexual* beings—and as people concerned about sexual health issues?

In light of the increasing number of HIV infections among teenagers and college-aged students, this seems not only an important, but even a pressing question. Recognizing the need to deliver appropriate messages *to* college-aged students (and those even younger), some educational groups and organizations across the country have attempted to use the mass media to discuss or model for youth ways to protect oneself (and others) from STIs. Greater awareness of the health risks posed by STIs has also prompted a more thorough discussion of sexuality issues on television, for instance—a discussion *including* information about safer sex. The Kaiser Family Foundation reported in February 2003 that "The third biennial *Sex on Television 3: Content and Context* study finds the amount of sex on television remains high, but TV sex is more likely than in previous years to include some reference to 'safer' sex issues such as waiting to have sex, using protection, or the possible consequences of unprotected sex" (Sex on TV3 http://www.kff.org/content/2003/20030204a/).

Educators and health activists realize, though, that television alone is insufficient as a medium for delivering a message promoting safety and health. For instance, the organizers of the New York-based project Living Beyond Belief (http://www.livingbeyondbelief.org/), recognize that it is often better if young people *themselves* talk to one another about topics such as sexuality and safer sex. As such, this organization promotes peer education specifically about HIV and AIDS: "Living Beyond Belief, created to carry on the legacy of Wayne Fischer, seeks to save lives by motivating NYC public high school students to be HIV/AIDS peer educators, advocates and activists by providing them with college grants and recognition for their life-saving work" (http://www.livingbeyondbelief.org/aboutushome.htm).

Activists are also well aware that the WWW is becoming a significant resource about health topics for many. Many people with access to the Internet are increasingly using the Web to search for information about a variety of health topics. Ronald E. Rice, co-editor of *The Internet and Health Communication: Experiences and Expectations*, reports the following:

> As part of their ongoing comprehensive surveys of Internet use, the Pew Internet and American Life Project (2002a) reported on use of the Internet for health issues (as of March 2002). They conclude that "many say the Internet has helped them or someone they know and very few report harmful effects from acting on bad information they found online." They found that 62% of Internet users (72% women, 51% men) have gone online to seek health information, with more going online for medical advice on any particular day than visit health professionals, although this still means that slightly less than half of Internet health information users seek such information more frequently than every few months. (http://www.com.washington.edu/rccs/bookinfo.asp?AuthorID=55&BookID=192)

Recognizing this increasing reliance on the Web, several national and local organizations focusing their attention on HIV/AIDS education and prevention have established Web sites to disseminate much needed, life-saving information. For instance, the site Gender and HIV/AIDS (http://www.genderandaids.org/) offers information tailored to the specific health needs of women, with particular attention paid to how woman are at risk for contracting HIV. Other sites focus on different populations. The Web site for the Minority HIV/AIDS Initiative (http://www.hiv.omhrc.gov) has been presented as a model at national conferences as a Web project that reaches many people with important information (more than 200,000 visitors in 2001) and that addresses the needs, concerns, and issues of specific populations of people.

Activists have also attempted to reach youth, as a general population, with images, messages, and information about HIV, and their efforts have been spurred by increasing rates of infection among all racial, ethnic, and gender categories of youth. In early 2003, Viacom and the Kaiser Family Foundation launched a collaborative educational media effort called "Know HIV/AIDS." The project's aim has been to raise awareness about the disease through a substantial media campaign:

> Taking advantage of the Kaiser Family Foundation's expertise, and the breadth and depth of Viacom's creative and distribution assets, the multi-year initiative encompasses the creation and dissemination of information about the HIV virus and its prevention through television, radio, outdoor, online and print media. The mission: To use the power of media to educate and compel people to act to protect themselves and to get tested for the virus-and to erase the stigma for those afflicted. (http://www.knowhivaids.org/utility_campaign.html)

The project directors were well aware, however, that many youth with Internet access look for information on the Web, so they created an attractive and engaging site: www.knowhivaids.org. The site offers information-rich resources, including an interactive quiz, advice about testing and prevention, and an invitation for Internet-connected youth to "get involved" with the campaign.

Other efforts are similarly noteworthy, particularly as they attempt to take advantage of as many communications platforms as possible to provide messages about sexual health. Brian F. Geiger, writing in 2003 for the *American Journal of Health Education*, notes how Yahoo! Groups can be used "to communicate with . . . students across a variety of settings . . . to download information and files, participate in synchronous discussion, link to reputable Web sites for information about specific health topics, and receive ongoing support and encourage" (54). One such site targeting American youth in particular is MTV's "Fight For Your Rights: Protect Yourself" Web campaign (http://www.mtv.com/onair/ffyr/protect/), which casts sexuality education and information about safer sex in loosely political terms; visitors to the site are told they have the "right" to know how to protect themselves from STIs such as HIV, and those rights must be

Screen shot of www.knowhivaids.org

defended and guarded diligently from conservative social forces seeking to squelch important safer sex information. Included on the site are articles about World AIDS Day, petitions promoting comprehensive sex education, links to other resources, and a sex quiz to test one's knowledge of safer sex.

Although I am sure that some young people have had input about the construction of all of these Web sites, it strikes me that none of them are composed, operated, and maintained necessarily by college-aged students themselves. As such, they offer images and information—representations of youth and text and images about taking responsibility for one's health and sexuality—that do not necessarily come *from* youth. The *peer* involvement promoted by Living Beyond Belief consequently seems missing, at times, on the Web. Given this, I want to cast the YOUth and AIDS Web Project as one in which my students and I attempted to create a space for college-aged students with Internet access to construct and disseminate both information *and* representations of youth engaged in thinking critically about HIV, AIDS, and related health topics. The students understood the necessity of developing such representations, and they noted their lack in mass media artifacts such as *American Pie*. But they also intuited, as the organizers of Living Beyond Belief do, that such representations might be more effective if they came from digital youth themselves—not from other adults, no matter how caring or invested.

Out of these energies and insights, the YOUth and AIDS Web Project evolved. I turn our attention now fully to that project, situating it within the pedagogical context that nurtured it—and that was ultimately transformed by the students themselves as they explored radical literacy and compositional practices.

THE *YOUTH* AND AIDS WEB PROJECT: SOME INITIAL ASSIGNMENTS

Pedagogically, my inspiration for creating writing courses about HIV and AIDS (which I launched during the winter term, 2001), arose in part to the so-called "social turn" in composition studies, which has produced a growing body of provocative scholarship that seeks to unpack the connections between discourse and politics, language and power, representation and social agency. In books as varied as *Left Margins, Reclaiming Pedagogy, Composition and Resistance, Social Issues in the English Classroom, Pedagogy in the Age of Politics*, and *Miss Grundy Doesn't Teach Here Anymore*, compositionists have theorized how the writing classroom can become a site of both emergent political awareness and critique. With this in mind, however-er, Bruce McComiskey claims in *Teaching Composition as a Social Process* that many of the theories put forth in the aforementioned books advocate for courses that are admittedly content-rich, but often at the expense of examining and integrating *writing* process into the political critique. To demonstrate how such work can be undertaken, McComiskey describes what he calls a "social-process pedagogy." For instance, McComiskey discusses how, in one set of exercises, students analyze college viewbooks for the ways in which they construct ideal students with the "right" values—values that the institution puts forward as desirable in its students; then students are invited to critique the distribution of such books and their own consumption of them. Ultimately, McComiskey has students create their own viewbooks in response to the critiques they have undertaken. Frequently, such analysis of circulating discourses (such as viewbooks) results in the production of letters aimed at intervening in the dissemination of representations and values that students find exclusionary or politically troubling. For example, in another set of carefully designed exercises, McComiskey describes how students examine the "culture of school[ing]" to excavate and explore both formal and hidden curricula, as well as the cultural values implicit in contemporary educational practices. After such examinations, students write letters to instructors, advising them about various classroom practices. Of course, to be effective, such letters must engage the discourses that circulate in the academic world, and McComiskey discusses how instructing students in navigating these discourses can strengthen their sense of agency in affecting change. Thus, McComiskey attempts to lead students through a writing process that moves from invention to *intervention*. In the process, students develop critical thinking and reading skills to understand how texts (and values) are constructed, understand how context and audience shape the reception of texts (and values), and think critically about how they can shape their own writing to contribute to and intervene in the discourses shaping values (and texts).

Ideally, I wanted to take some of McComiskey's creative pedagogical energy and apply it to my course, particularly in the crafting of assignments that would prompt and allow students to interrogate, understand, and contribute to the social discourses surrounding the AIDS pandemic and its potential effect on their lives and on the lives of other students and young adults. To facilitate thinking about HIV and AIDS and to stimulate ideas about developing content for the YOUth and AIDS Web site, students composed expository and argumentative texts that reflected critically on a variety of AIDS issues, and that relied on their own experiences, the experiences of academics and scholars, the insights and arguments of AIDS activists, and the expertise of other social thinkers. Each of the assignments for the course was also designed to prompt critical reflection about the collaborative Web site, which I hoped would be our collective project of *intervention*.

To accomplish this task—to move from invention to intervention, I knew that students would have to develop a strong consciousness about writing *for* a particular audience—their campus community—and that their writing about HIV and AIDS should take into consideration the needs, concerns, and interests of that community, particularly if we were going to create a useful Web site for UC students. Taking the student body as our community, we established our community's needs in a number of ways. First, we consulted local experts and worked with a UC professor of biology, who regularly teaches a course on HIV/AIDS and who, as part of that course, has been collecting for several years now information about student attitudes about HIV. His most recent survey (1999) revealed that slightly more than 30% of UC students polled were engaging in multiple sexual relations and just over 30% of students polled reported that they had "lied to someone for the purpose of having sex." Furthermore, in response to questions specifically about HIV, nearly 32 % said they were not worried "at all" about contracting HIV, and 34 % said they were only "a little concerned" (Meyer.http://www.biology.uc.edu/faculty/meyer/SexSurvey1999.pdf). Although the percentages of sexually active students were not especially high, the number who were not particularly concerned about contracting HIV seemed alarming—both to me and my students. Furthermore, to generate some of our own data, we created and used a survey (with more than 400 respondents) to "test" knowledge and attitudes about HIV and AIDS among our college's students. Although the survey results suggest that many students understand how HIV is contracted, many others think that AIDS is primarily a "problem" for homosexuals, the promiscuous, and intravenous drug users (http://oz.uc.edu/ ~ alexanj/survey.htm). As such, students seem in ignorance of statistics from the CDC, which suggest that the rate of infection among American youth has been increasing: "half of all new HIV infections in the United States are among people under 25" (http://www.cdc.gov/hiv/pubs/facts/youth.htm). Again, when students considered the "gaps" in knowledge that could lead to HIV infection among their peers, a "community need" became readily apparent.

But how could we attract and hold the attention of this community long enough to communicate our messages about HIV and AIDS? In an attempt to address this question, I began the course with a writing assignment that I hoped would introduce students to the significance of considering audience, effective organization, and visual rhetoric. I had students construct a pamphlet that (a) would be directed at a particular audience and (b) highlight the dangers of a specific STD. Furthermore, students also had to submit a short meta-commentary explaining what rhetorical choices they made when creating the pamphlet. The exercise seemed successful, in that ideas generated during the construction of these pamphlets were later utilized in discussions about the course Web site. For instance, students writing pamphlets about AIDS argued *against* using the red ribbon on their pamphlets because such symbols, they suggested, have become almost cliché, and they feared that their peers, therefore, might not take notice and might dismiss the pamphlet as irrelevant to their lives. Another student argued for using images of young people, both in the pamphlet and on the Web site; for instance, the first page of her pamphlet depicts a handsome young man with the following caption: "Think he's cute? Guess what else he is . . ." Upon opening the pamphlet, we read that ". . . he's HIV positive." Such consideration about organizing visuals and text vis-à-vis one another to create both dramatic effect and audience engagement prepared students to begin thinking about how visuals and text could best be utilized on a Web site targeting their peers.

For the remaining writing assignments for the course, I took inspiration from the work of Jan Zita Grover, who, in her essay "AIDS, Keywords, and Cultural Work," argues that many of the social and cultural dimensions of HIV and AIDS are often left out in discussions that pathologize or stigmatize individuals and their "problematic" behavior. For instance, she suggests that many, even those with the best intentions, "focus exclusively on the individual [with HIV] and his or her weakness, leaving unacknowledged the social relationships between individuals and their positioning by class, occupation, religion, politics, education, region. All responsibility, they propose, rests with the individual" (233). For Grover, such short-sightedness manifests itself in several ways. First, she maintains that "Too many cultural critics see AIDS only in terms of its representations, analyzing the films, television programs, and outpourings of the press as an index to 'what AIDS means,' ' how AIDS means,' while ignoring the relationship between these representations and the lived experience of people coping with AIDS" (232). And, secondly, in a related vein, she notes a "media blackout" about the often "difficult and heroic work" that many gay organizations and other ASOs perform to combat the spread of HIV and to care for those with AIDS (232). With these thoughts in mind, I created two writing assignments that I hoped would prompt students to consider HIV and AIDS in the context of a variety of "social relationships," and not just as an individual problem.

For one assignment, students composed profiles of a local agency dealing with AIDS and other STDs. Their profiles had to use print, electronic, and field research sources, and students often used hyperlinks in their documents as well as substantial quotations from interviews with agency personnel. The use of hyperlinks was inspired, I think, by the possibility of publishing the profiles on the site, and students' increasing willingness to incorporate hyperlinks into their word-processed documents helped them see the advantage of using links and gave them some ideas about the kinds of links they wanted to see in the Web site. Finally, students wrote longer argumentative pieces in which they explored, discussed, and critiqued various issues surrounding youth and sexuality in contemporary American society. Originally, I wanted students to evaluate a specific safe-sex or sex education program, but, by this point in the quarter, some students wanted to explore aspects of sexuality that had come up in class discussion but that didn't *directly* deal with STDs. Instead of stifling their creativity, I felt that it was beneficial to negotiate individually with students about their topics. As it turns out, many students chose to write about STDs and sex education, and several produced excellent essays about condom distribution in high schools—essays informed by continued class discussion about peer education and the need to address specific audiences with relevant information crafted for those audiences. Other students wrote exciting essays about pertinent topics, such as FOX's controversial "reality show," *Temptation Island*, in which "contestants" were tempted to cheat on their significant others. Interestingly, students who wrote about this show invariably addressed issues of safe sex, STDs, and peer attitudes about sex and sexuality. Because students wanted such essays on the site, one could argue that such work reveals an increased audience sensitivity: The students knew what kinds of subjects their peers would want to read about, and they felt they could, in the process of "hooking" their peer readers into their writing with interesting topics, introduce discussions and information about safer sex and HIV. Moreover, students were beginning to address issues of sexuality and HIV in particular social contexts, such as educational institutions and pressures from peers to date and perform sexually. Such discussions moved consideration of HIV from, in Grover's words, a focus on the individual to an examination of its "social relationships."

Finding a place for such work led us to intense and productive discussions about the site: what it would look like, what it would contain, and what it would really *do*. In conducting online research for their pamphlets and their profiles, students encountered a number of sites that address the dangers of HIV, but few seemed targeted to young adults. None of the sites we sampled, however, were particularly appealing to my students, so they actually became more invested in composing the site *after* seeing how few sites about HIV and AIDS seem geared toward youth. To emphasize our intended audience, we tentatively called the site "YOUth and AIDS" (located at http://oz.uc.edu/ ~ alexanj/What.html), and, throughout the term, we continued to brainstorm its overall function and purpose, as well as specific components to achieve those ends.

One of the first discussions we had about the site's construction involved its "menu," or the number and kinds of different items that students wanted to see represented in the site. We knew right away that we did not want the site to just be a list of facts and figures; rather, we wanted a site that young adults could feel comfortable moving around in. In many ways, the ultimate menu that we created ("info," | "agencies," | "profiles," | "service learning," | "art," | "YOUth & Sexuality," |"discuss," | "links") reflects the diversity and depth of discussions we had about what kinds of student-centered content and even images to include.

In terms of text, students knew that we would probably want to include at least *some* statistical information, but several argued against just a list of facts and figures. We reached a compromise by agreeing to put at least one or two rotating statistics (a "Fast Fact") on the menu page and by

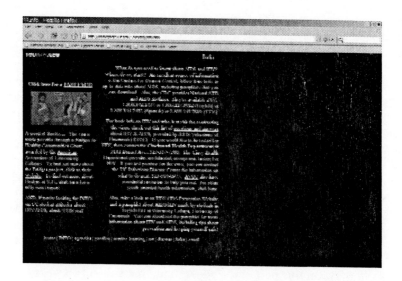

Screen shot of http://homepages.uc.edu/~alexanj/AIDSResources.html

constructing a page that linked to a number of other sources on the Web, all of which students discovered in their research for the course. In some ways, this "info" page is not particular interesting, and I'm curious to see how students in other classes will critique and alter it. Students also wanted their profiles of local ASOs to be published, so we constructed a page that links visitors to local agencies that deal with AIDS/HIV, and we agreed to have a rotating set of student-written profiles about particular agencies, such as Planned Parenthood or AIDS Volunteers of Cincinnati (AVOC).

The desire to publish the profiles of local agencies sparked another idea: including profiles of teens and young adults with HIV. Upon hearing about it, I eagerly encouraged such an innovation primarily because such profiles would, in Jan Zita Grover's words, begin to show the "lived experience of people coping with AIDS." Such a project seemed useful in both demystifying HIV and AIDS and in representing the disease not as an abstract notion but as a concrete reality, particularly for youth. The site initially included two such stories: One, an anonymous account of a student taking an HIV test for the first time, and the other, a "fictional" account of a student meeting an HIV-positive person. Students' interest in including such material speaks well, I think, to their understanding of the place of narrative, even portraiture, within the politics of AIDS, as well as their rhetorical sensitivity to their readers (Crimp, 118; Grover, 232). Moreover, these students suggested that it is important to dispel the myth that young adults do not contract HIV; including personal stories, students argued, might help.

In terms of visuals, students were particularly adept, I think, at creating and suggesting a series of opening pages that would capture the attention of their peers. The first page links to a quickly spinning counter set against a black background with the question, "What's this . . . ?", poised above it. Visitors "click" the counter to see another black page with multiple quickly-spinning counters, and they read the answer: "the increasing number of teens and young adults with AIDS . . ." This is an eye-catching entrance, and I worried at first that the effect was too "serious," even sinister. But students enjoyed the effect, and I must say that just about everyone I have shown the pages to since has responded positively, saying that the effect is quite "striking." Indeed, people invariably click to find out more, and they are taken to the main menu page.

In working on this part of the site, I think that students developed and demonstrated a wonderful sense of visual rhetoric, a sensitivity to the ways in which images convey and contextualize meaning. Moreover, as with the pamphlets, students generally insisted that AIDS ribbons not be present;

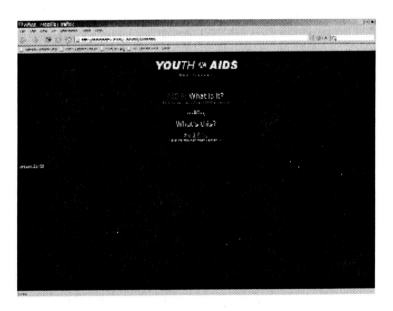

Screen shot of http://homepages.uc.edu/~alexanj/What.html

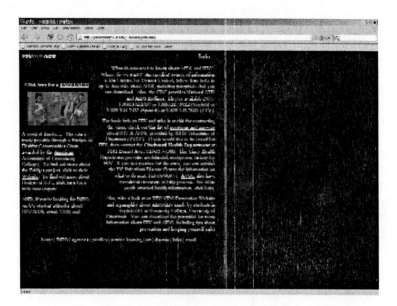

Screen shot of http://homepages.uc.edu/ ~ alexanj/Numbers.html

instead, several of them found the striking and attractive art work of AIDS activist Keith Haring on the Web, and we sought (and obtained) permission to use several of his pieces on our site. In fact, some students were so interested in this artwork that we created a whole page just about AIDS and Art, with several student essays about this important work. Again, this careful consideration of how the site needed to communicate with readers *visually* attests to the students' willingness—and increased ability—to consider multiple literacies in the production of meaningful Web sites.

FROM PEDAGOGY AND INVENTION TO ACTIVISM AND INTERVENTION: THE STUDENTS TAKE CONTROL

The initial *pedagogical* impulse behind the YOUth and AIDS Web Project was one of awareness and advocacy, the promotion and dissemination of information crafted for specific groups—a goal that some scholars characterize as a rudimentary form of online activism. As seen in chapter 6, Sandor Vegh suggests in his article, "Classifying Forms of Online Activism," that we can divide Web and Internet activism into three categories: "awareness/advocacy; organization/mobilization; and action/reaction. . . . These are progressive steps of online activism leading from basic information seeking and distribution to online direct action, better know as 'hacktivism' [which would include the last category, action/reaction]" (72). As an *activist* tool, the YOUth and AIDS site seemed primarily one of "awareness/advocacy," and the project has expanded as I have invited students in most of my subsequent courses to consider making contributions to the site, either in terms of articles and/or artwork for publication, and students in other classes have also contributed work, either as Web designers, authors, or artists. Expansion has occurred in other, unexpected ways, as well. As community agencies across the greater Cincinnati area have begun linking to the site, and as visits to the site continue to climb every month, I have begun to rethink how the project functions as an activist-oriented site—one in which the students' work contributes to the larger community's understanding of HIV/AIDS. A significant part of that rethinking has been spurred by the kinds of contributions students have made to the site within the last year. To wit, if the initial impulse and the original contributions emphasized *awareness*, more recent contributions reflect a move toward *mobilization* and even *reaction*. Along the way, students have used Web technologies in some surprising ways to explore the connection between ideology and information, the use of visual rhetoric as a literacy and activist tool, and the kinds of writing values that *students* want to forward as appropriate for crafting information about HIV and AIDS for other college-aged students.

In general, continued contributions have been sparked by a growing awareness of the connection between information and ideology, and the way information is constructed and disseminated ideologically. In late 2002, news reports from around the country alerted Web users to the fact that the CDC was altering the content of its Web site pertaining to HIV prevention. Specifically, information about the effectiveness of condoms in reducing the transmission of HIV seemed, in some cases, to be cast in doubt and, in other cases, removed entirely. One report characterized the change this way:

> The condom fact sheet previously said that abstaining from sex was the best way to prevent transmission of HIV and other sexually transmitted diseases, but it also stated that "for those who have sexual intercourse, latex condoms are highly effective when used consistently and correctly." The new version of the fact sheet, which was posted on Dec. 2, includes in its introduction that condoms "can reduce the risk of STD transmission. However, no protective method is 100% effective, and

condom use cannot guarantee absolute protection against any STD"
(*Democratic Lawmakers* . . .). (http://www.ppmarmonte.org/news/view-
er.asp?ID = 643)

In a way, such changes seem rather small, but their significance was not
lost on students. Whether they agreed or disagreed with the promotion of
abstinence-based or abstinence-only sex education programs, most could
quickly make the connection between an ideological shift in the Oval
Office and its concurrent impact on the dissemination of information
about such a politically "touchy" subject. Indeed, other reports we found
seemed almost dire in making the connection between shifting ideologies
and seemingly related changes in what kinds of information about HIV and
AIDS is disseminated:

> Until recently, a CDC initiative called "Programs That Work" identified
> sex education programs that have been found to be effective in scien-
> tific studies and provided this information through its web site to inter-
> ested communities.
>
> In 2002, all five "Programs That Work" provided comprehensive sex
> education to teenagers, and none were "abstinence-only."
>
> In the last year, and without scientific justification, CDC has ended this
> initiative and erased information about these proven sex education
> programs from its web site. "Abstinence-Only Education"
>
> (http://www.house.gov/reform/min/politicsandscience/example_absti-
> nence.htm)

Students' responses to this debate—which, as you can imagine, fueled
many pedagogically useful and productive discussions—were varied, and
subsequent contributions to the YOUth and AIDS Web site reflect both a
growing sense of writing as potentially interventive *and* a willingness to
engage various forms of Webbed writing to create "sites" of intervention.
Let's look at several student-driven projects that comprised their contributions and response to the CDC. Some are variations on assignments I gave;
others are original contributions.

Critical Link Lists

Part of some students' response to the ideological shift at the CDC, the
recasting and in some cases hiding of information to promote abstinence-

based or abstinence-only sex education, was a more substantial engagement with sites that provided a wide variety of information about HIV/AIDS—sites that would provide alternative views to that of the CDC. Indeed, given the growing awareness of how information is ideologically cast, even constructed, students wanted to ensure that visitors to the site could link to a variety of different sources of information. As such, they debated the contents of a large "link list" for the YOUth and AIDS site, which eventually including the following:

> For more youth-oriented info, check out YouthHIV, http://www.youth-hiv.org/
>
> Advocates for Youth, http://www.advocatesforyouth.org/
>
> Children with AIDS Project, http://www.aidskids.org/
>
> The Body at http://www.thebody.com/safesex.html
>
> For something a bit different, try MTV's sexual health quiz at http://www.mtv.com/onair/ffyr/protect/sexquiz.jhtml.
>
> The SEXplained Zone offers information ranging from forms of contraception, protecting people from STDs, to complete listings for clinics for sexually transmitted disease testing: http://www.sexplained.com/
>
> Teen Health Web sites is basically a link to other web sites that deal with sexual health information for teenagers. The site offers an advice link, a youth link, and many other links with very helpful and educational information about sexual health and testing: http://www.mihivnews.com/teenweb.htm
>
> The National Campaign to Prevent Teen Pregnancy site's primary audience is parents. The site gives useful information on preventing teen pregnancy as well as advice as to what to do if you are the parent of pregnant teen. The site offers very "real" images of what happens when a teenage girl becomes pregnant: http://www.teenpregnancy.org/

Pedagogically, this was highly useful as students had to debate the merits of the sites they forwarded, convincing the larger class group that the information contained in each was reliable, useful, and engaging for other youth with Internet access. To facilitate such discussions, I had students create annotated bibliographies for the sites they wanted to support, and we utilized both in-class discussion and Blackboard-enabled discussion postings to debate the various merits of several sites. In the end, students insisted that a diversity of information be made available via the YOUth and AIDS site.

Questioning Traditional Strategies

Some students also expressed dissatisfaction with some of the major ways in which AIDS activists have attempted to alert the public about the importance of battling HIV, and their critiques focused, surprisingly enough, on one of the oldest and most honored AIDS awareness campaigns in the country—the AIDS Memorial Quilt. As a simple in-class exercise in summarizing and incorporating outside sources, I asked students to search the Web and compose a brief article about the Names Project AIDS Quilt. Most students dutifully completed the assignment, producing competent summaries about the AIDS Quilt. One student, however, wrote a satiric commentary about the Quilt, claiming that the Quilt, however well intentioned, might just be "covering up" more important issues related to AIDS, HIV, and sexual politics in our country. More provocatively, he argued that some might be using the Quilt as a "security blanket" to mollify themselves with thoughts of the remembered dead as opposed to pushing for more radical and progressive ways of addressing how our pleasure-phobic society (a society that refuses to "throw off the covers") might be contributing to dampening or "covering up" important discussions of sexuality and sexual health, thus potentially contributing to the spread of the disease.

Certainly, I discussed with this student and the class that the piece produced was *not* a "summary" of the Names Project, but upon sharing the piece with the class for discussion, I was surprised at how many of the students responded positively to the piece (which was fairly well written) *and* how many of them suggested we post the piece to the Web site. Two things are noteworthy here. First, in sharing the piece, I was not only validating a dissenting student voice, but I believe I was also creating a space in which students could see what good, critical thinking and questioning could do and how powerful it can be in prompting us to think about issues that we might otherwise "cover up." Second, the students' interest in publishing the piece via the Web only reinforced my conviction that students not only want their voices to be heard but that they see the Web as a forum for disseminating, cultivating, and sharing their ideas.

Critical Visual Rhetorics

Other students focused their attention on the YOUth and AIDS site's "welcome page." Initially, as discussed earlier, the entrance page presented a question, "What's this?", followed by a rapidly spinning counter. When visitors clicked on the counter, they were taken to a page with rapidly spinning counters and the "answer": "the increasing number of teens and young adults with AIDS . . ." Although many found the entrance page quite striking, there was some growing criticism of it among some students who thought that it promoted and used the same kind of "fear-based" tactic they were seeing in increasing use on the CDC site. As such, one student, Dave, experimented with a very different kind of entrance page:

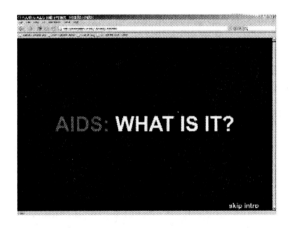

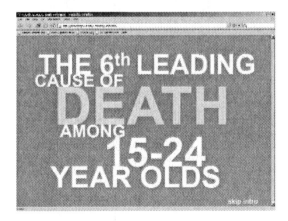

Screen shot—several panels of FLASH entrance from
http://homepages.uc.edu/ ~ alexanj/Flash.html

The change is significant—not just in terms of design, but in terms of what the design communicates about the content of the site. Specifically, I think the FLASH entrance attempts to move the visitor from a fear-based response to HIV and AIDS to an empowered position, one in which she is encouraged to "use [her] knowledge." After sharing and discussing Dave's work with different sections of writing courses, we decided to use the FLASH site, upon students' enthusiastic recommendation.

The FLASH site also raises some interesting questions about how students engage visual rhetoric. When Dave approached me about creating a FLASH entrance, he talked initially about creating a more visually-appealing site. I told him and the group of students he was working with, however, that they were not allowed to simply pull images from the Web and that they would have to secure signed permission from anyone appearing in a digital photograph they might want to use. Undeterred, Dave created a site that reveals, I think, a bit of sophistication in manipulating the visual dimension of text—or, put another way, in recognizing text as a visual medium. Patricia Sullivan, in her 2001 *Computers and Composition* article, "Practicing Safe Visual Rhetoric on the World Wide Web," argues that "Because print is absorbed visually, we can hardly avoid the fact that even when the text is the focus, as it is in print literacy, visual conventions carry meaning" (108) [http://www.writinginstructor.com/essays/webb3.html]. We can see some students' rudimentary understanding of this concept in Dave's construction of the FLASH site, particularly in the creative visual manipulation of text. The "downer message"—that AIDS kills—is rendered in fairly dramatic but nonetheless static text; in contrast, the messages moving toward empowerment actually *move*, encouraging students to explore the YOUth and AIDS site, develop knowledge, and use it accordingly. A substantial part of any collaborative Web project is going to be consideration of the site's visual dimension, and I was delighted that students wanted to tackle this—and tackle it intelligently—as part of their contribution to the effort. Furthermore, from an activist standpoint, such work signals to me yet another move from advocacy and awareness to potential mobilization, even reaction. Students are invited not just to accept the limited information distributed (by the CDC, for instance), but to explore a variety of information in helping them make informed choices.

New Writing Values

Certainly, not all students are proficient with FLASH, so many have contributed instead short pieces that are more like text-based articles, but even in these pieces, one can see, I think a critical engagement with the issues that explores how information can be shaped and cast to reflect a set of writing values that seek not to use information to "warn" and "intimidate," but to empower and mobilize for informed action. Some of our most productive discussions about such writing values occurred during the process of selecting and editing pieces for publication on the YOUth and AIDS site.

Before students wrote up pieces for submission and publication consideration, we brainstormed individually and collectively about the *best* ways that they could, based on their experience, reading, and research, talk to other youth with Internet access about HIV and AIDS. I suggested to the students that this brainstorming could form the basis of their selection criteria for choosing which submitted pieces would be published on the site. We compiled their thinking into the following "top 10" list:

Top 10 Ways to Talk to Youth About HIV and AIDS

1. Make it interesting. Use visual attractions, so the audience does not lose interest in your topic.
2. Don't try to scare us by statistics.
3. Tell us how it affects us directly. Use clear facts that anyone could understand.
4. Have a person with HIV or AIDS speak—not just some random person. I think that one thing that always sends a strong message is to hear of someone's struggles with the virus. It seems that the topic hits closer to home when someone standing in front of you is telling of how this has affected his or her life. Personally, as a young person, everything relates more closely to my own life that way.
5. Don't confront a youth about AIDS; gently talk to them, so you won't make them feel uneasy. Warn us, but not threaten us, about HIV and its effects.
6. Don't hesitate to use humor. Teens and young adults have no attention span, especially if they're being spoken to in a large group. Making things humorous is the best way to get their attention. If you can make them laugh, you'll be able to get your points across in a way they might actually remember. I know that it might not be the best idea to make AIDS or HIV a joke. But there are plenty of ways to be humorous and make jokes while talking about it.

7. The best way, I think, to talk to young people about these issues is for both people to be open and completely honest and non-judgmental, and to have facts and "myths" around so you can talk about them.
8. When talking to youth, have them be involved in the discussion. Make it safe for them to ask questions.
9. Don't sugarcoat anything.
10. Make us feel comfortable to want to talk about it.

What's engaging about this list is its emphasis on directness and the use of humor. As such, it is hard for me not to read the list as a reaction to—and refusal of—the CDC site's tentative and conservative approach. The students propose that, instead of limiting discussion, we need *greater* discussion of sexuality issues and topics.

If we look at some of the topics students chose to write about and submit, and which were then chosen for publication on the site by group discussion and selection via a discussion board, we see pieces on the following topics:

"AIDS and youth denial"
"HIV and tattooing and piercing"
"Myths about condoms"
"Negotiating healthy relationships"
"Tackling HIV/AIDS and Its Grip on Black Women"

The pieces reflect the kinds of subjects that these students want to hear about in relation to HIV, and most of the pieces are fairly straightforward in promoting knowledge awareness to informed choices as opposed to condemning or cautioning against certain behaviors. We can easily see this in increased discussions about tattooing and piercing—which is never forbidden; rather, students discuss safety precautions to take when pursuing various body modifications. Students' use of directness, nonjudgmental attitudes, and even humor in the pieces serves, I think, as a counterbalance to the loaded language of the CDC Web site. In a way, I believe these students were using a different *style* to communicate a very different ideology about talking about HIV and AIDS—a style characterized by openness as opposed to fear. They also reflect, interestingly enough, what queer activist Michael Warner has advised should be one of the golden rules of health and HIV awareness: "Prevention has to start by imagining a mode of life that seems livable, and in which decisions about how much risk can be tolerated will not be distorted by shame and stigma" (217). For Warner, "The prohibition against sexiness in HIV prevention is so powerful that people take it for granted, forgetting that it is even there" (200). What drives this prohibition is a sense of "shame" and "stigma" that our culture frequently associates with sex and sexuality. Students' nonjudgmental approach, I believe, highlights "how much risk can be tolerated" in various activities, without "distorting" such activities with "shame and stigma."

One final project we'll look at provides us with a challenging use of humor, even *edgy* humor, which exemplifies this favored style. To advertise free and confidential HIV testing on campus, two of the students, Dave and Travis, created a poster campaign, which one of the students later turned into a FLASH site.

Some might think that Dave and Travis' poster and FLASH announcement is a bit too *edgy*, perhaps even misguided, especially because some prevention specialists and activists warn against a "shaking your finger" approach about the consequences of risky sexual behavior. Warner, for instance, strongly advises against the use of shame or stigma in such educational efforts.

But I learned to read the site the way many students did—appreciating how its directness and its strange humor potentially undermine any explicit or implicit morality. Moreover, the use of visual rhetoric is intriguing and pointed. Anne Wysocki argues "that learning to analyze and compose rhetorically effective visual communication is not (simply) a matter of working only with whatever we have named 'images.' Effective visual rhetoric requires trying to understand and work with (or sometimes against) the expectations and assumptions and values of one's audience concerning ALL the visual aspects of a text" (182–83). In their original poster, and then again in the FLASH site, the students play with images, even play with our expectations of what is an appropriate use of those images, to create a striking message: Yes, HIV can kill, but that's no cause for finger-wagging and uptight seriousness; we can get an important message across with a bit of sarcasm. How so? The "staidness" of the characters used, clip art with a 1950s feel, the "Jack and Jill" of an ancient rhetoric, a by-gone literacy, suggests an old style of rhetoric and moralizing about STIs—a style that is, for these students, a proper subject of ridicule. The students torque the images, putting the innocent, even naïve Jack and Jill in the context of contemporary dangers of STIs. The resulting effect is, oddly, funny and thus creates a double message: You need to get tested for HIV, but you don't have to feel shame and stigma. Such an approach seems wisely predicated on an understanding that it is exactly shame and stigma that actually might *prevent* many from seeking out testing. As such, such contributions

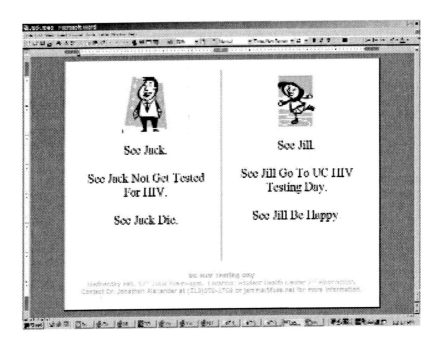

help move the YOUth and AIDS site from promoting a "shaming," "stigma-tizing" and, in Warner's view, a consequently distorting point of view about HIV and AIDS, to one of honesty—and to one that has attempted to *mobilize* readers a bit more than simply inform them.

CONSTRUCTING WEB SITES AS SERVICE-LEARNING PROJECTS: A QUESTION

Because the YOUth and AIDS Project has been one that we've character-ized as meeting and addressing a particular community need, as well as forwarding writing skills development in a particular course, it is worth con-sidering if such a project qualifies as *service learning*. I turn attention, if only briefly, to such a consideration, asking, can a collaboratively com-posed Web site serve as a service-learning project? To answer this question, we need first to work through a definition of service learning and some of the basic debates surrounding it as a pedagogical practice in writing instruction.

For many compositionists, service learning has become a powerful tool in creating courses that prompt student writing to become both community focused and critically reflective, particularly as writers narrate and meditate on their interactions with their communities. In such courses, students usually participate in some kind of "volunteer" project at a community agency and then compose journals, reflection pieces, critical essays, research projects, and even Web texts that use writing to interrogate community policies and practices and to reflect on the intersection of the personal and the political in specific communities. Drawing on language from the National Community Service Trust Act of 1993, Thomas Deans maintains that "service-learning is not volunteerism or community service; nor is it simply an academic internship or field placement. While service-learning may draw on these practices, it is at heart a pedagogy of action and reflection, one that centers on a dialectic between community outreach and academic inquiry" (2).

Two aspects of this definition merit comment. First, in many ways, the use of service learning to teach writing may be reflective of the "social turn" in composition, which, since the early 1990s, has produced a growing body of provocative scholarship that seeks to unpack the connections between discourse and politics, language and power, representation and social agency (McComiskey, 19 ff). By providing both scholars and students access to local communities and the agencies that serve them, service learning offers writers the chance to become directly engaged with the way in which a variety of personal and social issues are addressed (or *not* addressed) by the larger community.

Second, most service-learning practitioners insist that service-learning projects must meet the specific needs of *both* the courses in which they are used *and* the needs of the community or agencies "served" in the learning process—particularly if the projects are to address (or create) a "dialectic between community outreach and academic inquiry." Offering many examples, essays in *Writing the Community: Concepts and Models for Service-Learning in Composition* edited by Adler-Kassner, Crooks, and Watters, highlight, describe, and assess multiple service-learning projects and practices in a variety of composition courses. In general, essayists describe *two* specific kinds of service-learning composition: one in which students critically reflect (in journals, in argumentative essays, in research projects) on the knowledge gained from the experience of serving, and another in which students work with community agencies on specific writing tasks, such as the development of pamphlets, grant applications, brochures, and even Web sites. Some assignments combine both forms of writing; for instance, students might publish their critical reflections, research pieces, and writing for local agencies on the Web, creating sites that not only attest to their work in the community but also model for visitors to the site what actively engaged service and writing might look like. As an example, the service-learning Web site at University College, University of Cincinnati (http://www.ucollege.uc.edu/ServiceLearning/home.html) details information about various service-learning programs and offers links to community resources and student service-learning projects completed for local agencies.

Although some will invariably see this work as "volunteerism" and, as such, more focused on community service as opposed to the pedagogical goals of an individual course, the growing body of scholarship on service learning in the composition classroom suggests that many pedagogical benefits accrue for writing students engaged in such projects. Moreover, as the editors of *Writing the Community* suggest, students involved in service-learning courses are (a) generally more "motivated" in completing coursework and grappling with course-content issues and (b) can make more "connections" between the work they do in class and the "real world" (2–3).

Compositionists who use computers in their courses have begun to think critically about how service learning can productively be incorporated into their classrooms. Just recently, Alison Regan and John Zuern published an article in *Computers and Composition* in which they detail their service-learning project in a computer-mediated advanced composition course. The majority of the students' work with computers involved them offering computer tutorials at a local agency and "teaching people whose life experiences, levels of literacy, and exposure to technology were different from their own" (Web text). As such, students could meditate critically on the ways in which access to computer technology (or its lack) affects literacy. Some students also wrote Web pages for use in their literacy tutoring.

Regan and Zuern offer a good starting point in thinking about how computers can be used in the context of service-learning projects, and I am particularly interested in the notion of students constructing Web spaces for direct use in particular service-learning projects. Indeed, many community-based Web sites exist, and they provide valuable and sometimes even life-saving information to individuals about a number of topics. Many of these sites are student projects; for instance, in Web publishing courses offered at UC, instructors have had students identify, work with, and compose Web sites for community agencies that need Web sites but do not have the technical "know-how" to construct them. And, more specifically, in "Freshman Composition, the Internet, and Service-Learning," Floyd

Ogburn and Barbara Wallace describe a series of service-learning projects in which students "construct[ed] and publish[ed] profiles of Cincinnati-area social service agencies on the Internet" (68).

Clearly, some compositionists figure the Web as a useful and active component of the service-learning experience, offering students the chance to, in Paul Heilker's words, "experience writing as social action." Although such sites provide useful information, it is worth asking if their construction and publication qualify as *service learning* that meets the needs of both a writing course *and* a discernible community need. Or, to use Thomas Deans' definition of service learning, can student-written Web sites engage a "dialectic between community outreach and academic inquiry," facilitating both "action and reflection" about pressing social concerns? I believe, in certain circumstances, they can; and I would characterize the YOUth and AIDS Web Project as just such a site.

Some would argue, however, that the creation of this site is *not* an act of service learning, in that students did not *actively* meet the needs of specific, local community agencies. When I first presented an earlier version of this project at the 2001 Computers and Writing Conference, audience members debated about whether I could "legitimately" define the Web site as a service-learning project; much of the debate focused on the fact that students did not actually "work for" a particular agency, and thus did not perform "service" for a particular "community partner." Interestingly, some of the scholarship on service learning might agree, highlighting the necessity of "moving" the service component to a space "outside" the classroom. For instance, in "Rhetoric Made Real: Civic Discourse and Writing Beyond the Curriculum," Paul Heilker argues that "In order for students to experience writing as social action, we need to move the *where* of writing instruction to some place outside the classroom" (72). Heilker has in mind the kinds of writing that are done specifically for community agencies.

Although I respect Heilker's experience as a service-learning practitioner, I do not completely agree that this is the *only* way in which students can experience their writing as *socially* engaged or active—or as an act of service learning. My work with using e-zines and having students construct their writing assignments as Web spaces demonstrates to me that students writing for Web publication can and often do experience their work as addressing the interests and needs of a larger community. As one student wrote about this project on the Blackboard message boards,

> This assignment made me realize that alot of people out there have stds or sexual health problems. And I think it's a great thing that people dedicate their time helping people with diseases. I now know

options that I can go to to get help or recommend to my friends if they ever find themselves in a situation where they don't know where to turn.

Indeed, I would contend that having students compose for Web publication offers many, if not indeed all of the benefits listed earlier as accruing around service-learning projects.

For instance, Ogburn and Wallace characterize their work with students—publishing student-written profiles of local social-service agencies—as "indirect" service learning, in which, according to Connor-Linton, "students do not participate directly in field work, but (1) learn about some sector of the community through their teacher's own research and/or community service; (2) apply knowledge acquired through the course to create a service or product which helps to meet a need of the community; (3) critically analyze course content and social issues through the application" (107–108). Based on these criteria, some may characterize the YOUth and AIDS Web Project as a comparable project, offering an "indirect" service-learning opportunity. In many ways, however, although I was inspired by Ogburn and Wallace in the creation of my course, I attempted to "go beyond" their model in a few key ways.

First, students actively surveyed their specific community to shape the service—the informative Web site—that we hoped would begin to meet a community need. For instance, in response to the initial pamphlet about HIV and AIDS, students received feedback from other students (with more than 400 surveys collected in the first year of this project). Such feedback reported on the pamphlet's intelligibility, clarity, appropriateness for college students, and visual appeal; specifically, students learned that audience-appropriate visuals and student-sensitive language would "catch the attention" of students seeking information, and such feedback was incorporated into the construction of the site's visuals (bright colors) and images (clearly of college-aged students). As such, the service learning experience became recursive, with one community-based project leading to the development and refinement of another.

Furthermore, beyond simply supplying information, our hope was—and is—that the YOUth and AIDS Web site is a *participatory* and interactive medium. Students, and others in the larger Cincinnati (and Web?) community, are invited not only to visit the site but to contribute their writing and artwork as well. In this way, the site is not just a repository of information, but, we hope, has the potential to serve as a *forum* for finding, exchanging, and *creating* useful information for other students about sexual health. In fact, students in subsequent writing courses continue to solicit information about community needs and recursively (re)construct the site based on responses. For instance, at student urging, we continue to expand the section on "AIDS and Art," perhaps the most popular portion of the site among students—and the most frequently visited. In this way, I believe the site is not just an "indirect" instance of service learning, but a "direct" one as well.

Finally, students participating in this project *did* engage the larger, off-campus community by meeting with local agencies to discuss community needs and the best way to approach "sensitive" subjects such as HIV and AIDS, and student profiles of those community agencies reflect such discussions. Indeed, various community agencies and partners, such as AVOC and UC's Wellness Center, expressed interest in linking our course site to theirs as part of their ongoing effort to inform late teens and young adults, and several agencies pledged their willingness to provide direct service-learning opportunities for future students; such experiences have since been narrated and critically reflected in writing posted to the site. Moreover, my students' interest in having profiles from young people with HIV speaks to a willingness on the behalf of many of them to go to community agencies, work with youth who have HIV, and use their experiences to enhance the rhetorical—and potentially political—effectiveness of the Web site.

But, beyond these considerations, I argue that this Web project shifted my thinking about *where* service learning can take place; for, in working with my students, we began to revision the classroom itself, the site where the Web site was largely constructed, as both the "the *where* of writing instruction" *and* a site of community action. Post-process theorist Joseph Petraglia, in "Is There Life after Process?," asserts that "we have become much more interested in the ecology in which writing takes place than in the mere fact that writing is the outcome of a variety of steps and stages" (63). The great advantage, I argue, of creating a publicly and communally useful Web site is that the project engages *both* the "ecology" and the process of writing. In terms of process, my students and I had to pay particularly close attention to the audiences who might access the site; further, the fact that the site will need to be updated frequently draws attention to this situated writing endeavor as an ongoing, recursive process. In terms of the "ecology" of writing, much of the impetus for students to create this particular site arose directly out of discussion with young adults, many of whom maintain that it is often extremely difficult for them to discuss sexuality issues, with either their peers or older adults. At one point during our course, a student spoke eloquently about the need for "peer education," and her comments resonated with a discussion I had just had with a staff member of AVOC who told me that he was beginning to feel too "old" (at 28!) when talking to youth and that he therefore did not feel that he was "connecting" with youth when talking about HIV and safe sex. After talking about such issues with my class, we reasoned that our peer-constructed Web site might be one of the best ways to provide an important information service to youth with Internet access, who otherwise might avoid discussion about AIDS and thus increase their risk for contracting HIV.

CRITIQUES: "DOES THIS SITE REALLY WORK?"

All of our hopes for the YOUth and AIDS Web Project have prompted for me considerations of assessment, focused on one question that has lingered over the project since its inception: Does the YOUth and AIDS site actually *meet* the needs of the community it seeks to assist with its information? In many senses, this is not an easily answerable question—about *any* service-learning or community engagement project. We do know that the site averages nearly 2,000 "hits" a month since it first went live in January 2001, and many visitors—from the academic community *and* the larger Cincinnati community—have e-mailed to say how much they appreciate not only the information on the site but the ease with which one can navigate the site and find useful information. For instance, in an unsolicited comment, one visitor told us that the site is "well designed and the links were quite informative and useful." Other comments, sent in via email, have been similarly enthusiastic:

> To Whom it may Concern,
>
> I was directed to your AIDS awareness Web site from another place and I encountered a site about the artists of the world that are global AIDS activists.
>
> I think it's terrific that the word is getting out and people are finally beginning to understand what AIDS is and what it is not. I've known several gay and lesbian people and they are all wonderful and some are quite inspiring. I write poetry, and I saw that you were featuring a couple of poets on your site, Beth and Stefanie. I just wanted to say that they are good writers and I can feel the emotion in their words.
>
> Thank you again for providing this Web site to inform the public and by showing an outreach of unity to a world who's ignorance is long overdue to be 86'ed. Keep up the good work!

It's difficult *not* to feel a sense of pride when reading such an e-mail—in both my work as an instructor and, in particular, in my *students'* work as writers. Corroborating such an email is the fact that the YOUth and AIDS Web site was highlighted as a "creative use of technology" to promote health issues in a recently published article in *Community College Journal*, Charles Koehler's "Using Technology for Low-Cost/No-Cost Health Promotion." Koehler notes that this site is a prime example of one "of the many ways that a simple application of technology has made it possible to create effective, low-cost, health-related messages that can have a positive impact on the health and lives of our students. [Such have] transformed our students and our campuses" (18, 19).

At the same time, if only occasionally, other e-mails come through that offer divergent viewpoints, ones that critique our goals for the site. For instance, we recently received this message:

> Hello all,
>
> Your Web site is very informative. I can only hope it is making a differ-ence. Unfortunately I have an issue with it . . . I get the feeling you are not about stopping the epidemic of AIDS. Why do I say this . . . I never once saw the stand against indulgant [sic] sex. Condoms have been out long before AIDS . . . so, guess what, that cant [sic] be the answer to this problem. The only answer to getting a start on ending this prob-lem is bringing to a close (hah . . . never happen!!!) this sexual revolu-tion that started somewhere in the 60's and has been gaining followers ever since. Sex is abused by pretty much every single person, here in the US & overseas.
>
> Religion is the major staple in the society.
>
> My point to all this, it is very disappointing to see those that claim to be advocates for something but avoid saying what nobody wants to hear (i.e. DON'T HAVE SEX!!!!!!). Well, anyway, that was just my 2 pen-nies. I do like the site, espically [sic] the quiz's . . . hehe.

Certainly, this respondent is articulating one powerful view of how to address the spread of HIV and other STDs: Just tell young people to say "no" to sex. But, by this writer's own admission, it may not be possible to "bring to a close . . . this sexual revolution," so promoting abstinence as the *primary* message in a sexual health campaign seems short-sighted—and it has seemed so to the majority of my students as well.

Nonetheless, this e-mail raises what I think is *the* central concern I have about the YOUth and AIDS Web Project: "I can only hope it is making a difference." *Is* it? Does this site *work*? Measuring the effectiveness of any pre-vention campaign is fraught, particularly with Web activist work, which runs the risk of seeming fairly passive: Visitors to the site can point, click, and learn—but that does that translate into action, or changed attitudes and behaviors? Again, in response, I could point to increased visits to the site, which have been steadily rising throughout this past year; I could point to the number of times the site has been cited at national conferences or in national publications; I could point to e-mails we receive about the site, or notices that agencies have linked to it. Moreover, other faculty have begun using the site in their courses and have actively been passing its URL on to their students. In many ways, then, I would argue that our use of the Web, to provide specific, targeted information to the campus community, could be considered effective.

Reluctantly, however, I must admit that there is at least *some* reason to be skeptical about such Web-based activist projects *in general*. One inform-ant, who contacted me after I posted a request for sites dealing with queer youth issues, noted the existence of many programs across the country to address the sexual health needs of many different populations. However, she also suggested that much information placed on the Web about sexual health was *not* reaching intended audiences:

> What we have found is that a lot of the information on the web is total-ly unavailable to our clients and that most of it speaks around and not to our clients or those of us serving these communities, as I'm sure you've found. Overall, with the transgender program [for example], our staff has had to be face-to-face with everyone and every organization.

Certainly, the Web doesn't reach all populations potentially affected by HIV, and other potential drawbacks can be even more acute. Ironically, the Web not only provides information, but it also offers an avenue for many to facilitate sexual encounters, some of which are invariably unsafe. *The Advocate* reported in February 2003 on research presented at the 10th Conference on Retroviruses and Opportunistic Infections:

> Chat rooms on gay Web sites are becoming a common place for arranging risky sexual encounters, a new survey has found, and experts say the chat rooms could be playing a role in rising HIV infec-tion rates among gay and bisexual men. "The Internet is a new venue associated with high-risk sex," said Sabina Hirshfield, one of the study's authors. "It is a quick and easy way to meet partners."

. . . of 3,000 men surveyed who frequently visited the popular gay Web site Gay.com, 84% used the Internet to find sex partners. About two thirds reported recently having unprotected anal sex with someone they met online, while about one quarter of the men said they have had more than 100 sex partners during their lives. The majority of the survey respondents were college-educated white men. Half were under the age of 30.

Given such situations, the Web seems a double-edged sword—potentially facilitating the kinds of irresponsibility that lead to the spread of the disease that our course and Web project have been using the Web to try to prevent.

Such prevention work is often exacerbated by the provisional nature of many Web sites, many of which appear and disappear seemingly overnight. Sally J. McMillan, writing in "Survival of the Fittest Online: A Longitudinal Study of Health-Related Web Sites," notes that health "[s]ites created by individuals were least likely to survive while education and government sites were most likely to survive." Fortunately, because our site is connected to a growing university-wide commitment to address the spread of HIV among students, I have every hope that the YOUth and AIDS site will "survive."

But part of what may contribute to the "survival" of a Web site is perceived effectiveness in reaching intended audiences. McMillan says that many of her respondents noted "the importance of targeting rather than sheer numbers in measuring the Web site audience" (http://www.ascusc.org/jcmc/vol6/issue3/mcmillan.html). With this in mind, it has occurred to me that the only way to evaluate the "success" of such a project is perhaps to examine the context in which it was created—a pedagogical situation—and its primary "target"—my writing students.

So, how did students respond to working on this project?

In terms of the course, students seemed engaged and pleased with the project, particularly as they could see how their writing about their own communities was becoming part of a Web site that their peers could access and use. Throughout our discussions, several students made it clear that peer education, students speaking to other students particularly about "touchy" or intimate topics such as sexuality and AIDS, is much more effective than traditional sex education, where an adult often "lectures" about these difficult topics. Therefore, students were generally receptive to the idea of a student-created, student-directed Web site about HIV/AIDS awareness and prevention.

Participation on the Blackboard message boards was generally high. At times, I would devote class time to such exchanges, but increasingly I found that students would contribute to the message boards on their own time and without being told to do so. I divided the message boards into two categories: those dealing with general course and specific essay concerns and those addressing issues such as condom distribution in high schools and the reasons why young adults do and do not practice safe sex. Exchanges on the latter boards were especially lively and even provocative. Students seemed to feel free to express opinions, challenge one another, and even have fun during discussions touching on some of the more intimate aspects of their lives, such as the use of condoms and why some young adults choose not to practice safe sex.

In terms of their writing, students worked on a number of skills related to the writing process. Of course, some skills, such as using Web editors or learning rudimentary hypertext to create Web sites, may seem ancillary to the primary concerns in a composition class. But I argue that constructing this site underscored the significance and perhaps even facilitated the development of other skills germane to the writing process, such as editing, revising, and collaboration. At the most basic level, preparing documents and content for a Web site involves the deployment (and in some cases development) of numerous editing skills, as my students and I revisited these pages again and again, correcting spelling and grammar, checking links, revising text, and repositioning images against words. In this way, students began to see how much continuous editing—both "globally" and "locally," in terms of larger revisions and the minutiae of mechanics—is an ongoing process.

So far, so good—but the pedagogical question became even more complex for me: How do students grapple with issues of textual and visual rhetorics, considerations of audience, the politics of collaboration, and their own personal interests and agendas as they seek to construct a personally and politically effective Web text? I have answered this question for myself by taking note of how students in multiple classes in successive terms have benefited from examining and "updating" the site; students critique what their peers have done before them, suggest changes, and update content. As such, use of the site models a recursive approach to writing, perhaps more effectively demonstrating than anything else I have done in my composition courses the need to approach writing and meaning making as a process. And finally, our numerous discussions about the site—both in the classroom and via Blackboard message boards—helped all of us to develop a sense of the site as a collaborative endeavor. In a way, peer review of content and pages for the site became particularly significant as students discussed what they did—and did not—want on the site. Knowing that the site would one day be "public" made the collaborative process of peer review seem more "real" and, dare I say, more "authentic."

All in all, then, I think that the project fostered—and displayed—quite a bit of rhetorical sensitivity in that students thought critically about their audiences and considered how best to arrange and organize textual and visual material to engage the site's visitors. Much of this work was accomplished because constructing a publicly accessible Web site is embedded and grounded in a public situation. And I think that creating writing courses revolving around such "situated" endeavors parallels the service-learning experience that so many writing students benefit from when they "go into the field" to learn, reflect, and write. Such writing projects help writing students see their writing as connected to larger purposes and audiences, and they thus provide rhetorical situations that otherwise seem missing in more traditional composition courses, in which the instructor and other students often serve as the "artificial" audience for student writing. In "Community Service Writing: Problems, Challenges, Questions," Nora Bacon summarizes well the pedagogical benefits specific to the teaching of writing that many have discovered upon incorporating service learning into their composition classrooms: "Like WAC [Writing Across the Curriculum], community service writing demonstrates the enormous variety in written discourse and the degree to which the forms, processes, and purposes of writing are embedded in particular contexts" (53).

Invariably, every course project benefits from *critical* consideration of its aims and successes, and the collaborative construction of the Web site (and the course, for that matter) was a learning-process for both students *and* teacher. Indeed, while working on the site, we faced a number of challenges that led us to consider the *limits* of both collaboration and the Web as a tool for community action and intervention. For instance, some students were resistant to having the course focused so much on sexuality and, specifically, HIV/AIDS. Nora Bacon herself worries over the ways in which having students write for specific community agencies might set up situations that require students to write about material they are not particularly interested in, or even write from viewpoints that are not their own or that they do not share (45). Fortunately, the material in general was very engaging for students, so I believe this problem was minimized. However, I did worry that some students might express some homophobia, because AIDS is still, for many, a "gay" disease; and indeed, one student wrote in his third paper an anti-gay diatribe, suggesting that those who had AIDS probably deserved it. Certainly, one can turn such discussion to profitable use, and the classes had several good discussions about AIDS, (homo)sexuality, and stigma. These discussions, though, are often preceded by discomfort, for both students and teachers, but I would argue that discomfort should not preempt useful conversation, even about topics as "touchy" as sexuality and STDs.

And, in many ways, our creation of the YOUth and AIDS Web site was somewhat inspired by this "touchiness." One motivation for working on the site was to provide information to students and other visitors who might be too embarrassed or even ashamed to ask for it in person. In his conclusion to "Cyberspace and Disadvantaged Communities: The Internet as a Tool for Collective Action," Christopher Mele suggests that "online communication appears as a useful tool to challenge and even subvert differentials of power expressed as control over the access, transfer, and application of knowledge and information." Certainly, the intense shame people sometimes experience about their sexuality or sexual behavior, whatever its cause, acts as a form of "control" in our culture, denying access to needed information. One *possible* advantage of the Internet in general and the Web in particular is to provide information and, as Mele puts it, "bring . . . resources to bear on real and immediate problems"—which is what we hope the YOUth & AIDS site will do (305).

However, despite our attempt to address HIV and AIDS in a multifaceted and engaging way, we noted curious "silences" in our online presentation—silences specifically about AIDS and issues of race and ethnicity. Several students wrote throughout the course about the impact of AIDS on very specific communities, such as young white women and African Americans—groups at particularly high risk for the disease. These were excellent discussions, and students' attention to these communities reveals an awareness of the need to speak about community issues in specific, local terms, particularly if specific and effective action is to be taken. However, when turning to compose the Web site, I felt that such specific discussions were often left out. For instance, the pictures chosen for the site are mostly of White young adults; furthermore, no one suggested a link to discussions about race and sexuality, or the spread of AIDS among minority populations. I'm hoping that future classes in which I use and teach from this site will recognize these gaps and move to correct them with their own suggestions, either for site revision or expansion. Such moves would attest to an even more enhanced audience awareness than that demonstrated by students in the course I have described here.

Another nagging question about such work remains: How can a teacher evaluate and assess students' writing and skills improvement through such projects? In my course, I relied on our department's portfolio review process, in which students compile and submit for review a portfolio of their work, which is then evaluated on a pass/fail basis, with the teacher assessing a grade should the portfolio pass. Such portfolios usually consist of three substantive writing pieces, with drafts and revisions attached so evaluators can assess both effort and progress. In my case, students submitted their pamphlets, meta-writing essays about the pamphlets, profiles of local agencies, and critical essays about an issue involving sexuality and youth. As such, course grades could be based in large part on the compilation of a "traditional" portfolio; however, I cannot deny that students more actively involved in the Web project probably received more "brownie points" as I figured their final grades.

Ultimately, given all of the interconnections and apparent mutual benefits accruing from such a project, I have counted it as a pedagogical, technological, and even *activist* success. In his Foreword to "Activism and Marginalization in the AIDS Crisis," Peter K. Manning notes that "AIDS remains an ambiguous figure that enters and leaves the political stage, sometimes in the guise of debates about morality, sometimes about medical and social resources, and sometimes about the family and 'family values'" (xxiii). For a group of students, largely under their own volition, HIV and AIDS have become far less ambiguous; they have become subjects for written exploration, consideration, and action. But more than this, I believe that, for these students, the *Web* has become a place not just for the dissemination of information, but a site as well for both textual and visual activism and intervention.

CONCLUSION

THE FUTURES OF WRITING?
SPECULATIONS ON DIGITAL YOUTH,
LITERACY, AND TECHNOLOGY

In *Common Culture*, Paul Willis maintains that "Young people are all the time expressing or attempting to express something about their actual or potential cultural significance" (1). The new communications technologies have given many youth with Internet access *multiple* media for such expressions—and, if we pay attention, they are talking to each other, and sometimes to us, about their "potential cultural significance," particularly in terms of how technology can be used to communicate. Put another way, they are talking to us about *their* literacies. In fact, in *Channel Surfing: Race, Media, and the Destruction of Today's Youth*, Henry A. Giroux puts forth the following argument:

> Educationally and politically, young people need to be given the opportunity to narrate themselves, to speak from the actual places where their experiences and daily lives are shaped and mediated, such as alternative music spheres, neighborhood subcultures, mass-mediated electronic cultures, underground magazines, and other sites. Educators and others need to recognize the importance of providing opportunities for kids to voice their concerns, but equally important is the need to provide the conditions—institutional, economic, spiritual, and cultural—that will allow them to reconceptualize themselves as citizens and develop a sense of what it means to fight for important social and political issues that affect their lives, bodies, and society. (31)

Giroux makes a good, even noble point in this passage: As educators, activists, or those intimately concerned with issues of literacy, we need to make sure that students in our courses have sufficient spaces in which to experiment with, explore, and develop their own voices, with which they can speak to us about their own sociopolitical, cultural, and personal concerns. Giroux is concerned that images of youth in the mass media, in films, on television, and even in advertising either misrepresent youth and their concerns or model consumerist values that fritter away the energy, vitality, and creativity of youth in orgies of shopping. I cannot disagree with either his sentiment or his assessment of how our culture largely attempts to seduce youth into being more concerned about purchasing products rather than pursuing politics, more invested in fashion rather than interrogating fascist attacks on civil liberties. Chapter 7, on the YOUth and AIDS Web Project, offers an example of how, as a writing instructor, I attempted to create such an opportunity for "young people" to "narrate themselves."

At the same time, there is something ever so mildly patronizing about Giroux's comments. Note the passive voice in the first sentence just quoted: "young people need to be given the opportunity . . ." But by whom? The answer comes in the following sentence: "Educators and others need to recognize the importance of providing [those] opportunities . . ." Perhaps I am being a bit hard on Giroux, but I can't help but feel, after having written this book, that many youth with Web-authoring skills are already taking the opportunity to express themselves, and to "reconceptualize" themselves as citizens, in the work analyzed here. In e-zines, activist sites, community-building Webs, and even in personal homepages, young writers "voice their concerns," and experiment with ways to "develop a sense of what it means to fight for important social and political issues that affect their lives, bodies, and society."

My goal has been to note, trace, and analyze some of the ways that these writers voice their concerns, and how they are using the new communications technologies, particularly the Web, to do so. In the process, I think we have seen how a few distinct emerging trends have surfaced. The writers examined here display the following characteristics:

1. An interest and creativity in using multimedia to experiment with hyperbole, pastiche, parody, and irony as modes of critique.
2. An engagement with such rhetorical strategies for sociopolitical ends, critiques, or interventions.
3. A resistance to thinking of Web texts as global, but rather as more local interventions.

4. A willingness to situate, understand, and use Web texts vis-à-vis other communications venues.

The following briefly examines each characteristic to recap what has been found through analyses of individual works.

First, the sheer amount of Web writing seen here suggests that many digital youth are deeply invested in writing—and in expanding what we mean by "writing" in the "digital age." In general, the work seen here suggests what other scholars have pointed out about many diverse youth practices: Youth are hardly illiterate, and they deploy a variety of literacy practices to engage in the exploration and critique of many different ideas and views. For instance, Michele Knobel and Colin Lankshear, in their article "Cut, Paste, Publish: The Production and Consumption of Zines," note that "Zines provide firm ground from which to interrogate literacy education as currently practiced in schools and offer hard evidence that young people are not held necessarily in a 'consumer trance' or are without sophisticated critical capacities" (183). But more than this, the electronically enabled communications that have been studied in this book demonstrate that those "sophisticated critical capacities" embrace textual, visual, and multimedia literacies. Nearly every text examined in this volume has used multimedia formats, including the frequent and creative use of visuals and even video and sound. From Dave's "personal" homepage, asitshould.com, to the queer online youth community site Mogenic, digital youth are using a variety of media, facilitated by the Web, to articulate complex narrations about their lives.

And the majority of such narrations offer not just narration but *critique*—most notably of how youth have been represented in the past, or of what youth are "supposed" to be interested in. Using parodic and satiric textual, visual, and even aural thrusts, these composers parry bankrupt notions of youth as naïve, innocent, or unmotivated by social and political concerns, which leads to the second major trend that has been seen use of the Web as politically interventive. Certainly, substantial publication undertakings, such as that of XRay or YGA, show digital youth engaged in a variety of literacy practices, from narration to reportage to documentary reports—all used to forward their social and political concerns. But more than this, they are using the Web as a tool specifically to *enhance* the dissemination of their messages. In XRay's case, the Web is used to further problematize the delineation of information construction into "reporters" and "readers," and the XRay editors think of the Web as a forum for inviting readers themselves to actively participate in the creation and dissemination of "news." Likewise, the organizers of YGA invite visitors to write

and share their stories about growing up gay for distribution via the Web—
a publication project that could not otherwise be undertaken easily in print
without significant cost.

Although such projects highlight the hopes of these youth for using the
Web to enhance how some youth communicate their interests, insights,
and investments, it is also clear that other digital youth are keenly aware of
some of the limitations of the Web as a communications tool—limitations
that give the lie to the Web as a truly *global* platform for *comprehensive* construction and dissemination of information and ideas. Tim Covi's work
with the IMEMC is one prime example of how some youth are reconfiguring their use of the Web—not as a global tool, but as a local communications platform whose goal is to support the educational and activist mis-
sions of yet other media. Although this is one extreme example of reconfiguring use of the Web, I think we can see comparable literacy strategies
in other projects examined here. For instance, even *XRay*'s editors' use of
the Web is *in conjunction* with a print publication, with the Web component
supporting, augmenting, and enhancing the print version. Moreover, a project such as XRay, as well as Mogenic, YGA, and others, seem focused on
local events, issues, and politics. Although all benefit from having access to
points of information from around the world, each site seems targeted to
a local set of issues, as though the digital youth recognize that the Web is
perhaps best used to meet slightly less than global needs. Perhaps we are
seeing a strange form of remediation, to borrow the term used by Jay David
Bolter and Richard Grusin to describe how a newer medium's effects are
often mimicked by older media, such as television news programs broad-
casting reports in formats that look like Web pages. In addition to such
remediation of "older" media, we may be seeing ways in which the Web
itself is being re-mediated to take advantage of some of the power of television, for instance; certainly, using the Web to disseminate video feed to
television broadcasters says as much, if not more, about the continued
power of televised images in our culture as it does about the ability of the
Web to speedily supply such feed.

I think that such uses of the Web serve as a counter to Birkerts' or
Postman's insinuations that tech-based communications might short-cir-
cuit critical thinking and thus undermine literacy. Postman's fear that youth
who are "deeply conditioned by the biases of television" are essentially illiterate and "cannot organize their thought into logical structure" (38) seems
unsubstantiated, if not actually refuted, by the kinds of digital youth-produced texts seen here. Indeed, if we return momentarily to Nancy Kaplan's
definition of literacy—"the most important or highest form of literacy manifests itself as a sustained, critical engagement with ideas expressed verbal-

ly and presented in visible language" (220), we see, I think, that these youth *are* indeed undertaking a "sustained, critical engagement" with a variety of important social, political, and personal ideas. Granted, these writers are not producing *linear* texts advancing arguments as they have been traditionally understood. But their literacy practices are critical, interrogating important social issues—in often sophisticated ways. I argue that the use of satire and parody, facilitated through a deployment of irony, self-irony, pastiche, and hyperbole, shows a different kind of critical thinking at play—not its absence.

At the same time, use of the Web by these youth is hardly utopian. The writing and Web literacies examined in this volume suggest that some youth are well aware of the limitations of the Web, both as a communications tool and as a platform for launching or forwarding activist agendas. The Web has its place, but it is not supplanting other forms of communication, as Bolter's earlier work suggests. Actually, I argue that we are seeing more of a blending of traditional and electronically enabled literacy and compositional practices. The coupling of writing for the Web with other kinds of literacy practices suggests that digital youth are not abandoning the pleasures and rigors of text as much as they are using—to their advantage—all of the media platforms available for crafting and disseminating their ideas. Moreover, all of the Web composers discussed here seem attuned, at different levels, to the Web as a *hyper*real space—in which possibilities for radically transforming or at least impacting the "real world" are tempered by a realization of the Web's limitations, or by an understanding of the Web as a space more for rhetorical play and experimentation as opposed to cultural transformation. Think of Dave Myers' claim that he is not interested in changing anyone's life. Even when Web composers hold out hope for using the Web to advance various causes or to help build alternative forms of community, as with the editors of GoXRay.com, the hope is qualified; no one is putting all of their political eggs in one Web basket. Conversely, all of the Web composers *continue to explore and experiment* with different rhetorical modes, with different ways to manipulate and represent their notions of identity and community in the hyperreality of the Web. And, if their belief in the possibilities of the Web for articulating and building community aren't as utopian as those of Douglas Rushkoff in *Playing the Future*, their playfulness, creativity, and inventiveness speak at least to a continued understanding of literacy and composition—however transformed by the Internet—as powerful forms for self-expression and exploration of critical ideas and insights.

Granted—and this is a big granted—the youth discussed in these pages may be the exception, not the rule. It may be the case that many young people—our college-aged students, for instance—would rather go shopping online or play video games as opposed to sifting through HTML or FLASH to compose their Web sites. And in no way am I suggesting that people who are not "youth" could not deploy the kinds of literacy and compositional practices we have seen in these pages. They can, and do, I'm sure. But the energy and insights presented in the sampling (and I must stress *sampling*) of sites seen here, suggest to me that some digital youth *are* not only aware of the need to carve out a space to think sociopolitically, but they are more than willing to take advantage of existing media to do so— and to challenge themselves, their writing abilities, and their technological literacies in the exploration of yet other electronic spaces, such as sound and video clips, in which to express themselves and potentially reshape their words and worlds.

And, as seen in this analysis, much of this work has been done by these youth with a high degree of self-consciousness; they are keenly aware that they are *youth*, writing from a variety of alternative or subcultural vantage points, composing and disseminating thoughts about the dominant, mainstream culture. This is why I have not hesitated throughout the book to pit, if you will, that dominant culture's views of "youth" against what some digital youth are actually doing in their own e-spaces. I have found this useful in at least two ways: one, it reveals the shortcomings in a frequently utopian sensibility about the use of technology as fostering community, interactivity, and understanding; second, it points to some of the more subversive rhetorical modes, such as self-irony, hyperbole, and parody, that some digital youth use not so much to create community but to critique and understand the impact of technology on the dissemination of information.

Indeed, I think one of the most intriguing aspects of the work discussed in this volume is the degree to which some digital youth are using technologically enabled literacies, modes, and genres to critique both the culture at large and its romanticization of technology in particular. In "Media Knowledges, Warrior Citzenry, and Postmodern Literacies," Peter McLaren and Rhonda Hammer discuss the impact of media and the mass of information surrounding us on our conception of literacy, and they forward the concept of "critical media literacy" to capture the complex interactions between technology, mass communication, and meaning-making:

> Critical media literacy becomes the interpretation of the social present for the purpose of transforming the cultural life of particular groups, for questioning tacit assumptions and unarticulated presuppositions of our current cultural and social formations and the subjectivities and capacities for agenthood that they foster. Critical media lit-

eracy is directed at understanding the ongoing social struggles over the signs of culture and the definition of social reality—what is considered legitimate and preferred meaning at any given historical moment. (112)

The youth whose work was studied here offer us multiple examples of such "agenthood," fully engaged in raucous debates and provocative "struggles over the signs of culture and the definition of social reality." In particular, a questioning of genres—from rewriting the personal homepage, to pushing the boundaries of the definitions of "writer" and "editor" with e-zines, to problematizing concepts of sexual orientation identity and conservative views of sexuality education—Web-savvy youth seem to delight in the "struggle," and they take seriously the task of participating in the "definition of social reality."

This work—*their* work—has inspired me. Some youth *are* engaged—as writers, Web composers, and literacy mavericks. They speak to us both about their concerns *and* the many ways they are developing to express those concerns as technologically literate—and sophisticated—authors, composers, and designers.

Despite my enthusiasm, which I think has been evident throughout this book, I am left with a few nagging questions and concerns about the work seen here—questions and concerns that I feel must be addressed as I conclude this project.

First, who cares? Despite the variety of sites I analyzed, and the number of ways in which I believe digital youth are pushing the possibilities of Web literacies to explore challenging and innovative ways of representing their engagement with the world around them, I do wonder how many other youth actually read, assimilate, respond to, and appreciate the work that these youth are doing. This is no simple, throw-away question. If no one is reading this writing, then the work *is* limited in what it can accomplish, in whom it can influence. Just because you build it, doesn't mean anyone will show up, or, in this case, click "enter." I *do* know that many of the sites studied, such as GoXRay and Mogenic, have wide readerships; other sites, however, such as the personal homepages, are less frequently visited, as one might expect. Does that *decrease* their significance as indicators of emerging literacy trends? It might, even though I think I have demonstrated a similarity of attitudes and approaches across several chapters and several Web genres.

Second, what about all of the other forums, venues, and platforms, electronic and otherwise, that youth with Internet access and skills are using to experiment with writing, to challenge our—and their own—literacies, to provoke response through rhetoric? I'm thinking of chatrooms, texting, Instant Messaging, for instance, and a variety of other venues that need to be examined to assess how some youth are using new modes of communication and experimenting with literacy. There is not sufficient time nor space to explore these other electronic frontiers in this book, but the need to do so is critical, particularly as such platforms are used increasingly—and used creatively—by many youth.

Third, electronic literacies aren't the only literacies being explored and developed by youth with an interest in writing. In the introduction, I mentioned my visit to the Cincinnati Rock and Read Fest 2, which inspired me by showing the variety of ways such youth were disseminating thoughts, opinions, and ideas via the Web. At the same time, much of the work they were putting on display was in *print*. Paper zines, print journals, stickers, and posters were clearly popular venues for self-expression and literacy experimentation. A truly bold, innovative, and thought-provoking book might explore how youth with an interest in writing are using *all* of these forms and genres—electronic and print-based—to get their word, and words, out to the public. Tim Covi and the IMEMC give us an inkling of how some youth are re-conceiving the Web as a support system for other media. Continuing the discussion and analysis along these lines, and extending it to interconnectivity between the Internet and print could offer a more complex understanding of how some youth are engaging in and developing multiple literacies.

Fourth, I would be remiss if, at some point, I didn't counter my enthusiasm for the alternative literacy spaces that some youth are exploring with a recognition of and fuller discussion of the "corporatization" of the Web, or the continued dominance of White, Western, and middle-class voices on it. Throughout, I have tried to show how commercial spaces, from MTV.com to Gay.com, forward their own particular vision of youth, and as such have served as counterpoints to the seemingly more "authentic" voices of American youth. Of course, there is danger in forwarding notions of "authenticity," of suggesting that the youth-driven e-spaces examined here represent somehow more directly, more powerfully, and more accurately the interests, needs, voices, and visions of "youth"—surely a category too broad to be useful.

But commercial ventures are not without their uses. MTV, for instance, has been extraordinarily helpful in providing a variety of youth with much-needed information about sexuality, safer sex, the consequences of bigotry in our society, and the necessity of actively participating in democratic processes, such as voting. These are significant services to young people in our country. At the same time, however, the dominance of images of Whites, of writings by middle-class consumers, and texts by Westerners continues to suggest that the Web is still a fairly localized communications platform—local, that is, to the Western world. This is why I have emphasized the use of the Web by at least one minority group within Western culture—queer youth. Use of the Web by this group might model for other minority and marginalized groups a way of approaching and writing the Web for their own ends, purposes, and visions.

Fifth, I must also acknowledge that the sites I have studied, even lauded, have been ones that have taken a more "local" view, as opposed to forwarding an understanding of the Web as a global phenomenon—despite the fact that some sites *do* attempt to use the Web to more "global" ends. I have done this for two reasons. First, I can't help but think, as I have tried to show in this volume, that some of the most interesting, engaging, and thought-provoking uses of the Web are occurring on sites that are not necessarily concerned with altering the world at large, but are rather invested in more localized interventions. Even the IMEMC seems to target a particular group (Western, English-speaking journalists) with the goal of affecting change in one area (predominantly the United States). Granted, this is an ambitious goal, perhaps even one with potential worldwide consequences. But the focus is clear, and localized. Perhaps the forcefulness of the goal stems from the attention paid to a contained community, which suggests that change might best occur by focusing on specific communities and trusting in a ripple-effect to create or excite change in other communities and spheres of influence.

At the same time, I must admit that others, even those invested in youths' voices and visions, have nonetheless taken a broader view. One such enterprise is the nonprofit organization Teen Ink, whose popular Web site is designed to promote writing among youth with Internet access. The mission statement attests to what I think are some fairly admirable goals:

> Welcome to *Teen Ink*, a national teen magazine, book series, and website devoted entirely to teenage writing and art. Distributed through classrooms by English teachers, Creative Writing teachers, Journalism teachers and art teachers around the country, *Teen Ink* magazine offers some of the most thoughtful and creative work generated by teens and has the largest distribution of any publication of its kind. We have no staff writers or artists; we depend completely on submissions from teenagers nationwide for our content
>
> Every day, we offer teenagers the opportunity to publish their creative work and opinions on the issues that affect their lives—every-

thing from love and family to teen smoking and community service. Hundreds of thousands of students have submitted their work to us and we have published more than 25,000 teens since 1989.

The Young Authors Foundation, Inc. is a nonprofit 501(c)3 organization that supports all *Teen Ink* publications. The foundation is devoted to helping teens share their own voices, while developing reading, writing, creative and critical-thinking skills. All proceeds from the print magazine, Web site and *Teen Ink* books are used exclusively for charitable and educational purposes to further our goal. (http://teenink.com/ About/)

Certainly, some youth take advantage of this service, and I'm sure they benefit from it. At the same time, Teen Ink seems, well, scattershot—a venue for posting interesting stuff, but not a forum for putting literacy into action, for directing one's writing to a specific cause, concern, or agenda. We have seen the latter, I believe, throughout the pages of this book.

And, finally, some literacy educators and writing instructors will suggest that I'm tipping my hand a bit too much here, revealing my investment in activist-oriented literacies at the expense of other necessary, significant pedagogical concerns. They may be right. And such concerns are voiced—often eloquently, often movingly—by others in the field of writing studies who both appreciate what technology brings to the possibilities of being literate in the contemporary world and who realize that many students face some very basic skills deficiencies that keep them from participating fully in any number of social projects. Cynthia Jeney, for instance, wrote the following in frustration recently on a listserv designed to help participants explore the uses of various technologies in writing instruction. Her posting is worth quoting in full:

> From: cj < DrCeeJ@prodigy.net >
> Reply-To: techrhet@interversity.org
> Date: Sat, 04 Jan 2003 00:48:56 -0600
> To: techrhet@interversity.org
> Subject: [techrhet] Web Authoring Behaving Badly...
>
> So I'm splitting off completely from my old Web site teaching methods, the
> the semester starts in nine days and I may not even do ANY design stuff at all,
> it's going to be all about the writing this semester... maybe brutally so,
> I'm frustrated and intimidated and feelin' rebellious. It's a lower
> division course with no prerequisites, although most students who take it
> have had FYC. I'm not ever going to belong in the computer science
> department, I don't teach XML, java-script, server software, DHTML, ASP, or

> any kind of database programming, which means I'm not trying to teach
> students how to create the next E-bay or cars.com, or the ultimate Anime
> site (although that's all 90% of my midwestern Bible Belt Web authoring
> students have experienced on the 'net)...
>
> So.... I want ideas, support, detractors, discussion, criticism, agreement,
> and if possible URL's of Web sites whose WRITING (NOT pictures, NOT
> java-mouseovers, NOT animations, NOT rollovers, NOT frames, NOT
> "coolnesses") is most divine, most excellent, and exciting.
>
> I'm on the hunt myself, so if nobody responds, I *promise* this thread will
> not die... not yet....
>
> .... For the first assignment this semester, I'm seriously considering
> teaching rhetorical and grammatical sentence types, and assigning
> one-paragraph topics, then making them summarize to a truly great sentence,
> and then to three words... just to see if they can get attention without
> using dollar signs, naked pictures, or the F-word...
>
> ...Has anyone done a segment on those banners? The studies say internet
> users ignore them completely, and I personally think many of them are
> unethical and, well, crap... but perhaps a banner assignment could be
> useful rhetorically, anyway...
>
> I need guidance. I'm lost in a self-created, cynical, subversive wilderness...
>
> CeeJ

As a fellow technophile and writing instructor, I feel CeeJ's pain. And I love the tension in this posting. On one hand, she wants to return her students to exploring—and appreciating—the complexities and possibilities of rhetoric, at the level of the sentence. Such a desire arises understandably out of a recognition that many students take the easy way out when it comes to crafting prose or thinking about rhetorical effect: The "F" word, after all, has its limitations. On the other hand, note how she considers using Web banners as part of an assignment in rhetorical analysis. She doesn't want to let go of the powerfulness latent in e-communication, the rhetorical strategies that it enables, or the "teachable moments" about rhetoric that it offers.
Nor should she.

This is the double-bind of teaching literacy at this point in the development of networked communications technologies. We must both help students understand the power of rhetoric and the usefulness of basic literacy skills *and* give them a sense of what's "coming next" in terms of electronic literacies. Their survival in our part of the world might depend on it, as more and more businesses expect fluency in using electronic communications platforms, such as Instant Messaging, e-mail, and the Web.

The trick might be to combine both, as it seems some literacy specialists and writing instructors are doing. In a 2003 Cover Web for *Kairos*, contributors focused their attention on "Issues of New Media" (http://english. ttu.edu/kairos/8.1/), exploring how a variety of techno-rich media, from audio to video, could be used to address and expand students' literacy needs—and desires. In particular, Daniel Anderson's piece, "Prosumer Approaches to New Media Composition: Consumption and Production in Continuum," shows how Anderson encouraged students to work with new media, creating video projects and experimenting with visual argument (http://english.ttu.edu/kairos/8.1/binder2.html?http://cfcc.net/kairos/8.1/cov erweb/anderson/index.html). Anderson's hope is that students will become not just "consumers" but "prosumers" of media, using it to produce Web texts, video texts, and arguments that engage, explore, and expand their understanding of a variety of important issues. For example, some of Anderson's students composed complex video-based arguments that examined the pros and cons of standardized testing. For Anderson, offering such assignments has a real-world purpose: "Equipping students to participate in new media discourses empowers them to act in a world in which the knowledge currencies are increasingly digital." At the same time, Anderson is mindful of how his students will need to be able to compose texts in a variety of situations and circumstances, some still print-based, and he believes that his media-rich, prosumer approach helps to facilitate such learning: "In an interview the author suggested that composing the video gave her a better understanding of composition issues across genres."

Such work is exciting and forward-thinking. It shows a commitment to introducing students not only to a critical understanding of technology but to ways of using that technology to produce and forward their own voices, their own visions. It is also a potentially costly and time-consuming pedagogy, as schools must be able to afford certain technologies, and instructors must be willing to spend the time necessary to learn and develop pedagogies to use them. But this is also the kind of pedagogy that not only honors youths' voices, but aids them in transforming what it means to be literate in the "Information Age." As I have argued throughout this book, it also reflects the changes in literacy that many Web-savvy youth have been embracing for some time.

Perhaps, one day, we might catch up. We can do so by starting to pay attention to what some youth are already doing with the Web, with their writing, and with their literacies.

REFERENCES

"Abstinence-Only Education." United States House of Representatives. http://www.house.gov/reform/min/politicsandscience/example_abstinence.ht m (31 October 2003).

Addison, Joanne, and Michelle Comstock. "Virtually Out: The Emergence of a Lesbian, Bisexual, and Gay Youth Cyberculture." In Joe Austin and Michael Nevin Willard (eds.), *Generations of Youth: Youth Cultures and History in Twentieth-Century America*. New York: New York University Press, 1998. 367-378.

Adler-Kassner, Linda, Robert Crooks, and Ann Watters (eds.). *Writing the Community: Concepts and Models for Service-Learning in Composition*. Washington, DC: American Association For Higher Education Press, 1997.

Aikat, Debashis. "Cyberspace of the People, by the People, for the People: Predominant Use of the Web in the Public Sector." In Alan B. Albarran and David H. Goff (eds.), *Understanding the Web: Social, Political, and Economic Dimensions of the Internet*. Ames: Iowa State University Press, 2000. 49-72.

Alexander, Jonathan. "Digital Spins: The Pedagogy and Politics of Student-Centered E-Zines." *Computers & Composition* 19 (2002): 387-410.

Alexander, Jonathan. "Homo-pages and Queer Sites: Studying the Construction and Representation of Queer Identities on the World Wide Web." *The International Journal of Sexuality and Gender Studies* 7.2-3 (2002): 85-106.

Allison, Libby, and Kristine L. Blair. *Cultural Attractions/Cultural Distractions: Critical Literacy in Contemporary Contexts*. Upper Saddle River, NJ: Prentice Hall, 2000.

Anderson, Daniel. "Prosumer Approaches to New Media Composition: Consumption and Production in Continuum." *Kairos* 8.1. Spring 2003.

(http://english.ttu.edu/ kairos/8.1/binder2.html?http://www.hu.mtu.edu/kairos/
CoverWeb/anderson/ index.html (27 September 2004).

Anderson, Daniel, Bret Benjamin, and Bill Paredes-Holt. *Connections: A Guide to On-
Line Writing*. Boston: Allyn and Bacon, 1998.

Anderson, Daniel, Bret Benjamin, Christopher Busiel, and Bill Paredes-Holt.
Teaching Online: Internet Research, Conversation and Composition. New York:
Longman, 1998.

Bacon, Nora. "Community Service Writing: Problems, Challenges, Questions." In
Linda Adler-Kassner et al. (eds.), *Writing the Community: Concepts and Models
for Service-Learning in Composition*. Washington, DC: American Association For
Higher Education Press, 1997. 39-56.

Baron, Dennis. "From Pencils to Pixels: The Stages of Literacy Technologies." In
Ellen Cushman, Eugene R. Kintgen, Barry M. Kroll, and Mike Rose (eds.),
Literacy: A Critical Sourcebook. Boston: Bedford/St. Martin's, 2001. 70-84.

Batschelet, Margaret W. *Web Writing/Web Designing*. Boston: Allyn and Bacon,
2001.

Baudrillard, Jean. "Aesthetic Illusion and Virtual Reality." In Julia Thomas (ed.),
Reading Images. New York: Palgrave, 2000.

Baudrillard, Jean. "Simulacra and Simulations." In Mark Poster (ed.), *Jean
Baudrillard: Selected Writings*. London: Blackwell, 1988. 166-184.

Beach, Richard, and Bertram C. Bruce. "Using Digital Tools to Foster Critical
Inquiry." In Donna E. Alvermann (ed.), *Adolescents and Literacies in a Digital
World*. New York: Peter Lang, 2002. 147-163.

Bell, David. *An Introduction to Cybercultures*. London: Routledge, 2001.

Bennahum, David S. *Extra Life: Coming of Age in Cyberspace*. New York: Basic
Books, 1999.

Berlin, James. "Composition and Cultural Studies." In Mark Hurlbert and Michael
Blitz (eds.), *Composition and Resistance*. Portsmouth, NH: Boynton/Cook,
1991.

Berry, Wendell. "Why I Am Not Going to Buy a Computer." In Robert P. Yagelski
(ed.), *Literacies and Technologies*. New York: Longman, 2001. 103-111.

Bertens, Hans. *The Idea of the Postmodern*. London: Routledge, 1995.

Bey, Hakim. "Notes for CTHEORY." In Arthur and Marilouise Kroker (eds.), *Digital
Delirium*. New York: St. Martin's Press, 1997. 152-155.

Bey, Hakim. "The Temporary Autonomous Zone." In Peter Ludlow (ed.), *Crypto
Anarchy, Cyberstates, and Pirate Utopias*. Cambridge, MA: The MIT Press, 2001.
401-434.

Birkerts, Sven. *The Gutenberg Elegies: The Fate of Reading in an Electronic Age*.
Boston: Faber and Faber, 1994.

Bolter, Jay David. *Writing Space: The Computer, Hypertext, and the History of Writing*.
Mahwah, NJ: Erlbaum, 1991.

Bolter, Jay David, and Richard Grusin. *Remediation: Understanding New Media*.
http://www.lcc.gatech.edu/ ~ bolter/remediation/bk_intro.html (31 October
2003).

"Born Digital" A Wired Special Report." *Wired* 10.09. September 2002. http://www.wired.com/wired/archive/10,09/borndigital.html?pg = 1 (4 October 2004).

Branscomb, H. Eric. *Casting Your Net: A Student's Guide to Research on the Internet.* Boston: Allyn and Bacon, 1998.

Branston, Gill, and Roy Stafford. *The Media Student's Book.* London: Routledge, 1999 (1996).

"Bridges to Healthy Communities." American Association of Community Colleges. 2000-2001. http://www.aacc.nche.edu/initiatives/bridges/bridges1.htm (No longer available).

Castells, Manuel. *The Rise of the Network Society.* Malden, MA: Blackwell, 1996.

Charney, Davida. "The Effect of Hypertext on Processes of Reading and Writing." In Ellen Cushman, Eugene R. Kintgen, Barry M. Kroll, and Mike Rose (eds.), *Literacy: A Critical Sourcebook.* Boston: Bedford/St. Martin's, 2001. 85-103.

Cheung, Charles. "A Home on the Web: Presentations of Self on Personal Homepages." In David Gauntlett (ed.), *Web.Studies: Rewriting Media Studies for the Digital Age.* London: Arnold, 2000. 43-51.

Clark, Carol Lea. *A Student's Guide to the Internet.* Upper Saddle River, NJ: Prentice Hall, 1996.

Condon, William, and Wayne Butler. *Writing the Information Superhighway.* Boston: Allyn and Bacon, 1997.

Connor-Linton, Jeff. "An Indirect Model of Service Learning: Integrating Research, Teaching, and Community Service. *Michigan Journal of Community Service Learning*, 2.1 (1995): 105-111.

Crimp, Douglas. "Portraits of People with AIDS." In Lawrence Grossberg, Cary Nelson, and Paula Treichler (eds.), *Cultural Studies.* New York: Routledge, 1992. 117-131.

Crump, Eric, and Nick Carbone. *English Online: A Student's Guide to the Internet and the World Wide Web.* Boston: Houghton Mifflin Company, 1997.

Deans, Thomas. *Writing Partnerships: Service-Learning in Composition.* Urbana, IL: National Council of Teachers of English, 2000.

"Democratic Lawmakers Accuse Bush Administration of Political Bias in Deleting Information From New CDC Condom Fact Sheet." Planned Parenthood Mar Monte. 19 December 2002. http://www.ppmarmonte.org/news/viewer.asp?ID = 643 (31 October 2003).

Dery, Mark. *Escape Velocity: Cyberculture at the End of the Century.* New York: Grove Press, 1996.

Desmet, Christy. "Reading the Web as Fetish." *Computers and Composition* 18 (2001): 55-72.

Dibbell, Julian. "The Writer a la Modem, Or, The Death of the Author on the Installment Plan." In Robert P. Yagelski (ed.), *Literacies and Technologies.* New York: Longman, 2001. 112-118.

Dickson, Chidsey. "A Review of *Internet Invention: From Literacy to Electracy.*" *Kairos* 8.1.Spring 2003. http://english.ttu.edu/kairos/8.1/binder.html?reviews/dickson/index.html (27 September 2004).

Döring, Nicola. "Personal Home Pages on the Web: A Review of Research." *Journal of Computer-Mediated Communication* 7.3. April 2002. http://www.ascusc.org /jcmc/vol7/issue3/doering.html (31 October 2003).

"Douglas Rushkoff." Royce Carlton, Inc. http://www.roycecarlton.com/speakers/ rushkoff.html (August 2002).

Dyson, Esther. *Release 2.0: A Design for Living in the Digital Age.* New York: Broadway Books, 1997.

Ebersole, Samuel. "Uses and Gratifications of the Web among Students." *Journal of Computer-Mediated Communication* 6.1. September 2000. http://www.ascusc. org/jcmc/vol6/issue1/ebersole.html (31 October 2003).

Eco, Umberto. *Travels in Hyperreality: Essays.* Trans. by William Weaver. San Diego: Harcourt Brace Jovanovich, 1986.

Egan, Jennifer. " < lonely gay teen seeking same > ." *New York Times Magazine,* December 10, 2000: 110-113.

Eisenberg, Rebecca L. "It's All The Rave." *The San Francisco Examiner.* 22 June 1997. http://www.omino.com/ ~ dom/clips/ecstasyclub.html (31 October 2003).

Eisenberg, Rebecca. "The Two Doug Rushkoffs." *Rewired.* 30 June 1997. http://www.rewired.com/97/0630.html (31 October 2003).

"Episcopalians Approve Gay Bishop." CNN.com. 6 August 2003. http://www.cnn. com/2003/US/08/05/bishop/ (31 October 2003).

Faigley, Lester. *Fragments of Rationality: Postmodernity and the Subject of Composition.* Pittsburgh: University of Pittsburgh Press, 1992.

Faigley, Lester. "Understanding Popular Digital Literacies." In John Trimbur (ed.), *Popular Literacy: Studies in Cultural Practice and Poetics.* Pittsburgh: University of Pittsburgh Press, 2001. 248-263.

Fiske, John. *Media Matters: Everyday Culture and Political Change.* Minneapolis: University of Minnesota Press, 1996.

Foster, Derek. "Community and Identity in the Electronic Village." In David Porter (ed.), *Internet Culture.* New York: Routledge, 1996. 23-38.

Freccero, Carla. *Popular Culture.* New York: New York University Press, 1999.

Gamson, Joshua. "Gay Media, Inc.: Media Structures, the New Gay Conglomerates, and Collective Sexual Identities." In Martha McCaughey and Michael D. Ayers (eds.), *Cyberactivism: Online Activism in Theory and Practice.* New York: Routledge, 2003. 255-278.

Geiger, Brian F. "Use of Yahoo! Groups for Health Education." *American Journal of Health Education* 34.1 (2003): 54-55.

Gelder, Ken, and Sarah Thornton. *The Subcultures Reader.* New York: Routledge, 1997.

George, Diana. "From Analysis to Design: Visual Communication in the Teaching of Writing." *CCC* 54.1 (2002): 11-39.

George, Diana, and Diane Shoos. "Dropping Bread Crumbs in the Intertextual Forest: Critical Literacy in a Postmodern Age." In Gail E. Hawisher and Cynthia L. Selfe (eds.), *Passions, Pedagogies, and 21st Century Technologies.* Logan, Utah: State University Press, 1999. 115-126.

Gibson, Stephanie B., and Ollie O. Oviedo. *The Emerging Cyberculture: Literacy, Paradigm, and Paradox.* Cresskill, NJ: Hampton Press, 2000.

Gibson, William. *Neuromancer.* New York: Ace, 1984.

Gilliam, Jesse. Personal interview. 17 November 2003.

Giroux, Henry A. *Channel Surfing: Race Talk and the Destruction of Today's Youth.* New York: St. Martin's Press, 1997.

Giroux, Henry A. "Doing Cultural Studies: Youth and the Challenge of Pedagogy." In Michael Peters (ed.), *After the Disciplines: The Emergence of Cultural Studies.* Westport, CT: Bergin & Garvey, 1999.

Giroux, Henry A. "Teenage Sexuality, Body Politics and the Pedagogy of Display." http://www.gseis.ucla.edu/courses/ed253a/Giroux/Giroux3.html (31 October 2003).

Glatze, Mike. Personal Interview. 22 August 2003.

Godwin, Mike. "Cybergreen: Bruce Sterling on Media, Design, Fiction, and the Future." *Reasononline.* http://www.reason.com/0401/fe.mg.cybergreen.shtml (19 February 2004).

Goldberg, Amie, Michael Russell, and Abigail Cook. "The Effect of Computers on Student Writing: A Meta-analysis of Studies from 1992 to 2002." *JTLA: The Journal of Technology, Learning, and Assessment* 2.1 (2002): http://www.bc.edu/research/intasc/jtla/journal/v2n1.shtml.

Griffiths, C. J. "Activist at Heart." Tempercentbent: The E-Zine for GLBT Youth. http://www.tenpercentbent.com/article.php?dept = 3&article = 178&col = 23 (28 September 2004).

Griscom, Amanda. "New Media Savants Check the Pulse of Silicon Alley Vital Signs." *The Village Voice.* 19-25 January 2000. http://www.villagevoice.com/issues/0003/griscom.php (31 October 2003).

Grover, Jan Zita. "AIDS, Keywords, and Cultural Work." In Lawrence Grossberg, Cary Nelson, and Paula Treichler (eds.), *Cultural Studies.* New York: Routledge, 1992. 227-234.

Gruber, Sibylle. "The Rhetorics of Three Women Activist Groups on the Web: Building and Transforming Communities." In Laura Gray-Rosendale and Sibylle Gruber (eds.), *Alternative Rhetorics: Challenges to the Rhetorical Tradition.* Albany: State University of New York Press, 2001. 77-92.

Gruber, Sibylle, ed. *Weaving a Virtual Web: Practical Approaches to New Information Technologies.* Urbana, IL: National Council of Teachers of English, 2000.

Guernsey, Lisa, "A Young Writers' Round Table, via the Web." *New York Times.* August 14, 2003. http://www.nytimes.com/2003/08/14/technology/circuits/14peer.html?ex = 1061950041&ei = 1&en = 0384f06529293737 (31 October 2003).

Gurak, Laura J. *Cyberliteracy: Navigating the Internet with Awareness.* New Haven, CT: Yale University Press, 2001.

Hale, Constance, and Jessie Scanlon. *Wired Style: Principles of English Usage in the Digital Age.* New York: Broadway Books, 1999.

Halperin, David. *Saint-Foucault: Towards a Gay Hagiography.* New York: Oxford University Press, 1995.

Handa, Carolyn. "Digital Literacy and Rhetoric: A Selected Bibliography." *Computers and Composition* 18 (2001): 195-202.

Haraway, Donna. "Fractured Identities." In Patrick Joyce (ed.), *Class*. Oxford: Oxford University Press, 1995. 95-98.

Haraway, Donna. *Simians, Cyborgs, and Women: The Reinvention of Nature*. New York: Routledge, 1991.

Hawisher, Gail E., and Cynthia L. Selfe. *Global Literacies and the World-Wide Web*. London: Routledge, 2000.

Hawisher, Gail E., and Cynthia L. Selfe, eds. *Literacy, Technology, and Society: Confronting the Issues*. Upper Saddle River, NJ: Prentice Hall, 1997.

Hawisher, Gail E., and Patricia A. Sullivan. "Fleeting Images: Women Visually Writing the Web." In Gail E. Hawisher and Cynthia L. Selfe (eds.), *Passions, Pedagogies, and 21st Century Technologies*. Logan: Utah State University Press, 1999. 268-291.

Hayles, N. Katherine. *How We Became Posthuman*. Chicago: University of Chicago Press, 1999.

Hebdige, Dick. "Posing...Threats, Striking...Poses: Youth, Surveillance, and Display." In Ken Gelder and Sarah Thornton (eds.), *The Subcultures Reader*. New York: Routledge, 1997. 393-405.

Hebdige, Dick. *Subculture: The Meaning of Style*. London: Routledge, 1981.

Heiberger, Mary Morris, and Julia Miller Vick. "Building a Better Home Page." *The Chronicle of Higher Education*. 6 June 2003. http://chronicle.com/jobs/2003/06/2003060601c.htm (31 October 2003).

Heidegger, Martin. "The Question Concerning Technology." In David Farrell Krell (ed.), *Martin Heidegger: Basic Writings*. New York: Harper & Row, 1977. 283-317.

Heilker, Paul. "Rhetoric Made Real: Civic Discourse and Writing Beyond the Curriculum." In Linda Adler-Kassner et al. (eds.), *Writing the Community: Concepts and Models for Service-Learning in Composition*. Washington, DC: American Association For Higher Education Press, 1997. 71-78.

Heim, Scott. *The Metaphysics of Virtual Reality*. New York: Oxford University Press, 1993.

Hine, Christine. *Virtual Ethnography*. London: Sage, 2000.

Ho, Howard. "Novel Explores New Counterculture." *The Daily Bruin*. 30 November 1998. http://paradigm.asucla.ucla.edu/DB/issues/98/11.30/ae.ecstasy.html (31 October 2003).

Hoban, Mary T., Nan W. Ottenritter, Jan L. Gascoigne, and Dianne L. Kerr. *Campus HIV Prevention Strategies: Planning for Success*. Washington, DC: Community College Press, 2003.

Holeton, Richard. *Composing Cyberspace: Identity, Community, and Knowledge in the Electronic Age*. Boston: McGraw Hill, 1998.

hooks, bell. *Outlaw Culture: Resisting Representations*. New York: Routledge, 1994.

Jenkins, Henry. *Textual Poachers: Television Fans and Participatory Culture*. New York: Routledge, 1992.

Johnson, Steven. *Interface Culture: How New Technology Transforms the Way We Create and Communicate*. New York: Basic Books, 1997.

Jones, Steve (ed.) *Doing Internet Research: Critical Issues and Methods for Examining the Net*. Thousand Oaks, CA: Sage, 1999.

Jones, Steve, and Stephanie Kucker. "Computers, the Internet, and Virtual Cultures." In James Lull (ed.), *Culture in the Communication Age*. London: Routledge, 2001.

Kaplan, Nancy. "Knowing Practice: A More Complex View of New Media Literacy." http://iat.ubalt.edu/kaplan/ssgrr01.pdf (31 October 2003).

Kaplan, Nancy. "Literacy Beyond Books: Reading When All the World's a Web." In Andrew Herman and Thomas Swiss (eds.), *The World Wide Web and Contemporary Cultural Theory*. New York: Routledge, 2000. 207-234.

Knobel, Michele, and Colin Lankshear. "Cut, Paste, Publish: The Production and Consumption of Zines." In Donna E. Alvermann (ed.), *Adolescents and Literacies in a Digital World*. New York: Peter Lang, 2002.

Koehler, Charles. "Using Technology for Low-Cost/No-Cost Health Promotion." *Community College Journal* 74.1 (2003): 16-19.

Kolko, Beth E., Alison E. Regan, and Susan Romano. *Writing in an Electronic World*. New York: Longman, 2000.

Kowal, Donna M. "Digitizing and Globalizing Indigenous Voices: The Zapatista Movement." In Greg Elmer (ed.), *Critical Perspectives on the Internet*. Lanham, MD: Rowan and Littlefield Publishers, 2002. 105-126.

Kress, Gunther. *Literacy in the New Media Age*. London: Routledge, 2003.

Kress, Gunther. "Visual and Verbal Modes of Representation in Electronically Mediated Communication: The Potentials of New Forms of Text." In Ilana Snyder (ed.), *Page to Screen: Taking Literacy into the Electronic Age*. London: Routledge, 1998. 53-79.

Kryzan, Chris. Personal Interview. 5 November 2003.

Landow, George P. *Hypertext 2.0: The Convergence of Contemporary Critical Theory and Technology*. Baltimore, MD: The Johns Hopkins University Press, 1992 (1997).

Lanham, Richard A. *The Electronic Word: Democracy, Technology, and the Arts*. Chicago: University of Chicago Press, 1993.

Lasn, Kalle. *Culture Jam: The Uncooling of America*. New York: Eagle Brook, 1999.

Leonard, Andrew. "Hits on Zits." *Hotwired*. 2003. http://hotwired.lycos.com/packet/packet/leonard/96/47/index3a.html (31 October 2003).

Manning, Peter K. Foreword. In Michael A. Hallett (ed.), *Activism and Marginalization in the AIDS Crisis*. Binghamton, NY: Haworth, 1997. xvii-xxiiv.

Manovich, Lev. *The Language of New Media*. Cambridge, MA: MIT Press, 2001.

Mansfield, Nick. *Subjectivity: Theories of the Self from Freud to Haraway*. New York: New York University Press, 2000.

"Many Americans Think an HIV/AIDS Vaccine Already Exists." *NIH News*. 15 May 2003. http://www.nih.gov/news/pr/may2003/niaid-15.htm (31 October 2003).

McCaughey, Martha, and Michael D. Ayers. *Cyberactivism: Online Activism in Theory and Practice*. New York: Routledge, 2003.

McComiskey, Bruce. *Teaching Composition as a Social Process*. Logan: Utah State University Press, 2000.

McLaren, Peter, and Rhonda Hammer. "Media Knowledges, Warrior Citizenry, and Postmodern Literacies." In Henry Giroux (ed.), *Counternarratives: Cultural Studies and Critical Pedagogies in Postmodern Spaces*. New York: Routledge, 1996. 81-116.

McLuhan, Marshall, and Quentin Fiore. *The Medium is the Message*. New York: Random House, 1967.

McMillan, Sally J. "Survival of the Fittest Online: A Longitudinal Study of Health-Related Web Sites." *Journal of Computer-Mediated Communication* 6.3. April 2001. http://www.ascusc.org/jcmc/vol6/issue3/mcmillan.html (31 October 2003).

Meikle, Graham. *Future Active: Media Activism and the Internet*. New York: Routledge, 2002.

Mele, Christopher. "Cyberspace and Disadvantaged Communities. The Internet as Tool for Collective Action." In Mark A. Smith and Peter Kollock (eds.), *Communities in Cyberspace*. London: Routledge, 1999. 290-310.

Meyer, Ralph. The Fifth Annual Survey of Sexual Attitudes and Behavior of University of Cincinnati Students (AIDS Awareness Week–May 1999). http://www.biology.uc.edu/faculty/meyer/SexSurvey1999.pdf (31 October 2003).

Mitra, Ananda, and Elisia Cohen. "Analyzing the Web: Directions and Challenges." In Steve Jones (ed.), *Doing Internet Research: Critical Issues and Methods for Examining the Net*. Thousand Oaks, CA: Sage, 1999. 179-202.

Murray, Janet H. *Hamlet on the Holodeck: The Future of Narrative in Cyberspace*. Cambridge, MA: The MIT Press, 1997.

Nakamura, Lisa. *Cybertypes: Race, Ethnicity, and Identity on the Internet*. New York: Routledge, 2002.

O'Brien, Jodi. "Writing in the Body: Gender (Re)production in Online Interaction." In Mark A. Smith and Peter Kollock (eds.), *Communities in Cyberspace*. London: Routledge, 1999. 76-106.

Ogburn, Floyd, and Barbara Wallace. "Freshman Composition, the Internet, and Service-Learning." *Michigan Journal of Community Service Learning* (Fall 1998): 68-74.

Ong, Walter. "Writing Is a Technology that Restructures Thought." In Ellen Cushman, Eugene R. Kintgen, Barry M. Kroll, and Mike Rose (eds.), *Literacy: A Critical Sourcebook*. Boston: Bedford/St. Martin's, 2001. 19-31.

Padilla, Max. "Affirmative Access: A Gay Chicano Lost in Cyberspace." In Richard Holeton (ed.), *Composing Cyberspace: Identity, Community, and Knowledge in the Electronic Age*. Boston: McGraw-Hill, 1998. 121-122.

Pavlik, John V., and Steven S. Ross. "Journalism Online: Exploring the Impact of New Media on News and Society." In Alan B. Albarran and David H. Goff (eds.), *Understanding the Web: Social, Political, and Economic Dimensions of the Internet*. Ames: Iowa State University Press, 2000. 117-134.

Pearce, Sharyn. "'As Wholesome As...': *American Pie* As a New Millennium Sex Manual." In Kerry Mallan and Sharyn Pearce (eds.), *Youth Cultures: Texts, Images, and Identities*. Westport, CT: Praeger, 2003. 69-80.

Peck, Wayne Campbell, Linda Flower, and Lorraine Higgins. "Community Literacy." In Ellen Cushman, Eugene R. Kintgen, Barry M. Kroll, and Mike Rose (eds.), *Literacy: A Critical Sourcebook*. Boston: Bedford/St. Martin's, 2001. 572-587.

Petraglia, Joseph. "Is There Life after Process? The Role of Social Scientism in a Changing Discipline." In Thomas Kent (ed.), *Post-Process Theory: Beyond the Writing-Process Paradigm*. Carbondale: Southern Illinois University Press, 1999.

Pickerill, Jenny. "Weaving a Green Web: Environmental Protest and Computer-Mediated Communication in Britain." In Frank Webster (ed.), *Culture and Politics in the Information Age: A New Politics*. London: Routledge, 2001. 142-166.

Plummer, Ken. *Telling Sexual Stories: Power, Change, and Social Worlds*. London: Routledge, 1995.

Postman, Neil. *Technopoly: The Surrender of Culture to Technology*. New York: Vintage Books, 1993.

Regan, Alison, & John D. Zuern. "Community-Service Learning and Computer-Mediated Advanced Composition." *Computers and Composition* 17 (2000): 177-196.

Rheingold, Howard. *The Virtual Community*. http://www.rheingold.com/vc/book/ (31 October 2003).

Rhodes, Jacqueline. "'Substantive and Feminist Girlie Action': Women Online." *College Composition and Communication* 54.1 (2002): 116-142.

Rice, Jeff. "The 1963 Hip-Hop Machine: Hip-Hop Pedagogy As Composition." *College Composition and Communication* 54.3 (2003): 453-471.

Rice, Jeff. *Writing About Cool: Hypertext and Cultural Studies in the Computer Classroom*. New York: Longman, 2004.

Rice, Jeff. "Writing About Cool Web Site." Longman. http://www.ablongman.com/ricecool1e/about.html (11 February 2004).

Rice, Ronald E. Author's Response. Resource Center for Cyberculture Studies. http://www.com.washington.edu/rccs/bookinfo.asp?AuthorID=55&BookID=1 92 (31 October 2003).

Rice, Ronald E. *The Internet and Health Communication: Experiences and Expectations*. Thousand Oaks, CA: Sage, 2001.

Rollin, Lucy. *Twentieth-Century Teen Culture by the Decades*. Westport, CT: Greenwood Press, 1999.

Romano, Tom. *Blending Genre, A Hering Style: Working Multigenre Papers*. Portsmouth, NH: Boynton/Cook, 2000.

Rushkoff, Douglas. *Ecstasy Club*. New York: Riverhead Books, 1997.

Rushkoff, Douglas. *Playing the Future: What We Can Learn from Digital Kids*. New York: Riverhead Books, 1996 (1999).

Saco, Diana. *Cybering Democracy: Public Space and the Internet*. Minneapolis: University of Minnesota Press, 2002.

Sanderson, Duncan, and Andree Fortin. "The Projection of Geographical Communities into Cyberspace." In Sally R. Munt (ed.), *Technospaces: Inside the New Media*. London: Continuum, 2001. 189-204.

Schroeder, Christopher L. *ReInventing the University: Literacies and Legitimacy in the Postmodern Academy.* Logan: Utah State University Press, 2001.

Schroeder, Christopher, Helen Fox, and Patricia Bizzell. *Alt Dis: Alternative Discourses and the Academy.* Portsmouth, NH: Heinemann, 2002.

Selfe, Cynthia L. *Technology and Literacy in the Twenty-First Century: The Importance of Paying Attention.* Carbondale: Southern Illinois University Press, 1999.

Selfe, Richard J., and Cynthia L. Selfe. "Critical Technological Literacy and English Studies: Teaching, Learning, and Action." In Robert Yagelski and Scott A. Leonard (eds.), *The Relevance of English: Teaching That Matters in Students' Lives.* Urbana, IL: NCTE, 2002. 344-381.

Sefton-Green, Julian, ed. *Digital Diversions: Youth Culture in the Age of Multimedia.* London: UCL Press, 1998.

"SexInfo." University of California, Santa Barbara. 13 October 2003. http://www.soc.ucsb.edu/sexinfo/ (31 October 2003).

"Sex on TV 3: TV Sex is Getting 'Safer.'" The Kaiser Family Foundation. 4 February 2003. http://www.kff.org/content/2003/20030204a/ (31 October 2003).

Shaw, David F. "Gay Men and Computer Communication: A Discourse of Sex and Identity in Cyberspace." In Steven G. Jones (ed.), *Virtual Culture: Identity and Communication in Cybersociety.* London: Sage, 1997. 133-145.

Shields, Rob. *The Virtual.* London: Routledge, 2003.

Silberman, Steve. "We're Teen, We're Queer, and We've Got E-Mail. In Richard Holeton (ed.), *Composing Cyberspace: Identity, Community, and Knowledge in the Electronic Age.* Boston: McGraw Hill, 1998. 116-120.

Smith, Marc A., and Peter Kollock (eds.) *Communities in Cyberspace.* London: Routledge, 1999.

Stald, Gitte. "The World is Quite Enough: Young Danes, Media and Identity in the Crossing Between the Global and the Local." In Gitte Staid and Thomas Tufte (eds.), *Global Encounters: Media and Cultural Transformation.* Luton, UK: University of Luton Press, 2002. 125-150.

Storey, John. *An Introduction to Cultural Theory and Popular Culture.* Athens: University of Georgia Press, 1998.

Street, Brian. "The New Literacy Studies." In Ellen Cushman, Eugene R. Kintgen, Barry M. Kroll, and Mike Rose (eds.), *Literacy: A Critical Sourcebook.* Boston: Bedford/St. Martin's, 2001. 430-442.

Streitmatter, Rodger. "How Youth Media Can Help Combat Homophobia Among American Teenagers." Gay and Lesbian Alliance Against Defamation. 15 Nov. 2003. < http://www.glaad.org/programs/csms/initiatives.php?PHPSESSID = 5d5acde4f3cfe1e3983643aacb2bfae7 > .

Stroupe, Craig. "Visualizing English: Recognizing the Hybrid Literacy of Visual and Verbal Authorship on the Web." *College English* 62.5 (2000): 607-632.

Sullivan, Patricia. "Practicing Safe Visual Rhetoric on the World Wide Web." *Computers and Composition* 18 (2001): 103-122.

Tapscott, Don. *Growing Up Digital: The Rise of the Net Generation.* New York: McGraw-Hill, 1998.

Taylor, Todd, and Irene Ward. *Literacy Theory in the Age of the Internet.* New York: Columbia University Press, 1998.

Trimbur, John. *Popular Literacy: Studies in Cultural Practice and Poetics.* Pittsburgh: University of Pittsburgh Press, 2001.

Trupe, Alice L. "Academic Literacy in a Wired World: Redefining Genres for College Writing Courses." *Kairos* 7.2. August 2002. http://english.ttu.edu/kairos/7.2/binder.html?sectionone/trupe/WiredWorld.htm (31 October 2003).

Tsang, Daniel. "Notes on Queer 'n' Asian Virtual Sex." In In David Bell and Barbara M. Kennedy (eds.), *The Cybercultures Reader.* London: Routledge, 2000. 432-438.

Tuman, Myron C. *Word Perfect: Literacy in the Computer Age.* Pittsburgh, PA: University of Pittsburgh Press, 1992.

Turkle, Sherry. *Life on the Screen: Identity in the Age of the Internet.* New York: Touchstone, 1995.

Turkle, Sherry. "Seeing Through Computers: Education in a Culture of Simulation." In Robert P. Yagelski (ed.), *Literacies and Technologies.* New York: Longman, 2001.

Ulmer, Gregory. *Internet Invention: From Literacy to Electracy.* New York: Longman, 2002.

Vacker, Barry. "Global Village or World Bazaar?" In Alan B. Albarran and David H. Goff (eds.), *Understanding the Web: Social, Political, and Economic Dimensions of the Internet.* Ames: Iowa State University Press, 2000. 211–238.

Valovic, Thomas S. *Digital Mythologies: The Hidden Complexities of the Internet.* New Brunswick, NJ: Rutgers University Press, 2000.

Vegh, Sandor. "Classifying Forms of Online Activism: The Case of Cyberprotests against the World Bank." In Martha McCaughey and Michael D. Ayers (eds.), *Cyberactivism: Online Activism in Theory and Practice.* New York: Routledge, 2003. 71-96.

Vitanza, Victor J. *CyberReader.* Boston: Allyn and Bacon, 1999 (1996).

Vitanza, Victor J. *Writing for the World Wide Web.* Boston: Allyn and Bacon, 1998.

Wakeford, Nina. "Cyberqueer." In David Bell and Barbara M. Kennedy (eds.), *The Cybercultures Reader.* London: Routledge, 2000. 403-415.

Warner, Michael. *The Trouble with Normal: Sex, Politics, and the Ethics of Queer Life.* New York: The Free Press, 1999.

Weight, Gregory M. "Closetspace in Cyberspace." http://www.english.udel.edu/gweight/prof/web/closet/index.html (21 July 1999).

Weight, Gregory M. "queer wide web?" http://www.english.udel.edu/ gweight/prof/web/queer/form1.html (21 July 1999).

Willis, Paul. *Common Culture.* Boulder, CO: Westview Press, 1990.

Woodland, Randal. "'I plan to be a 10': Online Literacy and Lesbian, Gay, Bisexual, and Transgender Students." *Computers and Composition* 16 (1999): 73-87.

Woodland, Randal. "Queer Spaces, Modem Boys and Pagan Statues: Gay/Lesbian Identity and the Construction of Cyberspace [1995]." In David Bell and Barbara M. Kennedy (eds.), *The Cybercultures Reader.* London: Routledge, 2000. 416-431.

Woodward, Jeanette A. *Writing Research Papers: Investigating Resources in Cyberspace*. Lincolnwood, IL: National Textbook Company, 1997.

Wysocki, Anne Frances. "With Eyes That Think, and Compose, and Think: On Visual Rhetoric." *Teaching Writing With Computers*. Eds. Pamela Takayoshi and Brian Huot. Boston: Houghton Mifflin, 2002. 182-201.

Wysocki, Anne Frances, and Johndan Johnson-Eilola. "Blinded by the Letter: Why Are We Using Literacy as a Metaphor for Everything Else?" In Gail E. Hawisher and Cynthia L. Selfe (eds.), *Passions, Pedagogies, and 21st Century Technologies*. Logan: Utah State University Press, 1999. 349-368.

Yagelski, Robert. *Literacies and Technologies: A Reader for Contemporary Writers*. New York: Longman, 2001.

Yancey, Kathleen Blake. "Made Not Only in Words: Composition in a New Key." Conference on College Composition and Communication. San Antonio, TX. 26 March 2004.

"Young People at Risk: HIV/AIDS Among America's Youth." Division of HIV/AIDS Prevention. Centers for Disease Control and Prevention. 2 April 2002. http://www.cdc.gov/hiv/pubs/facts/youth.htm (31 October 2003).

Zeltner, Mark. "New Media and the Slow Death of the Written Word." *Kairos* 7.2. August 2002. http://english.ttu.edu/kairos/7.2/binder.html?sectionone/zeltner/NM (31 October 2003).

MAJOR WEB SITES DISCUSSED

Adbusters.org. 2003. http://www.adbusters.org (31 October 2003).

Advocates for Youth. http://www.advocatesforyouth.org/

Alienkult. http://www.alienkult.com/main.html

All Things Queer. http://www.rslevinson.com/gaylesissues/comingoutstories/blcoming_youth.htm

Asitshould.com. 2003. http://www.asitshould.com/ (31 October 2003).

Butch Dyke Boy. http://www.butchdykeboy.com/ (31 October 2003).

"Cannot find Weapons of Mass Destruction." http://www.coxar.pwp.blueyonder.co.uk/ (31 October 2003).

Can't Think Str8. All Things Queer: http://www.rslevinson.com/gaylesissues/comingoutstories/blcoming_youth.htm

The Center for Democracy and Technology. 2001. http://www.cdt.org/ (31 October 2003).

Cincinnati Youth Summit. http://www.cincyyouthsummit.org/

"Compy 386!" Everybody! Everybody! http://www.homestarrunner.com/sbemail64.html (31 October 2003).

CUMPOST: A Radical Faerie Site. http://www.interlog.com/~ matt634/cpost.html (31 July 2001).

Cybersocket. http://www.cybersocket.com/ (31 October 2003).

Definition Hip Hop. http://definitionhiphop.com/ (31 July 2003).

Friction Magazine. 2003. http://www.frictionmagazine.com/index.asp/ (31 October 2003).

The Funding Exchange. http://www.fex.org/home.html (31 October 2003).

Gay.com. 2003. http://www.gay.com/ (31 October 2003).

Gayscape. http://www.gayscape.com/ (31 October 2003).

Gay, Lesbian, Straight Education Network. http://www.glsen.org/

Gettingit. http://www.gettingit.com/ (31 October 2003).

Get Underground. 2003. http://www.getunderground.com/ (31 October 2003).

The Greater Cincinnati GLBTQ Youth Summit. 2003. http://www.cincyyouthsummit.org/ (31 October 2003).

Hyperreal. http://www.hyperreal.org/ 2002. (31 October 2003).

I-Mockery. http://www.i-mockery.com/ 2003 (31 October 2003).

International Middle East Media Center. 2003. http://www.imemc.org/ (31 October 2003).

It's Your (Sex) Life. http://www.itsyoursexlife.com/

Kaleidoscope. http://www.kaleidoscope.org/

Know HIV/AIDS. http://www.knowhivaids.org/ (31 October 2003).

LiveJournal. http://www.livejournal.com/ (31 October 2003).

Living Beyond Belief. http://www.livingbeyondbelief.org/ (31 October 2003).

Mogenic: Gay & Lesbian Youth Magazine. 2003 http://mogenic.com/index.asp/ (31 October 2003).

MoveOn.org. http://www.moveon.org/ (31 October 2003).

MTV.com. 2003. http://www.mtv.com/ (31 October 2003).

MTV.com FFYR [Fight For Your Rights] Protect Yourself. MTV.com. http://www.mtv.com/onair/ffyr/protect/ (31 October 2003).

Nguyen, Mimi. Worse Than Queer. 2003. http://www.worsethanqueer.com/ (31 October 2003).

Oasismag. http://www.oasismag.com/ (31 October 2003).

"The OFFICIAL Anti-Rave Site!" I-Mockery. http://www.i-mockery.com/antirave/ (31 October 2003).

Other. http://www.othermag.org/ (31 October 2003).

Outminds. http://www.outminds.com/

OutProud. 2003. http://www.outproud.org/ (31 October 2003).

Outright. http://www.outright.org/ (31 October 2003).

Planet Out. 2003. http://www.planetout.com/ (31 October 2003).

Planet Soma. http://www.planetsoma.com/ (31 October 2003).

Queertopia. http://queertopia.org/

Red Dog Sportswear. http://www.reddogsportswear.com

!... reX.caM. ...! http://www.rexsworld.com/ (31 October 2003).

Scarleteen. http://www.scarleteen.com/

Spacegirl. http://www.spacegirl.org/ (31 October 2003).

Spank! Youth Culture Online. 2003. http://www.spankmag.com/ (31 October 2003).

Tenpercentbent. http://www.tenpercentbent.com/

The UC [University of Cincinnati] Alliance. http://www.soa.uc.edu/org/algbp/ (31 October 2003).

United for Peace and Justice. 2003. http://www.unitedforpeace.org/ (31 October 2003).

XRay Magazine. 2003. http://www.goxray.com/ (31 October 2003).

XYmag.com. 2003. http://www.xymag.com/ (31 October 2003).

Young Gay America. 2003. http://www.younggayamerica.com/ (31 October 2003).

"YOUth & AIDS Web Project." University of Cincinnati. 2003. http://oz.uc.edu/~alexanj/What.html (31 October 2003).

Youth.org. http://www.youth.org/ (31 October 2003).

Youthpride (Atlanta). www.youthpride.org

YouthResource. http://www.youthresource.com/ (31 October 2003).

AUTHOR INDEX

SUBJECT INDEX

Printed in the United States
39270LVS00004B/91-126

9 781572 736511